D1551317

Patriots and Cosmopolitans

Patriots and Cosmopolitans

Hidden Histories of American Law

John Fabian Witt

Harvard University Press

Cambridge, Massachusetts, and London, England 2007

Library of Congress Cataloging-in-Publication Data

Witt, John Fabian.
    Patriots and cosmopolitans : hidden histories of American law /
John Fabian Witt.
        p.   cm.
    Includes bibliographical references and index.
    ISBN-13: 978-0-674-02360-4 (alk. paper)
    ISBN-10: 0-674-02360-9 (alk. paper)
    1. Judges—United States—Biography.   2. Lawyers—United
States—Biography.   3. Law—United States—History.   4. United
States—Biography.   5. Nationalism—United States.   I. Title.

KF353.W58 2007
349.73—dc22   2006049505

For Annie Murphy Paul

Contents

Introduction: The Features of American Nationhood   1

ONE: CREATIONS   13

The Pyramid and the Machine: Founding Visions
in the Life of James Wilson   15

TWO: EXITS   83

Elias Hill's Exodus: Exit and Voice in the
Reconstruction Nation   85

THREE: CRITIQUES   155

Internationalists in the Nation-State: Crystal Eastman
and the Puzzle of American Civil Liberties   157

FOUR: REACTIONS   209

The King and the Dean: Melvin Belli, Roscoe Pound,
and the Common-Law Nation   211

Epilogue: Law and the National Frame   279

Notes   287

Acknowledgments   383

Index   385

Illustrations

Fort Wilson, watercolor by Benjamin Evans   18

Giovanni Battista Piranesi, *Piramide di C. Cestio*   52

Solomon Hill and June Moore   130

Solomon Hill's home in Monrovia   151

The Hill-Moore family graveyard, 1977   154

Crystal Eastman, circa 1910   171

Woman's Peace Party demonstration, circa 1916,
New York City   186

Melvin Belli and Roscoe Pound   216

Introduction:
The Features of
American Nationhood

This book is a historical inquiry into law and the experience of American nationhood. Like so much else in early twenty-first century America, the book's beginnings can be traced to the morning of September 11, 2001. I was inside a voting booth in the Westbeth Building in New York City, an old factory turned artists' space along the Hudson River on Manhattan's west side. Until just a few years before, the waterfront along the Hudson in downtown Manhattan had been home to a bustling international maritime trade. Cargo, immigrants, emigrants, sojourners, and slaves all passed through the harbor in seemingly endless cycles of exchange. The Westbeth Building itself has a kind of world-historic importance, too. Early stages in the Manhattan Project's development of the atomic bomb—a technology that transformed the globe and threatens one day to destroy it—occurred in Westbeth during its years as the main research center for Bell Laboratories.

While I pulled voting levers to elect candidates for mayor and city council in the Corporation of the City of New York, the radio of the African-American police officer assigned to the 82nd Election District came alive with an improbable and panicked message. By the time I turned to leave the curtained booth (my hastily registered votes destined never to be counted), the officer had left the polling place and was running through the Westbeth courtyard toward Bank Street and toward the river just twenty yards away. From West Street along the river, he would have an unimpeded view on this brilliant cloudless morning of the World Trade Center buildings less than a mile to the south. We morning voters—about a dozen in all—followed, unsure of what exactly we would see, until there it was, a large, gaping black hole in the Trade Center's north tower, near the top but eerily centered in a way that made it seem unlikely to have been an accident.

Over the next minutes, hours, and days, the political entities in whose governance I had been participating when the first terrorist plane struck the World Trade Center took on extraordinary sentimental importance. Emotional attachments to the city became salient, to be sure. These were the connections to the millions of New Yorkers who shared in countless different ways the experiences and terrors of the towers' collapse. At the same time a less concrete, but equally urgent and in some ways more powerful, kind of attachment also made itself felt in the midst of the events of 9/11, a kind of attachment that Americans have felt for over two centuries but that has remained remarkably opaque in American history. For in addition to the attachments of the city, my fellow voters and I experienced with renewed strength the sentiments of the nation. American nationhood sprang to life and became something greater than the sum of its constitutive legal parts. Standing with my wife and neighbors on the street, watching as the second plane smashed into the south tower, and hearing panicked reports of black smoke in the nation's capital, we were instantly and deeply connected by bonds of shared national identity with millions of people we would never meet. Here was the imagined community of which students of nationalism write, experienced with an intensity and passion that made it clear that American nationalism was no less powerful for being imagined.[1]

In one way or another, all of us there in the street were bound up in American nationhood. In the shadows of the beginnings of the world's most awesome national defense project, on the shores of what was once one of the busiest international ports, we were voters, spouses, tenants, condominium owners, law enforcement agents, residents of the municipal corporation of the City of New York, and more—all legally constituted identities whose authority stemmed ultimately from the power of the nation-state. Even our racial and ethnic identities (witness the African-*American* police officer) were tied up in the technologies of nationhood.

Moreover, many of my neighbors and I felt ready in those moments, and for some time thereafter, to support extraordinary things we would never have contemplated before that morning. Suddenly there was talk of the propriety of torture: Would weapons of mass destruction in Central Park warrant its use? There was talk of racial profiling by law enforcement to single out likely terrorists (talk that is renewed in the cities of Europe and North America with each new al-Qaeda–supported attack). Constitutional constraints on government action suddenly seemed more malleable. My neighbors and I contemplated these steps and others if reasonably necessary to defend the American nation. I am not certain I am so ready to contemplate them again now, but who's to say that another such crisis would not prompt the same overriding commitment to the idea of the nation? I am an American nationalist. My national identity is inescapable—not that I try to escape it. I embrace it, it embraces me. This book is an attempt to begin to think about what that embrace has meant in American history and in the history of American law in particular.

In the community of nation-states, the United States stands out as distinctively organized around law. To be sure, nation-states around the world are defined in significant part by the norms and conventions of the law of nations, or "international law" as Jeremy Bentham renamed the law of nations in 1780. International law helps to determine nation-states' boundaries, their powers, and their obligations.[2] Yet the United States is distinctive among nation-states in that law has not merely defined its legal status in the international community. In the United States, law and constitutionalism have also created a people, the "We the People" of the U.S. Constitution's preamble. More than in any other nation-state around the globe, a robust national identity rests on a foundation of constitutive legal texts. The interpretation of these texts—the Constitution and the Bill of Rights—has been vested chiefly in the nation's jurists. As countless past observers of the American experience have noted, American nationhood thus rests in distinctively important respects on legal-constitutional foundations.[3]

Other nations rest on very different bases. Nationhood in Germany, for example, has long rested on an imagined community of shared descent. Nationhoods in France and the republics of Latin America rest on political foundations that survive constitutional revolutions and persist across successive legal-constitutional regimes. By contrast, the United States and the American nation have distinctively legal and constitutional foundations. Unlike descent or kin-based nationalisms, the United States claims no single ethnic or racial community organized around bloodlines. Unlike political communities that have maintained political traditions across repeated regime change from one constitutional order to another, the United States consists of a constitutional order that has persisted over time. If elsewhere nationhood has been an ethnocultural or political fact, in the United States nationhood has been a legal and constitutional fact.[4]

These legal foundations have often helped to obscure American nationhood rather than illuminate it. Indeed, the universalizing aspirations of law—its claims to be rooted in impartial reason rather than in partial or particular political projects—have made understanding American nationhood peculiarly difficult. Since its beginnings, the United States has been a nation that alternately asserts and denies its nationhood. In the Declaration of Independence, the Continental Congress announced that the United States would occupy a "separate and equal station" among the "Independent States" of the world. With its next breath, the Congress asserted the nation's adherence to universal truths applicable to all mankind. The United States has thus imagined itself from the outset as both distinct and universal at the same time. Indeed, those who focus on the United States's universal ideals sometimes deny that the United States counts as a nation at all.[5]

Yet the American attachment to universal ideals also lies at the heart of one of the most influential interpretations of law and American nationhood: Louis Hartz's magisterial and controversial *The Liberal Tradition in America*. In *The Liberal Tradition*, first published in 1955, Hartz diagnosed the American national condition as a monolithic tradition of "fixed, dogmatic liberalism" that was remarkably impervious to international influences. According to Hartz and his many followers, the liberalism of political philosophers like John Locke dominated American political ideas and animated American legal institutions. In Hartz's view, there was no better evidence of the United States's liberalism than the practices of the U.S. Supreme Court, which virtually alone among the courts of the world has long had the authority to enforce liberal principles by striking down laws enacted by the political branches. Judicial review, Hartz argued, "would be inconceivable without the national acceptance of the Lockean creed," which Hartz contended was embodied in the U.S. Constitution. For Hartz, then, the American legal tradition—in both its ideological content and its institutional structures—was paradigmatic of the United States's uncompromising and world-exceptional commitment to a classical liberalism.[6]

More recently, however, the pendulum has swung away from Hartz's view of monolithic exceptional liberalism toward more pluralist accounts of the American national tradition. Three decades of Hartz critics have sought to establish that American law and politics consist of many traditions, not one. Traditions of ascriptive racism, communitarian republicanism, hierarchical domination, and populist radicalism have existed alongside the liberalism that dominated Hartz's account.[7] Moreover, a new generation of commentators—many studying ocean-based regions, such as the Atlantic world and its Pacific counterpart—contend that nation-states were never more than "leaky containers" of people, ideas, and social forces. Of course the United States has had multiple traditions, they say. How could it be otherwise in a world in which the nation-state lacks the capacity to capture and contain intellectual currents or population flows? In the strongest versions of the pluralist and the globalizing accounts, the legal and political traditions of the United States are inevitably as multifarious as the traditions of law and politics the world over. The pluralists would have us think that national borders have been highly permeable with respect to political and legal change. The globalizers go even further, suggesting that the nation-state simply lacks the institutional capacity to carve out robust or distinctive traditions of its own in a world of transnational flows.[8]

The four yoked essays in this book—the "hidden histories" of the book's title—are loosely guided by the idea that neither of these views of American nationhood, neither the Hartzian nation of impervious law-based exceptionalism nor the pluralists' and globalizers' permeable nation of many traditions, quite grasps the relationship between nation and law in the United States.[9]

The legal history of American nationhood is characterized by both variety and constraint, multiplicity and limits, porousness and bounds. To put it differently and more precisely, American nationhood has carved out a tradition of bounded contingency in the law. "Bounded contingency" emphasizes the permeability of American borders to global influences. It emphasizes the many possible paths open to legal and constitutional development in the United States, the many possible national identities open to self-described Americans, and the many interests that may be advanced by invoking the nation. This is the theme of contingency. But bounded contingency also highlights the limits of American nationhood: the constraints created by American nationhood on the historical development of the law, on the political sentiments of Americans, and on the interests that have been able to invoke the nation successfully. This is the theme of boundedness.

As I use the term here, nationhood consists of at least two related phenomena. It encompasses the institutions of the *nation-state* and the sentimental attachments of identity and ideology that many call *nationalism*. In the United States, each of these senses of the term *nationhood* (institutional and sentimental) has been distinctively legal. The institutions of the American nation-state—its separated powers, its federal structure, its courts exercising the power of judicial review, and more—are the artifacts of a constitutional regime in whose interpretation and elaboration jurists have played a distinctively significant role. The sentiments of the American nation, in turn, are deeply (though not exclusively) bound up in the same legal traditions from which those institutions spring—the Constitution, the Bill of Rights, and the history of Anglo-American liberty, to name some of the most prominent.[10]

This book explores American nationhood in both the institutional and the sentimental senses of the term through little-known stories and forgotten characters during four defining moments in the development of American law. The first part of the book takes up the founding period of American constitutionalism, from the Revolution through the 1790s. Part Two turns to the Civil War and Reconstruction, a period in which the American nation reconstituted itself following its near collapse. Part Three takes up the critical moment around the time of World War I in which the modern American nation-state emerged. Part

Four focuses on the mid-twentieth-century growth of the modern American nation-state with its vast—and distinctly American—administrative apparatus. In each part, my aim is to describe some of the many ways in which American nationhood has fostered a wide variety of constitutional and legal practices while at the same time placing limits on institutional change and shaping the political and legal imaginations of those operating in its domain.

I have adopted biography as the organizing structure for the inquiry, for it is in the engagement of individual men and women with the American national tradition that the limits and varieties of American nationhood become apparent. As Alexander Hamilton rightly anticipated in 1787, a critically important element of American constitutionalism has been its remarkable (though not universal) success in attracting the "passions which have the strongest influence upon the human heart."[11] By starting with the stories of individual people, I aim to outline the capacity and limits of the American nation-state to take hold of the hearts and imaginations (the "hopes and fears," as Hamilton put it) of people living within its territory.

The book's case studies in law and American nationhood consist of five very different people from across the history of the United States. James Wilson—an American revolutionary, a delegate to the Constitutional Convention, an Associate Justice on the U.S. Supreme Court, and perhaps the least understood of the founding fathers—sought (often unsuccessfully) to imprint the United States with his own particular vision of American nationhood. Eighty years later, after the Civil War and Emancipation, a South Carolina Baptist minister named Elias Hill and thousands of other freedpeople wondered long and hard whether to commit themselves to an America that had enslaved them and barred them from citizenship. In the 1910s, politically forceful organizations led by people such as the charismatic, indefatigable, and now largely forgotten Crystal Eastman powerfully criticized the United States and the nation-states of the world more generally as dangerous legal entities that led inevitably to war. And in the middle of the twentieth century, individuals such as charismatic plaintiffs' lawyer and "King of Torts" Melvin Belli and former dean of the Harvard Law School Roscoe Pound mobilized the ideals and the institutions of American nationhood to shape and constrain the development of the American administrative state.

Each of these people engaged with the American nation-state in a distinctive way. Their lives make abundantly clear that the legally constructed American nation has appeared not in one monolithic guise but in many. American nationhood has been, to draw from Rogers Brubaker's writing on European nationalisms, a "varied and multiform" phenomenon, to which those in the United States have had equally "varied and multiform responses." The legal category of the American nation-state, in short, has been many things to many people at many times. It has defined membership status, determined institutions and rules for internal governance, set external borders, and established a foundation for bureaucratic authority. American nationalism has provided the basis for a collective democratic project among its citizens, as well as a foundation for self-defense and aggression against those it defines as outsiders. It has fostered the identity of self-identified Americans, and it has created institutions in which a wide variety of competing interest groups pursue a broad array of competing ends.[12]

And yet the contingency of American nationhood has been accompanied by bounds, its varieties haunted by limits. Even as American nationhood has been susceptible of many nationalisms, it has constrained and channeled the energies of patriots and cosmopolitans alike. Recent theorists of nationalism and cosmopolitanism have aspired to a rooted cosmopolitanism—one that combines local attachments with the universal principles of impartiality. But the lives of the four men and one woman described in the stories that follow were rooted in American institutions and traditions not so much by aspiration as by inevitability.[13] They were by necessity bound up in an American nationhood made up of both institutions and sentiments. The nation's institutions cut grooves into the future, channeling the historical development of the United States in certain directions rather than others. The nation's sentiments helped to define the values and ideas of even those who styled themselves its critics. To be sure, the individuals whose stories make up this book sought (sometimes successfully) to shape and reshape the nation's institutions and ideals. But such efforts were again and again made in the image of the nation they purported to alter. American nationhood and American law have produced each other in an ongoing reciprocal process of mutual formation.

Three clarifications may be useful here. First, an emphasis on nationhood in the history of American law is long overdue. For the past half century, writers setting out to describe the development of American law have focused predominantly on the relationship between law and society. Students of legal history have asked whether and in what ways society—that complex and unwieldy amalgam of social forces, cultural phenomena, economic pressures, and more—has shaped law. The difficulty with this approach, however, is that particular constellations of social pressures are almost always indeterminate with respect to law. Particular moments in the industrial revolution, for example, did not require or demand any particular set of legal arrangements. And so, studies in legal history repeatedly conclude that legal form is relatively autonomous from social setting. Society shapes law, of course, but it is virtually never a sufficient explanation of any legal regime, except in the most tautological sense. The law-and-society framework has accordingly lost much of its analytic power in recent years, for the answer to law-and-society's questions is almost always the same: society influences law, but does not determine it.[14]

Focusing on American nationhood furnishes a way of thinking about the history of American law that moves beyond the law-and-society approach. If society and economy have turned out to be indeterminate for law, nationhood—at least nationhood in the United States—is often not. Nationhood is bounded by institutions and deeply rooted sentiments, both of which have framed the contests over American law even as the law has had formative influence in their own creation. The institutions of American nationhood have created powerful constraints on legal and political development, while the sentiments of American nationhood have defined and marked off the limits of legal and political ideals.[15]

Second, the case studies presented here do not purport to follow representative characters, though the five people whose lives I describe sometimes were. Nor do they claim to explore the lives of national leaders, though sometimes they do. The approach I have adopted here is unruly, like the subject of American nationhood itself. The subjects of my studies in American nationhood and the law are people who at critical moments in the development of the American nation and American law illuminated the development of the nation-state, people who brilliantly highlighted the capacity of the nation to shape American law, American institutions, and American imaginations. Moreover, they are people who helped to make and remake the nation-state at some of its most critical junctures—often in ways that have eluded attention.

Third, I should add that the aim of what follows is neither to attack nor to champion American nationhood. In the course of its history, American nationhood has been alternately appealing and ugly, and often it has been both at once. But the point of this book is not to arrive at an accounting of the merits and defects of

American nationhood. I seek neither to defend American patrio-tism for the democratic and communitarian virtues it has sus-tained, nor to endorse cosmopolitanism for its liberal impartiality or its rejection of nationalism's parochial attachments.

The perspective that runs through these yoked essays on the history of American nationhood is rather one of hidden ironies, tragic compromises, and unanticipated consequences. At the out-set of the twenty-first century, the most sophisticated nationalists advocate liberal or civic nationalisms. The most nuanced cosmo-politans, in turn, call for what they style as rooted cosmopol-itanisms. The stories and characters in this book suggest that both of these competing values have animated the history of American law, sometimes for the better, sometimes for the worse. At key moments in the development of the United States, Ameri-can nationhood and American law have been powerfully shaped by contests between ostensibly indigenous values, on one hand, and ideas and influences from abroad, on the other.[16]

What follows are four explorations in the many histories of the legal category of the United States, a legal entity that has been shaped and reshaped over time, has been subject to historical pro-cesses, and has at the same time been a historical force of its own, powerfully shaping and reshaping the world around it. If the American nation-state of patriotic myth was founded in the heav-ens and is aligned with the natural principles of the universe, its human-made history—crafted from the tissues of the law—has inevitably been a good deal more various than the mythmakers suggest.[17]

One ☆ Creations

Few individuals better illustrate the power of national sentiment and the significance of nation-state institutions in the United States than the recessive, oft-forgotten founding father James Wilson. Known in his day as the most learned lawyer in revolutionary America, Wilson developed an elaborate, idiosyncratic, and grandiose vision of the place of the United States in world history. It was a vision so powerful that Wilson guided his own personal and professional life by its precepts. Yet this vision ultimately misunderstood the character of the nation-state he had helped to found.

The institutions set in place at the Constitutional Convention in the summer of 1787 created workaday mechanisms for the accommodation of competing social interests. But Wilson saw the American Constitution not as a humble arrangement for the adjustment of interests and factions, but as a design that perfectly embodied natural truths for all the ages. As a result, Wilson failed to grasp the distinctive promise that the institutions of the American nation-state held out to lawyers like himself. For Wilson, lawyer-jurists were to be the high priests of the Constitution's natural truths; but the real opportunity for lawyers in the United States was to become the brokers par excellence among competing interests and between those interests and the state.

Wilson's distinctive vision ultimately led him to an ignominious and destitute demise. His star-crossed career thus highlights by contrast the characteristic features of U.S. legal institutions, casting them into sharp relief against his highly idealized conception of the nation. Most of all, Wilson's life illuminates the power that the American nation has had from its very beginnings over the imaginations of its members.

The Pyramid and the Machine: Founding Visions in the Life of James Wilson

On Monday, October, 4, 1779, the Pennsylvania militia took the law into its own hands. British troops had evacuated Philadelphia over a year earlier, but the months that followed had grown only more difficult. Merchants ("monopolizers and forestallers," the crowd called them) had raised the prices of seemingly everything, most of all bread and other necessities. A few self-interested merchants seemed "Avariciously intent on Amassing Wealth by the Destruction of the more virtuous part of the Community." Now, on the first Monday of October, some two hundred members of the militia marched through the city's streets to "drive from the city" all those who were "disaffected" with the American cause in the Revolution and to confront any who dared to oppose the wartime price control ordinances that the Pennsylvania state government had been unable (or unwilling) to enforce.[1]

Over the preceding weeks and months, the militia's ire had focused on a few especially prominent Philadelphians, chief among them James Wilson. Wilson was by many accounts the city's most learned lawyer. Born and raised in Scotland near St. Andrews, where he attended the university, Wilson had come to Pennsylvania in 1765, lectured at Benjamin Franklin's College of Philadelphia, and then read law with the distinguished Philadelphia lawyer John Dickinson. Dickinson himself had been trained at Middle Temple in London in the 1750s, where the great English jurist William Blackstone had studied a decade earlier. In 1776, Wilson had been one of the fifty-five signers of the Declaration of Independence; indeed, his support for the Declaration is widely viewed as having thrown the closely divided Pennsylvania delegation over to the side of independence. Eleven years later, in the summer of 1787, Wilson would be among the most active delegates to the federal Constitutional Convention, second only to Gouverneur Morris in number of times speaking and to James Madison in the cogency of his ideas. Wilson would be one of only six men to sign both the Declaration and the Constitution. In 1789, George Washington would appoint Wilson as an associate justice on the first United States Supreme Court.[2]

Yet in 1779, Wilson was a natural target for the militia's frustrations. He had developed close ties to the colony's financial elite and in particular to Robert Morris, a leading merchant and financier of the Revolution who was widely suspected of engaging in hoarding and price-gouging in his flour and dry goods trade. Wilson—Morris's political ally, sometime business partner, and lawyer—had himself been accused of similarly shadowy commercial dealings by none other than the revolutionary radical Thomas Paine. And although he had cast critical votes for independence in the first days of July 1776, that same spring he had attracted radicals' attention as one of a number of prominent Pennsylvanians urging caution in the movement for independence from Britain. Shortly thereafter, Wilson, Morris, and others such as Benjamin Rush founded an organization known as the Republican Society, made up of what Rush described as "the ancient inhabitants of the state . . . distinguished for their wealth, virtue, learning and liberality of manners." The Republican Society opposed the state constitution of 1776, which the state's radicals had pushed through during the heady days of that rebellious summer. In turn, Constitutionalists (as the radical compact's supporters were known) suspected Republicans of secret loyalist leanings. These suspicions seemed confirmed when in 1778 and 1779 Wilson took a lead role defending Philadelphia Tories against charges of treason.[3]

As the militia started to march on Monday afternoon, rumors flew that they had made Wilson's impressive red brick house at the corner of Walnut and Third Streets their destination. As many as "thirty or forty" Wilson partisans—"some with Muskets some with Pistols"—rushed to defend Wilson's home, a building known ever since as "Fort Wilson." The militia arrived soon thereafter. "They marched on very slowly," recorded one observer, "until the Rear came nearly abreast" of the Wilson home. The threat seemed to have passed. But then, as the militiamen moved down Walnut Street, strong words were exchanged between the militia and Wilson's partisans. Shots rang out. Some said it was two lone members of the militia who fired first, "without any Command" from their leaders; at least one witness reported that one Captain Campbell, holed up inside the house, had fired first, angrily shaking his pistol and firing it "from the third story window."[4]

Regardless who took the first shot, what followed was perhaps the most dramatic riot of the revolutionary period. "The Militia attacked with great Resolution" and the "firing against the house" quickly became "incessant," reported one witness; the "fire became smart on both Sides," reported another. A "number of desperate-looking men" forced the doors and windows to Fort Wilson with iron bars and sledge hammers. The crowd rushed in through the smashed doors only to be repulsed by a barrage of gunfire from the staircase, though not before a Wilson defender named Colonel Chambers was pulled from the house and beset by bayonets. The crowd was turned back not a moment too soon. Charles Wilson Peale, whose leadership role among the state's radicals put him in a position to know, believed that the militia "most probably would have killed every one assembled within those walls" had they not been driven back. Just as the crowd brought a cannon within firing range, Joseph Reed (president of the state Executive Council and himself a member of the Philadelphia bar) rode in "cutting and slashing" with a detachment of

The residence of James Wilson, known as Fort Wilson, Third and Walnut Streets, as it looked in 1779, by Benjamin Evans, 1888. (The Historical Society of Pennsylvania)

the cavalry to drive off the attackers. The battle was over, but some six or seven people had been killed—only one of them, the pugnacious Captain Campbell, from among the Wilson partisans. Estimates suggest that between seventeen and nineteen more had been "dangerously wounded." Wilson "sallied out" unharmed, but lucky to have escaped so easily.[5]

*
*
*

Wilson's brush with crowd violence in 1779 raises one of the great questions to come out of the American Revolution. How did the members of the colonial American legal profession not only survive the revolution but "sally out" of the experience as leaders of the new republic? Lawyers quickly took up (in some cases resumed) lead roles in the politics of the new nation. Indeed, for many aspects of American legal practice it was, one New York lawyer observed, "as if the revolution had not happened" at all.[6]

These are striking facts. Lawyers rarely do well in revolutions. The French and Russian revolutions both witnessed the abolition of the legal profession of the prior regime, not to mention the criminal prosecution and execution of leading lawyers. (Eleven members of the elite Parisian Order of Barristers met their ends at the guillotine.) Moreover, in the mid-eighteenth century elite American lawyers such as Wilson were developing closer and closer ties to the English legal system. A number of leading Philadelphia lawyers had remained loyal to the crown. Many fled with the coming of the Revolution. How, then, as the eminent historian Richard Morris asked in 1931, could political leadership in the wake of independence "have been assumed by a group of men who were largely responsible for bringing America into subjection to the reactionary legal system of England"? Lawyers' extraordinary success in and around the time of the American Revolution is, in the words of distinguished historian John Murrin, "one of the strangest paradoxes of early American history."[7]

A major part of the answer lies in the institutional design of the new nation. For a generation now, students of the American Revolution have suggested that the behavior of crowds like the one that gathered at Fort Wilson is best understood by reference to the relatively flexible institutions of American governance. British colonial governments were notoriously incapable of vigorous response to popular mobilization in the decade before independence. By contrast, the legal institutions of the new republic managed, accommodated, and defused popular mobilization with remarkable success. The emerging constitutional scheme of the new nation embodied what historian Gordon Wood has called the "American science of politics." This was a politics that institutionalized and contained struggles among the competing interest groups, factions, and individuals in a pluralist, heterogeneous nation. In Wood's influential account, American constitutionalism thereby promised to hold off the cycles of decline that throughout history seemed to plague faction-ridden republics. The aim was to balance (as James Madison famously wrote in Federalist 10) the "various and interfering interests" that grew up "by necessity in civilized nations," thus channeling the contentious passions of the people into public-regarding forms.[8]

As the Fort Wilson incident makes clear, the capacity of flexible and accommodating governmental and legal institutions to defuse popular uprisings was especially important for lawyers, who found themselves repeatedly singled out by the revolutionary crowd. Shortly after the riot ended, the Pennsylvania Executive Council—headed by the same Joseph Reed who had rescued Wilson just days before—enacted precisely the price controls demanded by the crowd. Within five days of the incident the Council released one hundred barrels of flour for distribution to the families of militiamen. Shortly thereafter, all the participants (Wilson included) were pardoned.[9]

Yet what is striking about Wilson is that for all his exposure to factional conflict in revolutionary politics, he barely grasped either the new political science or its promise for the American bar. The leading historians of the American Revolution—Wood and others—have associated Wilson's ideas with the distinctive constitutional pluralism that emerged in the 1780s. But Wilson was not a pluralist. He was an almost fanatical idealist, whose ideas stood not in the constitutional tradition that became America's distinctive pluralism, but in the very different jurisprudential tradition of natural law and a closely related strand of the Scottish Enlightenment. Indeed, Wilson's vision for the new republic makes clear that the founding period was a moment of many competing conceptions for what the United States might be.

The animating motif of Wilson's conception of the American republic and his legal science was the pyramid. These Egyptian monuments, whose simple geometry had survived for ages, seemed to embody timeless natural reason. The pyramids thus held out to Wilson the promise of what J. G. A. Pocock has called an "escape from history." Like the pyramids, Wilson's United States would avoid history's cycles of decline and decay by a design of "timeless rationality." For pluralists like Madison, Hamilton, and many others among the founding generation, however, it was not the pyramid but the machine that came to symbolize the American constitutional experiment. In the machine, the founders of American constitutionalism hit upon a humble, workaday metaphor that would not escape from history but merely (in Pocock's terms) "tame" and contain it through a constitutional arrangement that would balance and accommodate social conflict.[10] In this view, the constitutional mechanics of the founding period would not transcend the republican cycle of freedom to tyranny, but merely establish effective arrangements for keeping the cycle at bay.

The distinction between Wilson's timeless pyramid and the pluralist machine-in-time not only captures two powerfully different conceptions of the character of the young American nation. It also illuminates a closely related point about the ways in which the fledgling institutions of American governance served lawyers well across the revolutionary period—and indeed ever since. The pluralist state of Madisonian constitutionalism turned out to be extraordinarily conducive to expanding the jurisdiction and the power of American lawyers. In part, this was because crowds like the one outside Wilson's house regularly targeted lawyers. Constitutional structures that could defuse the passions of the crowd thus had special significance for the American legal profession. More important, however, the mechanics of American constitutionalism created a set of state institutions that were exceptionally well suited to lawyering—institutions, as political scientists put it, that were "less tangible, more diffuse, and more interpenetrated by nonstate actors" than any in Western Europe. Mediating conflict among contending parties and the state is precisely what lawyers do, and American lawyers quickly took up lead roles in the pluralist competition of American constitutionalism. The institutional structures created by American constitutionalism, in the words of one student of the legal professions, created "vast opportunities for legal work" in the United States relative to other nation-states.[11]

Wilson, as we will see, never fully grasped the promise of Madison's pluralist institutions for the American bar. Nor in his own life was he ever able to take full advantage of the lawyering opportunities those institutions made available. Wilson's life seems to have been one of those instances of flawed theory catastrophically realized in failed practice. By the middle of the 1790s—for reasons closely tied to his idiosyncratic legal science and the particular conception of the American republic to which it gave rise—Wilson's life would become a tale of declension into legal blunders and financial disaster, rumors of corruption, and tragic demise. While still a sitting Supreme Court justice, Wilson would be imprisoned for his debts, contract malaria, lose his mind, and die a pathetic death as a virtual prisoner of his creditors in a dreary North Carolina inn. But for two decades before his ignominious end, there had been few more prominent lawyers in the new United States.

*
*
*

Law must have seemed an ideal career choice to the twenty-four-year old, newly minted Philadelphian James Wilson. In Scotland, where he was born in Fifeshire near St. Andrews in the year 1742, lawyers were taking up important leadership roles. After the Act of Union unified England and Scotland in 1707, the Scots had retained their distinctive and heavily Roman-law–influenced legal system. Scottish politics became subordinate to London. Law, as historians John Clive and Bernard Bailyn observed, "became the main ladder for public advancement" in post-Union Scotland. Yet from early in his childhood, Wilson had been intended by his father, a devoutly religious Scottish farmer of modest means, not for a life in the law but a life in the rigorous Calvinist Kirk of Scottish Presbyterianism. At fourteen, he won a sought-after bursary to the United College at the University of St. Andrews. By the age of nineteen he had entered St. Mary's College at St. Andrews to study divinity. Within a year, however, the death of Wilson's father brought an end to his religious studies. Wilson began to direct his own life along a new trajectory altogether.[12]

The Scotland in which Wilson was raised and educated was in the midst of that extraordinary outpouring of ideas and energies known as the Scottish Enlightenment. Even at St. Andrews, which was something of an intellectual backwater, Wilson learned of the ideas of such leading lights as Francis Hutcheson, David Hume, Thomas Reid, and Adam Smith. With a host of others, these men produced work in moral philosophy, epistemology, political science, jurisprudence, and economics so pioneering as to have "ruled the Western intellect," as one recent account has it, for most of the second half of the eighteenth century. After his father's death in 1762, Wilson made his way to Edinburgh, the center of Scotland's eighteenth-century intellectual ferment, where he found work in bookkeeping and accounting while taking at least one class—and perhaps more—at the great University of Edinburgh.[13]

By the summer and fall of 1765, when he was twenty-three, Wilson decided to leave Scotland for America. In this, Wilson was hardly alone. His childhood friend Robert Annan had left for the Pennsylvania frontier several years before, and Wilson emigrated during what more than one historian has called "the 'flood' of Scottish emigration" in the years leading up to the American Revolution. Once in the North American colonies, Wilson was able to use his Scottish education and connections to good effect. Wilson took up an appointment as tutor (a favorite post among newcomers educated in the Scottish universities) at the College of Philadelphia where William Smith, formerly of Aberdeen, served as the provost.[14]

Wilson would not remain at the college for long, however. In lawyer-rich Edinburgh, Wilson had come to understand that the law offered a path to prestige and power in England's eighteenth-century provincial outposts. As his friend Annan later recalled, Wilson thus arrived in Philadelphia with a firm idea of the "course he meant to pursue through life." Within a year, Wilson was reading law in the offices of John Dickinson, a leading Philadelphia lawyer. (Dickinson's own family tutor had been a Scottish immigrant named Francis Alison, who was in turn a student of Francis Hutcheson.) In 1767, Wilson gained admission to the bar, and he soon started his own practice. The legal profession was booming in Philadelphia when Wilson came to the bar. In the middle of the eighteenth century, the city was in the midst of a remarkable period of growth. But Wilson chose to head west, to the Pennsylvania frontier, to begin his law practice. From early 1767 to 1770, he lived and practiced in the small town of Reading, Pennsylvania. In the latter year, he moved to the more prosperous town of Carlisle, in the center of the province, where he stayed until his return to Philadelphia in 1778.[15]

That Wilson had not abandoned his view of the law's promise upon his arrival in the colonies says much for the development of the American bar in the middle years of the eighteenth century. Just a few years earlier, the prospects for highly educated lawyers in British North America seemed relatively dim.

An early nineteenth-century commentator exaggerated somewhat when he wrote that for much of colonial American history "no trace can be found of law as a science or profession." But he was not overstating by much. For the first century of British colonization in North America, the experience of the colonial bar had been one of marginalization and disrepute. A number of early colonial governments instituted limitations on legal fees to discourage the practice of law. Others prohibited the receipt of fees altogether by those who pleaded another's cause in court. Moreover, seventeenth-century American lawyers were virtually all attorneys-in-fact rather than attorneys-in-law. They had, in other words, no legal training and lacked formal admittance to the practice of law. In any event, there was usually little need for trained lawyers in the early colonial courts. Judges rarely had any legal training themselves, and lawsuits typically dropped the pleading formalities of the English common law, using (at most) simplified versions of England's highly technical system of common-law pleadings. Those who represented others in court often made ends meet as shoemakers, wigmakers, masons, and apothecaries.[16]

The colonial bar's marginalization was accompanied by ill repute. The first two practicing lawyers in Massachusetts in the 1620s and 1630s were promptly shipped back to England, but not before one had meddled with the jury in a case in which he was counsel. Lawyers were prohibited by law from serving on the colony's General Court until 1691; even then, no lawyer represented Boston until 1738. In New York, lawyers were simply not "thought to be useful." They were, as one New Yorker put it, "The unletter'd Blockheads of the Robe / Than whom no greater Monsters on the Globe." In the South, the Fundamental Constitutions of Carolina (written by John Locke) provided that "it shall be a base and vile thing to plead for money or reward." Virginia colonists described lawyers as "a parcel of wild knaves and

Jacobites"—which may often have been close to the truth given that many early Virginia lawyers were reputed to be English lawyers sentenced to transportation to the colonies after criminal convictions in England. Even lawyers and officials had a dim view of the profession. John Adams complained that the practice of the law had fallen into the hands of "pettifogging meddlers" who "stirred up many unnecessary suits." As Massachusetts justice of the peace Benjamin Dyer put it in the 1760s, lawyers seemed at best to "live upon the sins of the People."[17]

Lawyers in Wilson's Pennsylvania had shared the early colonial patterns of distrust and relative insignificance. Lawyers "have a License to Murder and make Mischief," explained a typical seventeenth-century Pennsylvania account. A visitor to the colony at the start of the eighteenth century reported—only slightly too enthusiastically—that "they have no lawyers." Proprietor William Penn, who had developed an abiding distrust of the common law after his indictment in England on charges of common-law riot in 1670, counted two lawyers in his province in 1700, though by 1706 there seem to have been between four and seven.[18]

In the first half of the eighteenth century, the best-known lawyer in all of the British colonies had been Philadelphia lawyer (and Scottish immigrant) Andrew Hamilton, himself a student at Wilson's alma mater of St. Andrews some fifty years before Wilson matriculated there. Hamilton gained wide fame for his rhetorical performance in the 1735 John Peter Zenger trial in New York, winning a jury acquittal that nullified New York's seditious libel laws. But one of the worst-kept secrets of the eighteenth-century bar was that Hamilton was more rhetorician than lawyer. As Chief Justice William Tilghman of Pennsylvania observed in 1823 about his home state, "it was a long time before she possessed lawyers of eminence."[19]

Indeed, the Pennsylvania bench was little more distinguished than the bar. Of fourteen men commissioned as chief justice of the Pennsylvania Supreme Court between 1684 and 1743, only four were lawyers. During those sixty years, no other judicial office in the province was graced by a trained lawyer. Instead, consistent with Quaker injunctions against litigation, and with the original proprietor's distrust toward the common law and the legal profession, Pennsylvania developed an elaborate system of arbitration by referees. "Immense numbers" of disputes were resolved by referees rather than judges right up into the early national period. Largely as a result, Harvard-trained lawyer and historian Charles Warren called the Pennsylvania legal profession "extremely rudimentary"—at least by the standards being set in places like Massachusetts and New York—"until about the middle of the eighteenth century."[20]

In the decade or two before Wilson's arrival in North America, the condition of the American legal profession began to improve. The sheer number of lawyers grew dramatically, and the bar began to develop new power both in their communities and in the courts. Indeed, as Murrin observes, American lawyers were at the leading edge of a pronounced colonial movement toward "Anglicization." The colonial bar, in Murrin's words, was "consciously restructuring itself along English lines." Rudimentary (and occasionally more formal) bar associations began to develop in places like New York (1729 and 1744), Rhode Island (1745), Massachusetts (1750s), and Virginia (1770s). Would-be lawyers from the colonies traveled to the English Inns of Court for training with sharply increased frequency; where only 60 American lawyers had been trained in the Inns of Court prior to 1760, over 115 were trained there in the sixteen years between 1760 and the formal onset of the Revolution. A number of colonies, including Massachusetts (1762) and New Jersey (1767), even formally adopted the English two-tiered bar of elite barristers admitted to the highest courts in the province and middling attorneys admitted to the lower courts. In Massachusetts, Governor Thomas

Hutchinson required "distinct gowns for judges, barristers and attorneys" in the traditional English fashion; New York established the same dress requirements just two years later. And along with English training, English hierarchy, and English garb came technical common-law pleading practices like those long used in the courts at Westminster—varied writs, special pleas, sophisticated demurrers, and the like, all of which began to appear more regularly in American courts. Indeed, in their haste to ape English ways, provincial lawyers often outdid their metropolitan models. Massachusetts lawyers, for example, reintroduced the long-obsolete medieval "writ of entry" in real property disputes, a writ that Blackstone was describing in England at virtually the same time as so extraordinarily technical as to have long since been replaced by more sensible remedies. With the exception of a few such excesses, as lawyer-historian Julius Goebel once noted, colonial lawyers in the 1760s and 1770s were not far behind their Westminster peers in the sophistication of their common-law pleading.[21]

The Pennsylvania bar came relatively late to the colonial Anglicization project. But Pennsylvania lawyers embraced it with exceptional fervor. The "real Bar," as Warren called it in his history of the American legal profession, developed beginning in the 1740s. Between 1742 and 1776, more than seventy-six lawyers were admitted to practice in the Pennsylvania Supreme Court. All three of the colony's chief justices during the period were trained lawyers. In the same years, Philadelphia lawyers quickly distinguished themselves by their skills in the technicalities of English legal practice. The College of Philadelphia, founded in 1751, sent more students to the English Inns of Court during the colonial period than Harvard, Kings College (later renamed Columbia), Princeton, and Yale combined. And by some counts, there were more lawyers with memberships in English Inns of Court practicing in the Pennsylvania courts than there were practicing in the courts of any other colony except South Carolina.

By "the time of the Revolution," as Roscoe Pound put it, the Pennsylvania bar stood out in American history as a "center of legal learning"; it had, as another student of the colonial bar has observed, an "unrivaled excellence."[22]

＊
＊
＊

The prosperity of American lawyers in the 1760s was no doubt as appealing to Wilson as their increased learning and prestige; perhaps more so. Members of the Anglicizing American legal profession were among the chief beneficiaries of the commercial growth of the period. They were, by one account, the wealthiest of all the professionals, with earnings on the order of ten times those of doctors and ministers, often "as much as the very wealthiest merchants and planters, with less risk, and greater odds in favor of acquiring and retaining fortunes." Not every lawyer could match New York attorney general John Tabor Kempe, who rose through his career in the law from relative penury to enormous wealth, with an estate worth an estimated £80,000, an amount surpassed by few in the colonies. But by the 1760s, many lawyers did well enough. In 1765 lawyers ranked second only to merchants in a listing of one hundred wealthy Philadelphians. Elite lawyers such as Wilson's teacher Dickinson, in particular, appear to have been doing exceptionally well.[23]

Late colonial lawyers like Kempe made most of their money from investment opportunities, such as land speculation, and from the business connections that came with their practice, rather than from legal fees. Indeed, opportunities in western lands seem to have been a prime reason Wilson left the booming port of Philadelphia to open his law practice on the frontier. Wilson's earliest cases, in 1767 and 1768, were typical of young, inexperienced practitioners: probate, guardian accounts in orphans' court, and other estate matters. Within just two years, such cases made Wilson one of the busiest lawyers riding circuit in Pennsylvania's rural county courts. Very quickly, however, his most important cases became land cases. Robert Morris retained Wilson to litigate important matters touching on his speculation in western Pennsylvania lands. At the same time, Wilson himself took advantage of his regular circuits around the state's western counties to begin buying up unimproved lands on his own account.[24]

Wilson's land speculations are critically significant if we are to understand him. By the mid-1790s, the lure of investment in western lands in eighteenth-century America would help to create one of history's great market bubbles; in 1796 and 1797, the bubble would pop, leaving a number of America's wealthiest and most prominent men—Wilson included—in debtor's prison. But for two and a half decades before that, beginning at virtually the very start of his frontier law practice, Wilson engaged in land speculation and a variety of related commercial schemes with a fervor that verged on mania. In a bewildering array of often overlapping partnerships and stock companies, Wilson purchased unsettled lands throughout the northeastern and central parts of Pennsylvania, through the state's Wyoming Valley and Schuylkill and Susquehanna Counties, and along the Pennsylvania side of the Delaware River from what are now Wayne and Pike Counties in the north, downstream into Northampton, Bucks, and Berks Counties. Further west in Pennsylvania, he acquired interests in hundreds of thousands of acres along the south side of the Ohio River. In New York, with three partners, he invested in hundreds of thousands of acres of land near current-day Binghamton (named after Wilson's partner William Bingham). He invested heavily in, and later directed, the Illinois-Wabash Land Company, whose land claims in what would become the Northwest Territory amounted to some 30 million acres, of which Wilson's share included about 600,000 acres. To the south, he purchased 56,000 acres in Virginia. Other land companies in which Wilson invested included the Canaan Company, the Indiana Company, the notorious Georgia Land Company (whose lands were in the corruption-plagued Yazoo land grant to the west of Georgia), and the equally notorious (if slightly less corrupt) Great Dismal Swamp Company. By the middle of the 1780s, Wilson was exploring the possibility of obtaining Dutch financing for an elaborate system of iron works, grist mills, sawmills, and forges along lands he owned near the Delaware River in northeast Pennsylvania, along with an elaborate bridge that would connect his Pennsylvania land with Trenton and New York to the east. By the end of his career as a speculator, Wilson's land empire stretched from upstate New York west into the Allegheny Mountains of Pennsylvania to as far south as Georgia and North Carolina.[25]

Wilson was hardly the only member of his generation to build up extended interests in western property. But Wilson's reckless speculation was as ambitious as that of any his peers. It was also more deeply rooted in a peculiarly Scottish Enlightenment theory of political economy. Out of the grinding poverty of seventeenth- and early eighteenth-century Scotland, Scottish Enlightenment thinkers made economic development a central aim. In particular, Francis Hutcheson, David Hume, and Adam Smith sought to revise the view that commercial activity pushed communities toward luxury, vice, and corruption. For centuries, the civic tradition in political economy and constitutional thought, stretching from Machiavelli all the way back to the Roman historian Polybius, had linked commerce with moral declension and the corruption of the state. The civic tradition held that the advancement of private self-interest in commercial life ineluctably eroded the public virtue required of citizens of a republic. Indeed, in histories such as Edward Gibbon's classic *History of the Decline and Fall of the Roman Empire,* the happiness of a free state seemed to have a peculiarly "precarious nature." With the passage of time, the martial virtue of even vigilant republics seemed to slide into a taste for luxury and vice. Commerce accelerated this slide to luxury, which in turn seemed again and again to have produced decline, corruption, and ultimately tyranny in what had formerly been free states.[26]

As Pocock has put it, "The great achievement of the Scottish school . . . was the recognition that a commercial organization of society had rendered obsolete much that had been believed about society before it." Commerce need not, Scots like Hume and Smith contended, be seen as a corrupting force. It might instead be an engine of civilizing progress. Hume insisted that "the greatness of the sovereign and the happiness of the state are, in a great measure, united with regard to trade and manufactures." For one thing, Hume argued, men tended to display more virtue in their private commercial affairs than in their political capacities. Moreover, according to Hume commerce and industry—the bêtes noires of the civic tradition—were politically valuable because they were more conducive than feudal hierarchies to a relative equality of wealth. Smith pushed forward along similar lines. For Smith, the pursuit of riches was driven precisely by the force of our sociability: "it is chiefly from this regard to the sentiments of mankind, that we pursue riches and avoid poverty," he wrote in *The Theory of Moral Sentiments,* published in 1759. Our own moral faculties provided a check on self-interest run amok, and so too did the general regard shared by men for their social reputation. Virtue and commerce, it seemed, might go hand in hand.[27]

Smith's *Theory of Moral Sentiments* and Wilson's own ideas about commerce each drew heavily on the earlier work of Francis Hutcheson. Writing in the first half of the eighteenth century, Hutcheson had argued that "the Author of nature has much better furnished us for a virtuous conduct than some moralists seem to imagine." Against John Locke's idea of the mind as a kind of "empty cabinet," Hutcheson contended that we have an interior sense—a moral faculty, or "moral sense"—that not only receives sensory impressions but makes judgments on the basis of innate moral precepts. Our ideas of good and evil and our conduct, Hutcheson explained, are supervised by this moral faculty as a kind of internal self-government, policing our pursuit of self-interest "so as to limit and counteract . . . the selfish Passions." The moral faculty, Hutcheson contended, provided an internal "ballance of publick passions against the private." Public-regarding virtues would be upheld by the moral faculty's careful "ballance of affections." As Scottish lawyer Lord Kames put it, "in the breast of man a tribunal is erected for Conscience." That tribunal—the moral sense—was "so nicely proportioned to our situation in this world" as to strike the perfect balance between man's social nature and his selfish nature. Human nature was thus "contrived in the most perfect manner for promoting the general good," the "limited powers of man" notwithstanding.[28]

By the lights of Hutcheson's moral faculty, self-interest and public virtue, which had seemed so clearly opposed to each other in the civic tradition, were in fact tightly bound together. Indeed, in Hutcheson's view (and similar ideas can be found in Smith's *Theory of Moral Sentiments*), private happiness and the well-being of others existed alongside each other in an infinitely iterating virtuous cycle. For the man who sought to advance his happiness, "the Observation of the Happiness of others" was a "necessary Occasion of Pleasure." It was the moral faculty that provided the engine for Hutcheson's dynamic cycle of happiness. The moral faculty registered the "Pleasures arising from Publick Happiness, and Aversion to the Pains arising from the Misery of others," making the observation of others' happiness a "necessary Occasion of Pleasure" for observer and subject alike. In turn, the personal pursuit of wealth and power required the "good-will of others." Only by obtaining the favor of others and "maintaining credit in society" could wealth and power easily be obtained.[29]

This was a startlingly novel theory. And it was precisely this theory, which revised the civic conception of human nature and consequently of the relationship between commerce and civic virtue, that Wilson found irresistible. Wilson developed the idea of the moral sense into a powerful license for his own private commercial activity. Following closely on Hutcheson and the related ideas of Scottish philosopher Thomas Reid, Wilson argued that we are endowed with an "internal sense," or "consciousness," that "gives us information of what passes within us." Most important, Wilson's "internal sense" carried with it an "innate moral sense" that distinguished between right and wrong. The inner sense was the locus of our moral faculty, the "most important part of our constitution." It "is intended to regulate and control all our other powers. It governs our passions as well as our actions." It "assumes authority, it must be obeyed." It even, Wilson contended, supplied the hidden connection that answered Hamlet's agonized question "What's Hecuba to him, or he to Hecuba?", forming a "secret chain betwixt each person and mankind." Like the inner faculty that distinguished harmony and dissonance in music, like the "inward eye" that discerned beauty in forms, the moral sense was "diffused through every part of life." Every human language spoke "of a beautiful and a deformed, a right and a wrong, an agreeable and disagreeable, a good and ill," and in doing so provided eloquent testimony that "all languages . . . suppose a moral sense."[30]

If Hutcheson was right, Wilson insisted, it followed that the old concerns of political thinkers about supposed tensions between self-interest and the public weal were misplaced. After the destructive self-seeking described by social theorists such as Thomas Hobbes and Bernard de Mandeville, the recognition of a moral faculty promised a powerful new engine of human happiness. "Self-love and social" were actually "the same," Wilson told grand juries and lecture audiences. The advancement of self-interest coincided perfectly, or so it seemed, with the advancement of social interest. The judgments of the moral sense, he argued, were "not merely superiour in degree but as superiour likewise in kind, to what is recommended by our other perceptive powers." Human beings "endowed with such a variety of senses and interfering desires" might well have appeared like a "fabrick destitute of order." But "possessed of" the moral sense, "all our powers may be harmonious and consistent." Self-interested passions were subordinate to the intuitive moral perceptions of the moral faculty. The passions, it followed, would not outstrip virtue. "Let man pursue his happiness and perfection," Wilson crowed, echoing Hutcheson, for "whatever promotes the greatest happiness of the whole, is congenial to the principles of utility and sociability: and whatever unites in it all the foregoing properties, must be agreeable to the will of God."[31]

It surely did not escape Wilson's attention that North America seemed to hold a special place in the new political economy of the Scots. Adam Smith identified enormous economic promise in America, where British colonies had experienced "rapid progress . . . in wealth, population and improvement." In particular, Smith saw enormous potential in the unsettled lands to the west. "The purchase and improvement of uncultivated land," he wrote, "is there the most profitable employment of . . . capital . . . and the most direct road to all the fortune and illustration which can be acquired in that country." Indeed Smith contended that "such land . . . is in North America to be had for almost nothing, or at a price so much below the value of the natural produce."[32]

Following the teachings of Smith's *Wealth of Nations,* Wilson advocated policies such as the creation of a national bank, which would "increase circulation and invigorate industry." Commerce, he quoted Smith, would be "'a sort of wagon-way in the air,'" which would "'enable the country . . . to increase very considerably the annual produce of its land and labour.'" Most of all, the open frontier seemed to Wilson to present investment opportunities virtually unparalleled in human history. On the American frontier, capital might be invested "with a Degree of Certainty and System unknown to Transactions of any other Kind." The uncleared wilderness might seem to present obstacles to the small-minded. But clearing the land was in fact only another opportunity, and the resulting timber another source of profit.[33]

Like Hutcheson and Smith before him, Wilson became entranced by the opportunities for a virtuous cycle of ever-upward economic progress that the western frontier now seemed to present. Each new farm to the west made possible yet another even as it increased the value of the one that had come before. "Every preceding Settlement, Improvement and Farm," Wilson insisted, "prepares the Way for those, which shall *succeed:* And every subsequent Settlement, Improvement and Farm bestows an additional Value upon those, which have *preceded* it." Surpluses from existing plantations would be carried forward to support new plantations in temporary need, whose demands would inure to the benefit of the plantations that had come before. Prosperity would thus cascade across the western frontier, across the Appalachians to the Great Lakes and down along the Mississippi. Indeed, as Wilson saw it, "the reciprocal and encreasing Advantages of progressive and extending Settlements may be carried to a Height and with a Degree of Rapidity not easily conceived." And of course such plans, Wilson noted, "will obviously admit of an handsome Compensation to all, who shall be employed in its several Parts." Once again a kind of virtuous cycle of ever-increasing prosperity would ensue:

> The Compensation will be not only handsome, but permanent and encreasing. A Compensation, handsome, permanent and encreasing, will command a Choice of Characters, well recommended by their Integrity and their Skill. Characters, so recom-

mended, will engage the Confidence of every one, whose Interest can be affected by their Conduct. This Confidence will operate as a powerful Motive for taking an Interest in a System, which will be thus skillfully and honestly carried into Execution.

Investments in American land, in short, would touch off the kind of self-sustaining reciprocal cycles of ever-increasing happiness that Hutcheson and Smith had described. Fostered by the moral sense, commercial exchange would provide the foundations for ever-increasing wealth and happiness. The first ring of plantations would support a second, which in turn would sustain a third, and so on.[34]

Virtuous cycles of ever-increasing prosperity meant that there was no necessary conflict between the kinds of private profit seeking Wilson pursued while riding circuit around Pennsylvania, on one hand, and the public interest on the other. Commercial exchange and public morality complemented one another precisely because the "pillars" on which commercial life rested— "the obligation of promises, agreements, and covenants"—were rooted in "our moral perceptions." If, as Wilson said, "self-love and social are the same," Wilson's own profits would redound to the benefit of the United States. If the "unnatural[ly]" low "price of improved land," as Alexander Hamilton wrote in Federalist 15, seemed to result from a "want of private and public confidence," it followed that the fate of the nation and the fate of land values ran together. Wilson might patriotically signal his confidence in the nation's fate by willingly purchasing all that he could get his hands on. In turn, as values rose with the nation's prospects, he would stand to reap the private gains from his public professions of patriotism. "If my Plans and opinions are well founded," he wrote to prospective Dutch investors in one of his land speculation plans, "I shall have an Opportunity of doing thereby much Service to myself, to my family, to my

Country, and to the Citizens of a Country with which it is the Interest of mine to preserve and cultivate the closest Connection and the most extensive Intercourse, public and private." And again, to a new set of investors he was courting: "It will be in the Interest of the *United States as well as of Individuals* to pursue the Settlement of Farms and the Establishment of States" to the west.[35]

*
*
*

The crowd that smashed Wilson's doors and wheeled up the cannon outside his home on October 4, 1779, does not seem to have seen it quite this way. The members of the crowd were considerably less confident that Wilson's economic interests so perfectly aligned with the interests of the revolutionary republic. For the members of the Pennsylvania militia, and for countless other Americans in the 1770s and 1780s, it seemed that the gains of lawyers and men of commerce often came at the expense of artisans, handicraft workers, and journeymen.

The question of lawyers' fate in the American Revolution is deeply bound up in one of the most mooted issues in American history. Was the American Revolution simply a legal and constitutional struggle over the principles of the British Empire? Or was it also a social struggle, pitting factions—perhaps even classes—against one another in a contest over control of the political institutions of the new republic? The Fort Wilson riot raised this question as vividly as any other single event in the American fight for independence. What is interesting to the student of the legal profession and of the Fort Wilson incident, however, is not what the character of the American Revolution turned out to be, but what alternative directions the Revolution might plausibly have taken. Hannah Arendt once observed that the relatively conservative course of the American Revolution was nothing short of a "miracle." She might have said the same about the remarkable good fortune of American lawyers.[36]

As early as 1774, patrician lawyer Gouverneur Morris of New York (and later Philadelphia) noted in typically caustic fashion that "the heads of the mobility grow dangerous to the gentry." William Smith, like Morris a member of the New York bar, feared that the "partial tumults" and mob government arising out of the Stamp Act would escalate into "a general Civil War"; by the 1770s he considered the "landed Interest" to be lucky if it could save its estates. In Massachusetts, Elbridge Gerry observed that the people "now feel rather too much their own importance"; it would, Gerry feared, require "great skill to produce such subordination as is necessary." Even the Declaration of Independence expressed concern about the "convulsions within" to which George III had exposed the colonies by dissolving the colonial assemblies and thus returning the legislative power "to the People at large for their exercise."[37]

In the run-up to the Revolution, American elites had begun a process of popular mobilization that required attentive and adept management—"great skill," in Gerry's words—lest it turn against them as it would at Fort Wilson. Yet Philadelphia's politically divided lawyers were among those least prepared to engage in the process of managing the tensions raised by the Revolution. For fifty years, Pennsylvania's proprietary party and the Quaker-affiliated assembly party opposition had been engaged in a pattern of political competition for the allegiance of the Scotch-Irish and working-class German immigrants. Each new political contest had caused the contending elites to mobilize ever wider segments of the population for support. As Fort Wilson made abundantly clear, however, that popular mobilization now threatened to turn against the divided elites who had begun it. Indeed, Fort Wilson was hardly the first such riot in Philadelphia. As long before as the 1720s, a crowd had attacked the home of Philadelphia grandee and judge James Logan, tearing off shutters, throwing bricks through the windows, and generally "threaten[ing] to level one of Philadelphia's most gracious structures." In 1742 riots had marred elections. In 1764 a group known as the Paxton Boys had led an angry and murderous march on the city, protesting the proprietary government's alleged failure to protect them from Indian depredations. To be sure, Philadelphia had seen relatively little rioting during the Stamp Act period. But that was largely a measure of the power of popular politics in Philadelphia, not a sign of its weakness. Merchants feared "a deluge of blood" if they were to try to evade the popular boycott of English goods prompted by the Stamp Act.[38]

To make matters more pressing, Philadelphia was home to some of the most wrenching demographic, social, and economic change anywhere in the colonies in the decade leading up to the Revolution. The city's population tripled between 1741 and 1775, from 10,360 to around 32,000. More and more Philadelphians had difficulty paying their assessed taxes. Poor-relief rolls increased from 9 people for every 1,000 in the early 1750s to 16 for every 1,000 in 1765 and 30 for every 1,000 in the first half of the 1770s. By 1776, the city's radical committees were issuing warnings that "great and overgrown rich men will be improper to be trusted, they will be too apt to be framing distinctions in society, because they will reap the benefits of all such distinctions." One such committee even argued that the "enormous proportion of property vested in a few individuals is dangerous to the rights, and destructive of the common happiness, of mankind." The radical committee proposed that the state should therefore have the authority to "discourage the possession of such property.[39]

Lawyers in Philadelphia and elsewhere were lightning rods in the popular politics of the Revolutionary moment. Distrust of the legal profession had developed in some colonies as early as the Stamp Act crisis, during which lawyers in Philadelphia (and elsewhere) sat out court proceedings rather than take the more radical step of carrying on with unstamped—and thus unauthorized—legal papers. New York radicals demonstrated against lawyers by dragging a goat—apparently a popular eighteenth-century stand-in for lawyers—around the city. In the North Carolina back country, Wilson's future colleague on the Supreme Court James Iredell noted that "the gentlemen of the Bar" were "objects of obloquy and denunciation" by those Iredell called the "poor and illiterate." The popular militia known as the North Carolina Regulators kidnapped lawyers and threatened them with death to stop debt proceedings and foreclosures, urging their followers to "shun [lawyers] as you would the pestilence." Meanwhile, "Liberty Boys" riots beset New Jersey lawyers involved in rent collection; courts were shut down, and crowds burned the outbuildings of at least three leading lawyers, who were themselves tried at popular insistence for abusing the rules governing legal fees. Crowds resisted legal process—often violently—in Vermont and Massachusetts. Lawyers ("the Oppressors of the People," as New York radicals put it) seemed "ever the most forward to promote the Measures of the Court" and to "extend the Prerogative of the Crown" when it was "consistent with their own Advantage."[40]

Once the Revolution began, lawyers disproportionately aligned themselves with the crown. This was especially true in the northeastern colonies, in which Anglicized bars had taken root most strongly. Twelve of twenty-five barristers admitted to the New York Supreme Court became Tories during the Revolution. Of forty-eight barristers in Massachusetts, nineteen were Tories and eight were Tory sympathizers; only fifteen could be labeled patriots, though four more seem to have been sympathetic to the patriot cause. Similar patterns repeated themselves throughout the colonies, especially after a wave of Revolutionary loyalty-test legislation excluded "men who are enemies to their Country" from the practice of law. The consequences were especially severe among the "giants of the bar," who were virtually all Tories. Whereas between 60,000 and 80,000 out of 2.5 million people fled as emigrés from Revolutionary America, 25 percent of the legal profession did so, including 150 leading lawyers and some 200 or so others of lesser standing. Leading lawyers seemed to have been "seduced" from the revolutionary cause "by the honeyed Mansfieldism of Blackstone," as Jefferson recalled in 1826, leaving what Roscoe Pound would later call "a huge gap in what had become a great body of lawyers."[41]

In Philadelphia, most of the city's leading lawyers ("all the lawyers of any considerable ability" in the city, as Joseph Reed described them in 1779) remained loyal to the crown. Prominent lawyer Joseph Galloway, for example, had supported the Stamp Act and had long urged closer union with Great Britain rather than independence. In December 1776 he even decamped to British lines and acted as an aid to General Howe in the British attack on his home city, later serving as a high official in the occupation government in Philadelphia. All in all, at least fourteen—and perhaps more—of the forty-five practicing lawyers listed in *Martin's Bench and Bar of Philadelphia* as having been admitted through 1770 were loyalists during the war.[42]

Even many nonloyalist lawyers in Philadelphia distanced themselves from the revolutionary cause. Benjamin Chew, William Tilghman, and John Ross remained neutral through the war years; Chew did so only after being arrested as a loyalist and paroled to New Jersey. Jared Ingersoll, who had served as the Crown's "Stamp-master" in New Haven before moving to Philadelphia, sent his son to finish his law education in London during the war. William Tilghman, who later became chief justice of the state supreme court, studied law with the neutral Chew and married the daughter of loyalist lawyer James Allen. Tilghman then sat out the Revolution outside the city at the Chestertown estate to which his family had removed. His kinsman Edward Tilghman, who would later marry Benjamin Chew's daughter, was an avid student of Lord Mansfield at Kings Bench in Westminster in the early 1770s, even as Mansfield was articulating views on Parliamentary sovereignty squarely opposed to those of the colonists. As hostilities got under way, William Rawle studied law in New York under loyalist John Tabor Kempe, and then rode out the rest of the Revolution at the Middle Temple in London. Even John Dickinson—known as the "penman of the Revolution" for his legal arguments against Parliament's taxing authority in *Letters from a Farmer* (1768)—attracted radical ire when he famously declined to sign the Declaration of Independence, hesitating in the end to break from the Crown. Many Philadelphians, in short, had good reason to believe that Philadelphia lawyers had "hesitated until too late to declare for independence and revolution."[43]

The months and years that followed independence barely put the city's lawyers in a better light. By the fall of 1776 Wilson was serving as the architect of the bar's attempt to sabotage the courts created by the radicals' new state constitution. Wilson and others created "an agreement . . . neither to practice or accept any office under the constitution," as lawyer Alexander Graydon later recalled. By 1778 and 1779, Wilson and another Philadelphia lawyer, William Lewis, had abandoned the abortive boycott only to become deeply involved in defending accused Tories in what eventually totaled 118 treason prosecutions. Ominously for the remaining members of the city bar, the Assembly in 1779 impeached conservative state judge Francis Hopkinson, a political ally of Wilson and Robert Morris. Though Hopkinson was acquitted (and was later made federal district judge for the district of Pennsylvania), his would be only the first of a series of impeachment proceedings against conservative state judges in Pennsylvania between 1779 and 1803, proceedings that foreshadowed the impeachment efforts that Thomas Jefferson's congressional allies would launch against federal judges after Jefferson's election in 1800. By the 1780s, even as crowd actions shut down courts across the colonies, the Pennsylvania Assembly redoubled efforts to discourage formal legal proceedings in favor of lay arbitration by referees. Western Pennsylvania farmers, echoing Daniel Shays's rebellion in western Massachusetts two years before, expressed increasing anger over the authority of high-handed courts in foreclosure and debt proceedings. A little more than a decade later, the Philadelphia *Aurora* was still decrying the "enmity" of lawyers "to the principles of free government," while politicians around the state debated eliminating the privileges of the bar. "All the eminent lawyers" in the city, reported young lawyer Charles Jared Ingersoll around this time, "have their eyes on one city or another, to remove in case of extremes."[44]

Philadelphia lawyers who took the side of independence realized full well the danger of the situation. Wilson wrote in 1776 to longtime political ally Andrew St. Clair that he saw a "very critical situation of public affairs"; the Revolutionary system of government threatened to produce the "same results" as the "tyranny from a foreign power" against which the Revolutionary legal arguments of lawyers like Wilson and John Dickinson had been aimed. Dickinson, too, warned of the "calamities" that threatened to result from the Revolution absent proper restraints. Anticipating the heroics he would need to perform in rescuing Wilson in 1779, Joseph Reed—also a member of the Philadelphia bar—reported in 1773 that he "every day perceive[d] it more and more difficult to repress the rising spirit of the people." "Frequent appeals to the people," Reed noted, would inevitably "in time occasion a change."[45]

*
*
*

The Fort Wilson incident usefully stands in for an entire generation of attacks—some legal, some rhetorical, some violent—on

Philadelphia lawyers in the Revolutionary period. Loyalists aside, however, neither Wilson nor many of Philadelphia's other lawyers removed themselves from the city. Despite the threats that had mounted against their authority in the Revolutionary period, lawyers in Philadelphia and elsewhere thrived in the early years of the republic. Twenty-five of fifty-six signers of the Declaration were lawyers. So were thirty-one of fifty-five members of the Constitutional Convention a little over a decade later, in 1787. Sixteen of the thirty senators who served in the first U.S. Congress were lawyers; two more were admitted to the bar but never practiced; and still another had been trained at the Inns of Court. In the House, twenty-seven of sixty-six representatives were lawyers; two more were trained at the Inns of Court; and five others served as judges in the state courts. At virtually the same time, bar admissions skyrocketed. Between 1776 and 1800, 211 lawyers were admitted to the Philadelphia bar. Pent-up demand for legal services combined with lawyer-loyalist emigration to create new opportunities in the wake of the Revolution. In late eighteenth-century Philadelphia and elsewhere, it seems, lawyers were already well on their way to attaining the exceptionally powerful role they have enjoyed in the United States ever since.[46]

All of this brings us back to Richard Morris's question and John Murrin's paradox: How is it that lawyers managed with such spectacular success to ride out the American Revolution? Wilson, for one, well understood the nature of the dilemma when he warned in 1776 of the "very critical situation" facing the newly independent nation. Managing the Revolution would be hard work. Yet, as he so often did, Wilson saw personal opportunity running alongside public need. For Wilson the Revolution opened up new possibilities as well as new risks. Here was a chance to become a Blackstone or Mansfield—or, better yet, a Lycurgus or Solon—of the new republic.[47]

From the outset, Wilson pursued the Revolution's opportunities with uninhibited and only thinly disguised ambition. Already in 1777, Wilson was campaigning for his appointment to the post of continental attorney general. The attorney general, as Wilson conceived the office, would represent the Congress in admiralty cases and in the investigation of public officials, and would give opinions on questions "in the civil and Maritime laws, and the Law of Nations." Congress never created the position, but a decade later Wilson took up the possibility of a similarly august position under the new federal Constitution. "My aim," he wrote to President George Washington in April 1789, "rises to the important Office of Chief Justice of the United States." The next year, he prepared a series of lectures that aimed to do for the American common law what Blackstone had done for the English in his lectures of the 1750s: state it in a systematic and conceptually coherent whole. Less than a year later, Wilson sought and obtained authorization from his friend and partner William Bingham, speaker of the Pennsylvania House of Representatives, to revise and digest the entire common law along with all of the statutes of the state. By December 1791, Wilson was importuning Washington to support Wilson's plan to create a still more ambitious digest of the laws of the United States, one that would ostensibly reveal the "Principles" of the nation's laws as well as "their Connexion" to one another.[48]

Few of Wilson's ambitious undertakings came to fruition. Washington did appoint him as an associate justice to the Supreme Court. But Wilson was three times passed over for the chief justice position he coveted. His lectures were never completed. Washington and the Pennsylvania senate each declined his offers to digest the laws.[49]

Despite their failure to be realized, however, Wilson's ambitions illuminate his view of the American Revolution as a jurisprudential opportunity of world-historical proportions. In revolutionary America, Wilson identified a chance to develop and institute a new political and legal theory to match the new economics of the Scots. Eighteenth-century Anglo-American constitutional thought had sought to balance the three component parts of society—monarchy, aristocracy, and commons. Each of these three parts had particular and characteristic interests, and balancing these interests was the aim of a republican constitution. But if Hutcheson's ideas about the moral faculty were right, there might be a private inner mechanism for the control of individuals' ambitions and interests. Public institutions might not need to balance those passions after all. Instead of simply serving as a kind of elaborate mechanism to hold off the decline of virtue, republican constitutions might become the embodiments of perfect virtue themselves.

In Wilson's view, recognition of the moral faculty meant that constitutional design and jurisprudence could at long last be founded on principles that would coincide perfectly with natural reason and justice. Constitutionalism no longer needed to satisfy itself with the second-best approach of mediating the corrupting effects of private passion. Even better, perfect laws would create the same kind of virtuous cycle of which the philosophers of the moral faculty were so fond. "As excellent laws improve the virtue of the citizens so the virtue of the citizens has a reciprocal and benign energy in heightening the excellence of the laws," Wilson told a Virginia grand jury in 1791. "Let the law diffuse peace and happiness, and innocence will walk in their train."[50]

Wilson regularly expressed his theory through a favorite metaphor: the pyramid. He first offered the pyramid image at the Constitutional Convention in Philadelphia in late May 1787. Elbridge Gerry had just seconded a proposal that elections to the House of Representatives be by the state legislatures rather than by the people. The defect of the Articles of Confederation, he insisted, was "the excess of democracy." George Mason conceded "that we had been too democratic," but feared that "we should run incautiously into the opposite extreme." Wilson took the floor to offer a striking new image. "He was," as James Madison recorded Wilson's words, "for raising the federal pyramid to a considerable altitude, and for that reason wished to give it as broad a basis as possible." Only a government with a broad popular foundation, Wilson seemed to be saying, could attain the heights of the Egyptian edifices. As William Pierce of Georgia recorded, "Mr. Wilson thought that one branch of the Legislature ought to be drawn from the people, because on the great foundation of the people all Government ought to rest. He would wish to see the new Constitution established on a broad basis, and rise like a pyramid to a respectable point."[51]

Wilson returned to the pyramid metaphor just a few months later at the Pennsylvania ratifying convention, whose proceedings he dominated. "A free government has often been compared to a pyramid," declared Wilson. "It is laid on the broad basis of the people; its powers gradually rise, while they are confined, in proportion as they ascend, until they end in that most permanent of all forms." And again the next year at the convention to create a new state constitution for Pennsylvania: "The pyramid of government—and a republican government may well receive that beautiful and solid form—should be raised to a dignified altitude." Government's "foundations must, of consequence, be broad, and strong, and deep." Wilson advised his fellow delegates that "the authority, the interests, and the affections of the people at large are the only basis, on which a superstructure, proposed to be at once durable and magnificent, can be rationally erected." And in the winter of 1790–91, Wilson conjured the image of the pyramid yet again, this time in his law lectures at the University of Pennsylvania: "The pyramid of government may certainly be raised with all the graces of fair proportion, and also with the more substantial qualities of firmness and strength." Later the lectures returned to the same point. Wilson reminded his audience that the people were "the only foundation" on which a "superstructure" as "durable and magnificent" as the "pyramid of government" could "be rationally erected."[52]

Wilson's pyramid metaphor aimed to do much more than advance the case for popular elections. The pyramids were a regular feature in eighteenth-century intellectual culture and debate. Hutcheson had used the pyramid to illustrate how the human faculty for the perception of beauty found its object in proportioned geometric forms. Thomas Reid and David Hume, along with many others, also used pyramid metaphors, often without labeling them as such.[53]

In particular, English and American writers had been using the pyramids for almost a century as the example par excellence of the capacity of human reason to build monuments that could resist decay. The "pyramids of Egypt," wrote late seventeenth-century Englishman William Winstanley in a book widely reprinted in the eighteenth-century American colonies, had "outlasted devouring Time." They were, as one English writer had put it, "proof against the attacks of time." Seventeenth-century writer and statesman Sir William Temple invoked the pyramids in just the way that Wilson would a century later: "the safety and firmness of any frame of government may best be judged by the rules of architecture, which teach that the pyramid is of all figures the firmest and least subject to be shaken or overthrown"; the government "which . . . takes in the consent of the greatest number of people and consequently their desires and resolutions to support it must justly be said to have the broadest bottom."[54]

Closer to Wilson's own time, Blackstone's *Commentaries on the Laws of England* had described the stable, graded status hierarchies of English society as a kind of pyramid. Blackstone noted that "the rude pyramids of Egypt have endured from the earliest ages," while "more modern" and "elegant structures of Attica,

Rome, and Palmyra" had "sunk beneath the stroke of time." English divine James Hervey wrote of the "stability" of the pyramids. English children's literature author John Adams, lifting passages from a French text that had yet to be translated into English, wrote that the "famous pyramids, which a number of writers suppose to have been built before the deluge, still resist the injuries of time, which has destroyed so many empires." The native guide in Samuel Johnson's *Rasselas, Prince of Abbissinia,* described the "pyramidal form" as "intended to co-extend its duration with that of the world": "its gradual diminution gave it such stability" as even to defeat earthquakes.[55]

Interest in the pyramids—and indeed in virtually all things Egyptian—flowered in Europe in the second half of the eighteenth century. Under the influence of architects and designers infatuated with Egyptian motifs, English estates sported faux Egyptian-style gates in the 1750s and 1760s. Influential Italian designer Giovanni Battista Piranesi decorated villas with Egyptian images in the 1760s and 1770s. And in the latter decade, Josiah Wedgwood began to make fine pottery inspired by Egyptian designs. At the same time, a vogue for pyramidal mausoleums struck England, France, and Sweden, producing pyramid-formed tombs for, among others, James King of the Royal Academy (1777), the Dowager Queen Louisa Ulrika of Sweden (1782), the Fourth Earl of Darnley (1783), and the Second Earl of Buckinghamshire (1794). Plans for a pyramid tomb in which to re-inter the Renaissance artist Titian were drafted in 1795 but never completed.[56]

For many in the new republic (including Thomas Jefferson, who had among his belongings a miniature model of the great pyramid of Giza), the symbolism of Wilson's pyramid was quite familiar. Americans celebrating the French and American alliance toasted a friendship whose "duration shall be that of the ages of a pyramid." William Hillhouse of Connecticut in 1789 pronounced Washington's immortal fame a "durable pyramid." Poets wrote of the monuments of ancient Egypt "that bid defiance to the arm of Time." "Babel's tower is gone, and these remain"; the pyramids were "beyond tradition's reach" and beyond "history" itself. Time had smote its scythe on the pyramids, but they "resist its edge." Even the Continental Congress got into the act in 1782, adopting the design of Wilson's friend Francis Hopkinson, which placed "a pyramid unfinished" on the Great Seal of the United States to signify "strength and duration."[57]

Of special interest in the seventeenth and eighteenth centuries, before modern archeological science dismissed such mystical rumors from polite company, was the possibility that the pyramids might allow at long last for a grand synchronization of history across the ages. Not only had the pyramids resisted the forces of time, they also promised to reconcile historical time. The pyramids seemed to have preceded, and thus survived, the great biblical flood. Dating the pyramids would therefore allow the student to locate the flood in a single chronology that set biblical history alongside the classics of Greece, Rome, and Egypt. The deluge and the desert would at last fit snugly alongside Troy and Athens and Rome in a coherently rendered chronological line. By the mid- and late eighteenth century, as James Wilson turned to the pyramid motif, this grand aspiration had produced a fad for genre paintings presenting views of Rome that merged classical ruins and Egyptian-inspired monuments, collapsing the millennia separating the early pharaohs from Rome.[58]

Among more scientifically inclined students of human history, historical synchronization regularly focused on identifying a systematic index to reconcile the jumble of inconsistent systems of weights and measures that cluttered the historical record. Human weights and measures, as historian of science Zur Shalev observes, had long been interpreted "as a divine gift to postlapsarian human society." But the divine gift seemed to have de-

Giovanni Battista Piranesi, *Piramide di C. Cestio.* Piranesi's eighteenth-century etching portrays a timeless pyramid alongside the time-bound ruins of antiquity. (Fine Arts Museums of San Francisco, gift of Ann Lafferty Pfeiffer)

clined into a Babel of competing measures. The English foot, the Hebrew cubit, the Greek *stade,* the Roman *stadion:* the accumulated experience of human history was broken up into disparate and irreducible metrics. Difficulties in translation from one system to another meant that ancient scenes might never be fully grasped in the absence of some common, transhistorical measure. The pyramids, however, seemed to hold out the promise of a temporal lingua franca for the inconsistent systems of measurement that crowded human history. Oxford scientist John Greaves, writing in the mid-seventeenth century, had fixed on the pyramids—"where traditions went uninterrupted from time immemorial and where time's effects were least destructive"—as holding the solution to the problem. Greaves believed that "the vicissitudes, and revolutions of times" had deprived his contemporaries of the wisdom of the ancients, but that "the Pyramids have been too great to be consumed." Virtually all ancient systems of measure had been applied to the pyramids; indeed, as seventeenth- and eighteenth-century students of the pyramids noted again and again, no one, ancient or modern, seemed able to visit the pyramids without taking down detailed measurements of the awesome structures. Modern measures might now carefully be reapplied, and the ancient measures thereby translated into new ones. The "ancient Mathematicians," Greaves conceded, had failed to use measures sufficiently precise as to eliminate all uncertainty in interpreting the measures of the past. But at the very least posterity would have no such difficulties with the modern metrics founded in the pyramid. Regardless of what happened to the European civilization, future generations would be able to use the pyramids (along with Greaves's calculations) to take the measure of the English foot as well as "the feet of several nations" whose measures Greaves had carefully recorded. The world's measurement schemes would thus be synchronized on the transhistorical template of the pyramids.[59]

English luminaries such as Isaac Newton, who had turned to Greaves's work as part of a failed attempt to measure the mass of the earth, studied Greaves's calculations at length. In the next century, the massive, sixty-five-volume *Universal History,* published in London in the 1740s, brought the systematizing zeal of the Enlightenment to Greaves's synchronizations. The *Universal History* (which described the pyramids as the "most permanent of all structures") dedicated dozens of pages of frontmatter to establishing the transhistorical reconciliations of weights and measures that would render the histories that followed truly universal. By the mid-eighteenth century, Greaves's work had made it into colonial American conversation as well. Greaves's *Pyramidographia* (published in 1646), for example, was in the collection of the Library Company of Philadelphia. And when Jonathan Edwards told a Massachusetts audience that measurement of "antient buildings . . . particularly the pyramids" had caused learned men to revise their ideas of the length of the Old Testament cubit, he was drawing heavily on work by Greaves. The knowledge unlocked from the pyramids, Edwards announced, revealed Noah's ark to have been twice its previously estimated bulk![60]

All of this provided the resonant context for Wilson's pyramids. By invoking the pyramids in the debate over the constitutional order of the new nation, Wilson was not merely holding out the promise of a durable constitutional order that might be able to hold off, at least for a time, the corruption that history inevitably brought. Such was the standard stuff of eighteenth-century constitutional thought. Instead, Wilson was saying that American legal science might at last uncover universal truths that stood outside of time altogether. According to Greaves, the Egyptians believed that the eternal and the contingent—the soul and the body—could be made to cohere. In ancient Egyptian religion the soul persisted only "as long as the body endured." The great achievement of the pyramids and of Egyptian embalming techniques was thus to have "found out wayes to make the body durable." Even the body, that most corruptible of time-bound creations, might be preserved for the ages. (This was precisely why late eighteenth-century Europeans were so entranced with the pyramid as mausoleum.) For Wilson it seemed to follow that states, too, need not be caught in the contingent stream of history. God would never have left the "rational and moral world . . . abandoned to the frolicks of chance, or to the ravage of disorder." Instead, the moral intuitions of the people ratified into law might stand as timeless monuments to transhistorical moral truths akin to the "Eye of Providence" atop the Great Seal's pyramid. This would be the American legal science by which the body politic would be made durable. All that needed to happen was for the moral sensibility of the people to be unshackled and recognized for what it was: a timeless guide to right. Thus empowered, American law would be like the pyramids, the ancient monuments of Egypt that had withstood the ravages of time where the ruins of the classical cities had not.[61]

The appeal of the pyramids was all the more powerful because it seemed to resolve a problem that had been at the center of common-law thinking for centuries: the tension between the historically accumulated wisdom of the common law, on one hand, and the pull of reason, first principles, and natural law on the other. For the age of Enlightenment, the common law lacked the appeal of rationality and system that could be found in the eighteenth-century law of nations and in the civil law, both of which purported to be made up largely of just such natural-law principles. ("Written reason," Blackstone called the civil law.) This was why Blackstone had aimed to move beyond the jumble of English law books like Coke's *Institutes* and the untheorized alphabetizations of common-law abridgments ("Bailment, "Bar," "Baron and Feme" . . .) to "extract a theory of law," as he put it, from the "mass of undigested learning" that was the common law. Blackstone sought to establish once and for all that the common law was a "science . . . universal in its use and extent." The project of his great *Commentaries* was therefore to find in the immemorial custom of the common law "noble monuments of antient simplicity" that held the "accumulated wisdom of the ages."[62]

In Wilson's hands, Blackstone's "noble monuments" to the transhistorical reason of the common law became "most permanent" pyramids. Wilson knew firsthand the methodlessness of common-law learning of which Blackstone complained. As a student under John Dickinson in 1766 and 1767, Wilson had been one of the last Americans to read law in the era before Blackstone brought clarity to the obscure "labyrinths" (Blackstone's word) of Coke's common law. Indeed, Wilson's legal education proceeded in the form of forbidding snippets of legal learning in virtually no discernable order whatsoever: "Lawyer," "Jurisdiction," and "Essoin"; "Infant," "Covenant," and "Error"; "Case, actions on," "Slander," "Issues," and "Will"; "Pleas," "Statute," and "Trespass vi et armis"; and so on ad infinitum.[63]

Yet for all Blackstone's systematizing energies, he seemed to Wilson to have sacrificed reason at the altar of the common law's accumulated irrationalities. In particular, Blackstone seemed to Wilson to have completely missed the Hutchesonian move that would make the synchronization of nature and history possible. Law, in Blackstone's definition, was "a rule of action" set by "a supreme irresistible, absolute, uncontrolled authority"—namely Parliament—in which . . . the rights of sovereignty, reside." But for Wilson, Blackstone's parliamentary sovereignty threatened to interfere with the moral sensibility of the people in which the reconciliation of history and reason promised to happen. When the people were unrepresented in the Parliament, there could be no assurance that their uncanny moral judgments would effectively be communicated up the structure of government to members who did not owe their position to colonial elections and who bore neither the "burthen" of an "oppressive act" nor the "happy effects" of a "wise and good law." The "one great principle, the *vital* principle" of government, Wilson told his lecture audience, was "that the supreme or sovereign power of the society resides in the citizens at large." The people "at large," in turn, could appoint no greater authority than itself, for it could not logically constitute a body "superiour to that authority, from which the derivation is made." Borrowing a metaphor from Lord Kames, Wilson observed that although the "source of the Nile continued still unknown," "the ultimate and genuine source" of sovereignty "has been found . . . in the free and independent man."[64]

An important qualification is in order here. Wilson's support for popular sovereignty, though championed by some later lawyers and political scientists as the epitome of revolutionary democracy, was not as thoroughly democratic as it seemed on first glance. Wilson believed that popular moral intuitions as to the ends of the state properly gave way to the reasoned leadership of men of superior abilities ("great characters"). Indeed, the appeal of the pyramid for Wilson was in all likelihood strengthened by the fact that most eighteenth-century images depicted pyramids that were considerably steeper than the famous Egyptian pyramids at Giza.[65]

But if Wilson's model of the pyramids did not embody as flat a democracy as some have suggested, it did vindicate the reason of the customary common law. As Wilson's Egyptian panorama of the pyramids and the Nile suggested, Hutcheson's moral sense supplied a way to establish transhistorical truths in ancient principles, whether in the immemorial common law or in the ages-old monuments of Giza. Custom, "of all the makers and teachers of the law," Wilson claimed, was the best lawmaker. When Wilson grafted the moral philosophy of the Scottish Enlightenment onto the common law's customary norms, he found the "perspicuous" solution Blackstone had sought to the tensions between time and reason. The moral faculty—"reason and conscience"— served as a kind of "divine monitor within us"; it created a moral sensibility "engraven by God on the hearts of men." The "instincts" with which people created custom were "the oracles of eternal wisdom" founded in "the voice of God within us." That was precisely the key to the common law's durability across the centuries. An "innate moral sense," Wilson explained further, "has been felt and acknowledged in all ages and nations." The "secret chain betwixt each person and mankind," as Wilson had called Hutcheson's moral sense, seemed to stretch across the ages. Custom was therefore not merely the accumulated contingent practices of human societies. It was instead "natural law," realized in time and articulated in the customary norms of people invested with an intuitive sense for distinguishing right from wrong. *"Sapientissima res tempus,"* Wilson quoted Francis Bacon—"Time is the wisest of things." Indeed, the common law was "nothing else but common reason—that refined reason, which is generally received by the consent of all." It was the product of a moral sense that had discerned just laws for as long as eyes had discerned color and ears had detected harmony. "Its foundations, laid in the most remote antiquity," contained "the common dictates of nature."[66]

This was the deeper meaning of Wilson's pyramid, and his listeners at the Constitutional Convention in 1787, the Pennsylvania ratifying convention, the state constitutional convention, and his lectures surely grasped his meaning. Time had been a force for "darkness" and decay in European politics, Wilson observed. Indeed, in the "vortex of European politics," government had "hitherto been the result of force, fraud, or accident." Within the domain of what Pocock has called "the dimension of contingency," even the balanced proportions of the constitutional republics and the Saxon common law had suffered the corrupting ravages of time. But Wilson claimed that "after the lapse of six thousand years since the Creation of the world, America now presents the first instance of a people assembled to weigh deliberately and calmly, and to decide leisurely and peaceably, upon the form of government by which they will bind themselves and their posterity."[67]

American law might thus at last capture history from unreason and accident to unlock the natural law encoded in the moral sensibilities of the generations. "Let us ransack the records of history," Wilson demanded at the state constitutional convention in 1790. "How few fair instances shall we be able to find in which a Government has been formed whose end has been the happiness of those for whom it was designed?" The Constitutional Convention of 1787, Wilson urged the assembled delegates, was "laying the foundation of a building, which is to last for ages." "A nation should aim at perfection," he announced in his law lectures, and the new nation that was the United States seemed poised at last to realize the timeless and universal principles of perfect reason, sweeping the common law clean of the historical bric-a-brac that obscured the right reason at its foundations. "When we view the inanimate and irrational creation around and above us, and contemplate the beautiful order observed in all its motions and appearances," Wilson rhapsodized, "is not the supposition unnatural and improbable—that the rational and moral world should be abandoned to the frolicks of chance, or to the ravage of disorder?" The legal order of the United States would indeed be a kind of city on a hill, but with common-law jurists rather than Puritan divines as its high priests. "By adopting this system," Wilson told the Pennsylvania convention to ratify the federal constitution, "we shall probably lay a foundation for erecting temples of liberty in every part of the earth." Like an ancient "monument from the Athenian commonwealth" surviving through the ages, American law would thus establish itself as "true law, conformable to nature, diffused among all men, unchangeable, eternal" even as it remained rooted in the customs and manners of the people. If only government would "honor human nature" by leaving "it to its own feelings," Wilson asserted, human nature would show itself "capable of those virtues that maintain public order, and of that prudence which insures public tranquility."[68] American government—like the pyramids—would embody a perfect constitutional geometry, a politics for the ages.

    *
    *
    *

Wilson's model of the pyramid was striking for its erudition and its learning. As we shall see in a moment, however, strikingly few among the nation's founders shared Wilson's vision. Indeed, Wilson's pyramid was remarkably ill suited as a basis for either crafting the institutions of the new republic or carving out a place in those institutions for the bar.

Wilson, perhaps better than any of his contemporaries among the founders, ought to have understood both the significance of social conflict in the new nation and the precariousness of the bar's position. Four years after his house was attacked in 1779, he watched a Congress beset by angry, unpaid soldiers flee from Philadelphia to Princeton. Four years after that, in December 1787, Wilson was burned in effigy by Pennsylvania antifederalists after the state convention ratified the federal constitution. He should have known that conflict is precisely what American lawyers have thrived on. This is what Justice Benjamin Dyer of Massachusetts had meant in the 1760s when he said that lawyers "live upon the sins of the people," and it is what Grant Gilmore was getting at two centuries later when he wrote, "In Hell there will be nothing but law, and due process will be meticulously observed."[69] The significance of the American bar in mediating conflict and dispute is simultaneously one of its most important social functions and a chief source of popular misgivings about lawyers.

Despite all this, Wilson almost completely failed to grasp the ways in which the heterogeneous people of the United States would have competing values and conflicting interests. "The people," he insisted in November 1787, would be "the panacea" of the new constitutional politics. Where Wilson's generation of constitution-makers aimed to develop a mechanics by which popular majorities would be inhibited from oppressing minorities, Wilson refused to admit this as a serious problem in constitutional design. "The majority of people wherever found ought in all questions to govern the minority," he told the assembled members of the Constitutional Convention in 1787.[70] *All questions!* So blithely confident was Wilson in the shared moral sensibilities of the people and in the capacity of a united elite to guide them that he insisted on the right of simple majorities of the people at any time to recreate, amend, or abolish their constitutions.

Indeed, Wilson's vision of a consensual moral sense writ large among the people left little room for the everyday work of American lawyers. To be sure, lawyers might serve as legal mandarins, using their special learning in the moral lessons of the ages to guide the ship of state along the path of perfection. This would have been the function of Wilson's proposed office of attorney general: to dispense advice on the law of nations. So too would it be the function of the lawyers on the federal bench, who would review the constitutionality of state and federal legislation. (Wilson even insisted that in this respect the courts of the United States could be traced "to Egypt," which created the "first . . . courts of justice.") Lawyers, in short, would have significant roles within the pyramid in the work of refining the moral sense of the people from base to pinnacle. But what Wilson failed to grasp was that the distinctive work of lawyers in the American state would be as agents in the conflicts that would arise at the intersection of the private and public spheres. In Wilson's view, the work of the common lawyer was peculiarly about a kind of natural-law learning. The lawyer was tied by a deep "principle of connexion" to the other "learned professions," "physick" and "divinity," and "especially" to the latter. Divinity and law were "twin sisters, friends, and mutual assistants" whose "two sciences run into each other." But as comparative students of legal professions have explained, where the American lawyer would be exceptionally successful was not in the role of legal mandarin but in taking up the work of conflict adjustment left by American governmental institutions to the private sphere.[71]

Fortunately for the future of the fledgling American bar, the working metaphor for the state and federal constitutions in the fifteen years after independence was not the pyramid but the machine. In the work of thinkers ranging from Hume and Adam Smith to Bishop Berkeley and William Blackstone, the machine had become the Enlightenment metaphor of choice for natural and human systems alike. And in constitutional debates in revolutionary America, the "mighty," "vast," and "great machine of government" (the "new flying machine," as some even called it) was invoked again and again.[72]

In part, the powerful appeal of the mechanistic metaphor was its Newtonian modeling. The machine of government might share in the universe's natural clockwork: what American ministers called the "noble . . . harmony" of the "machine of the universe." This is what John Adams implied when he famously recalled American independence as the moment in which "thirteen clocks were made to strike together—a perfection of mechanism, which no artist had ever before effected." And it is what Wilson's political ally Benjamin Rush meant when he spoke of the need "to convert men into republican machines."[73]

No better symbol of the Newtonian strand of American thought can be found than Philadelphian David Rittenhouse's world-famous orrery: a model of the solar system that reduced Newtonian laws of planetary movement to the carefully calibrated gears of human mechanics. (A more primitive orrery had long hung on the wall at the Library Company of Philadelphia, not too far from the Library's copy of Greaves's *Pyramidographia*.) Built in the same year Wilson was admitted to the Philadelphia bar, Rittenhouse's orrery seemed to Tench Coxe to epitomize "the motions of the spheres, that roll throughout the universe." Men such as Coxe, Jefferson, Madison, and Philadelphia watchmaker Robert Leslie thought that Rittenhouse's Newtonian mechanics might reconcile weights and measures across time and space more effectively than could the pyramid. If Newton was right, measuring the time that a vibrating rod or pendulum device took to complete its oscillation would allow the reproduction of uniform measurements of length. All one would need to ensure the translatability of a system of measure for posterity would be the duration of the oscillation and the longitude of the experiment; the length of the rod would naturally follow. In this Newtonian mode, a mechanical constitution might (like Wilson's pyramid) unlock universal and timeless truths of government.[74]

But machines were not always miniatures of a perfect Newtonian universe. The makers and ratifiers of the American constitutions viewed mechanical models with less than the unalloyed optimism that has been attributed to them by such writers as Leo Marx and Gary Wills.[75] Machines could be "complex and unwieldy." They broke down. As Adam Smith had observed, "vile rust" made "the wheels of society . . . jar and grate upon one another." A constitution-machine that could be started might also abruptly be stopped or "unhinged," grinding the "whole machine of government" to a halt. "Any one wheel," warned Charles Pettit, might easily be embarrassed "by the irregular or uncorrespondent motions of others." Not everyone could be a Rittenhouse, it seemed, and even the great Rittenhouse was frustrated with the relatively primitive solar system of his orrery.[76]

Indeed, the most elaborate founding-era mechanical description of politics adopted a humble, anti-Newtonian mechanical analogy—a "jack," or machine for turning the spit while roasting meat. In his well-known answer to John Adams, New Jersey inventor and early steamboat engineer John Stevens explained that "in government the weight or origin of power, is the people, and the people only; the jack is the machinery of government; the motions of which are regulated by adding a check or flyer." Stevens went on:

The weight is the power from whence the motion of every part originates. However complicated in its construction, tho' one wheel may be made to impel another, *ad infinitum,* yet without the weight, the machine must forever remain at rest. . . . But as the friction of the wheels will be greater in one part than in another; and as the meat, too, if not very nicely spitted, will give more resistance in one part of its revolution than in another; to counteract therefore the irregularities which these causes would produce in the movements of the machine, a flyer has been added, by the operation of which an equability of motion is all times preserved.

Constitutional mechanics could thus be a highly practical art. A constitutional machine would require, as Stevens put it, "cleaning or oiling" lest the "friction in some parts [be] increased." Stevens and others in the 1780s recognized mechanics as a distinctly human trade. As Oliver Ellsworth observed in the Connecticut ratification debate, if government was a mechanism, then some earthly first mover would be required to set the "unwieldy machine of government into motion." Absent some initial application of power, Ellsworth contended, the "machine of government would no more move than a ship without wind, or a clock without weights." To be sure, like Ezekiel's wheels, in the words of one American minister, some dreamed that governmental mechanics might take the form of the "machinery of Divine Providence." But the machine of the state might also take any number of less appealing forms. Antifederalists, for example, worried that the Constitution "put it in the power of its movers" to decide the government's direction. Moreover, awkward design "in a political machine must produce the same mischief as in a mechanical one," noted one delegate to the South Carolina convention, "throwing all into confusion." Defective design, Hamilton noted in New York, would "forever embarrass and obstruct the machine of government."[77]

Newtonian mechanics could and did provide useful metaphors to founders such as Madison. But those who talked of constitutions as machines recognized that mechanical devices could easily become dangerous. At best, machines were morally neutral, "incapable of all merit and demerit," as Richard Price put it in a pamphlet widely reprinted in America in 1776. Yet constitutional machines—"mere machines"—could also carry decidedly negative connotations, even in the Newtonian eighteenth century. Mechanism drove off volition and virtue, rendering "man . . . no agent, but a mere passive machine," declared Jonathan Edwards at midcentury. In 1789, the Pennsylvania Society for Promoting the Abolition of Slavery described slaves as "accustomed to move like a mere machine," with no "power of choice" and little "reason and conscience." Men driven by sinister forces were regularly described as "mere machines" or "mere political machines." The government-machine might be turned to equally sinister purposes. Its "dangerous machinery" might inflict "the first, & probably the last, wound" on our liberties, worried Samuel Osgood of the Continental Congress in 1784. Others warned that the constitutional machine might be "contrived . . . to use men's passions for the picking of their pockets" or to generate corrupt opportunities for speculation and patronage by "ambitious men." Significantly, critics of governmental structures—whether the Pennsylvania constitution of 1776 or the intrigue-ridden political diplomacy of 1780s European states—were as likely to decry those structures as pernicious "machines" as their supporters were to invoke Newtonian mechanics on their behalf. Madison, for one, often referred to the constitution as a "machine" precisely when he was concerned it would become a monstrously overcomplicated contrivance. The soulless machine, it seems, was a troubled metaphor even before nineteenth-century romanticism and Mary Shelley's *Frankenstein*.[78]

What men like Hamilton, Madison, and John Stevens understood, however, was that the Enlightenment's Newtonian machines were not the only positive model of a constitutional mechanics. When such men as these talked about the political machine, they were skillfully grafting a much older tradition of constitutional mechanics onto the Newtonian machinery. This was the civic tradition of constitutional balance that Scottish Enlightenment economists had revised and that Wilson had rejected in favor of the internal balance of the moral faculty. Looking back on the experience of classical constitutions, John Adams succinctly stated the received wisdom: "orders of men, watching and balancing each other, are the only security; power must be opposed to power, and interest to interest." According to this classical theory of constitutional balance, "Excess in one direction produces excess in another, until the oscillations of the 'balance' gather sufficient force to sweep away an inherently unstable system of government."[79]

The key move in the mechanics of *The Federalist* was to adopt the idea of the state as a mechanical balancing apparatus, but to update it. *The Federalist* adapted the constitution of balance from Adams's static hierarchy of orders—king, aristocracy, and commons—for a new world of commercial interest and economic faction. As John Stevens had noted, Adams's classical theory of balanced orders no longer suited the dynamic commercial world of 1780s America: "So fluctuating is the tide of human affairs, that in an instant the scales" of Adams's classical constitutional mechanics "would be jolted out of place." Men like Hamilton, Madison, and Stevens thus sought to adapt the old political science of balance to a new political economy. Their hybrid constitutional mechanics would serve to mediate not old status hierarchies but (in Madison's words from the Constitutional Convention) "different Sects, Factions, & interests, as they happen to consist of rich & poor, debtors & creditors, the landed the manufacturing, the commercial interests." The civic tradition, with its focus on vigilant resistance to commerce and luxury, would be revised for a commercializing, inevitably faction-ridden republic.[80]

The civic tradition's balancing machine did not seek to model the universe, inscribing in government universal truths for all time. (A mechanics by which human beings would seek to conquer time—the time machine—would have to wait another century for H. G. Wells.) Civic constitutionalism was more like John Stevens's cooking jack: a modest, time-bound enterprise, a practical and contingent mechanics. As Andrew Ellicott said of the constitutional "machine" of 1787, "I have no doubt but that it has both defects and excellencies"; like "any piece of mechanism," its "imperfections" would be "discovered when the machine is put in motion." The Constitutional Convention, Madison wrote in Federalist 37, had been "compelled to sacrifice theoretical propriety" for political compromise. The Constitution it had produced thus lacked "that artificial structure and regular symmetry which an abstract view of the subject might lead an ingenious theorist to bestow on a Constitution planned in his closet." Instead, its "checks and balances of power," as one Massachusetts convention delegate called them, aimed merely to withstand time by constructing a stable and balanced structure that would hold off the corruption and decay that history seemed so often to bring. The constitution-machine would allow a republic to weather the storms of time without reaching for the reconciliation of universals with history.[81]

This was a very different view of American constitutionalism from Wilson's. *The Federalist*'s updated civic tradition of balanced constitutions disowned the moral faculty Wilson had borrowed from Scots like Hutcheson and Kames. In Wilson's pyramid, inner moral equilibria substituted for outer constitutional balance. It did not necessarily follow that governmental institutions were to be ignored; but the implications for constitutional design were dramatically different. In particular, balances and checks (words Wilson rarely used) were less important in government than what Wilson called "flow" and the construction of a constitutional architecture that would refine the "flow" of government "from the people at large." The pyramidal structure of government would properly refine the moral intuitions of the people and funnel them into the constructive leadership of those Wilson called "men of abilities." Wilson thus fought hard against the Pennsylvania Constitution of 1776, which had established a unicameral legislature. Wilson objected not because the unicameral legislature lacked checks and balances, but because the absence of a second house inhibited the progressive refinement of the virtuous instincts of the people's moral faculty. Indeed, this is why the relatively steep slope of the eighteenth century's false image of the Egyptian pyramids appealed so strongly to Wilson. A pyramidal structure would allow the legislative branch to act as "an exact transcript" (a phrase that Wilson used twice at the Convention in the summer of 1787) of the "mind or sense of the people at large." For Wilson, constitutional design might thereby approach, and perhaps even reach, "theoretick perfection."[82]

Other members of the founding generation, however, saw the problem of balance in public rather than personal terms. Following Hume, who had urged that in the science of politics "every man ought to be considered a knave," Madison and Hamilton described human beings as governed by their "prevailing passions" of "ambition and interest." Legal institutions, in Hume's view, served as a check on the natural passions of human beings, which "no affection of the human mind has both a sufficient force and a proper direction to counterbalance." Hume here was squarely targeting Hutcheson's moral faculty, and Madison could not have said it better. Balance was not an inner mechanism ("conscience . . . is known to be inadequate"), but one that had to be designed into public institutions. "If men were angels, no government would be necessary," Madison famously explained in Federalist 51. Hume had warned, however, that the construction of government created yet another problem. If not properly checked, private interests would seek advancement through the mechanism of government "under pretence of public good." The key for Hume, then, was to create state institutions in which even "bad men . . . act for the public good," wittingly or otherwise. The passions, as Hamilton told the Convention in the summer of 1787, "must be turned towards general government." Madison's Federalist 51 followed closely. The machine of government would balance competing interests "by so contriving the interior structure of government as that its several constituent parts may, by their mutual relations, be the means of keeping each other in their proper places." Most famously: *"Ambition must be made to counteract ambition."* Constitutional design in the founders' mechanics was thus not about recreating the perfect operations of a rational universe. "Government itself" was merely "the greatest of all reflections on human nature," and people were no angels.[83]

There were, to be sure, points of intersection between the pluralist machine and Wilson's pyramid. Each promised a variation of what Gordon Wood has called "the end of classical politics."[84] Wilson and the partisans of the machine all thought that they had found distinctively American solutions to the cycles of decline that plagued the civic tradition. This overlap has led many commentators to miss the distinctive timelessness of Wilson's constitutional thought and to underestimate the extent to which the American science of politics remained firmly fixed (if more effectively balanced) in the stream of time. Where Wilson's pyramids purported to capture truths that stood beyond history, Madison's machine cobbled together something akin to what political scientist Charles Anderson has usefully called "mechanical liberalism." The machine constitution would "contrive mechanisms" to "channel the efforts" of a fallen and "self-interested people" into "the public good."[85]

Few theories of constitutional design have been better suited to placing the bar at the center of American governance than the "mechanical liberalism" of *The Federalist*. The Revolutionary crowd had critiqued lawyers as men who "live upon the sins of the People." Now those sins had been embraced and made a part of the very scheme of the constitution. Citizens might or might not be angels in their private lives, to be sure. But for the purposes of politics they would be fallen angels, and in the world of fallen angels, it would be lawyers who managed the effects of the passions.

*
*
*

Simply to say that the American science of politics offered a solution for age-old cycles of political decline does not quite tell us enough about the constitutional thought of James Wilson and his fellow founders of the nation. There was a critically important difference between solving the problem of decline in the "dimension of contingency" (Madison's solution) and solving it in the "dimension of continuity" (Wilson's).[86] What some of the framers had realized was that the new conditions of late eighteenth-century North America had not eclipsed long-standing problems of governance but rearranged them into new form. Theirs was accordingly a constitutional mechanics that sought to maintain itself in time, holding aside the question of timeless perfection. The mechanical constitution adopted David Hume's view that the "world itself probably is not immortal." "Perhaps rust may grow," Hume wrote, "to the springs of the most accurate political machine, and disorder to its motions." Wilson, by contrast, sought to explain to his new republican audience that the United States could capture moral truths that stood outside the contingent stream of time. "An enrapturing prospect opens on the United States," Wilson announced. "Happy country!" he crowed. Trained and educated in the common law and therefore in the moral judgments of the ages, Wilson believed that learned lawyers would form an expert cohort with special knowledge of the moral sensibility of human beings. It was a prospect, in Wilson's view, that was "eminently glorious."[87]

It was also preposterous. Wilson's legal science bore traces of the Panglossian excesses of Enlightenment optimism—excesses that, remarkably, his encounters with revolutionary crowds never caused him to call into question. Even Wilson's much-praised performances at the Federal Convention in the summer of 1787, the Pennsylvania ratifying convention in the fall of 1787, and the Pennsylvania state constitutional convention in 1789–90 are easily overestimated. Though Wilson's contributions were deeply learned, his interventions were often clumsy and ill calculated to advance his goals. His well-known speech on ratification, given in the Pennsylvania State House yard in October 1787, was a forceful statement of the case for the Constitution. But it drew widespread ire from antifederalists. And though Wilson's speeches dominated the Pennsylvania state constitutional convention, they too were not without their critics, who remembered Wilson's performance as "a pretty fiction" to which the audience had listened with only "somewhat more than a demi-conviction."[88]

In the years that followed, Wilson's own life quickly proved itself all too bound in time. History, it seems, would have its revenge on Wilson for his attempt to escape its grasp. The law lectures that he had begun just months before in an atmosphere of pomp and circumstance—with an audience that had included President George Washington and Vice President John Adams—ended with a whimper on April 17, 1791. Sympathetic biographers have suggested that Wilson failed to pick up the unfinished lectures in the fall because of his preparations for the massive digest projects he offered to take on for Pennsylvania and the federal government. The undertakings were truly massive. (Attorney General Edmund Randolph, on whose recommendation Washington declined Wilson's offer, called the U.S. laws project alone a "Herculean task.") But it was also true that the lectures, as Francis Rawle later reported, had not "entirely met the expectation that had been formed." Wilson had begun to develop a reputation as "given to repellant learning and possessed of a prolix and voluble wisdom." At the same time, he seemed too openly ambitious; John Adams diagnosed in him a "too frequent affectation of Popularity."[89]

Over the next six years, Wilson encountered failure in increasingly rapid steps. Though the Philadelphia *Federal Gazette* had pronounced him "destined . . . to fill the office of chief justice of the United States" and though some well-wishers sent him premature congratulations for his appointment to the post, he was passed over, once in 1789 and then again in 1795 and 1796 when John Jay resigned to become governor of New York and the nomination of John Rutledge foundered. As an associate justice, Wilson participated in only a few cases of lasting consequence. His total judicial output in eight years as a justice on the Court, as Wilson scholar Robert McCloskey noted, fills little more than twenty pages of the *U.S. Reports,* roughly the length of any number of Wilson's speeches on the constitution in the fall of 1787. Indeed, as a judge Wilson seems to have been best known for his self-aggrandizing erudition and the "flashy parade" he came to be associated with as he rode circuit in a "very handsome chariot" pulled by four horses. When the fifty-one-year-old justice rode into Boston on circuit and began to court the young Hannah Gray, John Quincy Adams wrote that Wilson had managed to render himself "ridiculous." "Mr. Wilson on the bench," as one sympathetic observer put it, "was not the equal to Mr. Wilson at the bar."[90]

Some would have thought it better if Wilson had not authored any pages in the *U.S. Reports* at all. When Wilson did have the opportunity to weigh in on significant issues, the reactions that ensued were often remarkably hostile. Calls for impeachment went out in the spring of 1792 when Wilson cited constitutional scruples and declined to serve as a pension commissioner in pension petitions by Revolutionary War veterans. Wilson's critics might better have reserved their anger for cases such as *Hollingsworth v. Virginia*, a suit brought by the Indiana Company of land speculators against the State of Virginia for refusing to recognize the company's title in Virginia lands. Wilson was a shareholder in the Indiana Company, but he never recused himself from consideration of the case. By 1795, the entanglement of Wilson's official responsibilities and his commercial activities had attracted wide public attention. In particular, Wilson was "reprobated . . . by all parties," as James Madison noted, for his involvement in the Yazoo land scandals. Members of the Georgia legislature had voted to grant land to companies of speculators in return for outright bribes in cash and stock. Wilson was deeply involved in the infamous Georgia Company, a chief beneficiary of the Georgia legislature's corrupt largesse. He had rights in almost two million acres of Georgia Company Yazoo lands. How could "a man acting thus deserve the confidence of his country," asked newspapers. The state of Georgia, complained a Georgia grand jury, could "expect no justice" in a court "where the judges [had] been guiding the . . . speculation."[91] Once again, Wilson's supreme confidence that his own interests coincided with the interests of the nation seems to have blinded him to the appearances his commercial activities betrayed.

Wilson's opinion in the case of *Chisholm v. Georgia* summed up his failings on the Court. Decided in February 1793, the case raised perhaps the most controversial question faced by the Supreme Court in the first years of its existence: whether a citizen of one state could haul another state into federal court or whether the principles of sovereign immunity sheltered states from the federal courts' authority. The Constitution seemed to speak clearly on the issue. Article III provided that "the judicial power shall extend . . . to controversies . . . between a state and citizens of another state" and "between a state . . . and foreign states, citizens or subjects." But in the state ratifying conventions, Madison and others had assured critics of the Constitution's language that the clauses in question merely authorized states themselves to sue in federal court and did not authorize the federal courts to entertain actions against them. The question was, as Wilson put it in his opinion, "of uncommon magnitude," not the least because of its implications for the enormous debts owed by the states.[92]

Here at last, Wilson seems to have thought, he had found an occasion to shape the jurisprudence of the new nation. But the case demanded a politically astute performance by the still-young Supreme Court—the kind of performance that the politically savvy John Marshall would give a decade later in the famous case of *Marbury v. Madison*—not a lengthy exercise in overwrought erudition. Wilson's opinion upholding the federal courts' jurisdiction took an hour to read. He brought his audience on a vast and discursive tour of "the principles of general jurisprudence" and the comparative "laws and practice of particular states and kingdoms" before at last getting to a conclusion that was (in his view) easily drawn from the "direct and explicit declaration" of the Constitution's text. He discussed the "original and profound . . . philosophy of mind" of Hutcheson's fellow philosopher Thomas Reid. He discoursed at length on the "perverted use" of certain terms in logic and metaphysics. He described the Norman corruption of the Saxon common law. He wrote of the lawsuit by Christopher Columbus's son Diego against the Spanish crown, and he touched on suits against governing authorities from Sparta and ancient Greece to the "Spaniards of Arragon" and "Frederic of Prussia." He digressed to reopen his long-standing criticisms of Blackstone's view of Parliamentary sovereignty.[93]

Theoretical speculation had once again gotten the better of

Wilson. He and his supporters had believed that "genius alone" could "supply the defect of precedent." But Wilson's opinion came almost immediately to stand for the high-handedness of a Court that purported to substitute genius for practical wisdom. The opinion, critics complained, was "too rarified for any but 'a few, a very few comprehensive minds'"; it was mere "tawdry ornament and poetical imagery," "more like an epic poem than a Judge's argument, . . . the rhapsody of some visionary theorist." Wilson's opinion seemed to display what one critic of Wilson's had earlier called "the bewildering eloquence of the bar," "deeply versed in all the intrigues of ambition." To be sure, it was completely consistent with much of what Wilson had said about sovereignty since the beginning of his legal career. Sovereignty was a "pernicious" term that diverted the science of politics from the true source of sovereign authority: the people. But for Wilson's critics, the opinion seemed merely to carry out Wilson's "political wish to annihilate the state governments." The opinion seemed to some the work of "monarchy men" aiming for "an opportunity of getting back from the government some confiscated property." William Davie of North Carolina complained that "a man looks in vain for legal principles or logical conclusions" in Wilson's opinion. Many predicted that "numerous" suits would "immediately issue from the various claims of refugees, Tories, etc." Within one day of Wilson's opinion and the Court's decision in *Chisholm,* Congress began proceedings to reverse the decision. Before two years were out, the states had finished the job by ratifying the Eleventh Amendment to the U.S. Constitution.[94]

Yet by the time North Carolina completed the ratification of the Eleventh Amendment by being the twelfth of fifteen states to approve it, Wilson's jurisprudential difficulties paled in comparison to his commercial ones. As early as the middle of the 1770s some had warned that Wilson's private speculations were leading him to act in ways "unworthy of his public character." Creditors such as the Bank of North America (for which Wilson did legal work) had been writing Wilson with occasional angry demands for payment from at least 1780 onward. For over a decade Wilson managed to hold them off through a blizzard of successive loans from an array of creditors that included Speaker of the Pennsylvania House William Bingham (for whom Wilson proposed to draft the laws of Pennsylvania), Benjamin Rush, and Tench Coxe. In the summer of 1787, even as Wilson took part in the Constitutional Convention, a sheriff in Northampton County began foreclosing on some of Wilson's Pennsylvania holdings. Political opponents began to contend that Wilson's "aspiring and grasping spirit [had] received a peculiar edge from his pecuniary embarrassments."[95]

In all likelihood, it was Wilson's mounting financial "embarrassments" and the "grasping spirit" they produced that kept him from being appointed chief justice. Wilson's allies sought in 1789 to dismiss such concerns. "Where will you find an American landholder free from embarrassments?" Benjamin Rush asked John Adams. But Adams and Washington preferred John Jay in 1789, not the least because of what Adams delicately called the "hazards" of Wilson's candidacy. By the time Jay resigned in 1795, Adams noted that "Mr. Wilson's ardent speculations had given offence" to too many. Over the several preceding years, Wilson's affairs had begun to spiral out of control. An audit committee convened at the request of William Bingham had concluded that Wilson owed Bingham substantial sums for which he had failed to account. The U.S. Senate delivered a crushing blow to Wilson's interests in the Illinois-Wabash Company by refusing to validate deeds derived from Indian land grants. Notes to the Bank of North America totaling almost $100,000 came due. Creditor suits threatened to destroy Wilson's highly illiquid empire. Indeed, when Washington followed Adams's advice not to nominate Wilson as chief justice in 1795 and 1796, he hardly needed to rely on rumor. In November 1795 Washington had been asked by Virginian Henry Lee to take notes drawn on Wilson as payment for Washington's share in the lands of the Great Dismal Swamp Company. Washington held off answering and then declined to take Wilson's notes. He "could not depend on converting them into cash."[96]

Yet no amount of difficulty seemed to deter Wilson from extending his holdings. Wilson's blithe confidence was simply extraordinary. Even as his finances began to collapse, he launched into the most ambitious plans of his entire career: an elaborate series of saw- and textile mills along the Lackawaxen River and Wallenpaupack Creek in northeast Pennsylvania. He called the development "Wilsonville." By July 1795 his agents reported that there were twenty-two houses, a substantial cloth mill, and a sawmill in operation there. A dye works and further sawmills would soon be up and running. Profits, Wilson ludicrously estimated, would surely be more than eight times the initial investment in a mere eight years.[97]

Wilsonville and the rest of Wilson's overstretched empire came crashing down in 1796. He could, he had long insisted to any who would listen, "come forward in *real force* . . . on a scale of great extent" if necessary. But in January, a bill drawn on his account for $1,000 was protested for nonpayment. By the summer, the situation was beyond repair. To be sure, Wilson was hardly alone in his financial distress. The land price bubble had burst, and Robert Morris and many others shared much of the distress. (In 1798, Morris would be forced to entertain George Washington from his well-appointed room in Philadelphia's Prune Street debtor's prison.) But Wilson fell especially hard. (Morris angrily wrote that it was "W–l–n's affairs," as he put it, that made "the vultures more keen after me.") By August, Wilson had confessed a "great number of judgments," wrote one correspondent, who added that "people speak freely of the situation he is likely to be in very shortly." A "scene [was] about [to be] exposed to public view & public animadversion," a business partner warned Wilson, that would be deeply "injurious in its consequences to thy Reputation & Interest."[98]

And so it was. In September 1796, Wilson was very likely jailed by one of his Philadelphia creditors. That may be why he failed to appear at the circuit court sittings for Delaware and Virginia in October and November 1796. In any event, Wilson was certainly jailed a year later, in September 1797, when creditors Simon Gratz and Isaac Hopper caught up with him in Burlington, New Jersey. (Wilson had failed to appear for the August 1797 term of the Supreme Court.) In the meantime, creditors attached and began auctioning off large swaths of Wilson's Pennsylvania holdings. Wilson spent most of his time during this period hiding from his creditors at an inn seventy miles outside the city.[99]

Yet to the last, Wilson held to his belief that the value of his land holdings would increase. Wilson was like the sucker in his own elaborately theorized financial pyramid scheme. Land values, he had long believed, would inevitably increase as confidence in the new nation's government grew and as Europe's excess population flooded North America's wide-open frontier. As values increased, the proceeds of loans secured with the next piece of land would easily pay off the loans on the one before it, leaving progressively larger surpluses. The virtuous cycles of Scottish political economy would be realized at last on the American frontier. It was only a matter of time, and for the theorist who had sought to escape time altogether, that time was always just around the corner.

After managing to secure his release from the Burlington jail, Wilson took to the Court's Southern Circuit in October 1797. Of the three circuits—Eastern, Middle, and Southern—the justices most dreaded the long, cumbersome Southern Circuit. For

Wilson, however, it promised some respite from his middle-colony creditors. Amazingly, Wilson also saw new investment opportunities. And just as he had ever since he rode the state circuit around Pennsylvania as a young lawyer in 1767, Wilson sought once again to snap up land he encountered along the way. These new prospects, Wilson wrote to his Philadelphia lawyer Joseph Thomas, were "favorable in a degree much exceeding my most sanguine hopes." A mere "twenty thousand dollars would, I believe, secure every thing: Ten thousand would secure a great deal." And yet a note of panic had crept into Wilson's voice: "You can have no conception of what importance it is to me to have some funds. . . . I can only repeat you can have no conception of what importance it would be. Without friends much must be lost." Even as late as May 1798, Wilson insisted to Thomas that there was "reason to believe" that his "exertions may be crowned with the most abundant success." Indeed, the apparent debacle might still be resolved "with safety to all, and advantage to many."[100]

Wilson's theoretical speculations had by now slid into delusion and delirium. When Pierce Butler filed a suit against him in February or March 1798, Wilson struck a deal that spared him from debtor's prison in return for what Butler called "parole" in a small inn at Edenton, North Carolina. (Butler's agents had warned Butler of Wilson that "if you rely on his honor, or trust him in any thing, he will certainly deceive you.") From that point onward, his young wife Hannah later wrote, Wilson's "mind [was] in such a state . . . harassed and perplexed, that it was more than he could possibly bear." Wilson began haranguing his son, Bird Wilson, demanding money and good news that Bird could not possibly supply. What Bird may well have known, but did not say, was that the talk had turned to the possibility of impeachment. As if to strike one final blow to Wilson's tattered dreams, in August his lawyer Joseph Thomas was discovered to be an embezzler, his long-standing frauds amounting to some $60,000. ("I am afraid this must unavoidably add to Judge Wilson's distress," wrote Wilson's colleague Justice James Iredell.) And on August 21, 1798, Wilson died. The immediate cause was malaria ("an intermitting fever," Hannah called it). But Iredell attributed it to "distress of the mind." Wilson had "sunk in so short a time" that others speculated "he hastened it by some unjustifiable means." As Philadelphia lawyer Jacob Rush wrote to his brother Benjamin, "What a miserable termination to such distinguished abilities."[101]

In the months before Wilson's demise, Benjamin Rush reported that Wilson—"deeply distressed"—had found one last refuge: "his resource was reading novels constantly." It was a sensible place for Wilson to go, for the novel had long been the genre of choice for the men of sensibility who developed the theory of the moral faculty. Twenty-five years earlier, Thomas Jefferson had recommended to his friend Robert Skipwith that "the entertainments of fiction" provided "an exercise of our virtuous dispositions" and "moral feelings." Wilson may well have felt, as Jefferson had intimated to Skipwith, that all too "few incidents" from life were properly calculated to excite the "sympathetic emotion of virtue" to which Wilson had attributed such power. At the end, literature stood like the common law as a repository of the ideal human moral intuitions that had failed Wilson in practice.[102]

We have no record of what novels Wilson turned to in the delirium of his final months and weeks. But it would be fitting if he had picked up Samuel Johnson's *Rasselas, Prince of Abissinia*, the novel in which the pyramids figured so prominently. *Rasselas* had been published in London in 1759. The Library Company of Philadelphia owned two copies of this English printing. An American edition had just come out in 1795. The novel explored an ancient line of thinking about the Egyptian monuments that

Wilson had heretofore ignored. Since at least Herodotus and Pliny, the pyramids had symbolized not just timeless perfection but also its opposite: reason and power declined into corruption, luxury, and tyranny. Eighteenth-century students of the pyramids estimated that some 600,000 slaves had been employed over twenty years to build what one such student called the "insignificant Pomp of the Pyramid." In turn, the pharaoh who built the great pyramid had been "torn to pieces in a mutiny of his people." Voltaire thus saw the pyramids as "monuments" to slavery, on which an entire nation had been forced to work to no discernable purpose. These were the pyramids that appeared in Johnson's *Rasselas,* their "dark labyrinths" cursed by ancient tyrannies. The Great Pyramid at Giza in particular seemed merely to have served "the satiety of dominion and tastelessness of pleasures, and to amuse the tediousness of [the pharaoh's] declining life, by seeing thousands labouring without end, and one stone, for no purpose laid upon another." If Wilson ever got to the next passage, he surely knew it spoke to him: "Whoever thou art, that, not content with a moderate condition, imaginest happiness in royal magnificence . . . survey the pyramids and confess thy folly!" Wilson had found himself in what John Greaves called "the maze of times, out of which we cannot . . . unwinde ourselves."[103]

And yet it would also be folly to dismiss Wilson's eccentric theorizing altogether. His tragic, star-crossed life powerfully illuminates the pull that the United States has exerted from the very outset on the imagination and sentiments of millions of Americans. Few among the founders lived out their lives hewing as closely to their visions for the nation as did James Wilson. Moreover, Wilson's particular conception of the nation illustrates by indirection the character of legal and political institutions in the United States. The institutions Wilson helped put into place created mechanisms not for the achievement of perfect eternal truths (as Wilson had hoped), but for the adjustment of conflict among competing conceptions of those truths. Ironically, though Wilson never quite understood it, this was an environment in which his profession would thrive. In a governmental system that allocated a distinctively large role in conflict adjustment to the private sphere, lawyers would soon play an exceptionally important role in brokering between competing interests.

To dismiss the search for eternal truths too quickly, however, would be to miss an important dimension of the history of the American nation. Ever since Wilson's pyramid dreams, the American nation and the constitutional regime around which it has organized itself have unfolded in what Pocock calls "a dialectical relationship between continuity and contingency," a dialectic between the accommodation of the passions, on the one hand, and the pursuit of the eternal on the other.[104] To be sure, Wilson's appeals to the eternal may have played a minor role in the institutional design of the nation as compared to Madison's science of political mechanics. Indeed, in the two-plus centuries since Wilson's pyramid, explicit references to timeless truths have been relatively recessive in the official materials of American constitutional law contained in the *U.S. Reports*. Generations of American lawyers have worked the constitutional machine to mill truth claims and passions into less combustible forms. But outside the official sources of constitutional law, many millions of Americans—abolitionists and civil rights activists, property rights advocates and pro-life protesters alike, along with countless others—have drawn on appeals to natural truths to shape the United States. These Americans have sought self-consciously to make the United States consistent with transcendent, noncontingent ideals of justice. Again and again they have given motion to the constitutional machine, often with considerably more success than Wilson ultimately enjoyed. We can trace their achievements to Wilson's legacy.

Two ☆ *Exits*

The United States is a nation of immigrants. The phrase is virtually a ritual incantation. Yet the United States is also a nation of exits and emigrants. Those who leave are typically omitted from the national histories; but ever since Benedict Arnold switched his allegiance, ever since the Cherokee fled the encroaching white republic, and ever since abolitionist William Lloyd Garrison described the Constitution as a covenant with death, individuals and sometimes entire groups have left the United States or abandoned their allegiances and affiliations with it. Immigrants from southern and eastern Europe at the turn of the twentieth century, for example, returned to places like Italy and Poland at rates approaching 40 and 50 percent. Detainees at Japanese internment camps in the 1940s formally renounced their citizenship. And since the 1960s a new generation of immigrants to the United States has created new transnational networks and new cross-border diasporic communities that do not adhere to traditional conceptions of national affiliation.

Many of these exits have been just that: clean exits. Immigrants returned to their native land, having used the labor markets of the United States to advance plans and dreams they had created before they ever set foot on U.S. soil. But many exits have been messy and partial ones, for the American nation has proven extraordinarily adept at shaping the ideals and values of those who purport to reject it. These partial exits are testament to the power of American national ideals to capture outliers, to set the bounds of political and legal discourse, and to encompass even those who would exit.

The emigration of a crippled former slave in up-country

South Carolina named Elias Hill was just this kind of messy exit. At the height of post–Civil War Reconstruction, even as it seemed that at last black Americans might live on terms of equality with whites, Hill and a large group of fellow emigrants left the United States for Liberia. Their aspirations and ideals, however, were powerfully influenced by the traditions and institutions of the United States. Those aspirations and ideals would shape both the future of Liberia and the history of the nation the emigrants left behind.

Elias Hill's Exodus:
Exit and Voice
in the Reconstruction Nation

Elias Hill left his home in the morning on the first day of November in 1871. For his entire life, for more than half a century, he had lived in the South Carolina Piedmont in the precinct of Clay Hill, among the gullies and ravines and rooted in the red clay soil of York County where Allison's Creek emptied into the Catawba River, flowing south and east through the South Carolina upcountry toward the Atlantic Ocean. On that morning, the last morning he would ever awaken in Clay Hill, Elias Hill set out down the road along the river toward the still-new railroad town of Rock Hill, twelve miles away. With him traveled a group of 167 freedpeople, all of them members of the nearby Sardis Baptist Church at which Reverend Elias Hill served as deacon and pastor. Many in the group had been slaves long before the town of Rock Hill even existed. With the exception of the very youngest children and Reverend Hill, who had lived as a free man since sometime around 1840, everyone in this company of travelers on that day in the fall of 1871 had been a slave little more than six years before.[1]

Some in the group rode on horses and in wagons. Others walked, their belongings having been sent ahead by Hill's nephew June Moore. We can be sure, however, that the man whom Moore and others in the Sardis congregation called "Uncle Elias" did not walk. From childhood, Elias Hill had been a cripple, suffering from what he described as rheumatism but was more likely polio. The disease struck his limbs, leaving his legs shriveled and virtually useless, and progressively attacking his arms. Ever since the end of the war, he had been ferried from place to place by friends and neighbors on a spring wagon to which an armchair had been attached. From the chair, Reverend Hill would preach to black Baptist congregations and teach reading and writing in poor black schools in the cotton communities of the Piedmont, between the Tidewater belt of the low country and the Blue Ridge Mountains that rise up in the state's northwest corner. This trip at the beginning of November 1871 would be considerably longer than his circuits around the Piedmont.[2]

At the same Rock Hill railroad depot from which York County's Confederate troops had departed to join the fighting at Fort Sumter, past the new store fronts, cotton dealers, and agricultural supply stores that had begun to spring up along Rock Hill's Main Street, and not far from the bus terminal in Rock Hill where John L. Lewis and a dozen other civil rights activists would experience the first violent encounter on their Freedom Ride through the South ninety years later, the freedpeople of Clay Hill climbed aboard a specially reserved first-class train car on the Charlotte, Columbia, and Augusta Rail Road. They were headed for Charlotte, North Carolina, and from there to Portsmouth, Virginia. In Hampton Roads Bay, in the waters just off of Portsmouth, they boarded the *Edith Rose,* a double-decked barque chartered by the American Colonization Society. In all, the *Edith Rose* carried 245 passengers—243 on the ship's manifest, plus 2 stowaways, who would be discovered only upon landing. Like Hill and his company, virtually all of the passengers except the very youngest were former slaves. And like Hill and his company, all of them were bound for Liberia on the west coast of Africa. Along with Hill, these black women, men, and children had concluded that they could not satisfactorily be citizens in the United States—even in the reconstructed United States of the post–Civil War moment. And so they were leaving in search of a nation-state to which they could more meaningfully belong.[3]

Elias Hill and the Clay Hill company of emigrants offer a rare glimpse into some of the ways in which the typically anonymous freedpeople of the American South thought about their new relationship to American nationhood. In particular, the story of Elias Hill and his group brings us about as close as we can get to the lives and thoughts of rural southern blacks who experimented in what historian Steven Hahn has called "grassroots emigrationism" from the United States. Hundreds of thousands of poor rural blacks expressed interest in leaving the United States for Liberia in the decade and a half after Emancipation. Many talked about Haiti or other destinations to the south. Still others argued about moving west to Kansas, or to Arkansas or Texas, or to Indiana or Oklahoma. In all of these debates, the freedpeople of the South were asking essential questions about the nature of political identification and citizenship in the American nation-state.[4]

Most freedpeople, of course, answered those questions very differently than the Clay Hill emigrants. That is part of what makes the Clay Hill company so fascinating. In the same month in which Hill led his York County group across the ocean to Africa, the South Carolina upcountry became center stage in the American national drama of black citizenship. Even as the Clay Hill emigrants climbed aboard the train for the coast and boarded the *Edith Rose* for Liberia, other freedpeople in the very same community were committing themselves to testify and serve as jurors in a battery of federal prosecutions that have come to be known as the Great South Carolina Ku Klux Klan Trials. The prosecutions, which targeted a Klan leader who years later would become the model for the hero of the infamous racist film *Birth of a Nation,* became critical early tests of the meaning of the Reconstruction amendments. For weeks the trials captured the nation's attention. And though few would have guessed it at the time, they would ultimately come to represent what many historians view as the high-water mark of the federal government's commitment to civil and political rights for black citizens in the Reconstruction South.

The story of the Clay Hill company emigrants suggests that even at the height of Reconstruction, the promise of a new black citizenship and the unification of the American nation-state were haunted by the prospect of emigration and by critiques of American nationhood. Indeed, even as federal authorities sought to establish a new national authority on their behalf, the freedpeople of Clay Hill showed a remarkably sophisticated grasp of the uses and limits of the nation-state, one that had deep roots in the intellectual traditions of the black diaspora. Exit and voice, social theorist Albert O. Hirschman's famous dichotomous strategies, collided in the South Carolina countryside, where renewed commitment to the nation existed cheek by jowl with exit from it.[5] For a century after the Clay Hill exodus, the American civil rights tradition would be influenced powerfully by varieties of exit. Indeed, exit would form one of the chief constitutional strategies of the all too often voiceless descendants of American slaves. That neither exit nor voice would work in November 1871 was something Elias Hill could not have been expected to know.

*
*
*

The Clay Hill precinct of York County, South Carolina, no longer exists today except on lists of the region's ghost towns. Most of what was once Clay Hill is now covered by man-made reservoirs installed in the early twentieth century to protect the fast-growing town of Rock Hill from spring floods along the Catawba River. What little remains is dotted by the lakefront properties of a white middle- and upper-middle-class commuter suburb of Rock Hill and Charlotte, North Carolina.

If we could transport them back in time, the area's current residents would barely recognize the place of Elias Hill's birth.

Hill was born a slave in 1819 in a tiny community set along a river that regularly spilled over its banks. His birth came exactly two centuries after a ship landed in Virginia with the first African slaves to arrive in British North America. His mother, a mulatto slave woman named Dorcas Hill, had been born thirty-nine years earlier, in 1780. Dorcas served as a house slave for the family of William D. Hill, a Revolutionary War hero, founder of the county seat at Yorkville, and owner of one of the only iron furnaces in the state. Upon William D. Hill's death in 1816, his son Solomon inherited Dorcas, and a few years later she served as the wet nurse for Solomon's son Daniel Harvey Hill. Daniel Harvey, who was born shortly after Elias, would go on to be a famously irascible, even erratic, Confederate general. In September 1862, as Robert E. Lee's troops marched north into Maryland, and as the great European powers were on the verge of recognizing the Confederacy as an independent nation, a copy of Lee's battle plans addressed to the very same Major-General Daniel Harvey Hill fell into Union hands near Antietam. In one of the most important turning points of the entire war, the famous "Lost Dispatch" helped the Army of the Potomac drive Lee back into Virginia. In the years after the war, Daniel Harvey Hill would become a bitter opponent of Reconstruction, all the while defending himself against accusations that he had carelessly cast aside the Lost Dispatch and thus decided the fate of the Confederacy. By the 1930s, local lore among upcountry whites—almost certainly false—had it that Daniel Harvey and Elias regularly met on the former's front porch in the years after the war to reminisce about the old days.[6]

Dorcas Hill, like her son Elias, had lived as a free woman since around 1840. As with many black people living as free in South Carolina in the last decades of the antebellum South, Dorcas had been closely connected to her former owners in the Hill family. House slaves were far more likely to be freed by their owners during these years than plantation workers. And as the manuscript census report for 1860 makes clear, Dorcas was a light-skinned black woman—a mulatto in the language of the census reports—who seems to have had one or more white ancestors. Dorcas herself may well have been patriarch William Hill's daughter. During Dorcas's lifetime, such connections were known to exist between white male members of the extended Hill family and female slaves. The father of Dorcas's great-grandson Thomas Simpson, for example, was a locally prominent white lawyer and the brother of the owner of Thomas's mother. Family legend on the black side of the Hill family long had it that Thomas was freed in 1861 at the age of five because he passed so completely for white.[7]

We can know much less about Elias Hill's father. When the census taker listed Elias and Dorcas in 1860, Elias's father was not listed as living in their household. He may have been dead, as he does not seem to appear anywhere in either the 1860 census or the 1850 census. In 1871, however, Hill described his father to a congressional subcommittee that had come to York County to take testimony on Ku Klux Klan violence. His father, he said, had been born in Africa and had been brought to the United States as a slave. Though Hill did not say when he had been brought from Africa, his father may well have been a victim of the illegal slave trade that flourished in South Carolina for decades after 1808, when the United States prohibited the importation of slaves from abroad. Sometime around 1840, Hill's father purchased his freedom for $150 from a Hill family estate (perhaps that of William D. Hill's son Andrew, who died in 1840). Not long thereafter, Elias's father purchased Dorcas. The Hill family insisted that if Elias's father wanted Dorcas, he had to take Elias as part of the bargain. Elias's father agreed, and Elias, Dorcas, and Elias's father appear to have lived thereafter as free blacks.[8]

As a legal matter, however, they were almost certainly still slaves. Since 1820, it had been illegal to manumit a slave in South Carolina. The state legislature could grant a special waiver authorizing a manumission, and since we cannot be sure of Elias's father's name the legislature may have done so for him. But it is unlikely. The legislature never granted such a waiver for Dorcas or Elias, and it seldom did so for anyone, notwithstanding a steady stream of petitions for more than forty years. As far as the law of South Carolina was concerned, then, it is likely that Dorcas and Elias remained slaves of the white Hill family. At best, they had become the slaves of Elias's black father. Though by the time of the 1860 census they were listed as free (he as "deformed," she as an eighty-year-old domestic), Dorcas and Elias had been consigned to a kind of lawless status.[9]

Nature and law had both been cruel to Elias Hill, and this is no doubt why the white Hill family insisted that Elias's father take Elias off of their hands. In 1826, at the age of seven, he was "afflicted," as he put it, by a crippling disease that attacked his legs. Later observers would describe the disease as "something like rheumatism." But it was more probably polio. (Nature may not have done all the work. Young Daniel Harvey Hill seems to have suffered from a mild case of a similar disease at around the same time, but Daniel Harvey recovered, perhaps in part because of the better care that was surely lavished on him.) Elias Hill "was never afterward able to walk." By the time he was an adult, his legs seemed "to be about the size of a man's wrist." Over time, Elias's arms were affected as well as his legs. Hill's limbs withered to such an extent that by the summer of 1871 one northern newspaperman commented that "his legs now resemble more the talons of a large bird than anything else, while his arms are so deformed and his fingers so contracted, that he has almost entirely lost the use of both." "His limbs are skin and bone, small as those of a child, and drawn up around his body like handles to a vase." "He presented the appearance of a dwarf," reported another observer, "with the limbs of a child, the body of a man." Hill's condition was such that he "could not help himself, but had to be fed and cared for personally by others." He was, all agreed, "utterly unable either to walk or crawl, and has to be carried in every instance." By his own account, he could barely "turn over in bed" without the aid of what he called his "prize stick," a device with which he moved himself around on a chair or in a bed. His hands were such that he could barely even write. He changed his manner of writing to accommodate his condition, from the ordinary thumb-and-forefinger style to a cruder grasp in a knot of fingers. By 1870, he had resorted simply to folding his hand "around the pen, and scribbling thus the best he can."[10]

Yet for all this, Elias Hill struck virtually everyone he met as "a remarkable character." Some even suggested that he was, "the most remarkable man in South Carolina." He had a "massive, intellectual head" (a "finely developed intellectual head," as another account had it) and "an intelligent, eagle-like expression." He had begun his education at around the age of eleven, picking up "an occasional letter of the alphabet" from "passing school children," eventually learning the alphabet, and ultimately becoming a fast and accomplished reader. His reading lessons, he told a reporter in 1871, had been "conned from the Bible." By the time he was an adult some claimed that "in all York County" there were not "a dozen better-informed men than old Elias, nor one with a stronger intellect." ("He had a mind that was far above the average of his race," remarked a racist York County editor looking back from the vantage of the 1930s.)[11]

In later years, local whites would claim to remember that Elias's white contemporary, Daniel Harvey Hill, had seen to Elias's education himself. A newspaper editor who had been a young child when Elias Hill left South Carolina wrote that Daniel Harvey had painstakingly taught the young, crippled slave to read Greek until "he could read it with the facility that English was read by the average scholar of his day." But this is almost certainly false. There is nothing in Elias Hill's later life to suggest that he read Greek. Moreover, teaching slaves to read—even to read English, let alone Greek—was illegal in South Carolina and had been since 1740.[12]

*
*
*

South Carolina's legal prohibition on teaching slaves to read did not technically bar teaching free blacks. When Hill began to live as free, however, there were exceedingly few free blacks in the state and even fewer in the South Carolina upcountry. Almost 98 percent of the black population in South Carolina in 1860—a black population that outnumbered the white population 412,320 to 291,300—was enslaved. Of the 9,914 free blacks in the state in 1860, almost half lived in one of three low-country districts: Charleston, Beaufort, or Georgetown. The vast majority of the remainder lived in the state's Tidewater belt along the Atlantic coast. Relatively few free blacks lived in the interior region of sandy pine barrens that separated the Tidewater from the Piedmont. Even fewer lived in the Piedmont, where free blacks made up a smaller proportion of the black population than in any other region of the state.[13]

Unlike the free black community of Charleston, which developed a substantial middle-class elite as well as significant black social institutions, such as churches and fraternal associations and schools, free and quasi-free blacks in the Piedmont like Dorcas and Elias Hill seem to have lived in close proximity to the region's slaves and to have shared in many of their loosely constructed social institutions. Piedmont free blacks were much more likely than their low-country counterparts to live among slaves, and many members of Dorcas and Elias's family remained slaves. When relatively independent free black settlements sprung up, they did so in ways that were as inconspicuous as possible and that in all likelihood closely resembled the black settlement at Clay Hill: "tucked away well off the main road" in "isolated cottages and shacks" that occasionally developed into small villages.[14]

The upcountry's already tiny and isolated free black community was further hemmed in by a dense network of discriminatory laws. Since at least 1740, the law of South Carolina had presumed that "every negro, Indian, mulatto and mustizo" was a slave absent proof to the contrary. Elias Hill, like all blacks living as free in the state, was required at all times to carry with him a certificate of freedom. Failure to have such a certificate made any free black subject to seizure by any white citizen. Hill's testimony, like the testimony of all free blacks, was inadmissible in court against white people. Hill could not even legally gather together with fellow free blacks. Since 1800, the South Carolina General Assembly had prohibited "assemblies and congregations" of "free negroes," including religious services and meetings "for the purpose of mental instruction"; in 1834, the General Assembly expressly prohibited free blacks from organizing schools. After the discovery of an apparent insurrection plot led by a free black man named Denmark Vesey in 1822, the assembly further required that all free blacks over fifteen years old have a white guardian. And though it is unlikely that Hill ever had any run-ins with the criminal law, if he had he would have found himself without many of the protections offered to white defendants. Free black criminal defendants were tried in slave courts without juries and were subject to considerably harsher criminal sanctions than were their white counterparts. There was no right of self-defense for a free black against a white person.[15]

The South Carolina General Assembly also sharply circumscribed free blacks' rights of movement. Immigration of free blacks into the state from the West Indies or anywhere else outside the United States was prohibited in 1794; by 1803, any free negro, mulatto, or mestizo entering the state from abroad risked being seized into slavery by the state as punishment. Between 1820 and 1822, a panoply of new laws restricted the mobility of free blacks in and out of the state. The General Assembly enacted a total ban on the immigration of free blacks. Free adult male negroes or persons of color living in the state who had been born outside of it were made subject to a $50 per year tax. Failure to pay the tax was punishable by sale for a period of years. Even free blacks born in South Carolina were affected. After 1822, free blacks residing in the state who left it for any reason were no longer "suffered to return."[16]

With one hand, the South Carolina General Assembly silenced the institutions of free black community life, chief among them voluntary associations, churches, and schools. With the other, it limited free black mobility. Perhaps the most important legal assault on the state's free black community, however, was the legislation that rendered the legal status of Elias and his parents ambiguous. Over the first half of the nineteenth century South Carolina's legislature made it progressively more difficult for slave owners to manumit their slaves. The assembly first regulated manumission in 1800, limiting it to slaves of good character who were able to gain "a livelihood in an honest way" and requiring that manumissions be executed by deed. Twenty years later, in the same statute that barred free black immigration, the assembly prohibited manumission except "by act of the Legislature." When determined slave owners circumvented the prohibition by conveying their slaves to a trust or executing a fictitious sale with the stipulation that the slave live "as if . . . fully emancipated," the assembly responded again, voiding the trusts that slaveholders had used to evade the law. As the case of Elias and Dorcas Hill illustrates, slaveholders were even then able to give their slaves a kind of quasi freedom. (The statute had "caused evasions without number," complained one lawyer in 1848.) Nonetheless, immigration restrictions and manumission limits had the effect of dramatically slowing the growth of the state's free black community after 1820.[17]

Such draconian legislative changes in the status of free blacks emerged out of a virulently racist view of the American constitutional order that was increasingly popular among whites in places like the South Carolina upcountry. Indeed, South Carolina distinguished itself throughout Elias Hill's lifetime as the most radical bastion of white proslavery values in the American South. "No other southern state," as historian James Banner has put it, "appeared quite so dedicated to the preservation of slavery and its distinctive way of life." South Carolina had both the highest ratio of slaves to free people and the highest percentage of whites owning slaves of any state. The state was home to many of the leading articulators of the creed of the Confederacy, including John Calhoun, the fiery secretary of war, vice president, senator, and theorist of the master class; James Henry Hammond, who famously declared on the floor of the U.S. Senate that "Cotton is king" and that the North, too, had a "mud-sill" class of laborers; and Robert Y. Hayne, whose fervor for southern states' rights in 1830 prompted a famous encomium to the Union by Daniel Webster ("Liberty and Union, now and for ever, one and inseparable!"). And while many southerners talked about nullifying federal laws that threatened southern interests, only South Carolina had actually purported to nullify federal law, doing so in 1832. The state came close to seceding from the Union in 1851 and 1852, and in December 1860 South Carolina led the secessionist charge months before Abraham Lincoln took office, making it clear that the state would go it alone if need be. It was no surprise that South Carolina fired the first shots of the Civil War at Fort Sumter in April 1861.[18]

If South Carolina was second to none among the states of the Union in its commitment to the slavery regime, the Piedmont region in which Elias Hill was born may have been the most powerful bastion of white Southern values in the state. Indeed, the Piedmont produced many of the state's most outspoken supporters of slavery. Calhoun grew up and practiced law in the lower Piedmont, in Abbeville on the Piedmont's far western end. Hammond's plantation was in Edgefield, in the southwestern reaches of the region. Edgefield also produced Preston Brooks (who memorably caned abolitionist congressman Charles Sumner on the floor of the House of Representatives in 1856), as well as the race-baiting governor and senator "Pitchfork" Ben Tillman (born in Edgefield in 1847). In 1902, the future senator and Dixiecrat presidential candidate Strom Thurmond would be born in Edgefield.[19]

At the northeast end of the Piedmont, York County stood out even within the region as one of the strongest redoubts for the values of the Confederacy. During the war, local whites established fourteen different Confederate infantry companies; according to local accounts, soldiers from the country's white male population suffered a higher percentage of deaths than soldiers from any other county in the state. Late in the war, as the Union gunboats pounded Charleston and as Union general William Tecumseh Sherman closed in on the state capitol at Columbia, whites from all around the state sought refuge in friendly homes in York County and elsewhere in the Piedmont. (Blacks migrated by the hundreds and thousands in the opposite direction, from the upcountry down toward the Union-occupied territories in the low country and the sea islands.) Indeed, it was to York County that Confederate president Jefferson Davis fled in the days after Lee's surrender at Appomattox. Davis stayed at the home of Dr. James Rufus Bratton along Congress Street in the county seat of Yorkville, where he and Bratton are reputed to have sat on the porch and bitterly reviewed what the war had done to the value of their estates. Forty years later, the very same Rufus Bratton would be immortalized as the model for the dashing hero Benjamin Cameron in *The Clansman,* the Thomas Dixon novel of white supremacy that was made into D. W. Griffith's film *Birth of a Nation.* Parts of the film were even shot in Yorkville, not far from the family home of Dixon's mother.[20]

The choice of York County was a shrewd one for writers and moviemakers seeking to capture the Old South. In the South Carolina upcountry, in places like York County, middling white slaveholders—farmers who typically owned fewer than twenty slaves and modest cotton farms—refined and adapted the constitutional theory of the founders, forging what was perhaps the most virulently racist form of U.S. constitutionalism ever to have widespread influence. For the white upcountry cotton planters of South Carolina, republican government rested—as it had in its classical eighteenth-century version—on the public participation of equal and upstanding citizens whose independence would ensure the virtue of government. Only independent citizens, the classical republican theory held, could avoid the dangers of factional strife and destructive partisanship that brought corruption and decay to republican government. "The truest prudence," insisted Edgefield's Hammond, "is, for men and nations, at all hazards to maintain their dignity and independence." It therefore seemed to men like Hammond that the political economy of slavery perfectly matched the imperatives of republican political theory. Slavery guaranteed the dignity, independence, and equality of white male citizens by effectively subordinating the laboring class—the inevitable "mud-sill" class, as Hammond put it. Racial slavery further marked off the subordinate class of labor with clear racial boundaries. As one of the most thoughtful historians of the South Carolina upcountry writes, slavery thus separated the "independent, enfranchised, white, and free" from the "dependent, politically impotent, black, and enslaved." And by creating the conditions for equality among the white citizenry, South Carolinian Henry William Trescot wrote in 1859, slavery seemed to have "realized the dream of political philosophers." White South Carolinian John Thompson put the same point more bluntly: "This Union," Thompson insisted, had been "formed by men for the white race, for white men and their posterity." Any other structure threatened to bring the republic crashing down into political ruin.[21]

As Trescot and Thompson made clear, it was crucial to the republicanism of the upcountry slaveholders that blacks—even free blacks—be excluded from citizenship. By the time Elias Hill was an adult, the republican constitutionalism of the white slaveholding class had fundamentally reshaped the law of black citizenship in the United States. For decades, the question of black citizenship had been the subject of ad hoc and often inconsistent treatment. All of that changed in the years after the Missouri Compromise of 1820. In 1821 and then again in 1843, U.S. attorneys general (one from Virginia, the other from South Carolina) opined that "free persons of the color" were "not citizens of the United States" but rather mere "denizens," or "sojourning strangers," to the American constitutional order. In South Carolina, Judge John Belton O'Neall of the state Supreme Court wrote that "the negro or his descendant is not, cannot be, a citizen" and that free blacks held a status below that of even an "alien enemy," who after all might become a citizen once hostilities had ceased. In 1846, the state Supreme Court squarely held that of the "three classes of persons" in the state—"freemen under the constitution," slaves, and "free negroes, mulattoes and mustizoes"—only those in the first category were citizens. "A firm and wise policy," the court reasoned, had "excluded" free blacks "from the rights of citizenship in this and almost every State in which they are found."[22]

In 1857, the position avowed by Judge O'Neall and the South Carolina Supreme Court was adopted and extended by the U.S. Supreme Court's decision in *Dred Scott v. Sandford*, authored by the Court's chief justice, Roger B. Taney of Maryland. *Dred Scott* announced that all those "whose ancestors were negroes of the African race, and imported into this country, and sold and held as slaves" were not and could never be made citizens of the United States. Taney's reasoning was famously weak, but his conclusions seemed to create a powerful barrier between free blacks like Hill and civic membership in the American nation-state. Taney determined that the thirteen states had not included free blacks among their citizenry in 1776 and that free blacks had not been among the citizens for whom the Constitution was ratified in 1788. The evidence on these points was hardly as strong as Taney made it out to be. But Taney reasoned (probably wrongly, as it turns out, at least with respect to the upper South) that the southern states would never have signed on to a Constitution that allowed free blacks to be citizens. Moreover, in Taney's view Congress's authority to naturalize noncitizens was "confined to persons born in a foreign country, under a foreign government." Black persons born and living in the United States therefore could not be made citizens under the U.S. Constitution because they had lived as noncitizens under the United States government. As the *Dred Scott* case's leading historian observes, Taney's reasoning led ineluctably to the conclusion that "American negroes, free and slave, were the only people on the face of the earth who (saving a constitutional amendment) were forever ineligible for American citizenship."[23]

The *Dred Scott* case famously generated a firestorm of opposition in the North, but among whites the black citizenship issue provoked relatively little controversy. Even Lincoln publicly agreed that blacks ought not be made citizens, though he contended that the states ought to have the power to decide the matter for themselves. By contrast, black people living in the United States reacted bitterly to the citizenship passages of the *Dred Scott* decision. No group better grasped the cumulative consequences of the *Dred Scott* ruling and the Fugitive Slave Act of 1850 than the United States's already beleaguered free black population. Indeed, historians of black nationalism have long observed that the 1850s witnessed an upsurge of enthusiasm among free blacks for emigration. To many free blacks, it increasingly seemed that Chief Justice Taney was right when he suggested that black people had "no rights which the white man was bound to respect." If that was so, then the choice for African peoples living in the United States seemed stark. "Shall we fly, or shall we resist?" asked 1850s black nationalist Martin Delany. And if the former, "Where shall we go?"[24]

*
*
*

Delany's question stands out in bold relief against conventional narratives of American nationhood. To invoke a national tradition is to invoke a set of powerful boundaries that mark off one constitutional system from others. It marks off the "we" and the "us" of countless national histories of the United States, histories whose imagined American readers stand inside that tradition as representatives of the same "we" that constitute the "We the People" in the preamble of the U.S. Constitution. Americans (like national audiences all around the world) are typically interested most of all in those who stay and whose commitments have helped to shape the traditions of the national community. Those who leave become not "we" but "they," exiled to some other tradition or traditions. "They" may be of interest to the parallel national development of some other national narrative, but they hardly have claims on the development of the nation they have left behind. Even worse, those who were "us" but become "them" are deeply suspect. To be "us" means to be bound by duties of loyalty and allegiance. "American citizenship," the immigrant, naturalized citizen, and later Supreme Court justice

Felix Frankfurter once wrote, entails "entering upon a fellowship which binds people together by devotion to certain feelings and ideas and ideals."[25] To have left those ideas and ideals behind implies a certain kind of treachery, even treason, a deficit of loyalty to those with whom the "we" of the American nation presumptively sympathize.

In politics and constitutional law, the nation-state also acts as a frame because nation-state politics is paradigmatically the art of voice, not of exit. As Albert O. Hirschman puts it, "exit is ordinarily unthinkable" as a strategy for change in institutions such as the nation. In American constitutionalism in particular, the Constitution created in 1787 has been remarkably effective in capturing the outer boundaries of the political scene. To be sure, some have agreed with abolitionist William Lloyd Garrison, who famously rejected the document as "an agreement with hell." The Civil War arose out of the most important such rejection (though some, like James Henry Hammond, advocated that the Confederacy adopt the U.S. Constitution wholesale). Yet with only a handful of exceptions, virtually everyone in American constitutional history has claimed the Constitution as theirs, choosing to work from within what has often proven to be a protean constitutional order remarkably open to change.[26]

The U.S. Constitution, then, creates a legal regime in which the question has typically not been whether to accept its terms, but rather what those terms mean. To step outside the constitutional framework, after all, is often literally treason. And even where exit does not warrant legal sanctions, it is open to charges of disloyalty and abandonment. At the very least, as many in the black tradition of American constitutionalism have argued since well before the Civil War, to advocate exit jeopardizes the cause of those who remain in the United States. To advocate exit, as white abolitionist William Goodell pointed out, seemed to suggest that it was "impossible for the colored race to enjoy the rights of freemen in this country."[27]

No one in the American tradition has better articulated the critique of exit than the escaped slave and abolitionist Frederick Douglass. To be sure, Douglass had a deep interest in Africa and the diaspora of African peoples. When he traveled to Egypt late in his life, Douglass claimed the glories of Egypt's storied past— its pyramids, its pharaohs—for those who in the United States were described as black. Several years before his death, Douglass served as the United States's minister to Haiti, one of the great nineteenth-century symbols of black nationalism. But from the 1840s onward, it was *American* nationalism that Douglass sought to deploy to the advantage of the people of African descent living in the United States.[28]

Nations, Douglass believed, were "the grandest aggregations of organized human power" that humankind had yet hit upon. They brought out "the world's greatest men" and inspired "the highest order of talent and ability." They were, he said, "the most attractive, instructive and useful" of human creations. Douglass thus became a lifelong critic of proposals within the black community to abandon the American nation-state. He pointed out that there were simply too many black people in the United States for exit to be a realistic option. The nation simply could not afford "such costly transportation." Any "attempt to remove them" would thus "be as vain as to bail out the ocean," as realistic as "sending missionaries to the moon." More deeply, Douglass saw in emigration schemes a kind of treachery. To advocate exit from a constitutional framework in which others had long struggled to create equality was "necessarily an abandonment of the great and paramount principle" that held "this Government"— the United States—"solemnly bound to protect and defend the lives and liberties of all its citizens, of whatever race or color." Exit was "an expedient, a half-way measure," a "premature, disheartening surrender," that "would make freedom and free institutions depend upon migration rather than protection; by flight, rather than by right." Exit left "the whole question of equal rights on the soil of the South open and still to be settled" and implied the "utter impracticability of equal rights." Instead, Douglass marshaled the obligations of loyalty to the nation-state on behalf of black freedoms. White Americans had failed to have "loyalty enough" and "patriotism enough" to "live up to the Constitution," he told the assembled crowd at the World's Columbian Exposition in Chicago in 1893. That failure was the chief source of the "Negro problem." By contrast, Douglass announced to audience after audience, "We Negroes love our country." For Douglass it followed that "the destiny of the colored American" was nothing less than "the destiny of America."[29]

Douglass's critique of exit resonated deeply in the nineteenth-century black community. In South Carolina in October 1871, in the very month in which Reverend Hill and the Clay Hill company were making final preparations for their departure, a Convention of the Colored People of the Southern States condemned emigration in much the same terms Douglass used. Emigration plans, the Convention declared, were treacherous and disloyal illusions. They emanated from "unscrupulous and irresponsible men," "enemies to the colored people" who were working to "induce them to leave the land of their birth."[30]

Yet by the time the Clay Hill company set out for Liberia, there had also been a long and distinguished line of people of African descent living in the United States who debated whether Douglass's was the appropriate attitude for blacks to strike toward the nation in which they lived. There was, of course, a long tradition of fugitive slaves and maroon communities from the earliest days of slavery; slaves had no doubt harbored aspirations to emigrate back to Africa from the earliest days of the first slave ships in the New World. By the late eighteenth century, small groups of blacks in New England—slave and free—were publicizing plans for emigration. Paul Cuffe, a wealthy black Massachusetts whaler and shipbuilder, explored Sierra Leone in 1811 and brought thirty-eight free black emigrants to Freetown on his return in 1816. Within a few more years, northern free blacks began forming emigration societies, such as the Haytien Emigration Society of Philadelphia, organized to aid black emigration to Haiti. And in 1821, Lott Cary, a free black man who had been born into slavery in Virginia, emigrated as a missionary to Sierra Leone and soon continued on to Liberia as one of the first emigrants to the American Colonization Society's proprietary African colony.[31]

Cuffe and Cary represented the leading edge of what historian Wilson Jeremiah Moses calls "the golden age of black nationalism." Led for the most part by literate free blacks in the North (many of them preachers), early black nationalists aimed to revive what they understood to have been a proud African civilization. That civilization had culminated in the great pyramids and cities of Egypt, and the Bible seemed to suggest it would soon return. The opening line of Psalms 68, verse 31 announced, "Princes shall come out of Egypt." Surely that meant a new African civilization was in the offing. Christianity, it seemed, would be the vehicle for the new African nationalism. "Ethiopia shall soon stretch forth her hands unto God," the verse concluded. Christianity promised to return civilization to Africa and to lift it up higher even than the European nations that seemed for the moment to have eclipsed it.[32]

Ironically, growing enthusiasm in the white community for black colonization helped to bring an end to much of the early interest in emigration among free blacks in the North. Established in 1816 to finance the colonization of free American blacks to the proprietary colony of Liberia, the American Colonization Society brought elite whites and new financial resources to the movement of American blacks to Africa. Its founding president was Bushrod Washington, George Washington's nephew and a former student in James Wilson's Philadelphia law office. Subsequent presidents included James Madison and Henry Clay. The United States's first great chief justice, John Marshall, whom colonization advocates proudly called "the father of the Constitution," spoke out in favor of the Colonization Society's efforts. And by the onset of the Civil War, the society had financed the passage of almost 10,000 blacks from the United States to Liberia. Yet free blacks participated in the society's ventures with increasing reluctance, and by the 1820s free black leaders were denouncing the society's programs. Many white southern supporters of the society aimed to rid the United States of the threatening presence of free blacks among their slave populations. White supporters of the society who opposed slavery often favored emigration in order to remove blacks from the country altogether. (The "removal" of the "free black man," wrote one such supporter, was "a matter of deep and abiding interest" and a "first step" toward the removal of "the blackest stain upon the bright escutcheon of American glory.")[33]

Even the dampening effects of the Colonization Society, however, could not overcome the powerful new impetus toward emigration that came with the harsh Fugitive Slave Act of 1850, the *Dred Scott* decision, and the panoply of new limits on black freedoms that arrived in the same decade. By the early 1850s a substantial number of free American blacks (including many who opposed the Colonization Society) were once again debating the relative merits of emigration to Canada, to South and Central America, and to Africa. Conventions to consider emigration plans met in 1852, 1854, 1856, and 1858, and men like Edward Wilmot Blyden, Alexander Crummell, Martin Delany, and Henry Highland Garnet emerged in the American black community as outspoken advocates of emigration. An estimated 20,000 blacks fled the United States to Canada during the decade. Almost half of the Colonization Society's pre–Civil War Liberian emigrants left during the same years. And when in 1859 a coup seemed to hold out new promise for the future of Haiti, many gave serious thought to leaving the United States for the nation that in the 1790s had become the world's first black republic. Some 2,500 American blacks moved to Haiti in 1861 and 1862.[34]

The common thread among those who made their way to Liberia or Haiti in the years leading up to and during the Civil War seems to have been a deep conviction that the United States would never admit a person of African descent to the rank of full citizen. Martin Delany, whom Frederick Douglass called "the intensest embodiment of black Nationality to be met with outside the valley of the Niger," observed pointedly in 1852 that "to imagine ourselves to be included in the body politic, except by express legislation, is at war with common sense, and contrary to fact." Delaney wrote, "We can have no rights here as citizens." It was thus "useless to talk about our rights," he insisted; blacks living in the United States were more akin to stateless peoples such as the "Poles in Russia, the Hungarians in Austria," or "the Welsh, Irish, and Scotch in the British dominions." Americans of African descent were without the political power that seemed to come when groups attained nation-state status. Indeed, it was precisely this status that had exempted Indians from the white-supremacist logic of the *Dred Scott* decision. As a people whom Chief Justice Taney described as "associated together in nations or tribes," Indians could be naturalized in the United States as if born in a foreign nation. From the Constitution's perspective, Indians were thus in the respect of citizenship "like the subjects of any other foreign Government" and could become entitled to the rights and privileges of U.S. citizenship on the same basis as "an emigrant from any other foreign people." As an unrecognized nation within a nation, by contrast, blacks had been almost completely stripped of any rights.[35]

A nation of their own seemed to offer American blacks a path to global stature and respectability. Just as nationalist movements had brought recognition to the subordinated peoples of European empires—just as the Greek independence movement, for example, had won the attention of the world in the 1820s—so too might black nationalism confer stature on the marginalized African peoples enveloped in the United States. As Delany put it, "the claims of no people" were respected until those claims could be "presented in a national capacity." Edward Wilmot Blyden, a West Indian black man and regular visitor to the United States who emigrated to Liberia in 1850, declared that "African nationality is our great need. . . . Nationality is an ordinance of Nature. The heart of every true Negro yearns after a distinct and separate nationality." Emigré recruiters for Haiti encouraged "the black and the man of color" to "seek elsewhere a home and a nationality" and argued that Haiti represented at last the chance to build "a great colored nation." And though many debated the relative merits of colonization, significant numbers of free blacks in the decade before the Civil War had come to agree that only African nationalism would allow "all colored men," as Professor M. H. Freeman of Avery College wrote in 1858, "to attain the full stature of manhood."[36]

Edward Blyden, in particular, encouraged blacks living in the United States to rethink the nature of their constitutional commitments. White Americans, Blyden urged, might look to the framers of the American Constitution as the quasi-mythical originators of American nationhood. But blacks in the United States, he suggested, ought to look to an alternative set of wise framers: the "framers of *our* Constitution," by which Blyden meant those who had founded the constitutional system of the black republic of Liberia. Martin Delany had powerfully criticized the idea that Liberia (a "pitiful dependency" of the American Colonization Society, he wrote) could serve as an independent black nation-state. In 1847, however, Liberia had become an independent republic, no longer the American Colonization

Society's proprietary colony. In black circles in the United States, the constituent documents of the new Republic of Liberia quickly took on great importance. To many, they seemed to announce the arrival of the kind of black nationalism that Delany and others had begun to discuss. "We the People of the Republic of Liberia," announced the Liberian Declaration of Independence, issued in 1847, "were originally the inhabitants of the United States of North America." There, however,

> We were debarred by law from all the rights and privileges of men. . . .
>   We were every where shut out from all civil office.
>   We were excluded from all participation in the government.
>   We were taxed without our consent.
>   We were compelled to contribute to the resources of a country, which gave us no protection.
>   We were made a separate and distinct class, and as against us every avenue to improvement was effectually closed. Strangers from all lands of a color different from ours, were preferred before us.

"All hope of a favorable change in our country," the Declaration concluded (and by "our country" the drafters meant the United States) "was thus wholly extinguished in our bosoms."[37]

The new Constitution of the black republic, ratified the same year, established the sovereignty of the Republic of Liberia as a black nation-state. "All men are born equally free and independent," announced the first section of the document's Bill of Rights. Yet the Constitution clarified that the freedoms to which all men were entitled did not include citizenship. The "great object" of the "we the People" who formed the black republic in 1847 was "to provide a home for the dispersed and oppressed children of Africa." Article V, section 13, of the Liberian Constitution therefore stipulated, "None but persons of color shall be admitted to citizenship in this Republic." As an international authority on Liberian constitutionalism would put it some decades later, the Liberian constitution thus used the term "People" in a special sense. It was "not synonymous with 'inhabitants.'" Nor did it even "include the native or recaptured Africans inhabiting the Commonwealth." Most important, "just as the word 'People' as used in the preamble of the American Constitution did not include the Negroes, whether slave or free, inhabiting the United States," so too did the Liberian Constitution permanently exclude from citizenship the republic's white inhabitants. If *Dred Scott* clarified that the United States's Constitution was one in which people of African descent could never be citizens, the Liberian constitution made the same move in reverse. Here was a constitutional order organized around race, but in the reverse image of black nationalism. Indeed, as the Colonization Society would later explain in words eerily similar to the pre–Civil War American law of black status, the Liberian constitution had created a nation that was "exclusively the black man's country, into which no white man can intrude except as a stranger or as a denizen."[38]

By the second year of the U.S. Civil War, Liberia's black nationalism was having powerful feedback effects on the black citizenship question in the United States. In December 1861 Lincoln called for formal recognition of Haiti and Liberia. The debate that followed made Liberian nationhood one of the first great tests of the Civil War's promise for black equality in the U.S. Congress. If the United States were to send ambassadors to Haiti and Liberia, Senator Garrett Davis of Kentucky warned, it would be necessary to receive their ambassadors in return. The international law principle of the equality of nations would thus effectively impose a form of racial equality on the domestic law of the United States. "If a full-blooded negro, were sent in that capacity from either of these countries," Davis exclaimed on the Senate floor, "by the laws of nations he could demand that he be received precisely on the same terms of equality with the white representatives from the Powers of the earth composed of white people." The black representatives of black nation-states would "demand admission upon terms of equality with all other diplomats" to social events, even in the salon of the President himself. If such representatives "had families consisting of negro wives and negro daughters, they would have the right to ask that their families also be invited to such occasions, and that they go there and mingle with the whites of our own country." If ambassadors were sent to Haiti and Liberia, Delaware senator Willard Saulsbury predicted, "some negro" would "walk upon the floor of the Senate of the United States" within twelve months.[39]

Diplomatic recognition of Liberia and Haiti—which is to say, recognition of black nationalism—gathered importance in 1862 precisely because, as Pennsylvania congressman Charles John Biddle declared, it went to "the very subject of this strife" between North and South: the place of blacks in the United States. For Democrats, the aim of the war effort was merely to "preserve the old frame of government, to rally it to the old affections." For Republicans like Senator Charles Sumner of Massachusetts, by contrast, the aim of the war was quickly becoming what Biddle derisively termed "political rights" and "an acknowledgment of the equality of the races." Opponents believed fervently that diplomatic recognition was "intended to introduce . . . the idea of negro equality" and would lead eventually "to a social equality with the free white people of this country." It was slowly dawning on the opponents of black equality in Congress that the war now threatened whites' "habitual sense of superiority to the African race."[40]

*
*
*

For many black emigrationists from the 1850s, the Civil War seemed to change everything. Indeed, the postwar prospects for black citizenship caused many of those who had turned to emigration in the bleak prewar years to come back into the fold of domestic politics. Their efforts, however, would be fiercely contested, and nowhere more so than in South Carolina.

Three constitutional amendments proposed by Congress and ratified by the states promised to transform the lives of blacks in the South Carolina upcountry and throughout the South: to free them, to integrate them into the nation, and to protect their rights with new federal authority. The Thirteenth Amendment barred "slavery" and "involuntary servitude, except as a punishment for crime." Proposed by Congress even before the close of the war, and ratified by the states in December 1865, the amendment promised, as Republican congressman James Wilson of Iowa put it, to "obliterate the last lingering vestiges of the slave system." Acting pursuant to its authority to enforce the new Thirteenth Amendment, and seeking to overturn the *Dred Scott* decision of 1857, Congress enacted the Civil Rights Act of 1866 over President Andrew Johnson's veto, declaring that "all persons born in the United States" were "citizens of the United States." Two months later, in June 1866, Congress proposed the Fourteenth Amendment. The amendment's first clause definitively reversed the citizenship ruling of the *Dred Scott* decision, making "all persons born or naturalized in the United States" citizens of the United States. This amendment, whose ratification was completed by the states when the Reconstruction South Carolina legislature voted to ratify it on July 9, 1868, provided (among other things) that no state could "abridge the privileges or immunities of citizens of the United States"; that no state shall "deprive any person of life, liberty, or property, without due process of law"; and that no state shall "deny to any person . . . the equal protection of the laws." Finally, the Fifteenth Amendment—proposed by Congress in February 1869 and ratified by the states a year later—provided that blacks would have a right to vote on the same terms as whites. Political voice in the American constitutional order, it seemed, would no longer be for whites only.[41]

The Reconstruction amendments offered men like Elias Hill the opportunity to raise new black voices in the reconstructed American nation. The opportunity to organize a new black citizenry seemed to play to Reverend Hill's greatest strengths. Virtually everyone who came into contact with Hill in 1870 and 1871 seems to have commented on his voice. He had "a clear, sonorous voice," noted the *Philadelphia Press*. According to the American Colonization Society, it was "a voice of unusual power and sweetness." And with his gift of voice added to his facility with language, crippled and dwarflike Elias Hill had become "a leader amongst his people." "Elias had such a powerful voice," remembered his nephew Thomas Simpson many years later, "he could be heard a long distance when preaching."[42]

Hill threw his energies into three of the great fields for black activism after the war: religion, education, and politics. He had been preaching to black congregations more or less illicitly since 1861. Once the war was over, Hill became a Baptist minister, traveling on his spring wagon around a circuit of churches in the Piedmont. He had a "license to preach," he said in 1871, referring to the licensing requirements that white South Carolinians sought to impose on free blacks immediately following the war. He also taught school in a one-room wooden schoolhouse in Clay Hill. More than sixty years later, former slaves from the Piedmont who had attended school for the first time during Reconstruction still remembered Elias Hill as "the only colored teacher in that section of the country." And by the winter of 1870–71, Hill had become the president of a York County council of the Union League, the most widespread and powerful black political organization among rural freedpeople in the South.[43]

Prospects for black political power in South Carolina were especially good. Blacks made up almost 60 percent of the state's population, outnumbering whites 415,814 to 289,667, a margin of more than 125,000. Some 314 blacks in South Carolina held public office at the state or federal level between 1868 and 1876, far more than in any other southern state during Reconstruction. The state's House of Representatives was made up of substantial black majorities from 1868 to 1876. Blacks were also a significant presence in the state Senate from 1868 to 1872, and black Republicans held a plurality over white Democrats and white Republicans in the state Senate from 1872 to 1876.[44]

Indeed, some of those who had been most committed to emigration in the 1850s came to South Carolina to help forge a new black citizenship in the reconstructed United States. Martin Delany—Frederick Douglass's "intensest embodiment of black Nationality"—went to South Carolina to recruit black men for the Union army, urging them to "rally around the flag." Delany would play a central role in the state's Reconstruction politics for another eleven years. James Redpath, a British abolitionist who had helped organize emigration to Haiti in 1861 and 1862, similarly appeared in Reconstruction South Carolina in the new role of superintendent of public education for the city of Charleston. And Henry McNeal Turner of the African Methodist Episcopal church, who had advocated emigration in the 1850s and would do so again in the 1880s and 1890s, worked as a Union League organizer in South Carolina in 1867.[45]

The great promise of black politics in South Carolina, however, produced white backlash. For many whites, the danger seemed all too real that the state's black majority might create what the editors of a Columbia newspaper called "an African dominion" in the United States, "a new Liberia" in the South. And so from almost the very moment of the war's end, South Carolina whites began a campaign to undo the Reconstruction constitutional amendments, to reimpose the white supremacy of the prewar South, and to silence the new political voice that the Reconstruction amendments had given to the state's black men. What followed was a pitched battle like few the nation had ever seen before—and indeed, like few the nation would see again—between competing visions of the postwar Constitution.[46]

The South Carolina Ku Klux Klan seems to have appeared in York County in late 1867 or early 1868. Its officers were leading men from the white community, including Rufus Bratton, who had hosted Jefferson Davis on his flight from Richmond in April 1865. Bratton was the leader of the York County Ku Klux Klan. He was born in 1821 at Brattonsville, his family's York County plantation, not more than about twelve miles south of Clay Hill. The cotton plantation, now a nostalgic historical center known as Historic Brattonsville, was one of the largest in the region. (In the 1990s, movie star Mel Gibson would use its picturesque grounds to make *The Patriot,* a film about the patriotism of the Scotch-Irish residents of the South Carolina upcountry during the American Revolution.) As an adult, Rufus Bratton moved to a grand three-story home on Congress Street, near the center of Yorkville. It was here, next to the elegant Rose Hotel and across the street from the county courthouse, that Jefferson Davis had stayed on his flight from Richmond in the spring of 1865, and it was here that in 1870 and 1871 Rufus Bratton organized the York County Ku Klux Klan.[47]

Other local Klan leaders were from the same Scotch-Irish families that had established area towns and a number of the region's most important churches. "In no other Southern county," historian of the Klan Allen Trelease writes, "did the Klan organize more fully or take over more completely." In the county seat of Yorkville alone, there were between three and twelve different Klan dens. In the county as a whole there were at least forty-five. "Nearly every white man," remembered one white county resident some years later, "was taken into it." The best estimates suggest that somewhere between 1,000 and 1,800 of the 2,300 adult white men in the county belonged to the Klan.[48]

In York and elsewhere in the South Carolina Piedmont, the Klan sought to restore the white slaveholder constitution of the pre–Civil War years. Echoing antebellum white South Carolina's claims of allegiance to what Klan members now began to call "the constitution of '89" and the "Union of our fathers," the Reconstruction Klan swore to uphold "constitutional liberty as bequeathed to us by our forefathers in its original purity." Similar organizations, such as local Councils of Safety, sprang up alongside the Klan, committing themselves to "labor for the restoration of constitutional liberty." The idea, as one Klan member freely admitted to a congressional committee, was to oppose the Reconstruction amendments to the Constitution and to resist "the freedom of the African race" as well as "their general equality before the law" and "their right to vote." As South Carolina's Republican attorney general put it in 1871, the Klan sought to restore "slavery as it existed in the Constitution of the United States" in 1857, the year of the *Dred Scott* case. The Klan was thus the postwar continuation of the antebellum slave patrol; the region's whites and blacks both understood it in just these terms. The Klan's aim, as a congressional report published in 1872 concluded, was to reestablish the institutions of the antebellum slave code and thereby to "recover what [southern whites] valued more than anything else—property in slaves and political power."[49]

Almost from its very beginning, the York Klan pursued the popular constitutionalism of the "constitution of '89" as violently as any Klan in the South. Indeed, the apogee of the Klan's popular constitutionalism in the Reconstruction South—what Allen Trelease calls the "climax of Klan terror" and "the most conspicuous theater of Klan activity in the South"—came in Elias Hill's York County in the winter and spring of 1870–71. For nearly eight months, from October into May, Klansmen engaged in regular weekly nighttime raids. "Hundreds of persons," according to a later congressional report, "slept in the woods from October until March" in fear of Klan attack. Investigators identified some 600 separate incidents of Klan-related violence between November 1870 and September 1871. The same period witnessed at least eleven murders, beginning with the brutal shooting and execution of a black man named Tom Roundtree in December, his throat slit with a bowie knife.[50]

One of the most horrific and well-publicized attacks was the raid on Jim Williams. Before the war, Williams had belonged to the upcountry South Carolina Rainey family. Escaping during the war, he had fought with Sherman's army and changed his name from Rainey to Williams. By 1870, he had become the bold and outspoken captain of one of York's three all-black state militia companies, chartered by the Republican Reconstruction state government. The federal government, Williams insisted, "had promised him forty acres of land, and they hadn't given it to him." And so, he was known to say, he would "carry on the war" to get what was coming to him. Some even claimed later to remember that he had ridden into Yorkville on sales day—the day of the monthly public auction at the county court—and announced from the steps of the Rose Hotel that "if ever the KKK came into his country very few, if any, of them would return to their homes." At the very least, he made clear, "he would be damned if he would vote for any white man."[51]

When Williams refused to give up the guns Republican governor Robert Scott had provided to the black militias in October, he was singled out. "We are going to kill Williams, and are going to kill all these damned niggers that votes the Radical ticket," announced the local Klan. On the night of March 7, 1871, a group of between forty and sixty white men gathered at a local muster field known as the "Briar Patch." They gathered there under the leadership of Rufus Bratton and Major James T. Avery, both veterans of the Confederate army. Bratton knew Jim Williams quite well. Through Bratton's mother, Harriet, whose maiden name was Rainey, Bratton was part of the family to which Williams had belonged under slavery.[52]

Many years later, in 1924, the grisly details of Williams's execution were recounted by Milus S. Carroll, one of the Klansmen who was there that night. Carroll, it seems, decided that his grandchildren and the "young people" more generally needed to know how the Klan had "saved our state from ruin" from the "lawless element" of the Republican Party. "Thousands and tens of thousands of the best men of the South," Carroll wrote for posterity, had "joined the Order." And when Williams "became a nuisance to the surrounding country" because of his refusal to surrender his rifles, the "York Klan under the leadership of Dr. J. R. Bratton" made plans to make an example of Williams. At Bratton's suggestion, Carroll recalled, the Klansmen found Williams hiding under his cabin's floorboards. As his wife looked on, they dragged Williams by a rope around his neck to a "large tree with a limb running out 10 or 12 feet from the ground." Carroll remembered how Williams had "pleaded and prayed." Most of all, Carroll remembered the ghastly manner in which the Bratton Klan had executed a leading man of the county's "lawless element." They forced Williams to climb up on the tree limb, one end of the rope around his neck, the other lashed to the limb. But Williams "refused to leap." A Klansman named Bob Caldwell, Carroll recalled, "climbed up and pushed Jim from the limb." Even then, "Jim grasped the limb," holding on for dear life until Caldwell "hacked his fingers with a knife, forcing him to drop." Williams died, Carroll told his grandchildren, "cursing, pleading, and praying all in one breath." A great victory had been won for law and order in the South Carolina Piedmont.[53]

As the Jim Williams raid indicated, perhaps the most dangerous thing one could do in York County in 1870 and 1871 was speak out against the violence. Black witnesses, it soon became clear, were "terrified" to appear before federal investigators. One federal soldier stationed in the upcountry claimed that the Klansmen "have scared the people out of their wits. They are afraid to speak above a whisper." Those who threatened to complain at the local courthouse were told that they would "never reach there alive." Black witnesses were ordered not to testify lest they become "the very next parties to be visited." "Leading men" in the white community told prospective black witnesses that next "it would be their day." Klansmen even killed one of their own when he was wounded and captured by local authorities after a night-time raid in nearby Newberry County.[54]

The Klansmen of York County thus made it abundantly clear that their mission was to suppress the new political voice that the Reconstruction amendments had given to the black men of the Piedmont. When Jim Williams had made threats, one federal official observed, the Klan had made certain that "his voice is hushed forever" and that he "will not reply again." Klansmen aimed literally to silence the freedpeople. "We silenced his court," one Klansman remembered years later in regard to an attack on a black judge living not far from Clay Hill. And in February 1871, this message was broadcast for all to see. In the very same railroad depot at Rock Hill to which Hill would lead his Clay Hill congregation in November, the Klan posted a notice. At the top were three stark letters: "KKK." Its text, as one black Rock Hill man later recounted, was chilling: "Your voices," the notice read, "shall be shut up." Shut up, it continued, "in a lonesome valley, where they will never be heard no more."[55]

South Carolina Republicans and the black women and men of Clay Hill, however, refused to be silenced. Within a week of Jim Williams's lynching, a company of ninety troops under the command of Major Lewis Merrill arrived in York, along with similar companies in Union and Spartanburg counties. Soon "the place," as a *New York Tribune* correspondent reported, "had the look of a town in war time recently captured by an invading army." A county that Sherman had skipped past on his march to the sea—a county that had been among the Confederacy's last redoubts—had finally come under military occupation. Within days, President Ulysses S. Grant called for legislation expanding the authority of the federal executive to address "a condition of affairs . . . in some of the States of the Union rendering life and property insecure." On April 7, 1871, the U.S. Congress resolved to create a Joint Select Committee of seven senators and fourteen representatives to "inquire into the condition of affairs in the late insurrectionary States." And on April 20, Congress enacted the legislation Grant had requested by passing the Ku Klux Klan Act. Through the spring and summer, the Joint Select Committee heard evidence of the Klan conspiracies that were sweeping across the South. In July, a subcommittee traveled to Yorkville and the South Carolina upcountry, where they heard testimony in the Rose Hotel, right next door to Rufus Bratton's home on Congress Street. And in October, relying on the Joint Select Committee's findings and at the urging of U.S. attorney general Amos Akerman, President Grant suspended the writ of habeas corpus in nine upcountry counties. Not coincidentally, Grant listed Elias Hill's York County first, out of alphabetical order. Within days, Major Merrill's troops began arresting accused Klan conspirators. By January 1872, Merrill would arrest some 472 Piedmont whites on charges of violating the constitutional rights of the freedpeople.[56]

A series of spectacular trials followed soon after the arrests. Klan indictments had come earlier in other states, but nowhere were there as many defendants as in the South Carolina upcountry. In sheer size, they were the biggest trials in the history of the federal courts to date. The grand jury of the U.S. Circuit Court for the South Carolina District, sitting in its November 1871 term in Columbia, indicted some five hundred separate defendants in eighty different bills of indictment.[57]

Defending the Klan conspirators were Reverdy Johnson and Henry Stanbery. Johnson, a former Maryland senator, had successfully argued the *Dred Scott* case in the Supreme Court on behalf of the would-be slaveholder. In 1866, he had sought to sabotage the Fourteenth Amendment on the Senate floor (it was, Johnson declared on the Senate floor, "an insult to th[e] states") and then cast a losing vote against the amendment's passage. Henry Stanbery had been Andrew Johnson's attorney general and later Johnson's defense lawyer in the Republican Congress's impeachment of Johnson in 1868. Both Reverdy Johnson and Stanbery were among the most distinguished—and most expensive—constitutional lawyers of the day. South Carolina's leading white Democrats, led by former Confederate general Wade Hampton III, had taken up a statewide, county-by-county collection that raised some $10,000 for the legal defense effort. Contributions quickly poured in from around the South. On the other side stood the state's Republican attorney general, D. H. Chamberlain, and the U.S. district attorney, Daniel T. Corbin, as well as U.S. attorney general Akerman himself, who spent substantial portions of the fall of 1871 in the upcountry to oversee the prosecution of the cases.[58]

The indictments, which were brought under the Ku Klux Klan Act and earlier legislation designed to enforce the Reconstruction amendments, quickly became important early tests of the new Reconstruction constitution. The great question was whether the Fourteenth Amendment had so dramatically augmented federal authority as to allow the federal government to protect freedpeople from violent conspiracies such as those waged by the Klan. In particular, the indictments charged that the Klan had conspired to interfere with black voting rights; to deprive blacks of the equal protection of the laws guaranteed to all persons, and the privileges and immunities guaranteed to all citizens, by the Fourteenth Amendment; and to deny black people the rights guaranteed in the Bill of Rights to security from unreasonable searches and seizures (the Fourth Amendment) and to bear arms (the Second Amendment).[59]

The difficulty, as Johnson and Stanbery were quick to point

out, was that for almost one hundred years enforcement of the criminal laws had been left largely to the states. And for more than three decades, it had been well established that the protections of the Bill of Rights could be invoked against the federal government, but not against the states. According to Johnson and Stanbery, the Reconstruction amendments had not so fundamentally reoriented the traditional federal-state relationship as to authorize the federal government to displace the states in the prosecution of criminal violence or to make the federal Bill of Rights binding on the states. The Fourteenth Amendment, furthermore, had given the federal government authority to remedy violations of rights only when those violations were committed by *states,* not when they were committed by individuals or groups of individuals acting in a private capacity. ("No State shall . . ." read the operative language of the Fourteenth Amendment.) Legislation such as the Ku Klux Klan Act, which authorized the prosecution of private individuals for violating the rights guaranteed in the Fourteenth Amendment, Johnson and Stanbery contended, was therefore unconstitutional.[60]

Akerman, Chamberlain, and Corbin argued to the contrary that the Fourteenth Amendment's object was "manifestly" to protect "the rights of the newly enfranchised citizens" from states that were "disposed to encroach upon" those rights. The Fourteenth Amendment, Corbin argued, thus imposed "the same restriction" against unreasonable searches and seizures and violations of the right to bear arms "upon the States that before lay upon the Congress of the United States." Moreover, as for the objection that the amendment empowered the federal government to act against states but not against private citizens or conspiracies, Corbin noted that Section 5 of the amendment had "lodged . . . discretion in Congress" to enforce the amendment by "appropriate legislation." Who could say that Congress had abused its discretion, he asked, by going right to the underlying private violence rather than punishing state officials for failing to live up to their law enforcement obligations?[61]

Ultimately, the Klan trials in November 1871 became a referendum on the relationship between the Fourteenth Amendment and the *Dred Scott* case that Reverdy Johnson had argued and that had placed black descendants of slaves outside the pale of U.S. citizenship. What the Klan conspirators aimed to accomplish, District Attorney Corbin argued to the juries, was to reestablish the Constitution of the *Dred Scott* opinion: "That Constitution," Corbin noted the Supreme Court had said, "meant this, that the black man had no rights that the white man was bound to respect." Johnson lamely objected that the Taney decision had said merely that the founders "at the time of the Declaration of Independence, and when the Constitution of the United States was framed and adopted," had believed that the "unfortunate race" had "no rights which the white man was bound to respect." But that was precisely Corbin's point. The Klan promised in its initiation oaths to restore "constitutional liberty in its purity, as bequeathed to us" by those very forefathers. The purity of what Corbin called the Klan's "ancient Constitution," he reminded the jurors, was code for the reimposition of the most virulently racist strands of the Taney opinion in *Dred Scott*. For Corbin, the central purpose of the Reconstruction amendments, and the Fourteenth Amendment in particular, had been to expunge Taney's ancient Constitution from the American constitutional order and to establish the descendants of American slaves as citizens of the United States.[62]

The most telling referendum on the legacy of *Dred Scott* and the Fourteenth Amendment, however, came not from the mouths of the congressmen who descended on the upcountry in the summer of 1871, nor from the legal professionals who litigated the Reconstruction amendments in November and December. It came instead from the mouths of the black witnesses who testified in the trials and the black jurors who served in them, and from the fifty-three black witnesses who came forward to testify when the subcommittee of the Joint Select Committee came to South Carolina.[63]

Elias Hill was among the most prominent of the witnesses at the subcommittee hearings. In late July 1871, Hill's nephew June Moore—a tall twenty-six-year-old whom whites described as "jet black"—helped him travel from Clay Hill and carried him into the Rose Hotel, where the subcommittee had just the day before begun to take testimony before hostile white townspeople. Even before he arrived, Reverend Hill seems to have been threatened by a white planter named Joseph Akins, who lived less than a mile from Hill's home and who warned Hill not to tell "on who had whipped him." Akins had good reason to worry that Hill would do just that. Since early May, Hill had been helping with Major Merrill's investigation of the Klan.[64]

At the subcommittee hearing in Yorkville, Hill told the story of his assault. Six members of the Klan arrived at his home between midnight and one o'clock on the morning of May 6. They were all disguised "with coverings over their faces," some in "a kind of check disguise on their heads" and one with a "black oil-cloth over his head." Perhaps because they knew Hill and knew he knew them, they sought to disguise their voices as well. They "came in a very rapid manner" and broke into his brother Madison Hill's nearby home. Madison, like so many others, was sleeping away from home, but they whipped his wife, Easter Hill, until she directed them to Elias's home across the yard. Bursting in, they grabbed Elias from his bed, pulling him by his arms into the yard between the two houses. Hadn't he ordered recent suspicious burnings of the cotton gins and homes of local whites? Hadn't he told "black men to ravish all the white women"? Hadn't he been president of the Union League, and hadn't he held night-time meetings of the Union League in his home? Hadn't Jim

Williams—whom they called Jim Rainey, using his slave name— been at his home and made speeches? Hadn't he been corresponding with Alexander Wallace, the Republican congressman?[65]

Hill remembered with special bitterness that the Klansmen had smashed his clock, a possession that had long been a marker of middle-class distinction in the South Carolina upcountry. They threatened to kill him, brandishing pistols near his head. "One caught me by the leg and hurt me, for my leg for forty years has been drawn each year." Hill told the congressional subcommittee that he had "moaned when it hurt so." He "made a moan every time" one of the men cut him with a horsewhip. "I reckon he cut me eight cuts right on the hip bone," which Hill explained "was almost the only place he could hit my body," given its shrunken condition. Even three months later, Hill's breast was still "sore from their blows," and there was a place on his left temple where he still felt the effect of his beatings. He tried to point it out to the congressmen, but his crippled condition prevented him from touching his head with his hands.[66]

The threats against black witnesses seemed to have taken their toll on Hill. As he testified, his voice cracked. Congressman Philadelph Van Trump, the lone Democrat on the subcommittee and the man who would later deride the black witnesses before the subcommittee as "persons of the very lowest grade of intelligence," demanded that Hill provide the names of his white Klan member neighbors. To give names in a public hearing, of course, was to invite reprisal, and this was precisely why Van Trump demanded them. Hill's voice—the voice that had impressed so many—suddenly changed "to a hoarse whisper." "Why do you whisper when you mention persons?" Van Trump demanded. "I feel afraid of others hearing," Hill replied. "We are always afraid now and careful." And yet Hill continued to speak, naming the names of whites who were his "near neighbors" and yet had openly rejoiced in the Klan's attack on him and his friends. He named J. L. Barry, and the Nealy family from across Allison's Creek, and J. B. Partlow. "You need not whisper," hectored Van Trump; Hill's voice had fallen into a whisper once again. Hill was "always suspicious in speaking of these things," he admitted. And yet, whispering or otherwise, Hill and his fellow black witnesses had spoken their piece.[67]

More black witnesses spoke up at the Klan trials later in the year. Fewer than fifteen years before, the Chief Justice of the United States had announced—at the urging of Reverdy Johnson, no less—that no descendant of black slaves could ever become a citizen of the United States. Now black men and women stood up as citizens and testified in Johnson's presence about acts of violence and intimidation to which they had been subjected. In each case, black witnesses spoke out against white defendants. Indeed, the courtroom seems to have been overflowing with black witnesses and jurors, many of whom seem to have watched the proceedings not just in their own cases but in others as well. As they looked on from the jury box and from the seats behind the counsel tables, dozens of black witnesses walked to the witness stand, described attacks on themselves, and named white attackers who were there in the courtroom with them.[68]

For six months, from Elias Hill's testimony in July through the Klan trials in November and December, a chorus of black witnesses raised their voices in the South Carolina upcountry. It was not easy, to be sure. But on the strength of such testimony, juries made up substantially of black men—two-thirds of the jurors who served in the trials were black, and every trial featured a majority black jury—repeatedly announced verdicts of guilty. By the end of the November term of the Circuit Court, juries entered verdicts of guilty for each of the five defendants put to trial by the prosecution. Fifty-four conspirators were convicted by guilty plea during the term. Eighteen more Klan conspirators were convicted after trial in the April 1872 term, and the court accepted eighteen additional guilty pleas. Three more jury trial convictions and four guilty pleas followed in the November term of 1872.[69]

Black voices seemed to have drowned out the white. In 1871 in the federal courts, as in the common-law courts for centuries, criminal defendants were barred from testifying in their own cases. The rationale for the rule seems to have been that the testimony of the defendant—like the testimony of parties to a civil suit, which was also judged incompetent—was unreliable. But the effect in South Carolina in 1871 and 1872 was to shut the mouths of whites. As Yorkville's leading newspaper noted bitterly, the federal circuit court decided that "the oath of the accused . . . could not be received as valid testimony." Accordingly, not one of the defendants testified in the Circuit Court in the November term of 1871 nor in any of the three terms that followed. White Klan members could only watch as black witnesses and black jurors convicted them one after another. The results were extraordinarily demoralizing. "There seems," wrote one white man in the fall of 1871, "to be a pall over everything." "The future of our section," complained the editors of the *Yorkville Enquirer*, "is now more gloomy than it has been at any time since the close of the war." As historian Eric Foner has written, the trials seemed to have "broken the Klan's back."[70]

Waves of flight by whites from their homes in the South Carolina upcountry followed the onset of federal arrests and prosecutions. Where just a few months before, black men and women from Clay Hill had spent nights hiding in the woods to evade attack, now Elias Hill observed that "affairs have changed right around." Now it was "the white people" who were "generally lying out in the woods at night" to evade arrest by federal troops. For many, the woods were not far enough. Indeed, in the fall and winter of 1871–72, an estimated 2,000 Piedmont whites ("many of our best young men," according to the *Yorkville Enquirer*) fled from the state to escape federal prosecution. And for some, even that was not enough. Rumors in the summer of 1871 suggested that the "pukes"—former Klan members who cooperated with the government—were being given money and transportation to Canada in return for their testimony. At virtually the same time, leading Klan members began to make the same journey, ironically following a trail beaten by generations of fugitive slaves before them. In May 1872, while awaiting a decision from the U.S. Supreme Court on the constitutionality of his indictment for the lynching of Jim Williams, Rufus Bratton fled to Ontario.[71]

*
*
*

And yet Elias Hill emigrated, too. On February 11, 1871, two months before Congress enacted the Klan Act, and five months before the congressional subcommittee arrived in Yorkville, Reverend Hill's close compatriots had sought to broker a compromise between the black community in Clay Hill and leading whites. Blacks and whites had met at a crossroads not far from Clay Hill. Rufus Bratton was involved on the side of local whites; June Moore, Elias Hill's young deputy, was there on the side of the Clay Hill black settlement. Jim Williams suggested that he would be willing to relinquish his militia weapons. Black Union League leaders agreed to cease nighttime meetings in order not to provoke white anxieties. And the white leaders seemed to give assurances—though the precise nature of these assurances appears to have been vague—that they would curb the Klan violence.[72]

The shaky truce was broken the very next day. Within twenty-four hours of the meeting, a race riot broke out in nearby Union County in which eight black men were killed by some 500 to 700 white men "in black gowns, with masks fitting tight to their faces." For the next month and more, the York County Klan went out on nightly raids, "every night raiding and shooting." Within the month, Bratton and the Yorkville Klan had lynched Jim Williams, and soon thereafter a group of Klansmen forced Elias Hill's nephews Solomon Hill and June Moore to publish public renunciations of their Republican Party affiliation in the local *Yorkville Enquirer.*[73]

The resumption of the nighttime raids in the wake of the February meeting at the crossroads caused Elias Hill to rethink the project of black citizenship in South Carolina. As he later put it, "the colored people [had] called a meeting with the hope that it would be the means of compromising or of pacifying the whites." Leading local whites had "pledged themselves at that meeting in February at the cross-roads," Hill told the congressional subcommittee in July, "to protect the colored people in case of outrage, and that they would come to their assistance, and use their influence in keeping it from that side of the creek which is our neighborhood especially." But the men whom Hill described as his "white neighbors" had since proven unreliable. Hill claimed that "every one of them was heard to rejoice . . . that so many were whipped" in subsequent attacks on Elias Hill and others in Clay Hill. As Hill explained, the Clay Hill freedpeople could no longer "take their pledges as good." They had "lost hope entirely since the whites pledged themselves at the meeting at the forks in the road . . . and then broke all those pledges." And so Hill decided, as Martin Delany had some twenty years before, to fly rather than resist.[74]

Hill made the decision to emigrate even before the Klan came to his door. "All the colored here has been under the dread of the Ku Klux Klan for the last 3 or 4 months," Hill wrote in April 1871, "& been beat & killed & had to lie out of house & beds." Given the circumstances, Hill continued, "hundreds & thousands" of freedpeople sought to "Embrace the 1st opportu-

Solomon Hill and June Moore, Elias Hill's two deputies, in a photograph taken in the 1880s or 1890s. (Liberian Collections Project, Indiana University)

nity to leave." They no longer believed it possible "for our people to live in this country peaceably, and educate and elevate their children to that degree which they desire." The members of the Clay Hill company, he explained, had worked tirelessly "For Good both in a political & Religious Sense." For all of this, they were "now dispised . . . and persecuted" by their former owners. Hill was hardly alone. Andrew Cathcart, a freedman and schoolteacher who had managed to accumulate a moderate savings, had his home ransacked in 1871. Indeed, at least twenty-one of the thirty-one households constituting the Clay Hill emigrant contingent either suffered Klan attacks themselves or had near relatives in York County who had. "That," Hill declared, "is the reason we have arranged to go away."[75]

Yet the question of where to go was not an easy one. From documents that Hill's local white Republican congressman Alexander Wallace had sent along, Hill concluded that "in some of the Western states these outrages are as bad as they are here." Local officials discouraged the Clay Hill congregation from emigrating at all; and a prominent white Presbyterian minister in the state, Dr. John B. Adger, warned that Liberians were "lazy and unenterprising." Nonetheless, Adger suggested that Hill and June Moore get in touch with the American Colonization Society.[76]

In early April, Elias Hill began to correspond with the Colonization Society. Hill's letters were written in the crude script of a crippled and shaky hand. The left margin of each line in his first letter to the Society began with a capital letter, as if "conned" (as Hill had described his reading lessons) from the psalters and Baptist hymnals he surely possessed. Within a short time, Hill's correspondence with the Colonization Society persuaded him that Liberia was the right destination. "In Liberia," it seemed, "there was greater encouragement and hope of finding peaceful living and free schools and rich land than in any place in the United States that I have read of." Africa seemed to Hill to be the "only refuge," the only place "for general peace, abiding peace and prosperity for me and my race, and for the elevation of our people."[77]

Two features of Liberia especially appealed to Hill and to others in the Clay Hill company. First, land was readily available. Ever since Emancipation, freedpeople in South Carolina and across the South had focused on the significance of real-property ownership as an indicator of freedom. And in Liberia rich farmland was readily available for allocation to emigrants from the United States. Every Colonization Society emigrant family would receive twenty-five acres of land, as well as six months' worth of supplies. Moreover, as Hill clarified with the Colonization Society, ownership meant that the black emigrants of Clay Hill would no longer need to worry about working for the profit of others, as they had under slavery, or even about sharing the fruits of their labor with landlords, as those who were tenant farmers or sharecroppers still did. "Every drop of perspiration" spent by a man laboring in Liberia was "for himself and his family."[78]

Liberia also seemed to offer Reverend Hill and the freedpeople of the Sardis Baptist church in Clay Hill an opportunity to participate in the black nationalist project that had thrived among free blacks in the North only a generation earlier. We can be fairly certain that debates over emigration and colonization reached the slaves and free blacks of the South Carolina upcountry. As Elias Hill's father's African origins suggest, slaves and free blacks in South Carolina maintained close connections to the West African coast. The African slave trade, for example, persisted longer in South Carolina than in any other state. (Three decades after the prohibition of the African slave trade in 1808, a close relative of South Carolina governor James Henry Hammond was still engaged in the trade.) And as historian Sterling Stuckey has observed, the durability of slave trading in South Carolina sustained the kinds of connections between South Carolina black culture and West African culture that elsewhere grew fainter in the decades after the official end of the slave trade. In addition, Reverend Hill may have heard rumors of the white upcountry Presbyterian ministers who as late as the 1820s had expressed support for colonization efforts. He may have known that South Carolina slaveholders occasionally used discreet, one-way passages for their slaves to Liberia to skirt the state's ban on manu-mission. By the 1850s, Hill might well have heard of occasional parties of emigrés from the Piedmont to West Africa, often trav-eling in church groups, including at least one group of some 160 free blacks in neighboring Lancaster County who emigrated to Liberia in 1853.[79]

The emigration of black church groups linked the emigrants from the Sardis Church congregation in Clay Hill (and the Lan-caster County emigrants of 1853 as well) to the Christian-influ-enced black African nationalism of the 1850s. The name "Sardis" itself referred to a precious stone God had instructed the people of Israel to use in the construction of the tabernacle after their flight from Egypt. Indeed for Hill the Old Testament story of Is-rael's exodus provided powerful inspiration for black nationalism. In the text of Romans 10:1, Hill drew on the Israel of the Old Testament as inspiration for the future of an African people who might be saved by an exodus of their own: "Brethren, my heart's desire and prayer to God for Israel is, that they might be saved." Generations of black nationalists had turned to Psalms 68, and there too Hill found inspiration for a powerful vision of Afro-centric Christian nationalism: "Princes shall come out of Egypt; Ethiopia shall soon stretch out her hands unto God." Draw-ing on both these texts, Hill wrote to the Colonization Society that he had "a long cherished desire . . . for the civilization & Christianizing of his race." His father, after all, had come from Africa, and Hill spoke warmly of the prospect of "dying on his fa-thers Native land." Here at last was an opportunity to achieve the black nationhood status that Martin Delany had thought so important. The west coast of Africa, wrote another upcountry South Carolina freedman in December 1871, was "our native land." It was "where the lord of heaven" had placed "our Fathers." Scott Mason, a member of the Clay Hill company, contended similarly that "the colored man never is and never can be really free until he sets his foot on the soil of his forefathers." Indeed, "nowhere else in the world save Liberia," Hill told one newspaperman in the summer of 1871, did black men "have a free and full opportunity" to develop into a "full and vigorous manhood." Hill was, as he put it on another occasion, "an enthusiast on the subject of his race"; as he conceived it, his "duty to the land of his ancestors and to his race demanded" that he emigrate.[80]

Such ideas about citizenship in the United States and about the prospects of Liberian emigration seem to have been widely shared among the rural freedpeople of the American South. Almost immediately after the close of the Civil War, the Colonization Society had begun to field "calls upon it for help to Liberia" that were "more numerous and more pressing" than ever before in its history. The wave of Klan violence that washed across the South in 1870 and 1871 and that reached its highest point in South Carolina renewed interest in Liberia and in emigration of a variety of kinds. By 1871, thousands of freedpeople were requesting assistance in emigrating to Liberia. In that year alone, "some twelve hundred people of color" applied for emigration through the Colonization Society, leaving the society with a waiting list of between two and three thousand applicants early in 1872.[81]

"The whole colored tribe seems to be aroused," wrote one Georgia freedman, who had organized a Freedman's Emigrant Aid Society. In North Carolina, a correspondent to the Colonization Society remarked at "the increasing spirit of emigration" among freedpeople such as himself: "I have never seen anything like it!" he exclaimed. Emigration requests poured in from 800 freedpeople from Decatur, Alabama; from 500 farmers in Mobile, Alabama; from 550 more in Selma, Alabama. In the town of Brunswick along the Georgia coast, 300 freedpeople announced their readiness to leave in March 1872, as did more than 400 from Pulaski County, nearer to the center of the state. "This part of the country is in a fever about Liberia," wrote a Georgia freedman named Enoch Parker, "and they are very anxious to go." As another freedman in Georgia put it in 1872, "we are citizens of the United States and we would like to leave hear."[82]

In the South Carolina upcountry, news of Elias Hill and the Clay Hill party generated powerful enthusiasm for Liberian emigration. As early as the spring of 1871 Reverend Hill reported that "hundreds & more" were "daily enquiring at us" how frequently the Society would provide passage to Liberia. J. D. Currence of Clay Hill predicted that in November 1872, 200 more emigrants would follow the first Clay Hill company; Currence promised 500 if Elias Hill and June Moore sent back "favorable newes from Liberia." Nelson Davies of Yorkville announced that he too desired to go "as soon as I can get ready," though he thought it might be "sum time" before his family would be able to be prepared. John Wallace, a pastor from nearby Union County, notified the Society that he had 40 emigrants willing to pay a total of $144.00 for passage to Liberia as soon as possible after Christmas 1871. By September 1873, a freedman named Reaves further downstate in Mullins Depot announced that "the people at this place are rejoicing more in Liberia than ever knew before." As the Colonization Society's board of directors observed, there seemed to have been "a great change in the disposition and wishes of the colored people of the South, touching the desirableness of seeking a home in their fatherland." It was "a most remarkable movement." The "colored people of the South" had "made more numerous and urgent applications for passage to Liberia" than even in the immediate wake of emancipation. From all across the South, correspondents told the Colonization Society almost exactly what Hill had said at the congressional subcommittee hearings in Yorkville in July and what one typical prospective emigrant wrote in December of the same year: "We are down here & cant rise up."[83]

It was increasingly apparent, however, that the Colonization

Society could barely afford to send a single ship each year, let alone the many ships that would be required to clear the waiting list of emigrants. The society had struggled for decades to finance its Liberia initiative. Emancipation only made things worse, and in 1871 and 1872 philanthropic financing for emigration dried up almost altogether because of the Great Chicago Fire. The society thus began to rely on would-be emigrants to help finance their own passage. The vast majority of freedpeople, however, could not even afford the trip to the Atlantic seaboard, let alone across the ocean. Economic obstacles abounded. Colonization Society ships left in November to take advantage of the best season for the passage. But cotton was often not out of the field until Christmas. For a time it seemed that Reverend Hill might not be able to bring along his company after all because of the timing of the departure during the cotton harvest: "they all pray," wrote Hill of his company, "if possible to delay the voyage as late as in novm. as possible." It would be only in late November at the earliest that they would be able to "gather & sell" their cotton crops. To leave before then often meant forgoing the returns from an entire year of farm labor; even when the crops were in early, they all too often fell short, leaving would-be emigrants with no savings at all. In addition, tenants needed to decide in October whether to rent land for the upcoming year, and they usually could not risk the chance that a November voyage would not go off as planned. The few who owned land often had to sell it under similar conditions of uncertainty. Indeed, virtually all the assets most freedpeople owned were ones on which they relied in their daily lives and with which they were loathe to part absent absolute assurances that the American Colonization Society could not provide.[84]

It did not help matters that many local black leaders and Republican politicians openly opposed emigration schemes, at least partly for fear that they would drain the community of their constituencies. "Som black folks"—especially those "that want office"—were "running a bout trying to stope bold pepole from going to Liberia," reported June Moore to the Colonization Society. Whites, too—"planters who wish cheap labor"—often resisted black emigration as it became clearer and clearer that the postwar South would depend on black labor. The Clay Hill company, for example, quickly learned that "the white folk," as June Moore described them, would not purchase the cotton of prospective emigrants.[85]

Against odds such as these, Reverend Hill worried that only "one hundredth part of those desiring" would possibly be able to emigrate "for years to come." Hill may have overestimated. Of nearly 4 million freedpeople living in the former Confederate states after the Civil War, only slightly more than 3,100 emigrated to Liberia in the ten years after the end of the war. Almost two-thirds of those emigrants left the United States in the first three years following Lee's surrender at Appomattox. By 1874 and 1875, only a very few former slaves—about two dozen—emigrated to Liberia each year.[86]

What separated the Clay Hill company from the many thousands of freedpeople who contemplated emigration—what allowed it actually to emigrate where tens of thousands of others could not—was money. Klan violence in York County seems to have been so extreme that it had driven even those freedpeople with property and investments in their community to want to emigrate. Hill called the Clay Hill emigrants the "most . . . well to do" blacks in York County, and the *Yorkville Enquirer* agreed, describing them as "the most industrious negroes" of the Clay Hill section and noting that "not a few of them had accumulated money" since emancipation. According to the York census taker in 1870, 23 percent of the households that would later make up the Clay Hill company had assets, as compared to merely 5 percent of the county's black and mulatto population as a whole. Before leaving for Liberia, Hill and several other members of the emigrant company were thus able to sell land for substantial sums. Both Hill and fellow emigrant Andrew Cathcart had received cash payments from the Reconstruction state government for opening schools. And local estate-auction records reveal both Hill and Cathcart among the high bidders for various substantial articles of personal property in the years before they emigrated.[87]

Unlike the vast majority of would-be-emigrant groups, then, the Clay Hill company was able to help finance its passage. Accordingly, the Colonization Society quickly promoted the Clay Hill group over thousands of applicants whose applications had come before. Even then, the Clay Hill company's emigration plan almost ended before it began when in Rock Hill the railroad conductor demanded advance payment for the unusual (and not entirely welcome) passage of almost two hundred poor black people to Virginia. The Colonization Society had promised to pay for their trip, but the railroad (which would later accuse the Clay Hill emigrants of stealing railroad equipment while aboard the train) demanded payment in advance. Only by coming up with over $900 in cash on the spot were the Clay Hill emigrants able to begin the first leg of their journey.[88]

For the next thirty-eight days, the Sardis Church congregation experienced an especially grueling ocean crossing on the *Edith Rose.* Two young children died during the course of the trip. The rest survived despite "many storms and much rough weather," "swift gales and a boisterous sea." The sea, Hill wrote, "was like hills and mountains." "Persons had to be tied in their beds," and ocean swells exaggerated "the usual sea sickness." "Women and children were seen staggering and falling down prostrate on the floor." But at last, in mid-December, the Clay Hill company saw the looming presence of Grand Cape Mount along Liberia's northern coastline. The next day the *Edith Rose* sailed past Cape Mesurado, which looms over the mouth of the harbor sheltering Liberia's capitol city, Monrovia. The cape was covered by dense green foliage from the coffee trees that covered the plantation of Joseph Jenkins Roberts, a Virginia-born emigrant to Liberia who just weeks before the *Edith Rose*'s arrival had become president of the republic.[89]

For Reverend Hill, arrival in Liberia marked the culmination of his aspirations for black nationhood. On landing in Monrovia on December 16, Hill gave a sermon based on his long-cherished passage from Romans: "Brethren, my heart's desire and prayer to God for Israel is, that they might be saved." The Clay Hill company, it seemed, had been saved, like Israel from Egypt. Within a matter of days, men from the company were exploring suitable lands near the settlement of Arthington, twenty-five miles up the St. Paul's River from Monrovia, just upstream from the river's famous rapids. Already there was one school there, with ninety-six students enrolled. The next year, another school was to be established near the settlement's Baptist church, where Hill was to be pastor. A small frame house was to be built for Hill that would allow him easy access to both the school, where he would be schoolmaster, and the church, where he would preach. By the middle of January, Hill himself had made the river voyage up the St. Paul's, and upon arriving in Arthington he gave a sermon based on nineteenth-century black nationalism's most important text from the Book of Psalms. "Princes shall come out of Egypt," read the scripture. Hill's distinctive voice rang out over the Clay Hill company, now some four thousand miles from the South Carolina Piedmont. Like the emigrationists of the 1850s, Reverend Hill saw the arrival of black emigrants in Africa as the first step toward the revival of African civilization. He finished the verse from Psalms: "Ethiopia shall soon stretch out her hands unto God." Reverend Hill had returned to the land of his father to create a new black Christian nation.[90]

In letters back to South Carolina freedmen, Hill reported

that he was "well pleased with the place & thinks he can live with ease." The emigrants were "all glad," he wrote, and he urged his correspondents to consider emigration. Elias Hill's nephews June Moore and Solomon Hill, in particular, seemed to be thriving. "I would say to you form my hart," June Moore wrote to the Colonization Society early in 1872, "that I well satisfied in Affrica and I Now if I Like I can make my Living in Liberia and make money too." Solomon Hill told the Colonization Society and the *Yorkville Enquirer* that he was "beter Sadisfide thean I Ever was" (the *Enquirer,* ever defending the idea of a golden age before the war, spuriously added "since Emancipation" to its printed version of the letter). "Pepole in Liberia," Moore reported back to the United States, could "bey Somebody if they Triy." A few years later, in 1876, Moore wrote to the Colonization Society that he was "only sorry that I did not come to Liberia the first year I was freed."[91]

*

*

*

June Moore's confidence that leaving the United States had been the right decision soon seemed prescient. The apparently sweeping victory for the black voices raised in the federal courthouse in South Carolina turned out to be fleeting. The prosecutions, to be sure, had produced convictions. Yet they had done so on exceedingly narrow grounds. Indeed, the court had dismissed as unconstitutional every count of the South Carolina Klan indictments except for the counts that charged conspiracy to violate blacks' voting rights. The Reconstruction amendments to the Constitution, the court held, had not extended the Bill of Rights so as to make its provisions apply to the states. Even in the voting rights context, the court ruled not that Reconstruction had added to the U.S. Congress's authority to protect the rights of the freedpeople of the South, but rather that Congress had always had the inherent power "to interfere in the protection of voters at Federal elections." That power, the court reasoned, had surely "existed before the adoption of either of the recent amendments." On the circuit court's theory, the Reconstruction amendments had added virtually nothing to the federal government's constitutional authority to defend the rights of the new black citizens in the South.[92]

Even more troublingly, the mass of Klan cases proved simply overwhelming for the federal courts of South Carolina. In 1871, the federal Circuit Court for South Carolina had already started to fall behind in the resolution of Enforcement Act cases. By 1872, the Circuit Court was simply swamped. More than 1,200 Enforcement Act cases were pending in the South Carolina federal courts at the end of the year. Over the next two years, the prosecutions collapsed altogether. At the end of 1872, a new U.S. attorney general, George H. Williams, instructed prosecutors to carry on in pending Klan prosecutions "only as far as may appear to be necessary to preserve the public peace." In April 1873, Williams simply instructed the district attorneys in South and North Carolina to suspend all Enforcement Act prosecutions. And in the summer of that year, a delegation of white South Carolinians, led by a man who would soon be appointed the Grand Cyclops of the South Carolina Klan, persuaded President Grant to extend clemency to those Klan defendants not yet tried and to pardon those who had been convicted and were still serving sentences. The last of the South Carolina Klan defendants convicted during the November term of 1871—Samuel G. Brown, a state judge and senior Klan member—walked out of the federal prison in Albany, New York, just before Christmas in December 1873. Occasional arrests of Klansmen continued. Max Steele, for example, whom Elias Hill had identified as a participant in Hill's own attack at the subcommittee hearings in 1871, was arrested in February 1874 for his crimes three years before. But his case came within President Grant's general amnesty program. Steele, the local newspapers reported, would not be prosecuted.[93]

The South Carolina experience proved to be a harbinger of things to come in the U.S. Supreme Court. The very first case decided by the Supreme Court testing the limits of Congress's new Fourteenth Amendment powers was none other than the prosecution of Rufus Bratton and James Avery for the murder of Jim Williams. The two-judge federal court in South Carolina had split on whether the Fourteenth Amendment authorized the federal government to bring indictments for traditional state-law crimes such as murder and had certified the question to the Supreme Court for guidance before bringing the case to trial. In the case that featured as a defendant the man who would become the model for the character of Ben Cameron in *The Clansman* and *Birth of a Nation,* the Court established a pattern that would continue well into the twentieth century: it ducked. On March 21, 1872, the Court sent the case—titled *United States v. Avery*—back to the Circuit Court for lack of jurisdiction. The appeal was not yet ripe, explained Chief Justice and former abolitionist lawyer Salmon P. Chase, until the case had come to judgment in the Circuit Court.[94]

It was only in the *Slaughterhouse Cases,* argued just weeks before *Avery* in January 1872 but not decided until April 1873, that the Supreme Court ("called upon for the first time to give construction to these articles") finally issued a ruling on the merits as to the meaning of the Fourteenth Amendment. The Court had put off a decision in the cases for well over a year. And when it ultimately decided the *Slaughterhouse Cases,* Justice Samuel Miller, a Kentucky-born Republican Lincoln appointee from Iowa, used the case to issue a sweeping statement for the Court on the Fourteenth Amendment's meaning in an area far removed from the controversies over the violent reimposition of white supremacy in the South.[95]

The *Slaughterhouse Cases* were not about the freedpeople at all, at least not in the first instance. They presented instead the claims of white butchers in New Orleans, who argued that a monopoly on slaughterhouses created by the Louisiana state legislature violated the new provisions of the Reconstruction amendments and in particular the clause of the Fourteenth Amendment that guaranteed "the privileges and immunities of citizens of the United States" against state interference. But Justice Miller's opinion for the Court in the *Slaughterhouse Cases* opened up a new chapter in the already intricate story of black citizenship. Writing for the Court, Miller rejected the claim that the slaughterhouse monopoly infringed on the privileges or immunities of citizens of the United States. There was, Miller reasoned, a "distinction between citizenship of the United States and citizenship of a state." Citing pre–Civil War practice, Miller explained that the great mass of civil rights were creatures of state law. The right to "protection by the government," for example, or the right "to acquire and possess property" or "to pursue and obtain happiness"—these were all "the privileges and immunities of citizens of the several States." The privileges and immunities of citizenship of the United States, by contrast, were relatively few, and well settled from long before the Civil War. (They included travel "to the seat of government" and protection "on the high seas" and even the privilege of the writ of habeas corpus and "the right to use the navigable waters of the United States.") Miller here relied on the authority of former Supreme Court Justice Bushrod Washington, writing in 1823, not long after becoming president of the American Colonization Society. In Miller's view this state of affairs survived the Civil War and the Fourteenth Amendment: rights such as those the butchers sought to vindicate—and indeed virtually all rights—"are left to the State governments" and could not be vindicated by the federal government after all.[96]

Miller effectively removed much of the force that the Fourteenth Amendment might have had for the freedpeople. Like the

New Orleans butchers, freedpeople too would have to look to the states to vindicate their basic rights, notwithstanding that the states had often been unable (and were increasingly unwilling) to do so. As Justice Stephen Field pointed out in dissent, Miller seemed to have revived the old ideas of none other than South Carolina's John Calhoun, who had insisted that state citizenship was primary and citizenship in the United States merely secondary. Indeed, the "shade of John C. Calhoun," as constitutional lawyer Charles Black would later observe, loomed over the proceedings from beginning to end. The "doctrines of Mr. Calhoun," counsel for the New Orleans butchers had insisted, were "struck at, and forever destroyed" by the Fourteenth Amendment. Yet the *Slaughterhouse* decision proved him wrong. The Kentucky-born Miller's opinion drew on precisely the white slaveholder constitutionalism that during most of Elias Hill's lifetime had helped to constrict the quasi-freedom of South Carolina's free blacks. Worse still, by doing so Miller had effectively invoked what District Attorney Corbin had described at the South Carolina trials of 1871 as the coded constitutionalism of the Klan. Miller, like Rufus Bratton and the York County Klan before him, had endorsed not the post–Civil War constitution of the freedmen but the pre–Civil War constitution of the slaveholders, what the Klan called the "constitutional liberty" that had been bequeathed to them by their forefathers in all its "original purity."[97]

The *Slaughterhouse Cases* signaled the beginning of the end of Reconstruction. In subsequent cases, the Supreme Court adopted the South Carolina Circuit Court's earlier holding that the Reconstruction amendments did not impose the federal Bill of Rights on the states. In *United States v. Cruikshank* and *United States v. Reese,* the Court also rejected District Attorney Corbin's argument that the Reconstruction amendments authorized the federal government to prosecute private violence in the South, holding instead that the Fourteenth Amendment merely gave the federal government authority over state (rather than private) action. At the end of 1876—merely three years after the last of the 1871 South Carolina Klan defendants was released from prison—the federal project of enforcing the Reconstruction amendments came sputtering to a halt.[98]

In the weeks after taking office in 1877, President Rutherford B. Hayes began to dismantle federal Reconstruction in South Carolina, abandoning the ambitious initiatives that Grant had begun six years earlier. To be fair, even Grant had begun to pull back from the Reconstruction ambitions of his first term. But in April 1877, Hayes ordered the withdrawal of federal troops from around the South Carolina statehouse. Governor Daniel H. Chamberlain, only five years removed from his efforts as prosecutor in the Klan trials of 1871, had become governor in 1874. For over four months after the gubernatorial election of 1876, he had refused to concede the election to Democrat Wade Hampton III, citing widespread violence and voter intimidation, which seemed especially acute in the upcountry Piedmont counties. But with the withdrawal of federal troops, Chamberlain turned over the state seal to the Democrats and Hampton.[99]

It was Hampton, of course, who had paid for the Klan defendants' lawyers in 1871. Opposing the constitutionality of the Reconstruction amendments, Hampton had been elected with the support of the so-called Red Shirts: assemblies of armed men from South Carolina's white rifle clubs, many of whom had been members of the Ku Klux Klan just a few years before. In Rock Hill, Hampton and the Red Shirts paraded down Main Street in celebration of the white "redemption" of South Carolina, past crowds waving Confederate flags and children dressed in the gray uniforms of the Confederacy, toward the railroad depot where the Clay Hill emigrants had embarked for Liberia five years earlier. For decades thereafter, local freedpeople and their descendants would refer to Rock Hill as "Bloody Town" because of the town's reputation for killing just about "anybody"—but especially the city's "colored people"—for just "about anything."[100]

*
*
*

The end of Reconstruction in South Carolina and in the nation as a whole produced renewed bursts of enthusiasm for emigration among blacks in the South. In South Carolina in 1877, Martin Delany once more took up the cause of emigration, founding the Charleston-based Liberian Exodus Joint Steam Ship Company to finance emigration to Liberia. By the end of the year, some 65,000 of the state's 400,000 black residents had registered their interest in emigrating with the Liberian Exodus Company. Leaders of that organization estimated the total number of South Carolina blacks desiring to leave as closer to 150,000. The American Colonization Society estimated in 1879 that a half-million blacks from the South wanted to emigrate to Liberia. Like the Clay Hill company in 1871, these individuals' motives were readily apparent. "We are no more than dogs here in S.C.," wrote would-be emigrants in 1879. "We have to keep our mouths shut."[101]

Yet for many, among them Reverend Elias Hill, exit proved as much a dead-end as voice. Colonization Society officials had long misled American blacks about conditions in Liberia. In particular, they had vastly understated the mortality rates of emigrants from malaria, which killed 20 percent of American emigrants to Liberia. Colonization Society publications, such as those that were sent out to the Clay Hill emigrants in the spring and summer of 1871, insisted that mortality rates were low, closer to 3 percent. The results were deadly for the already fragile Reverend Hill. In mid-January, as he was ferried upriver to Arthington for the first time, Hill came down with malaria, or what he called "the acclimating fever." For the next two months, Hill was unconscious for a "portion of the . . . time" and otherwise suffered alternately from "chills & fever." On March 28, 1872, Reverend Elias Hill died.[102]

Perhaps it was better that Hill did not see what transpired in the months and years after his death. In all, the death toll among the Clay Hill emigrants was devastating. Not long after Hill's death, June Moore reported, "A great meney of our folk has died off fast." According to Moore, one-third of the South Carolina emigrants were dead by May 1872. Moore believed, however, that "they did not die so mutch from Sickness" as from "Wanting to goe back to the States." As early as April 1872, four Clay Hill families were "preparing to return to America." They had refused even to go beyond the Colonization Society's bunkhouses at Monrovia, preferring to wait at the harbor for the next possible passage back. Within a month, Moore reported that everyone who was able to do so planned to go back. And by November 1872, the *Yorkville Enquirer* was reporting that "a number of the negroes who emigrated" had returned to the United States and were in Boston seeking to return to South Carolina. At least thirty-six of the emigrants would eventually return, among them Elias Hill's nephew Francis Johnson and his family; Madison Hill, Reverend Hill's brother; and Hill's nephew Thomas Simpson, who had been freed by the white Hill family in 1861 because of the lightness of his skin.[103]

Even in the short time he spent in Liberia, Reverend Hill had noticed that "the governmental affairs of the Republic" seemed to be "in great disorder." In fact, although Colonization Society officials had said nothing of the situation, the Clay Hill company had arrived in Liberia in the midst of a virtual civil war. Scandal had broken out over the draconian terms of a loan that President James Roye had arranged from a London bank and over amendments Roye advocated to the constitution that free blacks in the United States had so long admired. (Among other things, the amendments would have extended Roye's own term in office.) In late October 1871, supporters of Joseph Jenkins Roberts, who had served as the republic's first president, violently deposed Roye, firing a cannon at his residence and overwhelming government forces loyal to Roye. By the time the Clay Hill emigrants arrived, Hill learned that the "President, the Attorney-General, the Secretary of the Republic, the Secretary of the Interior, the Secretary of State, and the Superintendent of a certain county," as he wrote back to Yorkville, were "all in jail, on charges of robbing or otherwise defrauding . . . the Republic with a certain loan from Great Britain." Only two months later, just as the Clay Hill emigrants were settling into Arthington, Roye was brutally assassinated by a pro-Jenkins crowd that came upon him trying to escape.[104]

The Roye affair in 1871 marked the beginning of what would become Liberia's long decline. The previous forty years had been a period of relative commercial success. But by 1871, Roye was forced to look to foreign financiers because the national treasury was empty. For the next thirty years, political infighting and depressed agricultural markets plunged the republic into ever-deepening cycles of debt. By 1912, multiple defaults on loan payments going all the way back to the disputed 1871 loan pushed Liberia into an international receivership. A century later, after decades of civil war, assassinations, violent dictators, and horrific bloodshed, Liberia stands as a tragically and horribly failed state.[105]

Even so, the political collapse of the black republic might not have been the most disturbing thing about Liberia for Hill. In January 1872, Hill had noted that the "rich and well-to-do" American emigrant inhabitants of Monrovia exhibited "selfishness, disrespect, inhumanity and oppression" toward the "poor and ignorant" black natives. The natives, in turn, seemed to "work . . . at low wages" and were "oppressed by heavy burdens." Already, the Liberian-American elite had begun to exploit the cheap black labor of the native West African peoples. Such exploitation quickly became a pattern. By the 1880s, labor coercion by Americo-Liberians and cooperative tribal leaders in the Liberian interior would produce a booming supply of forced Liberian labor in the cocoa plantations of the Spanish island of Fernando Po. Government corruption allowed the trade in native labor with Fernando Po to flourish through the 1920s. A Firestone Rubber Company rubber plantation established in 1926 only increased the demand for coerced native labor. In 1931 the League of Nations would issue a report condemning practices that by the 1920s had effectively recreated African slavery in a republic established to abolish it.[106]

In all likelihood, the few Clay Hill emigrants who experienced their Liberia adventure as a success were deeply involved in the labor abuses for which Liberia would become infamous. Within a few short years of Elias Hill's death, the settlement at Arthington had become a "flourishing settlement" of between 600 and 700 residents. All up and down the St. Paul's River, Americo-Liberian settlers had become "mad on the subject of coffee." Hill's nephews June Moore and Solomon Hill quickly went into the business. In 1876, Moore wrote that he "had 9,000 coffee trees now, 3,000 of them bearing" marketable coffee beans. By the 1880s, visitors to Arthington described Hill and Moore as the "leading men of the settlement." Their firm, Hill & Moore, became one of Liberia's leading commercial institutions. Hill in particular became renowned as "the architect of his own fortune" who, through skill and hard work, though "beginning with no money," had grown his coffee plantation to some 180 acres. By 1889, he was said to produce more than 10,000 pounds of coffee each season, most of which Hill & Moore shipped back across the Atlantic to a Philadelphia coffee trader. As it grew, the firm of Hill & Moore expanded into ginger, sugar, and other goods, and by the 1890s the firm was reputed to do $100,000 in business each year. Together, Hill and Moore endowed a nearby Baptist Institute, which Moore's son Wallace attended before becoming a coffee planter and trader himself. Hill built a large brick and stucco house in Monrovia as a marker of his stature among the elite of the St. Paul's River planter class. After Hill's death, this mansion—built by a man who had sought to leave the United States behind—would become the home of the United States's diplomatic legation to Liberia.[107]

His nephews' successes came at a price that Reverend Hill would probably have found repellant. As one visitor to Arthington wrote in 1878, life among the "wealthier planters along the St. Paul's"—men like Solomon Hill and June Moore—looked disturbingly like "that of the Southern planter in the 'good old days'" before Emancipation. Even as early as the 1850s, it was being rumored that America-Liberian planters were enslaving the native peoples. Some even suggested that President Joseph Roberts worked slave labor on the lush Cape Mesuardo coffee plantations the *Edith Rose* had passed on the way into Monrovia's harbor in 1871. Edward Blyden, for one, interpreted the coup against President Roye and the reinstallation of Roberts as president in 1871 as a successful initiative to preserve America-Liberian, and largely mulatto, exploitation of the native Africans. If Blyden was right, it meant that the Clay Hill emigrants had left one civil war over race-based unfree labor for another. By the mid-1870s, planters along the St. Paul's River in places like Arthington routinely relied on coerced tribal labor. And indeed, for the next century and more one of the central stories of Liberian political economy would be the continued marginalization and exploitation of native peoples by the America-Liberian governing elite. "The discriminatory system in Liberia," a U.S. Peace Corps worker would write in the 1960s, "reminded me of segregation in Alabama."[108]

*
*
*

Between World War I and the Great Depression, some 1.5 million black people living in the South migrated to the North.

Solomon Hill's home in Monrovia was modeled on slave-owner plantation homes in the American South. Hill and some of those who stayed in Liberia ultimately accumulated considerable wealth, largely on the basis of unfree labor by indigenous Africans. (Liberian Collections Project, Indiana University)

There were, to be sure, recurrent bursts of enthusiasm for emigration to Africa. But even Marcus Garvey's Universal Negro Improvement Association in the 1920s did not in the end amount to much. The mass emigration of black people to Kansas in 1879 and 1880 similarly evacuated less than one-half of one percent of the blacks living in the South. The Great Migration to the North, however, fundamentally reshaped the demographics of the United States. In the three decades after the Great Depression, about 5 million more blacks moved to the North. This was migration within the nation, not emigration outside of it. But "nation" seems to have been a fluid notion for nineteenth-century black migrants, who moved to Kansas and Liberia alike as "emigrationists," not insisting on sharp distinctions around the boundary of the formal nation-state. As historian Steven Hahn noted, the Great Migration was a "social and political" phenomenon with "striking resemblances to the grassroots emigrationism" of the 1870s.[109]

Like emigrants from Clay Hill and elsewhere, African Americans who moved from South to North after 1910 did so in hopes of creating more meaningful lives against a background of racial subordination in the white South. And if the Clay Hill emigrants of 1871 did not find the kind of black nation in Africa about which Reverend Hill had dreamed, the Great Migration transformed the United States. As the dean of Howard Law School, Richard T. Greener, argued in the 1870s and 1880s, black emigrationists had been migrating across legal boundaries—lawyering with their feet—ever since the first fugitive slaves crossed from one colony or one empire into another in the earliest days of New World slavery. For the first seventy years of the republic, fugitive slaves had exploited the legal cracks and fissures of American federalism to help bring the constitutional order crashing down. The Clay Hill company of 1871 followed in the fleet footsteps of the fugitive slaves before them. And the Great Migration in turn stands in this tradition of mobility as a strategy by which the voiceless seek to change the world.[110]

Black migration in the twentieth century effectively realigned the nation's politics, once again making civil rights a national issue rather than a sectional one and helping to bring about a Second Reconstruction in the 1960s. Recent historians of civil rights have too readily treated this migration as a kind of "extralegal force" or as the "current of history" inexorably pushing away the Jim Crow era. But like the Clay Hill emigrants, the participants in the Great Migration were actively engaged in lawmaking. They were hardly impersonal social forces, but agents and lawmakers on their own, working in a long American tradition of making law through exit. The *Brown v. Board of Education* decision in 1954, the Civil Rights Act of 1964, and the Voting Rights Act of 1965 were all vindications, however partial, of the strategy of voice that many freedpeople in York County had sought to adopt in the fall of 1871. But each is almost unthinkable in the absence of the exits that reshaped the nation.[111]

In this sense, the Great Migration is tied in another way to the Liberian exodus of the 1870s. For in one respect, the Clay Hill folk were not exiting at all. The Sardis Church's black nationalism was not so much a rejection of American nationhood in favor of a separatist African alternative as it was an attempt to vindicate the principles for which the emigrants believed the United States properly stood. In 1871 Hill had explained to a white newspaperman that he "loved the United States" and "cherished" it as "his own native land." To be sure, he "felt a pride and an interest in the rising young negro Republic." But his vision for Liberia was built around the model of the American republic. It was thus Hill's "desire to see a United States of Africa arise," one that replicated many of the virtues of American nationhood.[112]

Hill's was therefore a kind of hybrid exodus, different than Israel's from Egypt in important ways, and deeply loyal to American ideals. In Hirschman's schema of exit and voice, loyalty functions as an aid to voice. It provides a reason to stay and speak up when exit might otherwise seem appealing. But for the Clay Hill company, loyalty led not to voice but to exit. Theirs was a loyalty that treated the boundaries of American nationhood not as limits for the political imagination, but as proxies for a set of powerfully attractive ideals. This was a loyalty not unlike that which Frederick Douglass had critiqued whites for lacking: "loyalty enough . . . to live up to the Constitution." It was an allegiance, at least in part, to what was best in the United States, an allegiance that seemed to require exit when voice was no longer possible. This is why Liberian independence began with a Declaration of Inde-

Hill-Moore Graveyard, Arthington, Liberia, 1977. Here lie the remains of Solomon Hill and June Moore. Left ro right: Rev. June Moore; Patsy Hill (September 1849–18 July 1882); Solomon Hill (stone placed in 1953). (Photograph by Max Belcher © 1988)

pendence, complete with a bill of indictments like the one that Thomas Jefferson had drawn up against England. This is why Liberia adopted a constitution largely drafted by American lawyers, a constitution with close parallels to its U.S. model. This is why the man who became president of the Liberian Senate in the same month Elias Hill arrived was named John Marshall after the first great American chief justice. Tragically, it may also be why Liberia so readily deteriorated into the ethnic apartheid of the American South.[113]

Three ☆ *Critiques*

If Elias Hill and the Clay Hill company sought to vindicate what they understood as the principles of the American national tradition, others have rejected the idea of national traditions altogether. In the first two decades of the twentieth century, an influential—though now usually forgotten—group of American cosmopolitans critiqued the nation and the nation-state as foolish ways of organizing the peoples of the earth. They sought not so much to leave the United States as to replace it and its sibling nations with what they called a "United States of the World." And so where other early twentieth-century writers such as Randolph Bourne famously defended a liberal version of American nationalism—what Bourne called "trans-America," an inclusive civic nation made up of many ethnicities—internationalist activists and lawyers such as the indefatigable Crystal Eastman argued against nationalism of any kind. Nations, contended Eastman and her fellow radical internationalists, created partial units of loyalty that distracted individuals from their universal obligations.

And yet, like Hill's exit to Liberia, Eastman's critique was powerfully reshaped by the nation. In the crucible of World War I, American national sentiment and American national institutions successfully channeled the cosmopolitan critique of Eastman and her colleagues back into the domestic frame. In the process, however, Eastman and other early twentieth-century cosmopolitans reshaped the trajectory of the American nation for the century to come. In ways that have been formative of the American national tradition and yet almost completely forgotten, the cosmopolitan critique of the nation-state lies at the beginnings of some of the United States's most cherished constitutional traditions.

Internationalists in the Nation-State: Crystal Eastman and the Puzzle of American Civil Liberties

A paradox haunts the history of civil liberties in the United States. The Bill of Rights notwithstanding, it took well over a century for the United States to develop protections for dissenting or unpopular speech. Both the phrase "civil liberties" itself and the civil liberties tradition as twenty-first-century Americans understand it— a body of legal protections for rights such as speech and assembly—date to World War I. Yet the years leading up to the war witnessed the emergence of powerful challenges to the very ideas of "rights" and "liberty" on which a civil liberties movement might be thought to depend. Indeed, many early architects of the civil liberties movement were themselves leading rights-skeptics and builders of the kinds of modernist legal institutions that sought to consign rights talk to a nineteenth-century past.[1]

One prominent solution to this paradox seeks to connect the advent of civil liberties to the distinctively American philosophical tradition of pragmatism and its jurisprudential analogues. Justice Oliver Wendell Holmes famously contended in 1919 that pragmatic uncertainty as to ultimate truths ought to lead nation-states to be reluctant to prohibit the expression of even apparently abhorrent ideas. "Time," Holmes wrote in his dissent in *Abrams v. United States*, "has upset many fighting faiths." It followed for Holmes that nation-states should establish the kinds of protections for speech and expression that Americans today would describe as central elements of the civil liberties agenda.

Yet until Holmes's suggestion in 1919, pragmatism had more often undermined rights claims. Pragmatic philosopher John Dewey scorned those who clung to "the individualistic tradition" of "early Victorian platitudes" about "the sanctity of individual rights." Critics noted that the problem of uncertainty to which Holmes pointed in *Abrams* cut both ways, calling into question not only legislative commitments to the suppression of particular ideas, but also the unyielding commitment to principle that underlay rights claims in times of crisis. And indeed, as American intervention in World War I approached, lawyers such as Raymond Fosdick (soon to become the first undersecretary general of the League of Nations) increasingly saw "natural rights" along with "Jefferson and laissez-faire" as just so many "mental trappings" from "a century ago." As Ernest Hemingway would write, the war had called into question the power of "abstract words such as glory, honor, courage, or hallow"—and, one might add, liberty and rights.[2]

A second way of resolving the civil liberties paradox sees in World War I what political scientist Samuel Huntington would call a moment of "creedal passion": a confrontation between the nation and its deepest values. Federal legislation effectively criminalized antiwar speech; the Post Office barred antiwar and radical literature from the mails; mobs brutalized and even lynched antiwar speakers; and federal agents and allied vigilantes led lawless raids on labor unions and radical organizations. Events such as these, the second account contends, touched off a movement on behalf of ideas about rights that Americans had long held but taken for granted. Yet there is remarkably little evidence of a long-standing American civil liberties tradition in nineteenth-century American law. As one historian puts it, the nation's civil liberties record instead "seems terribly dismal."[3] The civil liberties violations of the World War I period were not so different from those of the Civil War. As one prominent supporter of the war noted in 1918, Lincoln's "limitations of free speech" provided a model for the Wilson administration a half-century later. Indeed, American law had long been characterized by a wide array of practices that by later standards seem clear violations of important civil liberties. Southern states banned antislavery literature and speech. Congress stifled abolitionist petitions. Congress and the states alike prohibited the dissemination of birth control literature and sexually explicit materials. Laws prohibited entertainment on Sundays. Courts broadly enjoined peaceful labor picketing. And communities participated in repressing the free speech efforts of organizations like the Industrial Workers of the World (IWW). Historian Henry Steele Commager plausibly wrote of the period between 1789 and 1937 that there had not been "a single case, in a century and a half, where the Supreme Court has protected freedom of speech, press, assembly, or petition against congressional attack." Nineteenth-century American law, in short, seems to have borne out James Madison's warning that the provisions of the Bill of Rights would be mere "parchment barriers" to acts of government repression.[4]

The development of civil liberties in and around the period of World War I is thus difficult to explain by reference to home-grown traditions. Neither the philosophical tradition of pragmatism nor some supposed moment of truth for Americans' ostensibly deepest values provides a completely satisfying explanation of the modern civil liberties movement. Neither account, moreover, offers a solution to the paradox of rights claims in an age of skepticism.

We can begin to make sense of the beginnings of the modern American civil liberties tradition, however, if we take into account a legal and social movement that transcended the national boundaries of the United States and ultimately found fertile soil in American law. The modern civil liberties movement and indeed the phrase "civil liberties" itself have their roots in a pre–World War I cosmopolitanism in international law. In the late nineteenth century, internationalist lawyers had begun to question not just the abstract, metaphysical truth of rights claims but also the usefulness of that other great abstraction of nineteenth-century legal theory: the sovereignty of the nation-state. The civil liberties movement in American law thus did indeed emerge out of a pragmatist critique of abstract legal fictions. The relevant abstraction, however, was not so much the formal concept of rights as the formal concept of state sovereignty.

No one better captures the connections between the movement contemporaries called "internationalism" and the beginnings of the twentieth-century civil liberties tradition than Crystal Eastman. Though now largely forgotten, Eastman was an indefatigable and charismatic young New York lawyer who between 1913 and 1917 became one of the most important figures in the early twentieth-century American internationalist movement. In 1917, she founded with Roger Baldwin the predecessor organization to the American Civil Liberties Union. Yet a domestic civil liberties movement had not been Eastman's aim at all. For Eastman and a like-minded group of transatlantic internationalists, the world war inspired a struggle for new supranational legal structures to constrain the excesses of nation-states that the war had so plainly revealed. What Eastman would find, however, was that nationhood would vigorously and even violently defend its prerogatives. Much as Woodrow Wilson's League of Nations idea would falter in the face of nationalisms, Eastman would learn that the authority of law was deeply and perhaps even inextricably connected to the authority of the very nation-states she sought to eclipse. In the United States, the result was a cosmopolitan prewar internationalism that began with the aim of transcending the nation, but soon came to rely on civil liberties claims that could be rooted in the constituent documents of American nationalism.

*
*
*

Catherine Crystal Eastman hailed from the heart of the nineteenth-century American reform tradition. In the words of her brother, the eclectic aesthete and radical editor Max Eastman, he and Crystal grew up near the "center of gravity" of the "moral and religious map of the United States." She was born in 1881 in Glenora, New York, not far from where the Seneca Falls Convention had issued the Declaration of Sentiments in 1848 to mark the beginnings of the nineteenth-century woman's movement. Her mother, Annis Ford Eastman, attended Oberlin College, Ohio's center of abolitionist activism. Her father, Samuel Eastman, served and was wounded in the Civil War.[5]

Both Annis and Samuel became Congregational ministers in upstate New York, where they eventually moved to the Park Church in Elmira. The Park Church was among the nation's leading churches. In 1870, Mark Twain had married the daughter of a prominent Elmira family at the Park Church. The Church's abolitionist pastor, Thomas Beecher, belonged to one of the most prominent families in America. His sister, Harriet Beecher Stowe, the author of *Uncle Tom's Cabin,* was (in words attributed to Abraham Lincoln) the "little woman who wrote the book that started" the Civil War. His brother, Henry Ward Beecher, succeeded their father, Lyman Beecher, as America's most influential preacher. In 1889, upon Thomas Beecher's death, Crystal's parents jointly assumed the church pastorate that Beecher had held for thirty-five years.[6]

In Elmira, Crystal and her brothers Max and Anstice grew up in a home that embraced the tenets of nineteenth-century reform movements, the woman's movement foremost among them. At least in part at Crystal's insistence, the household "was run on feminist principles"; there was, as she later explained, "no such thing in our family as boys' work and girls' work." As a fifteen-year-old, Crystal read a paper—"Woman"—at a woman's movement symposium organized by her mother. Crystal's unfeminine behavior often scandalized the community. She wore "bathing suits without the customary stockings and skirts," her biographer writes, and she refused to ride horses sidesaddle. Taking the woman's movement's goal of woman's rights as their standard, Annis and Samuel Eastman organized their children's upbringing around their rights as individuals, unencumbered by the happenstance of such things as gender. As Annis told her children from early on, the ideal of the Eastman household, as well as of nineteenth-century American reform movements (from abolition to married women's property laws to temperance), was that each human being "be an individual." "Nothing you can gain," Annis warned them, "will make up for the loss of yourself." "Conformity with the crowd" was anathema when it involved the individual's "sacrifice of principle."[7]

By the late nineteenth century, however, the American reform tradition into which Crystal Eastman had been born began to lose its way. The abolition of slavery removed the tradition's greatest campaign, and although some abolitionists turned their attention to the "wage slavery" that accompanied free-labor capitalism, considerably less moral fervor coalesced around such alternative forms of labor exploitation. Harriet Beecher Stowe herself turned from writing antislavery novels to helping her son, Frederick, run a Florida plantation worked by poorly paid black agricultural workers. Closer to Elmira, Henry Ward Beecher had been brought low by the media spectacle of his apparent affair with the wife of a prominent parishioner. To be sure, the woman's movement that had begun at Seneca Falls continued. But the "New Departure" for women's suffrage and political equality that the leaders of the nineteenth-century woman's movement pursued beginning in the 1870s had sputtered; despite a modest string of successes in western states from 1887 to 1896, not a single state had enfranchised women between 1896 and 1910. As Max Eastman would later remark about Mark Twain, by the turn of the century Elmira and the nineteenth-century reform tradition seemed more and more like they "belonged to the 'old regime.'"[8]

In the new century in which Crystal Eastman came of age, many Americans were beginning to grope toward new ways of articulating the relationships between individuals and their communities—ways that purported to reject the abstract rights claims and individualism of nineteenth-century liberalism in favor of historicized conceptions of society and politics as organic, evolutionary, and deeply interdependent. Eastman plunged into the center of this new conversation. After graduating from Vassar College, and with the strong encouragement of her mother, Eastman entered Columbia University in the fall of 1903 to pursue a graduate degree in political economy. Although Eastman would spend only a year at Columbia, she took two courses each with the men who had made Columbia a center for the study of new ideas in economics and sociology: John Bates Clark, pioneering economist and cofounder of the iconoclastic American Economic Association; and Franklin Henry Giddings, one of America's leading sociologists.[9]

Clark, like many other prominent late nineteenth-century American economists, had done graduate work in economics in Germany in the 1870s, where he developed a deep respect for socialist ideas that emphasized cooperation over individualism. The German school of historical economics in which Clark studied argued that classical economists such as Ricardo and Malthus had failed to account for the apparent growth of poverty and inequality in industrializing economies. As history veered toward greater and greater interdependence among individuals, the German historicists argued, the state was required to take on wider and wider responsibilities in economic life. Clark quickly came to agree. By the time he returned to the United States, he was convinced of the "beauty" and "altruism" of "the socialistic ideal" as against the selfish advancement of the strong over the weak in individualism. Over time, Clark would pull back from his endorsement of socialist principles; by the time Eastman arrived at Columbia, Clark had become better known for his groundbreaking ideas in the field of marginalist economics. But Clark remained a committed, if moderate, progressive into the twentieth century.[10]

Giddings's influence on Eastman appears to have been still more important than Clark's. Giddings was a leader in the use of statistical techniques in the social sciences; as one scholar later put it, Giddings sought to make sense of social phenomena "in terms of chance and probability." As the holder of the first chaired professorship in sociology in the United States, Giddings conceived his subject not as the study of individuals in isolation but as the study of individuals in the groups in which they inevitably found themselves. Sociology was the study of "the phenomena presented by aggregations of living beings," Giddings wrote in an article that he drafted while Eastman was enrolled in his classes. Such aggregations, he argued, had enormous influence on individuals' behavior. Society, in Giddings's conception, was an "organization for the promotion of . . . efficiency by means of standardization and discipline," a "norm" that functioned to control "the variations from itself" such that individual behaviors would generally be found "clustering" around it.[11]

Given the structures of "social pressure" that constituted modern social life, Giddings taught his students that eighteenth- and nineteenth-century individualism and natural-rights ideas were simply beside the point. "The aggregation of human beings into communities," he wrote, necessarily occasioned "restrictions of liberty." Indeed, individualism in the nineteenth-century sense was little more than the "riotous use" of power by those who had it. Rights, in turn, were mere "legal forms of freedom" that had given rise to "conditions of great and increasing inequality." To be sure, Giddings was no socialist. "Utopian collectivism" was as distasteful to him as individualism run amok. But a "third and middle view," which combined the cautious use of the state with reasonable competitive freedoms, could ensure the proper mix of liberty and equality. Ultimately, the proportions of restraint and liberty that were "conducive to the general welfare" turned on the "normal social constraint" in the community and the "stage of its evolution" in history. This was the "supremely important question in all issues of public policy." Giddings had no doubt that the balance would be difficult to strike in particular cases. He was just as certain, however, that the instruments of the social policymaker were the insights of sociology and statistics, not old nostrums about rights and individualism.[12]

Eastman may not have imagined that she would put Giddings's ideas to use any time soon. In 1904, she left Columbia after what may have been either a bad final examination experience or an encounter with Giddings's increasingly dim view of the place of women in public life.[13]

She decided instead to go into law. A career in the law was a bold decision for a woman in 1904 and 1905. Of all the major American professions, law was probably the most unwelcoming to women. In 1873, when the U.S. Supreme Court upheld Illinois's refusal to admit Myra Bradwell to the state bar, Associate Justice Joseph P. Bradley explained that "nature herself" had made women unfit to join the bar; their "paramount destiny and mission," Justice Bradley wrote, was service as wives and mothers. Although Bradwell was eventually admitted to practice in Illinois after an 1873 change in the state's law, no woman was admitted to practice law in Eastman's home state of New York until 1886. By 1910, there were only 133 women among the 17,000 lawyers across the state, and only 558 women among the more than 114,000 lawyers nationwide. Even as late as 1920, women would make up 5 percent of all physicians and 4.7 percent of all scientists, but only 1.4 percent of all lawyers in the country.[14]

Columbia's law school did not admit women, but the law school at New York University did. By the time Crystal enrolled in 1905, New York University had become the leading school for training women lawyers in the United States. Crystal quickly became part of a close-knit circle of women lawyers, and she just as quickly developed a deep enthusiasm for the law. "I am even more wild than before to be a lawyer," she confided to her brother. By her second year at law school, she had emerged as one of the school's leading students—the second vice-president of the class, a champion of law school causes, and a friend of everyone from faculty members to the school janitor.[15]

But for Eastman, as for so many woman lawyers in the twentieth century, success in law school did not translate into professional success after graduation. She sought out a law office in which she could get "started with a good practice." "My mind is just tingling to get to practising law," she wrote to Max. She chose the representation of plaintiffs in negligence cases and personal injury suits as her specialty. Relatively few accident victims in the first decade of the twentieth century chose to sue. Moreover, practicing in the field offered little remuneration and even less prestige. Nonetheless, Eastman came to believe that in such cases "a lawyer has every chance of winning before a jury if he . . . knows the business." Yet she proved unable to get work even in this low-prestige and poorly paid area of the law. Her connections to a few reform-minded New York lawyers, including prominent socialist Morris Hillquit and leading labor lawyer George W. Alger, failed to produce employment prospects. In fact, the refusal of male lawyers to practice with women effectively kept her out of the profession altogether. Crystal Eastman would never actually practice law.[16]

Instead, after taking the bar examination, Eastman went to Pittsburgh in the fall of 1907 to begin what was scheduled to be a two-month investigation of industrial accidents and the law for the Pittsburgh Survey, a study of social conditions in the nation's most important industrial city. Her friend Paul Kellogg, an editor and progressive reformer with whom she had an ongoing flirtation, had hired her onto the project. Though her interest in practicing law initially made her a reluctant participant, she soon began to turn with more and more energy to the investigation of industrial accidents. Here was work that tapped both her legal training and her training in sociology. "Strange to say," she noted to her mother, "my spirits thrive on all this atmosphere of death and destruction." "Statistics," it turned out, the "records of tragedies" that she collected in the coroner's office, were not so much depressing as "interesting to me sociologically." Her two-month engagement turned into a full year, and she spent the first half of 1908 bringing Giddings's statistical approach to the study of work accidents, tabulating hundreds of injuries and fatalities into carefully presented tables documenting the human wreckage of the steel mills, coal mines, and railroads of western Pennsylvania.[17]

In fact, although Eastman seems to have had only the vaguest sense of this when she began the Pittsburgh study, industrial accidents provided an ideal field for bringing the new currents in sociological thought to bear on the law. When she arrived in Pittsburgh in the fall of 1907, the United States had experienced three decades of extraordinarily high industrial accident rates. Relative to other industrializing nations, American workplaces were characterized by lax and poorly enforced safety regulations. The law of employers' liability, moreover, imposed relatively few financial obligations on employers for injuries to their employees. These factors, among others, had combined to make American work accident rates far greater than those in western European nations. By the first decade of the twentieth century, leading lawyers, politicians, and muckraking journalists alike had begun to focus public attention on the problem.[18]

Critics of the law of employers' liability, as the law of torts in the workplace was known, argued that it was based in the nineteenth-century rights-based thinking that sociologists like

Giddings now described as anachronistic. Nineteenth-century jurists had sought to develop the law of torts as a kind of applied discipline in liberal political theory that would uphold each individual's right to act as he pleased so long as he did not do harm to others. Employees could generally recover compensation from their employers in work accident cases only if they could show that the employer had acted outside the scope of its rightful sphere of action by injuring the employee through some negligent or intentionally harmful act. If the employer had acted within its rights (or if the employee had acted outside his rights by a negligent act of his own), the employee could not recover. Employees' torts cases against employers thus turned on an inquiry into the relative rights and duties of the parties. Yet such inquiries all too often proved intractable. For one thing, it was extraordinarily time-consuming and costly to conduct trials into the nuances of the parties' behavior. Perhaps more troublingly, it seemed increasingly apparent that a significant percentage of work accidents could not be traced to the fault of anyone at all. Even when no one seemed to have acted outside of their rights, injuries occurred. Such injuries were simply the inevitable fallout from dangerous work, and whether or not they could be attributed to some individual or institution's fault, the existence of a grave social problem—the destitution of thousands upon thousands of families each year—seemed abundantly clear.[19]

Between 1908 and 1910, Eastman did as much as any American lawyer to direct public discourse about work accidents away from tortured inquiries into the rights and duties of employer and employee, toward the aggregate treatment of social needs. Beginning in the 1880s, western European nations—first Germany, then England, and then France—had enacted workmen's compensation statutes that sought to eliminate questions of right and duty, instead providing injured workers with a guaranteed insurance payment. Injured employees were not made whole in workmen's compensation programs. Compensation levels sought merely to provide for their needs, not to restore them to the status quo ante as if in response to a violation of their rights. But for Eastman, as for Giddings before her, talk of rights was largely a futile exercise. Employee injuries were not so much a problem of conflicting rights and duties as a problem of "national economy." "Each year" turned out industrial injuries, noted one student of work safety conditions, just "as surely as the mills ran full and the railroads prospered." Yet what Eastman called the "American System" of distributing accident costs "on the basis of old individualistic legal theory" made a "necessary national loss" into "an absolutely unnecessary amount of national deprivation." What was needed was nothing short of a revolution in the way American law dealt with the problem, and the statistical methods that Eastman had learned in graduate school were (she decided) "good stuff" with which to "start a revolution." Statistics would establish that "justice between individuals" was a quixotic aim in the work accident field. All the law could do was to seek "a distribution of the loss which shall be to the best interests of all concerned." Workmen's compensation statutes would vindicate the social interests that Eastman saw as the proper aim of twentieth-century accident law.[20]

Eastman's involvement in the Pittsburgh Survey brought her to the attention of the growing number of lawmakers interested in substituting workmen's compensation's insurance system for tort law's rights and duties. "The book of fame," as she put it to her brother Max, was opening up for her. By late 1908, she was actively sought for speaking engagements and articles on a topic that was quickly moving to the forefront of the political agenda. And in June 1909, at the suggestion of one of her professors at Vassar, Governor Charles Evans Hughes named her secretary to the Wainwright Commission, created to investigate the problem of work accidents in the state of New York and to recommend new legislation to address it. Her work on the Pittsburgh Survey prevented Eastman from participating as fully in the work of the Wainwright Commission as she might have liked. Nonetheless, Eastman drafted significant portions of the commission's influential report, and her imprint on the commission's work was abundantly evident.[21]

Even as the workmen's compensation movement got underway, however, the nineteenth-century legal tradition of liberal, rights-based jurisprudence seemed to obstruct efforts to rationalize the law of workplace accidents. Legislation purporting to regulate the employment contract seemed all too often to be struck down by courts as unconstitutional interference with rights of contract and liberty. Eastman, like many others, feared that constitutional provisions "originally intended . . . to safeguard the rights of the people" would now be used to strike down the important reforms contained in the workmen's compensation statutes. Sure enough, in March 1911, New York State's highest court struck down the state's new workmen's compensation law—the law for which Eastman and the Wainright Commission had worked—as a violation of employers' property rights. The rights tradition of American law had once again obstructed the sociological rationalization of the law.[22]

For many, the decision of the New York court set off a search for ways to accommodate workmen's compensation statutes to the constitutional rights of employers. For Eastman, however, the court's decision marked the end of her involvement in sociological law reform. The decision came at a difficult time for her. Her mother, Annis, had died of a stroke the previous October. In January, Eastman had come down with one of the illnesses that would plague her for the rest of her life, causing her to return home to Elmira and to break off her work with the Wainwright Commission. Soon after Annis's death, Crystal had married a young man named Wallace Benedict, who shared some of her interests in the insurance industry. But both she and Max,

Portrait of Crystal Eastman, photo by Arnold Genthe, circa 1910. (The Schlesinger Library, Radcliffe Institute, Harvard University)

who married at almost exactly the same time, seem to have rushed into their marriages in an attempt to compensate for their mother's death. Already in early 1911 Crystal was beginning to dread the impending move from the eclectic excitement of New York to "Bennie's" hometown of Milwaukee.[23]

One day after the New York court struck down the workmen's compensation law on which Eastman had labored, the infamous Triangle Shirt-Waist fire killed 146 people only blocks from Eastman's Greenwich Village apartment. Many of the dead were young women who had been working behind locked doors and ill-secured fire escapes at the Triangle Shirt-Waist Company.

The fire, she wrote Max, "sank into my soul," giving rise to a "constant stirring sense of tragedy and horror." Combined with the court decision of the previous day, the Triangle Fire seemed to pose starkly the ways in which the social reform of American law had run headlong into the institutions of the nineteenth-century state. Eastman's sociological skepticism about rights and her progressive-reform optimism about the capacity of rational, sociologically informed legal institutions now gave way to fiery radicalism. "Benevolent talk about workingmen's insurance and compensation" might "appease our sense of right," Eastman announced, but after events like the Triangle Fire "what we want is to start a revolution."[24]

Within two years, Eastman left Milwaukee—and indeed the United States altogether—for a European tour with Bennie in tow. In Europe, she would come into contact with the beginnings of an internationalist movement for woman's suffrage, a movement that sought to transcend the boundaries of the nation-states that had so long excluded women from full citizenship.[25] What she could not have guessed then was that the new internationalist venture on which she had embarked would soon bring her back around to the relationship between individual rights and the new institutions of the modern state. This time, however, she would be a crucial figure in the conversion of the internationalist impulse into the modern American civil liberties tradition. Through the looking glass of internationalism, Crystal Eastman would return to nineteenth-century rights claims as the quintessential strategy for resistance to the modern state that she had helped design.

*
*
*

On August 29, 1914, 1,500 women paraded silently down Fifth Avenue in New York City from Fifty-Eighth Street to Seventeenth Street. An "intense hush prevailed" along the parade route, reported the *New York Herald*, broken only by the "dirge-like roll of the muffled drums" that accompanied the marchers. Most of the marchers were "robed in black," wrote the *New York Times*. At the head of the parade, women carrying banners of doves and olive branches wore white with black armbands. "There were women of all nations," from India and China to Russia and Germany, "but they all wore the mourning symbol to show that" notwithstanding the war that had broken out in Europe, "they marched not as nations, but as sorrowing women together."[26]

The Woman's Peace Parade, which Crystal Eastman helped organize, marked the beginning of World War I. The parade also touched off a movement against American intervention in the Great War. Over the course of the next two years, the peace movement produced a host of organizations opposed to the war and to the United States's possible intervention in it. With Eastman's help, Chicago social worker and public intellectual Jane Addams and American woman's suffrage leader Carrie Chapman Catt formed the Woman's Peace Party in January 1915. Eastman herself—along with her old friend Paul Kellogg and the prominent settlement-house leader Lillian Wald—organized the American Union Against Militarism in December 1915 and January 1916. Similar associations (with almost all of which Eastman had significant contact) included the Union for Democratic Control, the People's Council, the American Conference for Democracy and Terms of Peace, the American League to Limit Armaments, the American Neutral Conference Committee, the Emergency Peace Federation, and the Fellowship of Reconciliation, all of which sprung up in the period between 1914 and 1917 in hopes of discouraging American entry into the war.[27]

The Woman's Peace Parade Committee and the organizations that followed in its wake formed the American wing of what international lawyer Nathaniel Berman calls "international legal modernism."[28] Indeed, when Crystal Eastman and colleagues like Addams and Wald took up the fight against militarism and war in 1914, their efforts were the culmination of more than four decades of ideas in the United States and in Europe about the development of new transnational legal structures. As the symbolism of the 1914 parade indicated, among the most important of these ideas was the notion that sovereign nation-states ought to be subordinated to international institutions.

Discussions among "internationalists," as they typically called themselves, often began with an observation that (in a variety of related forms) has continued to be made ever since, right up to twenty-first-century discussions of globalization. Technology, announced late nineteenth-century internationalists, had made the world a smaller place. As Eastman's teacher Giddings was fond of observing, the extension of "communication throughout the world" by means of a century of technological advances, from the steamship and the railroad to the telegraph, the telephone, and the wireless radio, had brought the nations, races, and civilizations of the world into closer contact than ever before. International treaties and fledgling international organizations followed. European nations signed a multilateral convention on telegraph communications in 1865. The Universal Postal Union came into existence nine years later, and in 1890 European diplomats crafted a uniform law for the international transport of goods by rail.[29]

All told, the century following the end of the Napoleonic wars witnessed the promulgation of an extraordinary number of international treaties: some 16,000, by one count. Many of these were traditional bilateral treaty agreements between states. An increasing number of them were multilateral lawmaking treaties on issues ranging from tariffs, copyrights, and patents to the treatment of war wounded. The crowning achievements of the late nineteenth-century international lawyers were the Hague

Conferences of 1899 and 1907. Initiated by Czar Nicholas II, who secretly feared that he would be unable to keep up in the European arms race, the conferences sought (among other things) to create international agreements for the peaceful resolution of disputes among nation-states. Although the agreements that emerged from the conferences were hedged with reservations, the First Hague Conference produced a Permanent Court of Arbitration for the peaceful resolution of international conflict. The Second Conference strengthened the Court of Arbitration and authorized the creation of an International Prize Court to decide disputes over vessels and cargo seized on the high seas. Much remained to be done, but many participants believed that much had been accomplished; in the words of the closing address of the Second Conference, the Hague Conferences had made the greatest progress "that mankind has ever made" toward "the maintenance of peaceful relations between nations."[30]

The Hague Conferences quickly captured the hearts and minds of international lawyers. Even before the conferences, the gradual development of international institutions had encouraged "a new professional self-awareness and enthusiasm" among international lawyers in Europe and in the United States, who became committed to spreading what a small but enthusiastic young group of European lawyers in 1867 called *l'esprit d'internationalité*. By the end of 1868, a cadre of international lawyers from England, Italy, and the Netherlands began publishing a professional journal, the *Revue de droit international et de législation comparée*. A professional association, the Institut de Droit International, was founded in Belgium in 1873. In the same year, another group of European international lawyers formed the Association for the Reform and Codification of the Law of Nations. Internationalism, in short, was developing an organized constituency with a professional self-consciousness.[31]

American internationalists followed fast on the heels of their

European counterparts. Beginning in 1895, peace advocates, leading businessmen, and international lawyers gathered for annual conferences on international arbitration at Lake Mohonk in the foothills of New York's Catskill Mountains to discuss alternatives to armed conflict. The next year, eminent figures in business, education, the ministry, law, medicine, and the armed forces held an American Conference on International Arbitration in Washington; they reconvened at a Second American Conference in 1904, at which labor unions, chambers of commerce, and the mayors and governors of dozens of cities and states expressed ardent support for the arbitration of international disputes. In 1905, a group of international lawyers at the Lake Mohonk Conference established the American Society for International Law. The American Association for International Conciliation was founded in 1906 to "awaken interest" in "international law, international conduct, and international organization." The New York Peace Society, established that same year, brought together men of affairs in New York City, as did similar associations in such places as Boston, Buffalo, Chicago, and Maryland. A National Peace Congress met in New York in 1907, spinning off new peace and arbitration advocacy groups of its own, including the American School Peace League, dedicated to teaching "broad ideas of international justice, universal brotherhood, and world organization" in American schools. In July 1910, wealthy publisher Edward Ginn founded the World Peace Foundation with a grant of $1 million, and in December of the same year Andrew Carnegie endowed the Carnegie Endowment for International Peace with a massive $10 million gift.[32]

From the proliferation of American international law and peace organizations came what one historian has called a "veritable flood of plans for world courts, world federation, and world government." Indeed, American international lawyers adopted an often utopian exuberance about the prospects for international order. The formation of international-law institutions and peace organizations led many American international lawyers—along with many of their peers across the Atlantic—to hope that they were watching the dawning of a "new internationalism" in which war between nation-states would be rendered obsolete as a mechanism for the resolution of international disputes. A century of relative peace seemed to have brought forth a new system of relations among states, symbolized by the Hague Conferences. In the Permanent Court of Arbitration, internationalists saw the progressive substitution of "the empire of law" for the anarchy of state rivalries. And with the example of the Hague Conferences before them, American internationalists found themselves involved in an increasingly heady new conversation about what Nicholas Murray Butler, following the European lawyers' *esprit d'internationalité,* began to call "the international mind."[33]

As early as 1889, Secretary of State James Blaine had described an agreement to arbitrate disputes among western hemisphere nation-states as the new "Magna Charta" of international peace. President William McKinley announced at his inauguration in 1897 that the "importance and moral influence" of arbitration among states could "hardly be overestimated in the cause of advancing civilization." Indeed, other commentators suggested that arbitration of nation-state disputes would complete the process of "substituting law for war," vindicate the possibility of a "spiritual evolution for mankind," and give life to an "all-embracing" idea of "brotherly love" and a "bond of union transcending national, racial or color lines." International arbitration would give rise to "nothing less than a court of the nations" to decide disputes among peoples "according to eternal principles of law and equity," argued President William Howard Taft. "Never before," announced an advocate of the "new internationalism," had "there been such a universal revulsion against force as a means of settling international quarrels." War, Andrew Carnegie declared on the formation of his Endowment for International Peace, had been "discarded as disgraceful to civilized men," much as dueling and slavery had been discarded in the century before. The "glorious example of reason and peace," President McKinley explained, would at last triumph over "passion and war." And, as leading American international lawyers such as Elihu Root observed again and again, the United States—as the world's greatest and freest republic—seemed to have an unequaled "power and influence" in this "new era of the law of nations" to bring about "peace and justice" and "human brotherhood the world over."[34]

Yet there were actually at least two distinct internationalisms at work in early twentieth-century American thinking. Many elite international lawyers—and preeminently Elihu Root—took up the orthodox version of American internationalism. As secretary of war in the McKinley administration and then secretary of state under President Theodore Roosevelt, Root helped to craft the United States's renewed engagement with the world after a century of relative isolation. He shaped U.S. authority and defended U.S. interests in Cuba, the Philippines, and Puerto Rico after the Spanish-American War. In 1907, he cosponsored a Central American Peace Conference that established the Central American Court of Justice. And in that same year he orchestrated American involvement in the Second Hague Conference. Indeed, for his efforts as secretary of state and as a U.S. senator thereafter, and for his work as the president of both the American Society of International Law and the Carnegie Endowment, Root was awarded the Nobel Peace Prize for 1912.[35]

Root viewed nation-state sovereignty as the foundational building block of international law. The law of nations, in Root's orthodox view, was organized around the practices and agreements of sovereign states. "The independence of nations," Root wrote in his Nobel Prize address of 1912, "lies at the basis of the present social organization of the civilized world." As "between two mutually exclusive sovereignties," he had explained three years earlier in a presidential address to the American Society for International Law, "each is supreme and subject to no compulsion on its own side of the line." The world was therefore ready neither for a "parliament of man with authority to control the conduct of nations" nor for "an international police force with power to enforce national conformity to rules of right conduct." Instead, people and organizations seeking to work for world peace, Root contended, were best advised to "stand behind the men who are in the responsible positions of government."[36]

In truth, even Root's nineteenth-century orthodoxy made room for international constraints on the sovereignty of nation-states. In Root's account, international law assumed the consent of all states to a minimal baseline standard of conduct. Nations "in the exercise of their individual sovereignty" were required to conform to "a standard of international conduct" deduced from the "universal postulate" that "every sovereign nation is willing at all times and under all circumstances to do what is just."[37] Like a Lockean social contract writ global, the implied consent of nation-states to this baseline standard created theoretical constraints on the sovereignty of states.

A second strand of American internationalism, however, focused much more explicitly on creating international constraints on the nation-state. Advocates of this second strand of internationalism argued that "to trust . . . traditional political 'organization' to create peaceful relations between nations" inevitably involved "reliance upon" precisely the "exaggerated nationalistic and power politics" that had caused crises between rival powers in the first place.[38] Radical internationalists like John Dewey and Jane Addams thus sought to move beyond the building blocks of nation-states to new international structures.

As Dewey's inclusion in the ranks of the radical internationalists suggests, this second approach to internationalism brought to bear the skeptical force of pragmatic thinking on the concept of the nation-state. Jane Addams warned that "nationalistic words" and "patriotic phrases" were "abstractions" with dangerous power. Disputes among nations, she argued, were like the international coordination of railroads, telegraphs, and commercial paper. They required solutions that "transcended national boundaries," and they could not be solved "while men's minds were still held apart" by the "national suspicions and rivalries" that nation-states so often generated. It was those suspicions and rivalries that made the legal fiction of nation-states—"artificial unit[s] of loyalty," as Max Eastman put it—so dangerous. Indeed, nation-state rivalries, argued Addams's colleague Norman Thomas, ensured that no nation could prepare to defend itself without "awaken[ing] suspicion" among its neighbors, who would be forced to "keep up a race in armaments" that would lead to regular "nationalistic struggles." What the radical internationalists offered instead, Max Eastman contended in 1916, was a world in which humanity would break the cycle of competitive rivalries to join together in "international union." War, he urged, might thus be eliminated "exactly as the wars of family and clan and city" had been "eliminated by national union."[39]

As World War I approached, Crystal Eastman joined the increasingly vocal cadre of radical internationalists who argued that nationalism (recently a positive force for the self-determination of peoples) had become a Trojan horse for militaristic arms races among the European powers. There were, to be sure, several different varieties of radical internationalism. Norman Thomas espoused a Christian-pacifist "internationalism based on the universal brotherhood of the children of God." Others came to internationalism from the perspective of socialist and communist critiques of the state. Still others were latter-day James Madisons, seeing in the relationships among states in the American federal system a principle that might be extended to nation-states in a transnational system. Some radical internationalists, like one American conscientious objector in August 1917, claimed simply that "internationalism" was their "only principle."[40]

What the eclectic array of radical internationalists agreed upon, however, was that nationalism all too often and all too easily gave way to militarism, an especially virulent form of nationalism. Militarism was "the aggressive spirit and unfriendly point of view toward other nations" that created "parochial hostility," "national aggression," and a "national psychology of fear," all of which led "inevitably . . . to conflict." In its place, Eastman and the radical internationalists advanced a conception of cosmopolitan democracy as the "mutual recognition of the rights of other men, irrespective of creed, color or national boundaries." Their aim was thus to create transnational institutions that would contain the threat of militarism by eclipsing the ostensibly unquestioned authority of nation-states in the orthodox nineteenth-century view of international law.[41]

Between August 1914 and March 1917, Eastman became perhaps the leading organizer of the radical internationalist movement in the United States. By early 1916, she was serving as the executive secretary of the American Union Against Militarism and as the chair of the exceptionally active New York City branch of the Woman's Peace Party. Both organizations adopted the positions of the radical internationalists, opposing the militarism of nation-state rivalries and supporting a world federation to transcend them. The Peace Party sought to serve as a worldwide "clearing-house" for internationalist ideas during the war. It urged the democratization of foreign policy, the abrogation of secret treaties, and the nationalization of arms manufacture so as to remove commercial incentives to instigating nationalist fervor. The American Union pursued a nearly identical program to "work against militarism" and "toward world federation, which alone would make disarmament possible, and which alone could really root out militarism."[42]

The American Union developed into America's most important radical internationalist organization, with Eastman (in Lillian Wald's words) as its "wonderful secretary." Eastman worked to ensure that all of the "energy and genius" of the American Union would "be directed toward putting this idea of a world federation into workable form, acceptable to all nations." As she conceived it, the American Union's aim was to "keep the ideal of internationalism alive and growing in the minds and hearts of the American people." Indeed, the organization's international program was lifted almost directly from the eclectic (and often not altogether consistent) array of ideas that American and European internationalists had bandied about for decades: self-determination; equal treatment for all nations; a "Society of Nations" developed through the Hague Conference; a "permanent Court of International Justice" to strengthen the existing Hague Court of Arbitration; reductions in armaments; the voiding of secret treaties; and the removal of restraints on international trade. Members of the American Union protested the war's diversion of public attention away from "World Peace based on International Agreement" and called for a "democratic federation of American republics as a step toward international government." They testified, as Eastman did before Congress in January 1916, against the creeping militarism that had created a dangerous arms race. And they urged President Wilson to take up the so-called Hensley Resolution in the Naval Appropriation Act of 1916, which authorized the President to convene a Conference of Nations for disarmament. Eastman and her colleagues advocated policies that they believed would move the world toward what Eastman described to Congress as "unnationalism": a "federation of nations" dedicated to "democracy, to peace, and to their mutual good will and friendship."[43]

Radical internationalist ideas were often utopian and impractical, to be sure. But they were no more so than many of the ideas that had been spinning out of internationalist conversations on both sides of the Atlantic for decades. Radical internationalism was a continuation of international lawyers' *esprit d'internationalité*. Indeed, the radicals of 1914 to 1917 drew their inspiration from virtually the same set of developments that had sent international lawyers into flights of fantastic rhetoric for the previous half-century. Like international lawyers since the 1870s, Crystal Eastman's Woman's Peace Party of New York City pointed to the development of the Universal Postal Union and the International Telegraphic Union and to the proliferation of international commercial associations such as the International Congress of Chambers of Commerce. Such institutions, Eastman and her colleagues contended, were harbingers of a coming internationalism. The world, it seemed, was growing smaller. According to orthodox and radical internationalists alike, it was "already in large measure internationalized." And like Andrew Carnegie just a few years before, Eastman and her colleagues cited the international condemnation of slavery in the nineteenth century as a demonstration of the moral progress that international action could achieve in the twentieth.[44]

Yet the same questions of nation-state sovereignty and of the citizen's obligations to work through official state channels that divided orthodox internationalists from radicals reappeared within organizations like the Woman's Peace Party and the American Union. In the latter organization, for example, leading members such as Lillian Wald and Paul Kellogg believed strongly in working through the national government to advance their internationalist aims. Congressional hearings, "personal work with congressmen," and discreet advocacy with President Wilson and his secretary of war, Newton Baker, were their preferred methods of action. The American Union therefore pursued a campaign of private advocacy and personal meetings with Wilson, Baker, and others in the Wilson administration into early 1917.[45]

Eastman, by contrast, represented the radical wing of even the nation-state skeptics in the internationalist movement. Friendly critics such as Wald suggested that Eastman was overly enamored of an "impulsive radicalism." (Members of the Peace Party quietly warned that she was too radical to "greatly help the movement.") Eastman's more confrontational tactics included propaganda campaigns, national speaking tours, and mass meetings. In the spring of 1916, she organized a public exhibit that included Jingo the Dinosaur ("All Armor Plate—No Brains," announced the collar on the papier-mâché caricature of militarist nationalism), whose aggressive personality and tiny brain had led to its own extinction. A speaking tour through the Midwest followed, reaching an estimated 40,000 listeners. By May, Eastman had collected the names of 5,000 supporters and distributed over 600,000 pieces of propaganda. Internationalism, she insisted, was a movement to be pursued by "the people acting directly—not through their governments or diplomats or armies."[46]

Internationally minded women like Eastman had good reason to adopt a stance of skepticism toward the official channels of the nation-state. As woman's movements in Europe and in the United States had observed throughout the nineteenth century, states had long excluded women from full membership. Annis Ford Eastman, for one, had noted years before that women (and especially married women) had at best a complicated relationship to the conventional categories of nation-state citizenship. Nation-states, she observed, had regularly disabled women from service as soldier, property owner, voter, officer of the court, or public official. Indeed, in 1916 Crystal Eastman encountered firsthand the liminal status of women in the modern nation-state when she divorced Bennie and married Walter Fuller, a British citizen whom she had met through their joint involvement in the early stages of the American Union. By virtue of a law enacted by Congress in 1907 and upheld by the Supreme Court in the year before Eastman's marriage, American women automatically took the nationality of their husbands. As a result, Eastman herself—though still living in the United States—was stripped of her U.S. citizenship when she married Walter Fuller.[47]

It should hardly be surprising, then, that many women adopted confrontational tactics—publicity, mass meetings, and direct action by the people—that skirted the official channels of the state. The state, after all, had made it exceedingly difficult for women to act through official channels. And just as many American women in the 1910s—Eastman included—were being drawn to the radical tactics of the British suffragettes, so too were they drawn to such tactics in the internationalist campaign against militarist nationalism.[48]

For Eastman and many other women in internationalist circles, women's persistent second-class citizenship highlighted the dangers of the nation-state and its nationalist symbols. In *Four Lights,* the magazine of the Woman's Peace Party of New York City, Eastman and her colleagues attacked the nation-state as a kind of artificial superstition. "Long ago," wrote one *Four Lights* author, "we drew 'imaginary' lines over our globe . . . we put deep-printed lines over latitudes and longitudes, believing that lines can separate the nations of the earth." Over time, those imaginary lines had hardened into divisions among peoples, "conceiving those across our crooked lines as hostages, enemies, or at best, remote and unlike peoples." The "foolish little boundaries" of imaginary maps, however, were now under attack from a band of "Internationalists" who were "as disturbing to your nationalistic Flatlander as the witches to Salem." According to the internationalist view, *Four Lights* contended, the "boundary lines of nations are as imaginary as the equatorial line"; the people on the other side were "neighbors and friends instead of strangers and

Woman's Peace Party members preparing for demonstration, circa 1916, New York City. Crystal Eastman is fourth from the left. (Peace Collection, Swarthmore College)

enemies." Indeed, the internationalist agenda, as Eastman and the *Four Lights* editors of the Woman's Peace Party of New York City conceived it, was no less than "to destroy geography" by "welding the nations of the world into the United States of the World."[49]

Women-led antiwar organizations had sharpened two decades' worth of growing skepticism about a nineteenth-century abstraction. But it was not skepticism about the abstraction of rights. It was instead skepticism about that other great nineteenth-century legal abstraction, the sovereignty of nation-states, which in internationalist circles had already come to seem little more than an abstract "relic from an earlier era," as international lawyer Louis Henkin would later describe it, made up of "fictions upon fictions." Here was one of the most dangerous of "a priori truths," in Addams's words, a fiction that inspired "violent loyalty" and caused "men in a nation, an army, a crowd" to do things "horrible as well as heroic that they could never do alone." The nation had become a kind of "metaphysical entity," complained Norman Thomas, "apart from the individuals who compose it."[50] Rights might have been a nineteenth-century idea newly vulnerable in an era of war and pragmatism, but so too was the sovereignty of states. As Germany resumed unrestricted submarine warfare in January 1917, conditions in the United States were right for a collision between the obligations of loyalty exacted by the nation-state on the one hand and internationalist ideals of cosmopolitan citizenship on the other. That collision would initiate the twentieth-century civil liberties movement.

*
*
*

It was one thing to question the form of the nation-state in 1916, to describe it as a dangerous legal fiction, and to call for its eclipse by new systems of international governance. But once the United States entered the war in April 1917, questions about citizens' obligations to the state were no longer merely theoretical. Among U.S. internationalists, intervention in the war thus touched off a scramble for a secure position between loyalty and internationalism. "After war was declared, we of course ceased all opposition to it," explained one member of the American Union. At the Woman's Peace Party, the reaction was the same: "All the activities of the Woman's Peace Party have been, of course, modified by the entrance . . . into the World War." And as far as Crystal Eastman's longtime friend Paul Kellogg was concerned, he favored "not blocking the prosecution of war, now that the decision has been made." For many, the obligations of loyalty to the nation-state seemed to trump the internationalist agenda. In the words of Elihu Root, "the question of peace or war" had "now been decided by the President and congress." "The question no longer remains open," Root concluded, and it had become the duty of American citizens "to stop discussion upon the question decided" lest criticism weaken the power of the nation to "succeed in the war" it had entered. As William R. Vance, dean of the University of Minnesota Law School, summed up in 1917, "wartime was no time to quibble about constitutional rights and guarantees." Indeed, the mere "suggestion" of opposition to conscription—a position that had formed one of the American Union's deepest commitments—now seemed to many Americans no different than "treason," and its advocates "traitors" to "be dealt with accordingly."[51]

Whether the American Union would be able to identify an intermediate position between loyalty and internationalism seemed to turn in large part on the Wilson administration's wartime stance toward the radical internationalists. As a rhetorical matter, at least, Wilson often allied himself with radical internationalists such as Addams and Eastman. As far back as the 1880s, Wilson had tentatively endorsed the idea that the world was witnessing a gradual evolution toward "confederation" among states on the model of the United States. He taught international law at Princeton in 1892. In 1908 he joined the American Peace Society. And once war broke out in 1914, he appealed to Americans to remain "neutral in fact as well as in name" while privately endorsing the idea of "an association of nations" and opening a dialogue with peace organizations such as the Carnegie Endowment and the League to Enforce Peace. In 1916, Wilson privately assured a delegation from the American Union that he was working toward a "joint effort" on a global scale to "keep the peace"; two months later, he came out publicly in favor of the principle of a "League of Peace" by which the "nations of the world" would "band themselves together to see that . . . right prevails." In his famous "Fourteen Points" speech to the Senate in January 1917, he called again for an international "concert of power which will make it virtually impossible that any such catastrophe should ever overwhelm us again."[52]

In these respects, at least, Wilson's vision for a postwar order often looked remarkably like that of internationalists in the American Union. To allow nationalistic ambitions to shape the peace, Wilson seemed to believe, would merely ensure the resurgence of the national rivalries that had caused the war in the first place. Instead, Wilson urged a peace based on the "equality of rights" among nations, "free access" for all nations to the seas and to international commerce, and limits on armies and on "military preparation." Moreover, many of his public addresses seemed (like Eastman's antimilitarist tactics) to skirt the official channels of nation-state diplomacy. Wilson spoke eloquently of reaching "the peoples of Europe over the heads of their Rulers"; as he told one correspondent, his "Peace without Victory" speech was addressed not to the Senate, nor even to "foreign governments," but to "the people of the countries now at war." Wilson, in short, seemed to have embraced the hopeful idealism of the prewar internationalist spirit. Leaders of the American Union and the Woman's Peace Party thus saw in Wilson's bold internationalist rhetoric of 1916 and 1917 their own aspirations for postwar international order. Even as late as the beginning of 1918, for example, Crystal Eastman and her brother Max supported the president, endorsing "his demand for an international union, based upon free seas, free commerce and general disarmament."[53]

In practice, however, Wilson proved to be an ardent believer in Root's orthodox approach to the relationship between states and individuals in the law of nations. Wilson claimed that the United States had entered the war to pursue the "vindication of right, of human right," and the "rights of mankind." But those rights were to be advanced on the international stage by vindicating the rights not of individuals but of sovereign nation-states. "We shall be satisfied," Wilson told the assembled joint session of

Congress, when human rights "have been made as secure as the faith and the freedom of nations can make them." In the final analysis, Wilson's internationalism aimed to ensure the "rights and liberties" of "nations great and small," and in particular "the most sacred rights of our nation." His "concert of free peoples" was just that—an association of peoples organized in nation-states for the purpose of bringing "peace and safety to all nations."[54]

When the war came to the United States, Wilson became a powerful (if occasionally reluctant) believer in the overriding power of citizens' obligations of loyalty to the state. War, he warned Frank Cobb of the *New York World* in March 1917, would require "illiberalism at home to reinforce the men at the front." "The Constitution," Wilson continued, "would not survive" a war, and "free speech and the right of assembly would go," too. By May 1917, merely a month after American entry into the war, Wilson had already begun to shut down the conversations that he had helped to start about the shape of postwar internationalism. Such conversations, he warned, were "very unwise" while the war was still pending.[55]

With the Wilson administration's approval and encouragement, state and federal governments enacted new legislation to enforce the loyalty to the nation required of citizens. In February 1917, Congress had debated legislation to punish those who intentionally caused disaffection in the armed forces or who intentionally interfered with military operations. With the declaration of war on April 6, such legislation became a virtual certainty. Congress authorized selective conscription, which Wilson put into effect by requiring the registration of all men between the ages of twenty-one and thirty. The Espionage Act, enacted June 15, authorized criminal prosecution of spies and of anyone who obstructed recruitment or enlistment or who caused or attempted to cause insubordination or disloyalty in military or naval forces. Materials violating the Espionage Act or otherwise "urging treason" were "declared to be nonmailable matter" not to be delivered by the postmaster general. The Trading with the Enemy Act limited commerce and communication with enemies of the United States. Amendments to the Espionage Act in May 1918 prohibited disloyal or abusive language about "the form of government of the United States" or about its flag, uniforms, or military or naval forces. From Montana and Texas to Minnesota and Nebraska, similar developments produced dozens of new laws at the state and municipal levels banning outward opposition to the war.[56]

Postmaster General Albert S. Burleson and Attorney General Thomas Gregory enforced the new legislation with an enthusiastic abandon that the *New York World* called "an intellectual reign of terror in the United States." "May God have mercy" on dissenters from the nation's war plans, thundered Gregory, "for they need expect none from an outraged people and an avenging government." Between 1917 and the end of 1921, the federal government would commence more than 2,000 prosecutions under the Espionage Act. Burleson shut down dozens of foreign language newspapers pursuant to authority granted him under the Trading with the Enemy Act. Newspapers such as the conservative socialist *Milwaukee Leader* were denied mailing privileges. Burleson denied mailing privileges to seventy-five newspapers by the fall of 1918. Even the eminently respectable *Nation* was barred from the mails on Burleson's order until Wilson intervened. The August 1917 issue of Max Eastman's avant-garde journal *The Masses* was declared nonmailable by Burleson and Gregory for its antiwar cartoons and its opposition to the draft. After an order by U.S. District Judge Learned Hand requiring Burleson to mail the issue was stayed and overturned by the Court of Appeals, Burleson revoked *The Masses'* second-class mailing privileges altogether for the publishers' having missed an issue and thus having failed to remain a "periodical" within the meaning of the second-class mail law.[57]

Private and quasi-private patriotism was often as powerful

a force as the authority of the state. Ad hoc vigilante gangs and ultranationalist patriots—organizations such as the American Defense Society, the American Protective League, the National Liberty League, the Liberty League, the Knights of Liberty, the American Rights League, and the Boy Spies of America—smashed antiwar demonstrations, interrupted pacifist speakers, and lynched men suspected of pro-German leanings. The more respectable National Security League held events urging national loyalty and condemning those whom former President Theodore Roosevelt called "weaklings, illusionists, materialists, lukewarm Americans and faddists of all the types that vitiate sound nationalism." National Security League addresses were supplemented by the thousands of speakers ("Four Minute Men," as they were known) who operated out of the federal government's Committee on Public Information (CPI). Headed by former journalist George Creel, the CPI spearheaded a massive propaganda campaign, including an extraordinary 75 million pamphlets and as many as 6,000 press releases, virtually all broadcasting the importance of national loyalty in time of war. As one Security League speaker summed up the message of the patriotic campaign of 1917, the nationalist view was that "citizenship means everything or nothing." Loyal citizens "should refrain from fractious criticism," speakers cautioned, and should openly display their support for the war effort lest they be mistaken for "unconditional traitors" who hid treasonous attitudes beneath outward neutrality. In the new wartime atmosphere, those whom Roosevelt and his nationalist allies scorned as "professional internationalists" were most at risk. Treasury Secretary William McAdoo declared in October 1917 that advocacy of internationalism during wartime was, "in effect, traitorous." Others expressed the same sentiment in less civilized fashion, scrawling slogans like "Treason's Twilight Zone" on the doors to the American Union's offices.[58]

For Crystal Eastman and her American Union colleagues, the

wartime atmosphere of mandatory loyalty to the nation-state made it extraordinarily important to determine "the logical, courageous, and at the same time law abiding" role for internationalists. "Extreme patriots would force us to go out of business," she observed, yet "extremists of another sort" would surely put them all "in the federal penitentiary." Many items on the American Union's prewar agenda were now "impracticable," opposition to the war not least among them. As the spring of 1917 wore on, however, a new role seemed increasingly available. President Wilson had "turned his back on civil liberties," as historian John Blum has argued, "because he loved his vision of eventual peace more."[59] But if Eastman's wing of American internationalism was right about the drift toward militarist nationalism, nongovernmental organizations like the American Union would have to be able to articulate views other than those approved by the state. The conversation about postwar internationalism that Wilson himself had helped to start would have to be continued, whether Wilson approved of it or not. Yet if radical antimilitarists were to carry on their advocacy of a new internationalism to replace the nation-state, they would have to establish some kind of protection from the very authority they sought to displace.

In the spring of 1917, civil liberties emerged as the solution to the dilemma of the internationalists in wartime. Civil liberties provided the position between jingoist patriotism and treasonous internationalism for which the American Union had been searching. As American Union member John Haynes Holmes would later remember, American entry into the war meant that disarmament and attendant internationalist goals were, "for the time being at least," a "lost cause." "But lo," he continued, "as though to engage our liberal efforts afresh, there came suddenly to the fore in our nation's life the new issue of civil liberties." As early as April 1917, the American Union called for an "immediate anti-conscription campaign" and "cooperation in the defense of free speech and free assembly during the war." Americans might no longer safely argue against the war effort, but they could surely work "to prevent and oppose all those extreme manifestations of militarism" that seemed certain to follow in war's wake: "the brutal treatment" of the conscientious objector, "the denial of free speech," and "the suppressing of minority press." The resolution of the internationalists' crisis, in short, was to fight "the general abrogation of civil liberty" that the war among nation-states had brought in its wake. Indeed, such work, American Union leaders argued, was "the logical consequence of what we have been doing for two years."[60]

As the organization put it in a press release in the fall of 1917, a "Union Against Militarism becomes, during war time, inevitably a Union for the Defense of Civil Liberty." In late June 1917, the Conscientious Objectors' Bureau of the American Union, which had tentatively been formed two months earlier, was remade into the "Civil Liberties Bureau." Within weeks, "civil liberties" had become the "chief war work" of the nation's leading radical-internationalist organization.[61]

The name of the new Civil Liberties Bureau emerged out of the same transatlantic internationalism from which the American Union had arisen. Though the term "civil liberty" had long been central to Anglo-American law and political theory, eighteenth- and nineteenth-century lawyers and political writers only sparingly and erratically employed its disaggregated form, the plural "civil liberties." The phrase had been popularized just a year earlier by the British National Council for Civil Liberties. Walter Fuller, Eastman's new husband, was closely connected to the British organization (he would later become its corresponding secretary). With the establishment of the Civil Liberties Bureau, the American Union adopted the National Council's coinage as its own. Roger Baldwin, a recent addition to the American Union staff and head of the new Civil Liberties Bureau, would later recall that the Bureau's name represented "the first time that the phrase 'civil liberties' had been so used in the United States."[62]

The phrase seemed well tailored for inveterate rights skeptics such as Eastman. The term "civil liberties" promised to break down the abstraction of "civil liberty" into its specific and concrete component parts—"free speech, free press and free assembly," as Eastman put it. Indeed, the phrase accomplished for the American Union what influential legal theorists of the same generation sought to do for legal thinking more generally. Early legal realists such as Yale Law School's Wesley Hohfeld argued that nineteenth-century juristic abstractions such as "liberty" had contributed to dangerously sloppy legal reasoning. Legal slogans such as "right," "property," and "liberty," Hohfeld insisted, contained a multitude of discrete legal relations. Those relations, in turn, were best understood in disaggregated terms, not in the language of conceptual deduction and abstract principle. Disaggregated "civil liberties" claims thus seemed well designed to mediate the tensions that rights claims posed for those in internationalist circles who had been critical of rights-based thinking only a few short years before. The phrase "civil liberties" would substitute for the older idea of "civil liberty" in a new Hohfeldian age of pragmatic skepticism about legal abstractions.[63]

Most important, for Eastman the civil liberties initiative represented not a new set of rights-based ends, but rather a continuation by other means of the American Union's prewar internationalist agenda. Now that war had materialized, the defense of civil liberties seemed a necessary precondition to the advancement of internationalism. Norman Thomas argued that "the country which [suppresses civil liberties] will never commend democracy to the world." Eastman further contended that all nations needed to "be democratized before a federated world can be achieved." At the very least, it seemed clear, as a small but growing number of people ranging from the members of the Woman's Peace Party of New York City to Senator Joseph I. France of Maryland noted, that "full free and continuous discussion" of matters of great public import—the nation's war aims, peace terms, and treaty negotiations—required "freedom of the press" and "freedom of speech."[64]

Early efforts in the Civil Liberties Bureau thus adopted civil liberties as a strategic tool for the advancement of internationalism. The Bureau's earliest efforts were often not so much authentic expressions of a commitment to the virtues of a domestic Bill of Rights as they were a means to internationalist ends. Roger Baldwin of the American Union put it most cynically when he instructed a colleague "to get a good lot of flags" and "talk a good deal about the Constitution." Baldwin was perhaps more cynical than most. But his strategic appropriation of constitutional rights as symbols of American nationalism captured the spirit of the organization's turn to civil liberties in 1917. The American Union had advocated international institutions for years precisely because those institutions seemed better able than nation-states to secure human freedom and democracy. In 1917 the organization's members found themselves compelled by the war to make those claims in new "civil liberties" terms, but their aims remained the same.[65]

During the summer and fall of 1917, Eastman worked alongside Roger Baldwin in the American Union's civil liberties activities. As Baldwin would later recall, Eastman had been his "first associate in World War I days." Together, they defended conscientious objectors and antiwar agitators. Eastman even developed an ambitious plan of test cases to try the "actual testing of the right of free speech" in those places in which it had been limited.[66] And yet Baldwin emerged as the leader of the Civil Liberties Bureau. It was a development that had significant implications for the internationalist agenda and the fledgling civil liberties movement.

*
*
*

Eastman missed the early weeks of the American Union's wartime move to civil liberties. On March 19, 1917, she gave birth to her first child, Jeffrey Fuller. The birth appears to have had lasting effects on Eastman's health. She had always been susceptible to sickness. When Eastman was three, she and her older brother Morgan contracted scarlet fever. Morgan died, and though Crystal survived, she regularly suffered debilitating illnesses thereafter. In 1911, she was forced to break off her engagement with the New York state employers' liability commission because of illness. In April 1916, she became ill during the American Union's Truth About Preparedness Tour and was ordered to be "kept strictly in bed" for several weeks. With Jeffrey's birth, Eastman developed a "chronic disease of her kidneys," as Max later described it, that would plague her until her death. By March 1921, she would be forced to resign from the executive committee of the Civil Liberties Bureau's successor, the American Civil Liberties Union. "I have always been too tired," explained the otherwise energetic Eastman. She would die just seven years later, in 1928.[67]

Eastman's complicated pregnancy forced her to take off more than two months beginning in mid-March 1917. They were a critical two months, spanning the beginning of American involvement in the war, and Eastman knew it. "I am crazy to get back on the job," she wrote shortly after Jeffrey's birth. There would be, she feared, "nothing left for me to do" by the time she got back. Most troublingly, Eastman feared that in her absence the American Union would turn away from its radical-internationalist agenda. Baldwin, in particular, had suggested a new direction for the group that Eastman found wanting "in a great many respects." She had hoped to meet with Baldwin before giving birth to Jeffrey and going to Atlantic City to convalesce, but Walter and her physician insisted that she not.[68]

During Eastman's absence, which continued into early June 1917, Baldwin had indeed begun to establish himself as the new force in the American Union. His extraordinary energies matched Eastman's. Like Eastman, he had begun his career as a sociologically informed architect of the modern administrative state. After graduation from Harvard College, he had gone to St. Louis to found the sociology department of Washington University and to run a neighborhood settlement house. While in St. Louis, Baldwin became actively involved in the reform of the city's criminal courts. What workmen's compensation had been to Eastman, the new juvenile courts and probation systems were to Baldwin: socialized systems for modernizing nineteenth-century law. Like workmen's compensation programs, juvenile courts aimed to replace cumbersome inquiries into individual rights and moral culpability with regimes of social-scientific expertise designed to treat social problems and manage populations. Expert "professional standards," in Baldwin's words, would replace traditional adjudication, which Baldwin had come to think of as simply "judicial interference." While Eastman was counting injured workers in Pittsburgh, Baldwin helped to found the National Probation Officers' Association. A few years later, he coauthored what would quickly become a leading text in the field of juvenile justice.[69]

Despite their similar backgrounds in progressive-era sociological reform, Baldwin and Eastman quickly developed an "uneasy" relationship. For one thing, Baldwin's Harvard education and inside connections in the Wilson administration made him both more inclined and better positioned than Eastman to engage in the kind of discreet advocacy with government officials that colleagues like Lillian Wald favored. Moreover, Baldwin came to the work of the American Union with an essentially domestic outlook. While Eastman toured Europe, met with international woman's suffrage leaders, and encountered European radicals in the cosmopolitan setting of New York City, Baldwin had gone to the relatively insular St. Louis. His frame of reference in the area of civil liberties was therefore not, as Eastman's had been, the internationalist outlook of the woman's suffrage movement. Instead, Baldwin had developed the outlook of a domestic reformer, involved in such fights as the National Association for the Advancement of Colored People's efforts to fight municipal housing segregation. To be sure, in his first months with the American Union, Baldwin supported its core internationalist agenda. And much later in life, Baldwin would become deeply involved in the United Nations's work for international human rights. "Nations," he would suggest in the 1970s, were "downright silly." As Eastman had suggested sixty years earlier, Baldwin would contend that national boundaries were imaginary divisions of people into "geographical units" bounded by arbitrary lines and protected by armies. But in 1917, Baldwin's arrival served to exacerbate increasingly acute differences within the American Union over the question of internationalism.[70]

For a few months, tensions between Baldwin's and Eastman's theories of civil liberties took a back seat to a larger conflict that drove such figures as Lillian Wald and Paul Kellogg out of the American Union altogether. Wald and Kellogg had never been convinced that the civil liberties strategy offered a viable solution to the American Union's wartime dilemmas. After the declaration of war, Wald and Kellogg—like Root and Wilson—believed strongly that the obligations of national citizenship required support for the war effort. The civil liberties campaign engineered by Baldwin and Eastman, in their view, veered too close to making the American Union "a party of opposition to the government." Over the course of the summer, Wald and Kellogg struggled to bring the American Union around to Wald's less confrontational approach. By September, however, Wald, Kellogg, and a number of others felt that they could not "remain if the active work for Civil Liberties is continued." Eastman and others in the American Union insisted that the organization was not "embarking on a program of political obstruction," that it was merely working "against hysterical legislation, and for peace." But the subtleties of the distinction were lost on the disgruntled Wald-Kellogg wing of the American Union. By October 1917, both Wald and Kellogg had resigned.[71]

Divergences between Baldwin and Eastman quickly resurfaced once the split within the American Union was complete. By the fall of 1917, the prevailing atmosphere of mandatory patriotism made it virtually impossible for the Civil Liberties Bureau to advance Eastman's brand of internationalism. After complaints from high-ranking members of the military, Secretary of War Newton Baker cut off contact between the War Department and the Civil Liberties Bureau in May 1918. Three months later, the Department of Justice raided the Bureau's offices and seized its papers. Courts began convening grand juries to investigate "foreigners" and "soap-box orators." Max Eastman was put on trial not once but twice during 1918 for his work on *The Masses* (the juries deadlocked both times). Baldwin himself was arrested for refusing to register for the draft, convicted, and sentenced to one year in prison.[72]

Around the country, attitudes toward internationalists deteriorated further. Herbert Bigelow, who had spoken on behalf of the American Union's Truth About Preparedness Campaign in the spring of 1916, was kidnapped and brutalized in November 1917. The *Grand Rapids Press* labeled the American Union and allied groups "seditious," and the *New York Tribune* called them dangerous "enemies within." By August 1918, Theodore Roosevelt was singling out "internationalists" as playing into the hands of "German autocracy." Elihu Root would soon announce that "internationalism" had become a threat to "the authority and responsibility of nations," including the United States.[73]

In the face of nationalist coercion, Baldwin led the Civil Liberties Bureau—now formally divorced from the American Union and renamed the National Civil Liberties Bureau—in what Norman Thomas called a "new direction" for civil liberties. The moral imperatives of nationalism had recast internationalism as treason. As Roger Baldwin explained to one supporter in September 1917, "internationalists and radical peace organizations" had come under tremendous pressure to purge "German names" from their lists of officials. Things became all the more dire after the November 1917 Bolshevik revolution in Russia. "Worldwide Anarchist Plot," screamed headlines, linking the "Bolsheviki" to the IWW and to "revolutionists" around the world. As the prosecutor at the 1918 Espionage Act trial of Eugene Debs said in his closing argument to the jury, "Pitch all the nations into one pot with the Socialists on top and you've got internationalism." By 1919, the federal government initiated deportations of suspected alien radicals back to Russia. The infamous Palmer Raids on suspected radicals quickly followed, beginning in November of that year, as did the similar Lusk Committee Raids in New York State soon after. By December 1919, President Wilson, who had been a willing but unenthusiastic supporter of Burleson's and Gregory's enforcement actions during the war, was calling for a peacetime extension of the Espionage Act. Even Lillian Wald, who had so carefully extricated herself in the summer of 1917 from the possible appearance of opposition to the war effort, would find herself in 1919 still trying to defend her patriotism.[74]

Between Baldwin's domestic frame of reference and the extraordinary pressures being exerted against internationalism, it is hardly a wonder that the National Civil Liberties Bureau began to pull back from its internationalist beginnings. The great virtue of the civil liberties campaign as a wartime program was its ostensibly patriotic connections to the nation's constitutive legal traditions. Under Baldwin's leadership, the National Civil Liberties Bureau seized on those traditions to advance a conception of civil liberties increasingly stripped of internationalist trappings. Gone were the appeals to do away with the abstraction of the nation-state as a political form. Gone were the calls for civil liberties as both the necessary precondition for, and the purpose of, new structures of international governance. In their place, Baldwin substituted civil liberties claims couched in the language and traditions of American nationalism. Affiliates were urged to celebrate the 130th anniversary of the signing of the U.S. Constitution in September 1917. The Bureau's challenges to the federal conscription regime, Baldwin assured, aimed not to obstruct the draft but merely to ensure that the first draft since the Civil War "not take place without the highest authority in the country passing upon it squarely." Propaganda against the draft, Baldwin explained, would cease and be replaced by work narrowly confined to "the lines of legal defense." "Let us be patriots in the true sense," exclaimed a Bureau-affiliated lawyer from Chicago, perfectly capturing the organization's newly bounded legal horizons. In the Bureau's devotion to national ideals, a press release from the fall of 1917 declared, "we believe ourselves to be patriots, no less sincere and earnest than those who lead our armies to France." The "cause of civil liberties," Bureau leaders insisted, was "loyal" to the "American ideal" of freedom. Even Crystal Eastman took advantage of the opportunities afforded by patriotism: "there is no more patriotic duty than to keep democracy alive at home," she announced. Democracy, she concluded, meant the protection of "ancient American liberties."[75]

By the time the Bureau held a conference on its civil liberties agenda in January 1918, the forceful internationalist voices of just a year before had become muted. Rather than talk about the relationship between civil liberties and international legal institutions, Baldwin and his colleagues focused on the protection of civil liberties in wartime as a "test of the highest type of loyalty"—loyalty not to global citizenship or to the idea of world federation, but to self-consciously national ideals.[76]

Three further conferences in the next year—one still widely remembered, the others now more obscure—made clear the extent to which internationalist energies had waned. The year 1919 brought renewed hope to internationalists in the United States and across Europe. The Paris Peace Conference began in January, with Wilson promoting the internationalist idea of a League of Nations. At the same time, Jane Addams and the women's branch of the internationalist movement assembled at Zurich in a renewed showing of the radical internationalism that had characterized the Woman's Peace Parade during the early stages of the war. Eastman did not attend; leaders of the Zurich conference feared that the scandal of her divorce from Bennie and quick remarriage to Walter Fuller would undermine the respect accorded to the conference. And though many internationalists bitterly opposed the indemnities imposed on Germany by the Treaty of Versailles in June, the treaty nonetheless established what many internationalists had advocated for decades: a League of Nations "to promote international co-operation and to achieve international peace and security."[77]

At the war's end, the National Civil Liberties Bureau seemed poised to preside over a similar rebirth of its own internationalism. In June, as the Paris conference wound down, the Bureau proposed an "international conference for the restoration of civil liberties." The conference, to take place in New York in October, would reach out across national boundaries to begin the process of reconstituting prewar internationalist alliances. The Bureau arranged to cosponsor the conference—to be called the Anglo-American Tradition of Liberty Conference—with its British counterpart and namesake, the National Council for Civil Liberties. Indeed, Eastman and her husband, Walter Fuller, with whom she had moved to London several months before, took the lead in organizing the British side of the event. Moreover, early signs suggested that the conference would resonate powerfully with the internationalist tradition. Arthur Ponsonby of the British antiwar organization Union for Democratic Control suggested that the conference might help create the "foundation of an enlightened and democratic internationalism." B. N. Langdon-Davies of the National Council for Civil Liberties similarly assured his American counterparts that although the conference would focus on Anglo-American liberties, it would not cut against "the wider internationalism we all seek." Early plans called for the conference to focus on such issues as "International Aspects of Civil Liberty" and topics like "Why Freedom Matters—International Co-operation."[78]

In some respects, the conference was a smashing success. Though Eastman's old teacher Franklin Giddings refused to come (Giddings had supported U.S. intervention in the war), leading figures in American law such as Zachariah Chafee Jr., Felix Frankfurter, and Roscoe Pound of the Harvard Law School, all of whom were assuming important places in the early history of civil liberties in American law, came down from Cambridge for the event. Their prominence and their close connections to men on the Supreme Court and in the White House meant that support for the protection of civil liberties had moved from the eclectic margins of radical internationalism into the corridors of power.[79]

From the internationalist perspective, however, the conference failed. Wilson had struggled mightily since his return from Paris to persuade the Senate to ratify his internationalist treaty. At the Anglo-American Tradition of Liberty Conference, too, internationalism foundered on the shoals of nationalist passions and difficult details.[80]

The conference was full of the high rhetoric of prewar internationalism. Speakers denounced "old assumptions of sovereignty and national honor" as ideas that "belong to the Middle Ages." "Liberty is not national," delegates declared, and they called for an internationalist system that would move beyond the "territorial basis" of the nation-state and beyond the "nationalistic segregation of peoples." But in the new era of the League and the Paris Conference, the platitudes of prewar internationalism were no longer sufficient. Concrete proposals for international structures were the order of the day. Yet the extraordinary complexity of the international question and the impracticality of internationalist ideas quickly became apparent. Delegates who favored gradual evolution toward internationalism clashed with those who urged immediate internationalist initiatives. Socialists clashed with liberals. Protonationalists from colonized regions like India and Ireland insisted on the priority of national independence over international structures, even as internationalists sought to subordinate nationalism to transnational institutions. Finding "a formula between nationalism and internationalism," as Norman Thomas put it, proved impossible. By the final day of the conference, those in attendance were riven with dissension. The conference, Thomas warned, was "in danger of being lost in an unnecessary bog." Debates over internationalism threatened to "wreck" the conference, cautioned another participant. And so they did. Just four weeks after Wilson's devastating stroke ensured the demise of the League of Nations in the U.S. Senate, the last gasp of wartime radical internationalism collapsed in a mess of differences and recriminations.[81]

What the assembled participants in the Anglo-American Tradition of Liberty Conference could agree on was the value of civil liberties. Within a few months of the close of the conference, Baldwin reorganized the National Civil Liberties Bureau as the American Civil Liberties Union. The ACLU would continue to monitor international events, including the demise of the British

National Council for Civil Liberties in 1920. But almost from the moment of its founding, Baldwin and the ACLU sought to obscure the organization's internationalist beginnings. The Bureau, the ACLU's organizers contended in 1920, had not been an "antiwar organization," but rather an organization that "insisted on American constitutional rights." Already in 1920, the center of attention for civil libertarians had shifted away from the question of war resisters and opposition to militarism to the problem of the "radicals, especially the I.W.W. . . . and the Socialists." "Radicalism, not the attitude to the war," now seemed the motivating factor in most instances of attacks on civil liberties. The ACLU thus organized itself to defend "peaceful picketing" and "trade unionism" and to fight discrimination against radicals and labor unions. Just as the ACLU would later purge communists from its ranks, the early ACLU had washed itself clean of its internationalist origins.[82]

*
*
*

What is striking about the development of a new language of civil liberties in American law between 1917 and 1920 is that it took part in both the modernist and the traditional idioms that the war occasioned. Historians have long debated the cultural consequences of the Great War. Some hold that the attempt to make sense of the brutal violence of modern nation-states touched off a deep shift toward the ironic and the modernist. Others argue that the war occasioned a powerful return to traditionalist rhetorics as a mechanism for coping with the apparent senselessness of the war. In Jay Winter's influential formulation, for example, the war revived "a number of traditional languages" expressed in "unusual and modern forms."[83]

Like Winter's distinctly modern traditionalists, lawyers such as Crystal Eastman responded to the war and to the rise of newly powerful state institutions by reinvigorating the familiar languages of rights and liberties that they had only recently rejected as Victorian anachronisms. For Eastman and her colleagues, the turn to rights advanced a strikingly modernist project in international law. The abstraction of rights seemed to offer a way to contain the dangerous abstraction of state sovereignty. Eastman's internationalist appropriations of a traditional language of rights and liberties, in other words, were themselves deeply ironic. With her fellow internationalists, she sought to pick and choose among the totems of a national tradition so as strategically to advance a cosmopolitan modernist agenda, identifying the abstraction of rights as more useful (and less dangerous) than the abstraction of sovereignty. The new civil liberties movement of the twentieth century was thus the product of a kind of double disillusionment with the fixtures of nineteenth-century legal thought—rights and states. And yet in the searing heat of wartime patriotism, internationalist modernism quickly gave way to more straightforwardly traditional arguments rooted ever more deeply in the trappings of American national identity. The traditional language of rights overwhelmed the internationalist agenda that the rhetoric of rights had been marshaled to advance. Indeed, within a few short years, Baldwin's recrafting of the civil liberties movement would obscure almost completely the movement's beginnings in international law.

Eastman herself refused to compromise with the imperatives of the nation-state. As John Haynes Holmes later remembered, Eastman "could not, or more likely would not, surrender the idealism" that had brought her to the internationalist cause. She never embraced the Bill of Rights and civil liberties as wholeheartedly as Baldwin did—strategically or otherwise. The First Amendment, she wrote from London, had "never" been "any good in a crisis"; it had "never been proof against a strain." As labor unions, socialists, and the ACLU turned to civil liberties to advance their causes, she contended that those safeguards had never been "of much practical value in protecting the poorest workers." Especially after U.S. military intervention in Russia in 1918, Eastman's own views radicalized dramatically. By 1920, she adopted a form of Bolshevik communism. A "capitalist state," she wrote, would never "maintain democratic institutions against its own interest." Even in the woman's movement, in which she had worked for legal change since childhood, Eastman lost hope in the reform possibilities of the law. Feminism could "most assuredly" not accomplish real sex equality through legal change, she argued; sex discrimination was instead a problem "of education, of early training." "We must," she concluded, "bring up feminist sons."[84]

Eastman, it seems, had encountered the limits of lawyering. In her day, as still a century later, the authority of law and of lawyers derived principally from the very sovereign states that she sought to critique. Lawyering therefore seemed to come with powerful institutional limits. To be sure, nation-state institutions were not immune to change. The United States's constitutive legal documents, after all, provided the materials with which Eastman and her colleagues built the modern civil liberties movement. Moreover, in the succeeding decades international lawyers—walking in the footsteps of internationalists before them—would make painstaking progress in establishing cosmopolitan human rights norms to constrain the prerogatives of sovereignty.[85] Yet national institutions have also proven powerfully resistant to the transformations that Eastman and the radical internationalists aimed to bring about. American lawyer-modernists have turned awkwardly to the abstraction of civil liberties for almost a century now. They have done so in substantial part to fend off the abstraction of nation-state sovereignty.

Four ☆ *Reactions*

The first three parts of this book have been histories of what political theorist Bonnie Honig might call "democracy and the foreigner." They have been stories of foreign influences in the American nation, whether Scottish Enlightenment ideas, pan-African nationalism, or European-inspired cosmopolitanism. They have been stories of the containment of these foreign influences, but also of the capacity of such influences to reshape the American nation. They have, in short, been stories of the making and remaking of the American nation in the hidden histories of its engagement with the foreign and the transnational.

This last part of the book moves forward in time to the middle of the twentieth century. In particular, it takes up the story of the early stirrings of that most American of lawyers: the plaintiff's-side personal injury lawyer. Unlike the earlier histories, this is a story of reactionary American nationalism—a history of the powerful legal institutions of the American nation-state and the sentimental attachments that have arisen out of them. As James Wilson never quite understood, the decentralized and permeable institutions of the Madisonian nation-state have repeatedly fostered the development of well-organized interest groups that have powerfully influenced the decisions and directions of government. The genius of the trial lawyers was to seize on the Madisonian legal institutions from which they had sprung and to defend those institutions—the jury trial, federalism, and the common law in particular—as constitutional and ideological traditions at the heart of what it means to be American. And so, beginning in the 1950s, trial lawyers wielded American nationalism against the ostensibly foreign intrusion of administrative welfare programs that threatened to displace them. In the hands of a charismatic and well-motivated group, American legal institutions became the ingredients for powerful nationalist arguments against cosmopolitan reform.

What follows is a story about both the bounds and the distinctive possibilities of American nationhood. As in other developed nation-states, nationhood in America has served as an important source for the collective identity that generates support for social welfare programs. But in the United States, national traditions and institutions have also resisted such social welfare programs, especially those describable (rightly or not) as foreign to the nation's character. Out of these traditions and institutions (and with the trial lawyers' willing assistance) new private mechanisms for the provision of social welfare have sprung up that are sometimes brilliant, often deeply flawed—and nothing if not distinctively American.

The King and the Dean:
Melvin Belli, Roscoe Pound,
and the Common-Law Nation

The friendship between Melvin Belli and Roscoe Pound is surely among the most startling and yet unremarked-upon relationships in the annals of American law. By the middle of the twentieth century, Roscoe Pound was considered by many the world's greatest living legal scholar. Early in his career he had pioneered an influential new school of socially oriented legal thought in the United States known as "sociological jurisprudence." For twenty years, from 1916 to 1936, he served as Dean of the Harvard Law School. He participated in numerous prominent law-reform commissions and was an associate of jurists on the U.S. Supreme Court and state supreme courts around the country. Between 1910, when he arrived at Harvard as a professor, and the early 1950s, when he retired from teaching, Pound taught countless future leaders of the American legal profession and dozens of future governors, congressmen, and judges. In the law, his prestige was virtually unmatched. And from the first decade of the twentieth century until well into the 1920s, Pound lent that prestige to the project of designing what was among the most important developments in the twentieth-century American state: the rise of administration as a fourth branch of American government alongside the legislature, judiciary, and executive.[1]

Melvin Belli was perhaps the most flamboyant, outlandish, self-aggrandizing, and scandal-plagued American lawyer in the half-century after World War II. Named "King of Torts" by *Life* magazine in 1954, Belli was the public face of a segment of the bar that suddenly became a new force in American politics in the postwar period: the trial lawyers. Belli was legendary in his hometown of San Francisco and around the world for his courtroom theatrics. He was, many said, "a Barnum" of the bar, turning courtrooms into "circus rings." Throughout the 1950s, his name was indelibly associated with trial lawyers' remarkably successful push for increased damages awards in personal injury cases, what Belli called "the adequate award." Outside the courthouse, Belli celebrated favorable jury verdicts by firing cannons and running the Jolly Roger up a flagpole atop his offices. The offices themselves—lined with framed copies of the checks Belli had won for his clients—were decorated like "the parlor of a bordertown bordello at the turn of the century." Belli ran with gangsters, rock-and-roll celebrities, and Hollywood stars. He acted in movies, and even produced one. He preached the gospel of the three-martini business lunch and advised readers of the *Wall Street Journal* that to "show a little class" they should "throw a broad in" along with the drinks. He was regularly sought out for television appearances, and he sought them out just as eagerly. Indeed, so great was Belli's fame—especially after his spectacularly unsuccessful 1964 representation of Jack Ruby for the murder of Lee Harvey Oswald—that the Belli Building in Jackson Square became one of San Francisco's leading tourist attractions.[2]

Belli and Pound relished their friendship for its stark contrasts. Belli loved to regale visitors with stories of how Pound, then in his eighties, preferred to stay at the younger Belli's baroquely adorned apartments on Telegraph Hill rather than at San Francisco hotels, much to the dismay of the mandarins of the American Bar Association and the Harvard Law School. On one such occasion, Pound addressed the bawdy Policeman's Ball that Belli hosted each year, speaking to roars of approval from the assembled officers about the idea that "law and order begins at the end of a policeman's billy." Belli liked most of all to tell the story of Pound and the "beautiful strawberry blond" who called on Belli late one night at the apartments that Belli had decorated like a "high-class Swedish massage-parlor." Not finding Belli, she reportedly curled up at the bedside of the octogenarian, pajama-clad Pound while he "discoursed on Henry VIII and the laws of Edward II and the Boston Red Sox's chances of winning the pennant."[3]

Yet what brought together the King of Torts and the Dean of Harvard was more than carousing and surprising juxtapositions. The relationship between Belli and Pound holds clues to one of the great questions of American law and politics. Why is it that the United States channels so much modern social policy through the institutions of the eighteenth- and nineteenth-century state? In particular, why have courts and private institutions played central roles in the kinds of social programs that comparable western nation-states perform through public administrative bureaucracies?[4]

As Pound understood better than anyone else in his generation, the growth of public administrative bureaucracies was among the signal developments of European and North American nation-states in the modern era. Between the late nineteenth century and the end of the New Deal, reformers in industrializing nations engaged in what historian Daniel Rodgers has described as an extended transatlantic dialogue about social insurance and the administrative state. Yet industrial-age conversations about the new social politics left fewer lasting traces in the United States than in western Europe. European civil service bureaucracies expanded exponentially to create the paradigmatic welfare states of the twentieth century. The United States, by contrast, vested central social policy functions in courts and in private entities such as employers, the legal and medical professions, commercial insurers, and philanthropic organizations. In the United States, the social policies of the modern state—health insurance, old-age pensions, poor relief, and bankruptcy protection, to mention only a few—were often poured like new wine into the old bottles of common-law courts and private institutions.[5]

No one worked harder than Melvin Belli and Roscoe Pound to ensure that the new social policy functions of the mid-twentieth-century state would be channeled into existing institutions. Indeed, for a little more than a decade, Belli and Pound worked to carry out a project each of them had come to hold dear: limiting the spread of the administrative state and expanding the common-law field known as the law of torts, the body of Anglo-American judge-made legal principles governing bodily injuries and other wrongs to the person. By the 1950s when they met, Pound had completed the arc of his thinking on the question of administration, transforming himself from sociological prophet of a rising administrative state to bitter critic of the New Deal and its associated institutions. In the freewheeling Belli, Pound saw the salvation (however unlikely) of a distinctly Anglo-American tradition of individualistic liberty under law in a world turning ever more decisively from courts and law toward administration and continental collectivisms. In turn, Belli found in Pound the perfect spokesman for the fledgling organization that some would eventually come to call "America's most powerful lobby": the Association of Trial Lawyers of America, or ATLA.[6] Under the stewardship of Belli and Pound, ATLA and its predecessors lobbied with great success against the expansion of administration into the domain of the common law of torts.

The genius of Belli and Pound was to see the strategic opportunities American nationhood made available to the legal profession. Indeed, theirs is a story of American nationhood three times over. The pluralist institutions of the Madisonian nation-state created significant and often lucrative opportunities for private groups, such as the trial bar, to play the role of broker between citizens and the state. Moreover, these same decentralized institutions (federalism, separation of powers, bicameral legislatures, and more) created multiple veto points at which private interests could obstruct reform that threatened to dislodge them, as administrative agencies threatened to dislodge the trial bar.[7] In turn, the legal and constitutional bases of American nationhood provided a ready-made rhetoric that could be marshaled in defense of the pluralist and decentralized institutions of the nation-state. Belli and Pound seized on these institutions—the very institutions from which groups such as ATLA had sprung—and invoked them as a national tradition to be defended against foreign bureaucratic intruders. Indeed, for over a decade, Belli and Pound worked together to mobilize a powerful nationalist campaign on behalf of the long-standing legal institutions of the American nation-state for which the trial lawyers had become a chief constituency—the jury trial, the common law, and the courts chief among them.

In the process of invoking American nationhood, Belli and Pound helped to reinvent the courts and the common law—and in particular the tort system—as a highly decentralized, sometimes brilliant, often deeply flawed, and always distinctively American system of privately organized social insurance. In the hands of the trial bar, the law of torts would become one more instance of social insurance and regulatory functions performed by private institutions—a sprawling social policy system of insurance companies, lawyers, claims adjusters, and courts amounting to $250 billion each year by the early twenty-first century, about the same as the annual cost of the Social Security old-age pensions that form the heart of the New Deal's administrative legacy. Even as the New Deal limped toward what historian Alan Brinkley has called "the end of reform," Belli, Pound, and the trial lawyers brilliantly rehabilitated and transformed Franklin Roosevelt's promise of social security and economic freedom, re-

Melvin Belli (far left) and Roscoe Pound (second from left) at a NACCA
meeting in the 1950s. (Association of Trial Lawyers of America)

casting the New Deal ideal of economic security in common-law
terms and reorienting important swaths of American public policy back toward the courts of the eighteenth- and nineteenth-
century American state.[8]

Yet if Belli and Pound thought they were upholding the ostensibly individualist traditions of the American common law against the spread of administrative bureaucracy, they were sorely mistaken. Wherever the trial lawyers managed to hold off *public* administration, irrepressible new forms of *private* administration grew up like peculiarly domestic kudzu in the shadow of the common-law courts. Indeed, even as Belli and Pound trumpeted tort law's capacity to preserve common-law virtues and individualized justice in a modern era of giant institutions and creeping state bureaucracies, American tort law gave rise to a decentralized and often invisible system of private administration that duplicated many of the bureaucratic mechanisms for which Belli and Pound had excoriated the administrative state. In the American nation-state, administration would persist. But unlike the administrative apparatus of many other western nation-states, it would be administration in private hands.

*
*
*

Administrative agencies and bureaucratic commissions could hardly have seemed further away from the American frontier setting of Roscoe Pound's childhood. Nathan Roscoe Pound was born in 1870 in the prairie town of Lincoln, Nebraska, when the young city and the new state were only three years old. Pound's father, Stephen B. Pound, hailed from upstate New York, about midway between Rochester and Syracuse. After being admitted to the bar in 1863, the elder Pound practiced law for three years in New York and then lit out for the frontier. By 1869, Stephen Pound had become one of the leading lawyers in Lincoln. He was elected the first president of the Lincoln Bar Association and served as a judge in the Nebraska courts, first on the county probate court and later on the state district court, where he served for thirteen years. As a member of the 1875 Nebraska state constitutional convention, Stephen Pound is said to have been the chief drafter of the state's broad takings clause, protecting property not merely from being taken for public use without just compensation (as the Fifth Amendment in the United States Bill of Rights provided), but also from being damaged in the course of public activity without such compensation.[9]

Stephen Pound's wife and Roscoe's mother, Laura Biddlecome Pound, came from an old New York and New England family that could trace its American roots back into the seventeenth century. Removed by marriage from relatively cultured New York to the prairie in Lincoln, Laura Pound sought to cultivate learning and manners in her three children, Nathan Roscoe and his two sisters, Louise (born in 1872) and Olivia (born in 1874). Under the circumstances, Laura did remarkably well. She brought about as much culture into the Pound home as frontier conditions permitted. She installed a blackboard on the dining room wall, the better to teach her children. Beginning at a tender age, Laura and Stephen instructed Roscoe in foreign languages, including German and Latin. And Laura made certain that such Nebraska notables as writer Willa Cather were counted among the Pound family's friends.[10]

Roscoe entered the University of Nebraska in 1884 at the age of fourteen, receiving a bachelor's degree in botany in 1888 and a master's degree in the same field a year later. For a tiny prairie university, Nebraska provided Pound with a remarkably cosmopolitan education. In particular, botanist Charles E. Bessey, who arrived in Lincoln the same year Pound began his university studies, brought the latest theories in Darwinian science to the Nebraska frontier. Bessey would go on to be a nationally recognized figure in the sciences; in the 1880s he was at the forefront of the movement in American universities to reconceive the study of biology in light of Darwin's evolutionary theory. Under Bessey's influence, botany quickly became the most exciting field of study at the university. Pound just as quickly became one of Bessey's best students. Pound himself even published several notable works in the field in the 1890s. In 1897 he was awarded a doctorate in botany and became the director of the Nebraska Botanical Survey.[11]

Botany was Roscoe's early passion, but Stephen Pound wanted his son to follow him into his law practice. And so in what would not be the last time he changed direction to please others, young Roscoe did just that. After reading law in his father's law office and taking several law courses at a local trade school, Roscoe traveled east to Cambridge, Massachusetts, to study law at Harvard in the fall of 1889. In Cambridge, it seems, the younger Pound decided that the law might hold as much intellectual interest as botany. By all accounts, his teachers—including constitutional lawyer James Bradley Thayer, prominent Boston lawyer John Chipman Gray, and legendary teacher James Barr Ames—left deep and lasting impressions on the young Pound. Yet under pressure from his father once again (this time to take up his father's practice), Roscoe returned to Lincoln after a year at Harvard. For the next five years, Pound practiced law while continuing his botanical pursuits in his after-hours. Pound developed a substantial law practice. His clients included the new corporations and railroads that were expanding their presence in the Nebraska frontier. Once he even tried and won a case against the prominent populist politician William Jennings Bryan, who soon after ran unsuccessfully for president on the Democratic Party ticket in 1896, and then again in 1900 and 1908.[12]

Pound's exposure to Harvard, however, had persuaded him that the world had in store for him things that he had come to think of as bigger and better than practicing law in Lincoln. In 1895, the University of Nebraska's new law school appointed Pound as an instructor. Four years later, Pound was promoted to assistant professor, and in 1903 the regents of the university elected him dean.[13]

Once again, the little university in Lincoln provided Pound with a stimulating intellectual environment. During the years he spent teaching law in Nebraska, Pound came into contact with new thinking that was revolutionizing the social sciences just as Bessey and his colleagues had sought to revolutionize the natural sciences. Edward Alsworth Ross, one of America's most dynamic young sociologists, arrived at Nebraska in 1901 after being fired from Stanford University. Ross's progressive views had antagonized Stanford's benefactors, but what was Stanford's loss was Nebraska's gain and Pound's opportunity. Ross was as versed as Bessey in the implications of Darwinian selection for his field. Moreover, Ross was deeply interested in the evolution of law as a mechanism for what he called "social control." Law, Ross believed, was "the corner stone of the entire edifice of control." And yet, as Ross understood it, the law was increasingly embattled in its project of imposing order on the social life of the industrialized modern era. "Its ponderous and slow-moving machinery," Ross wrote, was "far too clumsy to be relied upon"—or at least to be relied upon exclusively—to give order to the swelling populations and fast-growing industries of modern America.[14]

Ross's ideas about the clumsiness of the law—its ponderous processes and cumbersome workings—became the central theme of Pound's thinking for the next two decades. Years later, Pound would even publish a series of lectures using Ross's theory as its title, *Social Control through Law*. (For his part, Ross dedicated his 1921 book *The Principles of Sociology* to Pound, whom he called "prince of law teachers.") More immediately, Pound's friendship with Ross helped to forge the theory of "sociological jurisprudence" for which Pound would soon become famous.[15] If Ross the sociologist wrote that the law was losing its grip on modern social life, Pound the lawyer saw sociology as the way for law to reclaim its authority. The law, Pound concluded, needed to adopt sociological approaches to modern problems—approaches that traded awkward legal processes for efficient mechanisms of social control.

As Pound looked around at the law in the first years of the new century, the administration of justice seemed to be undergoing precisely the kind of evolutionary transformation that Bessey and Ross described in biology and sociology. "Throughout the English speaking world," Dean Pound explained in a 1923 Wisconsin bar association address, the rise of a new form of "administrative justice" seemed plainly evident. New administrative tribunals seemed to be "set up every day somewhere." Existing administrative bodies were being expanded and strengthened just as often, typically at the expense of traditional Anglo-American common-law courts like the one over which Pound's father had presided for more than a decade. Everywhere one turned, Pound wrote, "commissions and boards, with summary administrative and inquisitorial powers are called for, and courts are distrusted." Such modern imperatives as "public utilities, factory inspection, food inspection, tenement-house inspection, and building laws," Pound concluded, had compelled the United States to turn more and more from traditional legal institutions to new forms of "administrative prevention." In each of these areas, Pound believed, experts would be able to transform the "legal ordering of society" into "a great series of tasks of social engineering" to be "worked out in the sociological laboratory."[16]

Pound was hardly the only observer of American law to note the rise of a new kind of administrative body in American governance. State regulatory commissions for the banking and insurance industries sprang up in the 1850s and 1860s. New England states established commissions for the regulation of railroad traffic in the years around the Civil War; railroad commissions spread into the midwestern states in the 1870s. At the federal level, the Interstate Commerce Act of 1887 created an Interstate Commerce Commission for the regulation and oversight of interstate railroads. The 1906 Pure Food and Drug Act vested new authority in executive-branch departments to collect and examine commercial foods and drugs and to make rules and regulations for doing so. The Federal Trade Commission Act of 1914 created an administrative body to prevent unfair competition in interstate commerce. On a smaller scale, state mothers'-pension programs and the federal Children's Bureau ushered in new administrative bureaucracies. Systems of juvenile justice, plea bargaining, probation, indeterminate sentencing, and parole did the same for the criminal law. And between 1911 and 1920, workmen's compensation programs like the one supported by Crystal Eastman in New York created bureaucracies for the administration of the law of work accidents in some forty-two states. By 1948, when Mississippi became the last state to enact a workmen's compensation statute, every state in the United States had replaced the common-law system of tort law in work accidents with an administrative workmen's compensation scheme.[17]

This new phenomenon—this "conspicuous feature" of the new structures of American governance—posed daunting challenges for the constitutional system designed by such men as James Madison and James Wilson. For about a century, the United States had been what Pound called a "common-law polity." The common-law tradition rested on jury trials and adversarial legal processes. Neutral, common-law judicial umpires arbitrated between claims advanced by private parties. The whole system relied heavily on "individual initiative to secure legal redress and enforce legal rules." And as Alexis de Tocqueville famously noted during his tour of the United States in the 1830s, nineteenth-century Americans seemed to call on the common-law courts again and again to answer important questions of social policy.[18]

In Pound's sociologically influenced view, however, the common-law polity of Madison and Wilson had outlived its useful life. The conditions of the industrial age had exposed the limits of legal action in the common-law system and now cried out for the displacement of law by more efficient modes of modern administration. Trials before juries of laypeople, for example, required that the law develop elaborate evidentiary rules to police against the admission of unreliable or unduly prejudicial material. Some questions might be so complex and intricate that juries could simply not be expected to answer them (certainly not to answer them consistently). The private initiative on which the common-law courts relied had proved just as unsatisfactory. Individual litigants could hardly be expected to "set the law in motion" against either powerful business firms or the increasingly powerful state. Individuals were hopelessly overmatched by such powerful opponents. The common law's tradition of private enforcement, Pound concluded, was simply "not equal to the task" of administering justice in the twentieth century.[19]

In 1906, while still dean at Nebraska, Pound collected the critiques he had drawn from Ross into one of the most influential American criticisms of the common-law method ever delivered. Standing before the assembled self-styled guardians of the American common law at the annual meeting of the American Bar Association in Minneapolis, Pound delivered an address entitled "The Causes of Popular Dissatisfaction with the Administration of Justice." To be sure, Pound noted at the outset, "dissatisfaction with the administration of justice" was "as old as law." Nonetheless, he insisted, at the beginning of the twentieth century the "peculiarities" of Anglo-American law had generated widespread distrust and frustration with American governance by promoting legal form over the substantive administration of justice. In particular, Pound argued, American constitutionalism had wrongly favored common-law institutions where more efficient administrative management was required.[20]

The common-law tradition, Pound told the American Bar

Association's assembled delegates, depended too heavily on the private initiative of individuals to set it in motion. Indeed, the tradition of private control over the legal process, which Pound labeled the "sporting theory of justice" (making famous a phrase borrowed from Dean John Henry Wigmore of the Northwestern University Law School in Chicago), had become a chief source of popular dissatisfaction with the administration of justice. The "common-law doctrine of contentious procedure," Pound announced, "turns litigation into a game." The common-law theory, Pound had written in an article published a year earlier, was "that of a fair fist fight, according to the canons of the manly art, with a court to see to fair play and prevent interference." In practice, however, the common-law trial too closely resembled a cockfight in which the litigant whose bird had "the best pluck and the sharpest spurs" won. Worst of all, the sporting theory had transformed into a grave defect what Tocqueville had considered a distinctively American virtue three quarters of a century before. Under the influence of the sporting theory, American law had essentially committed important questions of law and public policy to the gamesmanship of private parties. Notwithstanding the grave defects of lay juries and private enforcement, the common law had made matters of great public import into "legal questions" to be resolved "as incidents of private litigation."[21]

In Pound's view, the central error of the common law was to rest so much responsibility in the hands of private parties without inquiring into social conditions that might hinder private enforcement. The "individual is supposed at common law," Pound observed, "to be able to look out for himself and to need no administrative protection." But the equality among parties on which the system of private enforcement relied was a chimera. The common law's individualism ignored that under modern social conditions "theoretical equality" was belied by the brute fact of actual and ubiquitous social inequality. Viewed sociologically, the theoretical equality of the parties gave "certain litigants a conspicuous advantage." Pound affirmed the claim of sociologist Lester Ward—a mentor of Pound's friend Edward Ross—that "much of the discussion about 'equal rights' was thus utterly hollow." Pound agreed with progressive economist Richard Ely that legal equality was a "mere juggling with words and empty legal phrases." For too long, Pound argued, the common law had adhered to "purely juristic notions of the state and of economics and politics" rather than adapting to "the social conceptions of the present."[22]

Justice, Pound contended (quoting the progressive economist John Commons), was "not merely fair play between individuals," but "fair play between social classes." In place of the "legal idea of justice" as "the liberty of each limited only by the like liberties of all," Pound thus proposed that the law reorganize itself around the sociologists' social-utilitarian theory of social justice: "the satisfaction of everyone's wants so far as they are not outweighed by others' wants." In Pound's conception, the question of the twentieth century seemed to be whether "the mass of mankind should have a right, not merely to pursue, but to realize the greatest possible measure of happiness," regardless of individual inequalities of skill, intelligence, and strength. And so, one year after his American Bar Association address, Pound spoke with cautious approval of "the drift toward equality in the satisfaction of wants rather than equality in freedom of action." Equality of results, not just equality of opportunity, was the new "standard of justice." Indeed, the new "watchword" of the law seemed no longer to be "freedom of will" or "freedom of individual activity," but rather the "satisfaction of human wants" and "a standard of living . . . as shall make possible a full moral life" for each individual. It was no longer enough "to give to everyone a free road, relieved of physical interference by the strong and protected against fraud and deception." "Social interests," not rights, were accordingly the guiding principle for Pound's conception of a sociological approach to remaking American law.[23]

Pound's thinking about the shift from courts to administration drew heavily on examples from the continental European civil-law tradition. (Laura Pound's early instruction in foreign languages paid off handsomely for her son.) As Pound noted in 1907, the tendency to adopt sociological methods and administrative procedures was "already well-marked in Continental Europe." Indeed, by the early part of the twentieth century, the imbalance between law and administration seemed to be a peculiarly American or Anglo-American phenomenon. Common-law thinking, Pound contended in articles and addresses alike, all too often took historically contingent legal principles peculiar to the Anglo-American tradition and invested them with the status of natural truths, spuriously converting the particular and partial principles of the common law into "fundamental conceptions of all legal science" or "the legal order of nature." The result was a self-destructive common-law chauvinism. It was "a grave reproach to American legal science," Pound insisted, that the new developments in jurisprudence "upon the Continent, are all but unknown to us." In the past, Pound contended, it had "been no bar to the reception of ideas into our law that they were modern or that they came clothed in a foreign tongue." To the contrary, the view that "sees danger in any contact of common law with modern Continental philosophy is wholly out of line with the best traditions of American legal science." Indeed, Pound noted, one needed "only to look at the law lectures of James Wilson" at the time of the nation's founding to see how thoroughly American conceptions of the relation between the individual and the state were the product of interactions between the common law and the Dutch and French jurists of the seventeenth and eighteenth centuries.[24]

The continental civil-law tradition seemed to Pound to offer an alternative to the common law's reliance on private initiative. Moreover, administrative commissions on the Western European model promised to substitute the new sociologically based economics Pound had learned from Ross and Ely for the classical and conservative economics of the Anglo-American common law. Where the common-law courts seemed to be *individualistic* institutions designed for a minimalist, night-watchman state that guaranteed only a narrow class of negative rights, the incipient administrative institutions of the twentieth century seemed to be *social* institutions, designed to serve the positive needs of modern citizens.

Pound's 1906 American Bar Association address drew him to the attention of leading lights in the law, including Dean Wigmore at Northwestern. In 1907, Pound left Lincoln, Nebraska, for Chicago to join the Northwestern faculty. Two years later, he moved across town to the University of Chicago, and one year after that Dean Ezra Thayer at Harvard tapped him to return to Cambridge as a member of the Harvard Law School faculty. At each stage in his journey back across the Midwest, Pound encountered new opportunities to develop and apply his sociologically inflected analysis of the common law and administration. Chicago in particular was a hotbed of reform. In part through the sociological connections of his Nebraska colleague Edward Ross, Pound met and began to work with progressive economists such as Richard Ely, as well as progressive reformers like Paul Kellogg and William Hard, both of whom had played important roles in the enactment of workmen's compensation legislation. A former student introduced Pound to Jane Addams's Hull House operation, where he was soon giving lectures. Through Addams, in turn, Pound began to work with the Chicago Juvenile Court, a pathbreaking institution in the administration of sociological justice. And in 1916, Pound defended the progressive Child Labor Act in the case of *Hammer v. Dagenhart*. The statute was struck down by the Supreme Court, but Pound's bold (if unsuccessful) arguments at the trial court stage cemented his place as a leading member of the progressive reform community.[25]

Pound's tireless lecturing around the country, his pithy and emphatic style, and his interactions with leading progressives of the day made him an inspiration for a rising generation of lawyers dedicated to increasing the capacity of the administrative state. His American Bar Association address launched a movement to overthrow the "sporting theory of justice," a movement that came to partial fruition in a new Federal Code of Civil Procedure enacted in 1938. The Brandeis Brief of 1908, named after its author, progressive lawyer Louis Brandeis, famously adopted Pound's emphasis on sociological fact over legalistic theory to defend successfully the constitutionality of a maximum-hours law for women workers. And Pound deeply influenced young progressive lawyers, including Felix Frankfurter, who joined the Harvard Law School faculty in 1914 and who would go on to be one of the architects of the New Deal through his relationship with Franklin Roosevelt. Frankfurter joined the Harvard faculty because of Pound. "With Pound there," he wrote to Judge Learned Hand in 1913, working with the Harvard faculty would present the opportunity "to fashion a jurisprudence adequate to our industrial and economic needs." Indeed, Frankfurter and the New Dealers among his students—men like James Landis and Thomas Corcoran—continued for decades to draw on Pound's ideas to establish new administrative institutions in the American state.[26]

Yet even as Pound's influence grew and even as a new generation of critics of the common law (many of whom styled themselves "legal realists") followed in his path, Pound began to draw back from many of the positions he took well into the 1920s. There had always been a conservative streak running through Pound's thinking on administration and the common law. The evolutionary model of legal development he had drawn from Charles Bessey's botany courses encouraged Pound to think favorably of growth and change from common-law beginnings. But Pound's theory of legal evolution did not necessarily countenance radical departures from the law's historical foundations. Like his old Nebraska colleague Edward A. Ross, who eventually became concerned that his theories of social control threatened to extinguish the individual altogether, Pound worried about abandoning the kinds of legal checks on the power of the state that had been the hallmark of the common-law system for centuries. What was needed, Pound asserted in 1908, was a pragmatic middle way between the dangers of "State omnipotence" on the one hand, and the "atomistic and artificial view of individual independence" on the other.[27]

Pound's conservative streak grew stronger as he grew older. Perhaps it was the influence of Northwestern's John Henry Wigmore, who sought to reform the judiciary rather than replace judges with bureaucratic administrative officials. Perhaps it was the effects of his Harvard deanship, which by the end of his twenty-year stint had become riven with bitter personality conflicts. Maybe it was the death of Pound's first wife, Grace, in 1928. Or perhaps it was the sharp differences between the temperamentally conservative Pound and the enthusiastic members of a new school of legal thought that claimed to follow in his footsteps, the so-called legal realists. In Pound's 1931 exchange with Columbia Law School legal realist Karl Llewellyn, for example, Pound inveighed bitterly against what he viewed as the "polemics" and "dogmatic rejections" characteristic of the realists' views of American law.[28]

Among the best explanations for Pound's drift away from administration may be the psychological insight offered by Willa Cather when she observed Pound in Nebraska in the 1980s. The same theory was advanced again in 1948 by a young and soon to be famous lawyer named William Kunstler. Cather and Kunstler both sensed in Pound a powerful conformity and a deep urge to please. Cather thought Pound was filled with "a petty traditionary sort of enthusiasm." Pound, she wrote in a University of Nebraska newspaper, sought most of all "to perpetuate his own name and fame." Kunstler, who in the 1960s would become a celebrity in his own right for representing civil rights workers and political radicals, suggested that underneath the charisma and the scholarly bravado, Pound seemed to have a "strange and deep shyness" that made him a deeply conformist person. As a self-consciously nonconformist New Yorker, Kunstler thought this trait characteristically midwestern. But whatever its origins, the prairie-born Pound had sought to please and impress from the time he left botany for law to accommodate his father. From at least the time of his 1906 American Bar Association speech, Pound seems quietly to have thrilled at the adulation of his nationwide audiences of jurists. What Pound perfected in his American Bar Association address and in the years thereafter was the ability to situate himself right at the boundaries of his audience's tolerance—to provoke, but never to disturb, to be iconoclastic and forceful but never radical or revolutionary, to startle while confirming his audience's deepest convictions.[29]

As the legal realists and other self-styled radicals outflanked him to the left, advancing more and more audacious criticisms of the common-law tradition, it became harder and harder for Pound to capture the attention of bar association and Harvard alumni audiences with mild reformist messages, no matter how forcefully articulated. Pound had been willing even in the first years of his career to moderate his progressivism when a conservative audience demanded it ("he wanted to please them," writes his biographer N. E. H. Hull).[30] By the 1930s, right-leaning addresses seemed to draw the most attention. Alarmist defenses of the common-law tradition against the incursions of the radicals, it seemed, offered a new way to engage lawyer audiences, titillating them while producing the adulation and approval that Pound (as Cather and Kunstler shrewdly noted) so desperately sought.

By the early 1930s, what another of Pound's biographers has called "the creative period" in Pound's intellectual life gave way to increasingly vituperative denunciations of the very jurisprudential ideas for which Pound had once stood. Indeed, by the middle of the decade, Pound's conservative streak had turned deeply reactionary. In the spring of 1934, Pound created a storm of controversy by praising Hitler for his opposition to socialism. (As Charles Beard incisively observed, Nazi Germany had been courting Pound's attentions for months.)[31] Closer to home, after resigning from the Harvard deanship in 1936, Pound became one of the most outspoken opponents of the New Deal and its new administrative agencies.

The New Deal brought out Pound's lurking conservatism. The Pound of the first two decades of the twentieth century might have been expected to look with sympathy on Franklin Roosevelt's economic bill of rights. From his presidential campaign in 1932 onward, Roosevelt echoed Pound's early theory of political economy as the science of the "satisfaction of human wants." During his presidency, Roosevelt made "security" the watchword of his economic plans—plans that culminated in the Social Security Act of 1935, providing collective insurance against the risks of old age and unemployment. Again and again, Roosevelt emphasized the social interest in ensuring that Americans, and indeed people around the world, experienced "freedom from want." In 1943 and again in his State of the Union address of January 1944, Roosevelt issued what he styled a "second Bill of Rights": a basic charter of economic freedoms that would establish "a new basis of security and prosperity." Roosevelt's New Deal vision of economic freedom and social security seemed to realize the shift Pound had described decades before, from an economics of freedom to an economics of satisfaction and security.[32]

Yet for all the parallels between New Deal ideas and Pound's early sociological jurisprudence, the increasingly dyspeptic Pound was anything but sympathetic with Roosevelt's program. Working with the Republican National Committee and the American Bar Association, Pound led a frontal assault on the administrative law being created by Roosevelt's New Deal. The President's expansion of administration, Pound contended, was "thoroughly in keeping with the Marxian idea of the disappearance of law." Administrative action, Pound wrote in a widely discussed American Bar Association report in 1938, proceeded lawlessly, without notice to or hearings for the interested parties. Administrators seemed to make determinations according to caprice and prejudice rather than reasoned analysis of the evidence. Agencies dangerously combined rule-making, investigative, prosecutorial, and adjudicative functions, and as a result tended to construe legal questions in their own favor and against the individuals who fell within their jurisdiction. They "yield[ed] to political pressure" and "administrative convenience" at "the expense of the law," alternating between partisan politics and "a perfunctory routine" that was almost as bad. Absent the rigorous oversight of administration by common-law judges (the very judges whose limitations Pound had been among the first to highlight), Pound insisted that "we may as well give up all pretense of being a constitutional democracy and set up an avowed dictatorship."[33]

Roosevelt's New Deal marked a high point in the federal government's support for a new generation of social rights, but Pound would have none of it. The welfare state—or the "service state," as he described it—too closely resembled a "charitably minded pickpocket." The Wagner Act and the New Deal regime of collective bargaining between labor unions and employers, Pound announced, conferred odious special privileges on union leaders, illegitimately immunizing them from the legal duties incumbent on their fellow citizens. Pound condemned the administrative agencies and bureaucracies that the "service state" necessarily seemed to entail as inimical to the rule of law. Courts simply would not be able to enforce the new social rights that Roosevelt's New Deal seemed to promise. Could a poor man sue to gain relief from his poverty? It seemed clear to Pound that the answer was necessarily a resounding no. The "service state could never be attained through the courts or other legal means," he declared. Any attempt to implement a new economic deal for the United States would therefore inevitably entail dangerous expansion of discretionary administration. In the 1950s, Pound even opposed the election of Republican presidential candidate Dwight Eisenhower on the ground that Eisenhower had refused to say that he would roll back New Deal welfare policies.[34]

Pound's prestige, his charisma, and his fondness for appreciative audiences—precisely the traits that had endeared him to progressive reformers—soon made him a senior statesman of the anticommunist far right. By the 1950s, he had become deeply involved with the angry fringe of the China lobby, which was pushing for the investigation of the State Department's actions in the communist takeover of China in 1949. At around the same time, he was serving as vice-chairman of the Council Against Communist Aggression, an anticommunist organization with close ties to the far right John Birch Society. (The decisions of American administrative agencies, he wrote to the Council's corresponding secretary, were a "veritable chamber of horrors" filled with "lawless high-handedness.")[35]

Pound seemed to have adopted as his own what the historian Richard Hofstadter would soon call "the paranoid style."[36] As Pound moved into his seventies, he might have been discounted as just one more right-wing opponent of the New Deal reorganization of American government. But as Roosevelt haters faded from the scene, Pound's powerful longing for appreciative audiences and his increasingly vituperative defenses of the common law caught the attention of a new group: the trial lawyers. In what would be the final chapter of his extraordinarily productive and eccentrically varied life, Pound hitched himself to a quickly emerging and—with his help—increasingly powerful interest group that coupled his vitriolic opposition to the administrative state with the resources and energies of American interest-group politics.

*
*
*

Melvin Mouron Belli was born in 1907, in Sonora, California, at the southern end of what had been California Gold Rush country only fifty years before. Like the prairie town of Lincoln, Nebraska, in which Pound had grown up, the mountains of northern California must have seemed far away from controversies about administrative commissions and the twentieth-century state. Lincoln at least boasted a university and a handful of intellectuals like Charles Bessey, Edward Ross, and Willa Cather. Sonora, by contrast, could have been the setting of a cowboy western. As Belli later described it, the town had been "settled by quick-thinking, self-reliant young men who didn't play it safe and didn't go by the book."[37]

Belli's "pioneer family," as he called it, fit right in. His tough-as-nails grandmother, Anna Mouron, was known locally as the first woman pharmacist in the state of California. Belli's father, Caesar Arthur Belli, was a nattily dressed, sometimes flamboyant local banker, vintner, and investor, who chafed against the constraints imposed by a disapproving wife. As his investments turned south, Caesar began to drink and have affairs. Prohibition only made matters worse for the wine business, and Caesar went bankrupt while his only son Melvin was a teenager. Leonie

Mouron Belli played the role of the doting mother and proper wife, whose moralizing strictures prompted rebellion in husband and son alike.[38] Melvin, it seems, spent much of his life—and most of six marriages, all but the last ending in divorce—in rebellion against his mother, trying to vindicate the life his father had charted before him.

From an early age, Belli seems to have made rebellion against authority his central life project, and he soon identified law as a powerful mechanism for rebellion. Pound's contemporary and Frankfurter's correspondent, the great Judge Learned Hand of the United States Court of Appeals, once said that he dreaded litigation "beyond almost anything else short of sickness and death." But Belli thrived on it. As a student, he sued the high school principal for withholding his diploma after drunkenness caused him to miss his own address as class valedictorian ("I was attacked by a bottle of whiskey," Belli later pleaded). High school officials promptly delivered Belli's diploma, and his fascination with the power of litigation had begun. Once you knew "how to handle it," Belli said of the law, it turned out you could "have a lot of fun" with it. "When I realized that," Belli recounted, "I knew I'd be a lawyer."[39]

After four years at the University of California at Berkeley filled with fraternity high jinks, Belli attended Berkeley's School of Jurisprudence from 1930 to 1933 and entered into his career as gladiator of the courtroom. His early work was in criminal defense. From the start Belli sought out cases that would garner public attention, and criminal defense work was certainly capable of doing that. Yet Belli soon identified personal injury law as a field in which his flair for the dramatic could be yoked to a more lucrative future than criminal defense could afford. In 1943, he won his first plaintiff's verdict in a personal injury case. Chester Bryant, a cable-car employee of the Market Street Railway Company, was injured when the cable apparatus powering two crossing cable cars became tangled. Belli invested $300 for a model of the cable car to demonstrate to the jurors exactly what had happened. He then used a blackboard to take the jurors step by step through the injuries his client had received and the damages they had caused, including pain and suffering. Lo and behold, the jury came back in Bryant's favor with a verdict of $27,500, of which Belli probably kept somewhere between $9,000 and $14,000.[40] Belli had learned the power of courtroom dramatics, and he had taken his first step toward becoming the nation's most famous plaintiffs' tort lawyer.

By the 1950s, Belli's courtroom theatrics in tort cases had become legendary. The *Washington Post* reported that he was part lawyer and part actor. He typically arrived at the courthouse looking like a cross between a robber baron and a court jester. He painted and repainted his Rolls Royce beige, purple, silver, black, and rose. ("Even a Rolls shouldn't be boring," Belli explained.) His standard courtroom outfit was a dark double-breasted suit (the finest from London's Savile Row) with a red silk lining over a custom-made shirt with a ruffled front and diamond studs. Robin Hood cuff links appeared at his wrists. On his feet he wore ankle-high, high-heeled, and perfectly polished black snakeskin "Congress gaiters" made to order by Peal's of London. He carried a wine-red velvet briefcase.[41]

Belli's courtroom behavior was as flamboyant as his dress. He provocatively wrapped the prosthetic of an amputee client in butcher paper, painstakingly unwrapping it in front of the jury to create the impression that it contained his client's own lost leg. He lifted a morbidly obese 682-pound client through the courtroom window with a crane, ostensibly to display the man's helplessness to the jury. He paraded a jury past the luridly exposed breasts of a client whose enhancement surgery had gone badly awry. And when he won a judgment, Belli seemed likely to stop at nothing to get the money that was coming to him and his client. On one occasion, he even obtained a writ of execution against the San Francisco Giants for one "Willie Mays, a prime asset of the San Francisco Giants" (Belli also attached liens on the team's "bats, balls, gloves, uniforms, and bar whiskey").[42]

Yet Belli's practice was not made up merely of courtroom theatrics. The tort field in which Belli began to work was shot through with doctrines inherited from the nineteenth century that sharply limited the liability of defendants ranging from landowners to charitable hospitals to product manufacturers. From the early 1940s on, Belli aimed to abolish these liability-limiting doctrines and to make the law of torts friendlier to injured plaintiffs.

One of the very first cases Belli tried was a case that would come to be known as "the case of the exploding bottle"—*Escola v. Coca-Cola Bottling Company.* Belli represented waitress Gladys Escola in her suit for damages suffered when a bottle of Coca-Cola exploded in her hand. Product liability cases were notoriously difficult for plaintiffs to win. It was often impossible to prove the negligence necessary to win product liability claims, and plaintiffs in California regularly lost such cases. Belli insisted, however, that the mere fact that the bottle exploded was evidence from which a jury might draw an inference of negligence by the bottling company. Against the weight of prior decisions going the other way, the California Supreme Court upheld Gladys Escola's claim on just these grounds. The doctrine on which Belli relied— the doctrine of *res ipsa loquitor* ("the thing speaks for itself")— seemed primed to open up the field of product liability for victims of defective products.[43]

Indeed, the *Escola* case did even more for the law of product liability than Belli could have hoped. Justice Roger Traynor, who was one of Belli's law teachers while Belli was a student at Berkeley, wrote a concurring opinion arguing that courts should abandon altogether the requirement that plaintiffs show the negligence of the product manufacturer or distributor. It should be enough, Traynor contended, that the Coca-Cola Bottling Company placed the bottle on the market and that the product then caused injury. As a distributor of Coca-Cola bottles, Traynor reasoned, the bottling company was better positioned to prevent the injury than were users like Gladys Escola. Moreover, the bottling company was better positioned to spread the loss among the pool of Coca-Cola purchasers. The company could simply charge slightly higher prices to its customers and thereby create an ersatz insurance system for those customers unlucky enough to be injured.[44]

Traynor's concurring opinion in *Escola* ultimately proved more influential than the ostensibly authoritative opinion of the court. It presaged what would be a generation of torts cases that transformed manufacturers' responsibility to people injured by their products. Over the next two decades, Traynor's idea of strict liability, or liability without negligence, rippled across American tort law. Lawyers and judges in the torts field would spend much of the next half-century working out its implications.[45]

Cases such as *Escola* suggested to Belli that plaintiffs' tort lawyers could remake the law. (The "winds of change" were "blowing through the world," wrote Belli on the occasion of the *Escola* decision.) Lawyer-entrepreneurs, Belli argued, might make the common law into a system of justice that could work for the individual even against insurance companies and giant corporations. To be sure, the lawyer might be "a gladiator for sale to the highest bidder." But that was not a flaw in the adversary system so much as its genius. Hired-gun gladiators, Belli argued, could ensure that the "total war" model of trial by battle would lead to the rigorous presentation of the facts to an impartial jury. As Belli put it on more than one occasion, "the sparks of conflict" could be counted on to "shed the light by which justice may be seen." And with the help of the contingent fee, under which mid-twentieth-century plaintiffs' lawyers took between one-third and one-half of the awards they negotiated or won for their clients, the gladiator for hire might be turned to the service of the wronged individual. Even if the only motive for serving the public good was money, Belli wrote in defense of the plaintiffs' bar, "still we must serve well or we won't make money." The adversary system thus need not produce the dysfunctions Pound had identified in 1906. It might instead redound to what Belli—now sounding not unlike the young Pound—called the "greatest social benefit."[46]

Belli's insight was to realize that in the field of personal injury, solving the inequality of position that had soured Pound on the adversary process did not require replacing the common law with administrative alternatives. The personal injury claim, Belli realized, was susceptible to being treated as "a commodity to sell," to which all of the techniques of modern mass marketing might be applied. To be sure, the "economic system," Belli wrote in his autobiography, seemed to be "stacked against the little man." Giant firms had "unbelievable amounts" of money. They "had entire firms of lawyers to help them in their struggle," while there were "damn few attorneys ready to fight on the other side." But if the plaintiff-sellers of personal injury claims could have the same sophistication, similar economies of scale, and as much expertise as the defendant-buyers, the inequality of plaintiff and defendant in the personal injury field could be resolved by market solutions instead of administrative ones.[47]

And so Belli made it his mission to even up the sides in litigation between the one-shot individual litigants and the sophisticated repeat players. Where Pound and his fellow critics of the sporting theory had argued that inequality between the parties doomed the adversarial system of the common law to systematically unequal results, Belli saw opportunity for ambitious plaintiffs' representatives. If Belli could make personal injury cases pay, if he could make a living in them, and if lawyers like him around the country could take up the market opportunity provided by tort law, "then maybe the poor man in America could have as much justice as the rich man" without the bureaucracies of the administrative state.[48]

*
*
*

Even Melvin Belli, with all his ambition and self-confidence, could not level the playing field of the courtroom on his own. When he sued tobacco companies for causing cancer in his smoker-clients, for example, he lost every time—nineteen times, to be exact. Defendants in such cases had far more at stake than any one plaintiff (the defendant who lost, after all, would likely be subject to many more suits), and the deep pockets of such defendants often made them too powerful, even for Belli. Worse yet, the performance of his peers in the trial bar inevitably affected the outcomes of his own cases. When other plaintiffs' lawyers failed to extract the highest value from their cases, they dragged down the going rates for verdicts and settlements. Belli liked to say that just "one award" could raise the standard for damages appropriate in a particular jurisdiction. But by the same token, a single low award could reduce the damages available. In the contingent-fee system, those lower awards went straight to the plaintiffs' lawyer's bottom line. What was needed, it seemed, was a mechanism for organizing the plaintiffs' bar—a mechanism for improving its image and for creating institutions on the plaintiffs' side that would approximate the information-sharing, loss-spreading, and expertise advantages that the repeat-play defendants and insurance companies typically brought to the personal injury claims process.[49]

In 1946, a small group of workmen's compensation claimant lawyers at a Portland, Oregon, meeting hosted by insurers and employers' representatives (just one of many institutions for the sharing of information and the coordination of legislative efforts among the defense bar) established the National Association of Claimants' Compensation Attorneys. The energetic organizer of the NACCA was a Boston workmen's compensation lawyer named Samuel Horovitz. Like many claimants'-side personal injury lawyers in the first half of the twentieth century, Horovitz was Jewish. Unlike many personal injury lawyers then or now, however, Horovitz had graduated from Harvard Law School. After a short stint as an insurance company claims adjuster in the 1920s, Horovitz switched sides and began to represent the Massachusetts Federation of Labor and its members in workmen's compensation matters. Two decades later, Horovitz was among the NACCA's founding members.[50]

By 1949, Horovitz was spreading the gospel of NACCA membership far and wide. He even took his family on a three-month, 10,800-mile tour across the South and the Southwest in a silver aluminum Airstream trailer to establish local chapters and branches of the NACCA. On the "Silver Bullet Tour," as plaintiffs' lawyers would later remember it, "Sam the Vacationer" made a name for himself as a Jewish "Billy Graham of the plaintiffs' bar." His meetings with local trial lawyers were like the revival meetings of evangelical ministers, and the unlikely Horovitz signed up hundreds of new members to the organization. The organization "sprang like wildfire" from state to state. From a membership of 35 lawyers in 1947 and 300 in 1948, the organization grew to some 5,000 lawyers in 1956, more than 7,000 in 1961, and almost 22,000 in 1967. Where 30 members had shown up at the 1948 meeting of the NACCA, some 500 members appeared at the 1950 convention, and some 1,200 at the 1954 convention in Boston. The new members established separate regional meetings of the NACCA, while prominent plaintiffs' lawyers and NACCA officers went on national tours to add even more members and chapters.[51]

If Horovitz had created the NACCA as a kind of tent revival

for the plaintiffs' bar, Melvin Belli elevated the group to what plaintiffs' lawyers like Sam Charfoos of Michigan would later remember as "legal ecstasy." Belli joined the NACCA in 1949 at its Cleveland convention, and within just a few short years observers commented that "when personal injury men think of NACCA it is generally Melvin M. Belli they have in mind." In 1951, the NACCA elected Belli president of the organization. With his Hollywood good looks and powerful charisma, Belli barnstormed around the country speaking to bar associations on the growth and progress of the plaintiffs' bar.[52]

Belli's membership marked an important turning point for the NACCA. Workmen's compensation lawyers had founded the organization to increase the clout of claimants and their representatives in the administration of workmen's compensation programs. Belli realized that the organization could offer some of the same benefits to plaintiffs' lawyers in the tort system. Indeed, the organization could not only help workmen's compensation lawyers reform the administrative system, but also give common-law tort lawyers new lobbying clout with which to hold off the further spread of the administrative systems that threatened their livelihood. In 1960, the organization changed its name to the National Association of Claimants' Counsel of America to de-emphasize the workmen's compensation focus. Just four years later, the organization stripped away all trace of its administrative beginnings when it renamed itself the American Trial Lawyers Association, later amended to Association of Trial Lawyers of America.[53]

Under Belli's leadership, the organization that would become ATLA lobbied judges and legislatures for liberalized tort liability rules. "We need legislation," Belli announced at the 1954 NACCA convention in Boston. "We need a lobby." Judge-made law, too, it turned out, was susceptible to the influence of well-organized interest groups. NACCA regional and national conventions were scheduled and organized so as to bring in as many judges and legislators as possible, all of whom were afforded princely treatment.[54]

Perhaps more important still, however, were the systems of education and information sharing that the NACCA established. Networks of information sharing, recalled one member of the founding generation of the modern plaintiffs' bar, were the tools with which the early entrepreneur-lawyers fashioned tort law "into a real weapon for the consumer." The NACCA's mailing list alone provided a new way to coordinate lawyers with litigation service providers such as investigators, medical analysts, and expert witnesses. But the organization quickly became much more than just a mailing list. By 1952, observers were calling the NACCA conventions a traveling "postgraduate school" for lawyers, teaching techniques that Belli and a small group of others had pioneered. At that summer's convention in the fabulous air-conditioned Shamrock Hotel in Houston ("Houston's Riviera," as it was known to Texas oilmen—or a "tragic imitation of Rockefeller Center out here on the prairie," as Frank Lloyd Wright called it), Belli established what came to be called the "Belli Seminars": two-day sessions immediately preceding each NACCA convention, at which the requisite Belli carousing and bedlam were joined with valuable training in the latest advances in trial and settlement practices. From 8:30 in the morning to midnight each day, Belli's "famous pre-Convention courses" brought together lawyers from around the country to share information on expert witnesses, product defects, and more.[55]

The spirit of the Belli Seminars spread through the organization. In 1958, NACCA president Al Julien established a rudimentary filing system of index cards kept in shoeboxes in his New York office. NACCA members contributed information about cases they had litigated, listing effective plaintiffs'-side expert witnesses and sharing especially effective cross-examination material with which to impugn defense experts. In turn, members could access Julien's index cards for help with new cases. Within a few short years, Julien's shoeboxes had grown into the "ATLA Exchange," a massive collection of information for the plaintiffs' bar that collected in one centralized location evidence against "a rogues gallery of products liability defendants."[56]

Most of all, Belli and the NACCA focused their sights on raising damages awards and settlement values in the tort system. From the very first issue of the *NACCA Law Journal,* published in 1948, NACCA members decried the "meagre verdicts" that they claimed were all too typical of the tort system. Samuel Horovitz and the *NACCA Law Journal*'s editors took it upon themselves to publish reports of verdicts or settlement amounts in excess of $50,000 in hopes of bringing out models that would support higher verdicts in subsequent cases. When Belli came on board as president in 1951, he made raising damages awards the central focus of his organizing efforts. "If awards were low in some states," Belli thundered, "by God" he would "bring them up." And, of course, because Belli and his colleagues were paid on a contingency basis, higher awards translated into higher fees.[57]

Belli's article "The Adequate Award," published in 1951 in the *California Law Review,* aimed to raise the dollar values involved in personal injury cases across the board. Baseball players were being paid $100,000 a season; racehorses were being sold for $300,000; paintings and violins went for half a million dollars. Yet personal injury damages awards, Belli asserted, had failed to keep up with increased prices for everything, from haircuts and housing to college and Cadillacs. Instead, "appallingly inadequate verdicts" typified the field of personal injury. Belli assembled reports of as many "adequate awards" as he could, reciting the essential facts of the underlying injury and noting the jury award that had been granted to compensate for those injuries. Searching across California and in states around the country, Belli compiled not just jury awards reported in the decisions of appellate courts, but also the more numerous jury awards that had not made it into appellate reports but were known to local pockets of personal injury practitioners familiar with the cases. The aim, as Belli made abundantly clear, was to ensure that personal injury plaintiffs were restored to dignity by awards commensurate with the damages incurred and "restorative by today's economic standards."[58]

The efforts of the plaintiffs' bar seem to have paid off many times over. By the middle of the 1950s, organizations of defendants and their lawyers were noting with some trepidation the beginnings of an ominous upward trend in damages verdicts, one that they attributed increasingly to the advocacy of Belli and his colleagues in the NACCA. "Mr. Belli and his cohorts are no fly by nights, no flash-in-the-pans," wrote the editors of the *Insurance Counsel Journal*. Increasing damages awards were only the beginning of the story. Led by the Supreme Court in Belli's home state of California, courts around the country in the 1950s and 1960s liberalized tort liability. Product liability decisions like the one Belli worked on in the *Escola* case dramatically expanded the potential liability of sellers and manufacturers of consumer products. As ATLA's onslaught on the stingy rules of nineteenth-century tort law continued, courts reversed and abolished the old liability-limiting rules, leaving landowners, product manufacturers, and charitable hospitals subject to significantly increased liability. And between 1950 and 1959, the total paid into the American tort system increased from $1.8 billion to $5.4 billion, almost doubling as a share of the U.S. economy from .6 percent to 1 percent of gross domestic product. During the 1960s, the American tort system grew at an annual rate of just under 10 percent, closing out the decade as almost 1.5 percent of the gross domestic product.[59]

In virtually every important instance in which courts expanded tort liability toward more liberal standards of recovery, NACCA and ATLA members were involved as counsel for the plaintiff. Following close behind Belli's *Escola* victory, ATLA lawyers smashed through common-law limitations on product liability. ATLA lawyers broke down the old common-law rules protecting landowners from liability for dangerous conditions on their land and charitable hospitals from liability for the malpractice of their doctors. They dismantled the requirement that victims suffer physical impact in cases of emotional injury. They pushed into new frontiers such as the liability of auto manufacturers for vehicles that proved uncrashworthy. And they supplied a new generation of crusading consumer rights' advocates—people like Ralph Nader—with information about unsafe products. The pathbreaking Nader campaign against the Chevrolet Corvair *(Unsafe at Any Speed)* drew on information Nader gleaned from litigation planning sessions at the NACCA.[60]

One of the NACCA's most important projects even raised the interest of Roscoe Pound, for in its new guise as an organization of tort lawyers, the NACCA and its successors had begun to fight not for the reform of administrative programs like workmen's compensation, but for their limitation and abolition. Any time that administrative compensation proposals threatened to spread into areas governed by the common law of tort, the NACCA could be counted on to object vociferously. From the perspective of the common-law plaintiffs' lawyer, administrative systems that promised to sharply limit lawyers' fees were anathema. And that conviction brought the country's fledgling trial lawyers—a group that had begun as an organization of claimants' lawyers working in the administrative system of workmen's compensation—together with an aging, but still extraordinarily energetic, Roscoe Pound.

*
*
*

The NACCA's "greatest coup," chroniclers of the plaintiffs' bar would later recall, was signing up Roscoe Pound. Pound and Belli met in 1951 when Belli opened his presidential speaking tour for the NACCA with an address Sam Horovitz arranged at Harvard Law School. The next year, Pound spoke at the NACCA Western Regional Conference in Los Angeles and applauded plaintiffs' lawyers for improving the administration of justice. Pound appeared again at the NACCA Convention in Houston in August 1952. And in July 1953, on what would later be described as a "fortuitous day" for plaintiffs' lawyers everywhere, the NACCA appointed Pound editor in chief of the *NACCA Law Journal*. The man whom Horovitz and the NACCA announced as "the nation's foremost legal scholar" took up an office in Horovitz's plaintiffs'-side law firm in Boston.[61]

In part, Pound seems to have been motivated by financial concerns in his retirement. He had long complained that his Harvard pension was inadequate, and according to Pound the *NACCA Law Journal* position provided him with much-needed additional income. Yet money may not have been the primary reason Pound joined the NACCA. By the early 1950s, Pound seems to have been increasingly isolated, and even lonely. Pound had wanted to have children, but neither he and his first wife Grace, who died in 1928, nor he and his second wife Lucy, whom he married when she was forty-eight years old, ever had any. (His two sisters, neither of whom ever married, did not have children either.) Moreover, Pound's status at Harvard was increasingly uncomfortable. Tensions from the end of his deanship continued to simmer, and for many of his colleagues, as Pound knew, his continued presence at the institution had become irksome. His colleagues described him as "nuttier and nuttier," and by the early 1960s, Pound privately described his place at the Law School as "embarrassing."[62]

At the NACCA, by contrast, Pound's prestige ensured celebrity status. The trial lawyers provided an organization of like-minded compatriots for the aging critic of administration. NACCA members and staff lawyers gushed and fawned over him at virtually every opportunity. Indeed, NACCA officials paid homage to Pound as a demigod among men even in their daily correspondence with him, proclaiming him second only to Socrates and complimenting him on his "astonishing vigor." Thomas Lambert, who succeeded Pound as editor in chief of the *NACCA Law Journal,* told the octogenarian former dean that he made "Hercules seem a sick-abed stripling and flyweight by comparison."[63]

What the NACCA gave Pound was the kind of appreciative and rapt audience of lawyers that Pound had sought out from the beginning of his career. Indeed, from the early 1950s until Pound's death in 1964, Melvin Belli and NACCA founder Samuel Horovitz came to figure as perhaps the most significant connections in Pound's life. Belli visited Pound regularly through the 1950s whenever he was in Boston on business. Horovitz, in particular, who lived in Boston and who had been a student at Harvard while Pound was dean, assiduously cultivated Pound's friendship. Between sometime in the early 1950s until shortly before Pound's death in 1964, Horovitz lunched each Saturday in Pound's home in Watertown, Massachusetts, just west of Cambridge. ("See you Saturday as usual," Horovitz scrawled on countless notes to the former dean in the 1950s.) After Pound's wife Lucy and his sister Louise died in quick succession, Horovitz appears to have been Pound's closest friend. When the Harvard-Yale football game was played in Cambridge, Horovitz would drive Pound to "The Game." On weekends, the Horovitz family would often have Pound to dinner. On such occasions, Ernst Bogusch, the executive director of the NACCA, would chauffeur Pound to the dinner and drive him home afterward. (Bogusch was also Pound's tenant; he rented the small house next door to Pound's larger Watertown home.) Horovitz spent the summer and fall of 1962 compiling a scrapbook of the former dean's press clippings and greeting cards. By 1963, a year before Pound died, Horovitz was keeping Pound in touch with his remaining sister, Olivia, handling his health insurance, keeping up his correspondence, and overseeing his medical care.[64]

For the NACCA, the addition of Pound was the capstone of a long campaign to bring prestigious figures in the law academy and the bench into the organization. Even before Pound joined as editor, Horovitz and the NACCA made grants to Pound as well as other scholars, such as Mark DeWolf Howe at Harvard, Arthur Larsen at Cornell, Stefan A. Riesenfeld at the University of Minnesota, Reginald Parker at the University of Arkansas, and Wex Malone at Louisiana State University. But nothing the NACCA had done before came close to matching the star power that Pound provided. The former dean was a whirlwind of activity. Picking up where Belli's 1951 national tour had left off, Horovitz and Pound barnstormed across the country, addressing bar association meetings and law school audiences and organizing the nation's plaintiffs' bar. Previous NACCA tours had exclusively targeted plaintiffs' lawyers, a traditionally low-status segment of the bar. Now Pound and the NACCA speakers he accompanied were met by large audiences of "the Judiciary, law school professors, local dignitaries, and lawyers from every field of legal endeavor." With Pound at their helm, Belli crowed, trial lawyers and the NACCA were now "about as shady and unsavory" as "the Harvard Law School."[65]

Pound resigned from his formal position as an NACCA official after two years. Harvard Law School's alumni, as its dean Erwin Griswold later recounted, "weren't too happy" about Pound's relationship with the trial lawyers. Dean Griswold identified a foundation grant that could substitute for Pound's NACCA salary and brought Pound back into his office in the Law School's Langdell Hall.[66]

Yet if Pound resigned his editorship at the NACCA, his ties to the NACCA grew stronger. Horovitz's weekly lunches with

Pound at the Watertown house continued apace. Notwithstanding his age, Pound remained extraordinarily energetic on behalf of the NACCA and the trial lawyers throughout the 1950s. Pound continued to travel, write, and speak widely on behalf of the NACCA, sometimes overseas in places like Ireland and Rome for NACCA junket-conventions, and often closer to home at NACCA national conventions and NACCA state chapter meetings from Oklahoma and Illinois to Pennsylvania and Massachusetts. The indefatigable Pound often gave multiple speeches in each city he visited, regularly speaking before law schools, civic groups, and bar associations multiple times each day. He lobbied on behalf of NACCA-favored judicial appointments. He weighed in on important cases. He broke out his Harvard Law School stationery to provide supportive legal opinions for members charged with ethics breaches by hostile local bar associations. And at Horovitz's encouragement, Pound wrote a glowing introduction to Belli's 1954 book, *Modern Trials*. The book's distillation of the techniques taught in the Belli Seminars and elsewhere, Pound wrote, made it "an indispensable book" for the modern trial lawyer. ("You have indeed a monumental work here," Pound wrote privately to Belli.)[67]

Belli and Pound corresponded regularly and even intimately in the 1950s on matters such as Belli's speaking engagements, the former dean's activities, and the newly dubbed King of Torts's cases. ("Dear Belli," the dean addressed his chummy letters.) Belli regularly sought out Pound to review briefs on especially delicate legal points. In 1955, for example, Belli brought Pound into the cases he was just starting to bring against tobacco companies on behalf of cancer-victim cigarette users. Indeed, through the NACCA connection, prominent plaintiffs' lawyers from around the country regularly sent along queries to Pound on complex points of law. On some occasions they even cited Pound's letters as legal authorities to the courts before which they were arguing.[68]

On Pound's NACCA speaking tours, even those who opposed the NACCA came out to see the man many of them called the "Father of American Jurisprudence." Judges from the high courts of numerous states and from the federal appellate courts—many of them Harvard Law School alumni from Pound's years as dean—now appeared at plaintiffs' bar gatherings that featured Pound as a speaker and honoree. In New Orleans, the mayor gave Pound the keys to the city. Pound's picture appeared on the cover of local plaintiffs' lawyer publications across the country. And state and local trial lawyers' associations around the nation made him an honorary member.[69]

In 1956, the trial lawyers cemented their relationship to Pound by purchasing Pound's Watertown home and turning it into a research center and think tank bearing Pound's name. The Watertown house had become too much for the aging Pound to handle, and so Horovitz gave Pound $25,000 for the home and donated it to the NACCA. Pound moved into the Commander Hotel in Cambridge, across from the Harvard Law School campus. The former Pound home became the headquarters of a new Roscoe Pound–NACCA Foundation, which beginning in the fall of 1956 served as a tax-exempt research adjunct to the NACCA.[70]

The purchase price of Pound's home was almost certainly worth every penny. Indeed, the cost of Pound's utility bills, which the NACCA paid for about a year before Horovitz purchased the home, was surely worth the money, too. Right up until shortly before his death in 1964, Pound continued to be deeply involved in, and exceedingly useful to, the NACCA. Through Pound, the NACCA maintained and indeed expanded its connections to the corridors of power in the state capitals and in Washington, D.C. Every October Horovitz and the NACCA threw birthday celebrations for Pound, attracting favorable press attention for the trial lawyers in addition to well-publicized goodwill messages to Pound and his hosts from Supreme Court justices, state supreme court judges, governors, and distinguished jurists at the finest law schools around the nation. (In 1960 alone, U.S. Supreme Court justices Hugo Black, William Brennan, Tom Clark, William O. Douglas, and Felix Frankfurter all sent their greetings.) Yale Law School's Fleming James gave the inaugural address at the Roscoe Pound–NACCA Foundation. And in 1961, Pound served as honorary chairman of the annual NACCA convention at which U.S. Supreme Court Justice Tom Clark delivered the opening address. By late 1962, Clark's chambers at the Supreme Court featured a photograph of Pound, Clark, and several NACCA officers on the occasion of Pound's ninety-second birthday. Thanks to Pound, the status-starved trial lawyers of the NACCA had at last reached the inner sanctums of American law.[71]

*
*
*

The trial lawyers were as useful for Pound as he was for them. In the trial lawyers and the NACCA, Pound identified an organization ready to join him in his battle against the encroachment of administration on the domain of the common law. By the 1950s, Pound had come to think of the choice facing industrialized nations as a stark one: adjudication or administration. The United States could either maintain its long-standing traditions of the rule of law or adopt the dangerous bureaucracies of modern collectivism.

Trial lawyers, Pound explained around the country, were a crucial common-law bulwark against modern totalitarianism. Common-law lawyers such as Sir Edward Coke had fought off the despotism of the Stuart monarchs in the seventeenth century. Three centuries later the trial lawyer held out the promise of doing the same in the worldwide battle against bureaucratic socialism and the "administrative machinery of the state." Lawyers practicing corporate law in the large urban law firms of the middle of the twentieth century, Pound believed, had become highly paid bureaucratic functionaries in the private sphere, office-based "client caretakers," as Pound put it. The traditional elite of the American bar had thus lost much of its vitality. But in the new trial lawyers' organization, Pound saw the old spirit of the common-law lawyer. The trial lawyer, Pound told audiences around the country, was "the uncompromising and inveterate foe of absolutism" and would resist the encroachments of the totalizing state "until communism or the millennium" brought an end to law altogether. Indeed, Pound believed that the trial lawyer distinguished the United States from continental Europe (and particularly the totalitarian states of Europe), where lawyers occupied a "subservient secondary position." In the energies of the NACCA, Pound found a "tough-minded independent body of lawyers willing and ready" to fight off totalitarianism of any stripe.[72]

And so, for most of the last decade of his life, Roscoe Pound's central project became working with Belli and the NACCA to hold off the spread of administrative agencies and government bureaucracies into the sphere of the common law of torts. From the beginning of Pound's involvement with the NACCA, the organization had opposed the expansion of the workmen's compensation administrative model to areas still governed by tort, such as maritime work and railroad employee injuries. Legislated benefit schedules, they insisted, had proven too susceptible to erosion by inflation and employers' political influence. And from 1949 onward—the year of Belli's admission to the organization—opposition to the spread of workmen's compensation and support for the common law of torts became the central pillars of the NACCA. The trial lawyers opposed American Bar Association resolutions to put railroad workers under state workmen's compensation programs, and they opposed congressional and AFL-CIO proposals to create new federal workmen's compensation administrations for railroad workers and seamen.[73]

By the early 1950s, the NACCA began to fight against administration on a new front, in the law of automobile accidents, and once again Pound performed yeoman's work for the organization. Since the 1910s, reformers and legislators around the country had shown interest in administrative automobile-injury compensation schemes modeled on workmen's compensation. The defects of the common law, in the view of no-fault compensation system supporters, were almost exactly as Pound had described them in 1906. The private law of torts relied too heavily on the scattershot private initiative of an uneven trial bar. It generated cumbersome and expensive legal processes and attendant delays in the compensation of needy victims and their families. And for victims who could not establish the fault of another driver, tort often produced no compensation at all. Administrative compensation systems, by contrast, would replace the costly and time-consuming fault determinations of the common law with streamlined administrative processes. Drivers would participate in mandatory insurance pools much like those that many employers were required to participate in by workers' compensation programs. When injured in an automobile accident, participating drivers would simply recover compensation from their own insurance policies rather than having to file tort claims on another driver's policy.[74]

By the 1950s, serious proposals to enact administrative compensation programs for automobile accident injuries were making headway in state legislatures across the United States. No-fault compensation bills even made it onto the congressional agenda. To many midcentury observers of American law, it seemed that such administrative compensation schemes would sweep away large swaths of the common law of personal injury in fields ranging from the law of accidents on common carriers and the law of utility company accidents to the law of injuries, in medical care.[75]

Administrative compensation proposals for automobile injuries, however, now faced opposition not merely from insurers, who had long opposed them, but also from the newly organized trial lawyers. As one ATLA official history recounted some years later, defending "the civil jury system" from administrative automobile-injury schemes was central to the organization's lobbying efforts. And from as early as 1952 at the NACCA's Houston convention, Pound was the organization's leading spokesman on the issue. Indeed, although Pound had opposed administration in virtually all its forms since at least the end of the 1930s, the substance of his criticisms subtly shifted to accommodate the interests and win the approval of the plaintiffs' bar. In 1940 and 1941, his chief complaint with administrative compensation systems was that they "put the claim of the workingman on a higher plane of value" than the claims of others. Under the auspices of the NACCA, by contrast, Pound now denounced administrative compensation schemes as establishing arbitrary and "grossly inadequate" schedules of compensation.[76]

Pound's connections with the personal injury bar also caused him to rethink his early criticisms of the mid-century expansion of tort liability. Pound had been highly critical of the Justice Traynor opinion in Belli's *Escola* case, describing it caustically as adopting the "doctrine of the involuntary Good Samaritan." In less than a decade, however, and with no hint of an explanation for his switch, Pound came around to seeing Traynor's *Escola* opinion as an "exceptionally able" one that had adopted the "just course" for the law of torts.[77]

Indeed, by 1961 Pound's commitment to the common law of torts as superior to its administrative alternatives was so strong that he viewed the "agitation" to commit personal injury claims to administration and take them "out of the protection of justice according to law" as the paradigmatic case in the contest between law and administration. Around the country, the plaintiffs' bar took up Pound's defense of the "individual liberty" of "our common law system" as against the "direct state action" of the "welfare or service state." Belli's best-selling books denounced the "assembly line justice" of administrative compensation systems. NACCA officials warned against "administer[ing] euthanasia to our revered jury system." From California to Pennsylvania, trial lawyers raised the rallying cry of the Anglo-American jury system (it had sprung Eve-like "from the side of society itself") in opposition to new administrative compensation schemes and anything resembling incursions on the adversarial trial in the personal injury field. By 1960, virtually the entire legislative program of the NACCA annual convention was designed to resist the creation of compensation schemes for automobile injuries. NACCA president Lou Ashe (Belli's law partner in San Francisco) systematically purged from the convention program any who held heterodox views on administrative justice in the automobile injury area.[78]

If the early twentieth-century rise of administration in American law borrowed liberally from foreign models and transatlantic reform dialogues, Belli, Pound, and the trial lawyers deployed powerfully nationalistic and often starkly xenophobic rhetoric to hold off administration. The young Pound had spoken favorably of borrowing new methods from the legal systems of continental Europe. But by the late 1930s, Pound's vituperative writings against the New Deal leaned heavily on associating the New Deal with foreign socialism. The welfare state, he announced bitterly, had "Marxian socialism and absolute government in its pedigree" and had "grown up with the totalitarian state." The administrative approaches of the Roosevelt administration, he insisted, rested on the very same "Marxian idea" that underlay the claim of the Soviet jurists that there were no laws, "only administrative ordinances and orders." The same Pound who only a few short years before had accepted honors from Hitler's government now warned that the New Deal threatened to produce "a Duce or Fuhrer or superman head administrator." At best, Pound suggested acidly, the new administrative agencies of the twentieth-century American state were based on the traditions of French lawyers, who lacked the same commitment to liberty that marked the common-law jurist. At worst, the administrative methods of the New Deal state had placed the nation "on the high road to Moscow."[79]

As the Cold War set in, Pound's critique of administration embraced ever more fervently the kinds of common-law chauvinism he had rejected decades earlier. "The common law," Pound wrote, was the "precious inheritance of English-speaking peoples." That common-law tradition, in turn, had reached its highest point of development in the U.S. Constitution and Bill of Rights, and its preservation would be necessary if the United States was "to be spared" the abuses of the administrative state—what Pound called "a season of Oriental justice." The Pound who had once adopted a moderate cultural relativism as to legal systems now became convinced of the distinctive, world-historical virtue of the common law as "the frame of mind of English-speaking peoples." The Anglo-American tradition, Pound insisted, was distinctively committed to "the supremacy of law." It was thus incumbent on the American common-law lawyer to reject "ideas of public law, derived from Continental Europe." The continental approach to law would have a "profound effect on our polity." Yet as Pound saw it, too many American lawyers seemed to be contemplating what Pound described to an NACCA audience as "the complete giving up of the nationalism . . . of the Anglo-American lawyer of the last century." "The Anglo-American," Pound warned, needed to maintain "his American allegiance" rather than experiment with the "exotic theories" of administrative law "recently imported from continental Europe."[80]

Both Belli and Pound warned that tinkering with the institutions of American law threatened to have dangerous repercussions for the American nation. Law, Belli insisted, was the "muse" that shapes "a country's whole national character and direction." The common law, Pound wrote, was the "universal and enduring element" binding together the "different English-speaking peoples." For Belli that same common-law tradition was the "great heritage" of the United States, "the legal cement" that held America together. In the United States in particular, the common-law process tied twentieth-century Americans to the founding fathers and the great figures of Anglo-American history. Belli the lawyer was thus, by his own account, at once a lawyer and "a true American," for it was the everyday work of lawyers and judges to commune with the national tradition. Common-law judges and lawyers consulted "Blackstone and Daniel Webster," they summoned "the shades of Chief Justice John Marshall and Oliver Wendell Holmes," and they weighed "the words of Milords Coke and Mansfield." They were, in sum, nationhood embodied, and thanks to them, Belli concluded flatly, "ours is indeed the best legal system in the world."[81]

Together with Belli and the trial lawyers, Pound turned his nationalist critique of administration toward no-fault administrative compensation proposals. The civil jury and the common law, Pound contended, represented the Anglo-American legacy of legal liberty, of which the United States was the highest realization. The displacement of tort law and its system of jury trials by administrative compensation systems thus promised to promote dangerous foreign administrative commissions over home-grown institutions. Alongside Pound, Belli noted that "the American system of justice ultimately consists of putting twelve ordinary citizens in the jury box." For Belli, "the face of America" was not the President, the national capital, or the Washington Monument or a flag or memorial. The United States was embodied "above all" in "the faces of those twelve jurors" sitting in jury boxes in courtrooms around the country. No-fault automobile-injury commissions, by contrast, made "Stalin's calendar pronouncement of 'Five Year Plans' seem democratic by comparison." Administrative commissions for automobile injuries and the accompanying abolition of the jury trial were but steps on the path toward what Belli called a "Big Brother" state; they were manifestations of what rhetorically savvy trial lawyers around the country began to call the "red-shift" of American governance toward administrative absolutism.[82]

The strategic value of nationalism for the American trial bar became most readily apparent at the end of the 1950s when the Warsaw Convention on airline liability came up for renewed action in the U.S. Senate. The Warsaw Convention, which the United States had ratified in 1934, limited the liability of airlines for deaths arising out of international flights to $8,300. In 1955, an agreement reached in the Hague among some member states (known as the Hague Protocol) would have doubled the liability limit, raising it to $16,600. For the NACCA, however, the principle of limited liability was anathema, and so the plaintiffs' bar—with Pound's help behind the scenes—urged the President and the Senate not to ratify the new limits, and indeed to denounce the treaty altogether. Following closely in the footsteps of Belli and Pound, NACCA lawyers argued that limiting liability was "repugnant to the very spirit of American society." In the Warsaw Convention, contended NACCA lawyer Stuart Speiser, "the basic legal rights of American citizens" had been "adjudicated by a gathering of foreign diplomats." In particular, Speiser complained, the Convention took from American common-law juries the power to assign values to the lives of crash victims on the basis of individualized determinations. Once again, the common-law system of jury trial was under attack, only this time the "destruction of civil rights" had been accomplished "by an international treaty." As Speiser put it, "if we allow the Warsaw Convention to stand, we leave the dikes open for the complete erosion of our hard-won personal civil rights." The first victims might be "in our courts," Speiser warned feverishly, but who was to say that eventually the attack on American rights would not reach right into "our very homes"?[83]

As the Warsaw Convention controversy suggested, NACCA leaders like Belli, Pound, and Horovitz sought to bring to a close the cosmopolitan dialogue that had accompanied the rise of administration a half-century before. NACCA leaders traveled around the world to talk about law and law reform. But now they did so as nationalists exporting an American model of legal institutions in what they saw as a worldwide struggle between the Anglo-American common law and its foreign administrative competitors. Modern international law, Pound insisted as he traveled the globe, threatened to lead to worldwide "administrative agencies" that "should not have the name of law." In 1955, Belli toured Asia, touting the social importance of the trial lawyer everywhere he went. There were, Belli proclaimed on such occasions, only three necessary prerequisites for a free society: habeas corpus, "a common law jury of 12 neighbors," and "a free trial bar." "Give me these," Belli intoned, "and I will assure you a democracy." Take them away, "and I will show you a government . . . such as the Soviet." Horovitz, too, traveled as a proselytizer for the trial lawyer and for law as against administration, going on an around-the-world trip in 1961 through Rome, Tel Aviv, Tehran, Bombay, New Delhi, Lahore (Pakistan), Benares, Calcutta, Rangoon, Bangkok, Manila, Hong Kong, Tokyo, and Honolulu. By the late 1950s, even the annual birthday parties that the NACCA hosted for Pound had become forums for the discussion of the worldwide contest between law and administration. Year after year, Pound took the occasion of the NACCA festivities to warn against the trend toward "a great super-government."[84]

Even as Belli and Pound sought to marshal American institutions to close out the cosmopolitan dialogue of the New Deal, they brilliantly adapted the New Deal language of economic security for their fight against no-fault administrative compensation systems. Pound had helped to pioneer the sociological policies that culminated in Roosevelt's plans for social security. Belli had even worked for the National Recovery Administration early in the New Deal. Yet even as the New Deal sought to replace courts, juries, and trial lawyers with efficient bureaucratic agencies, the trial lawyers contended that those same common-law institutions could best carry out the vision of the New Deal. Belli and Pound aimed to do nothing less than graft Roosevelt's ideas of economic freedom onto the common law and the courts. Pound insisted that "the courts in the common-law world" were developing the law of torts as a common-law mechanism "to maintain the general security" independent of the "social service state." In Belli's view, the personal injury lawyer—not the administrative state—was best positioned to provide what he called "'social security' . . . for the personal injury victim." In Belli's reworking of the New Deal conception of economic security, it was the "adequate award" that secured economic freedom and dignity for the working man and his family. Roosevelt's right to security became, in Belli's hands, a constitutional right to be "free from pain and suffering."[85]

Indeed, through the charisma and energy of Belli and Pound, the NACCA sought to appropriate and reinvent the legacy of the New Deal. Again and again, in addresses and in books and articles, Belli adopted the Four Freedoms of Franklin Roosevelt's great speech as his own. "Man's travail in gaining his economic freedom," wrote Belli in 1956, had been just as arduous as the path to political freedom. "Freedom from hurt and poverty and hunger" had not come automatically with the industrial revolution. According to Belli, man had wrested economic freedom "from the machine, from the factory, from capital." The new economic freedom, Belli insisted, consisted of "the right of dignity of life and limb," and the battle to secure it had been fought not by the administrators of the New Deal but by trial lawyers in the courts.[86]

The great virtue of tort as a common-law alternative to the administrative state, as Pound saw it, was that it seemed capable of balancing "the security of life and limb" with the "free individual." Around the country, fledgling plaintiffs' organizations took up the cause of tort law as a substitute for—and bulwark against—administration and state insurance. Belli, for example, contended in 1951 that "were it not for the personal injury lawyer, the state, the federal government, and the county hospitals would have to accept the burden of rehabilitation." Unlike state bureaucracies, however, tort law and the common-law trial lawyer offered the promise of what the plaintiffs' bar called "security with freedom."[87]

Trial lawyers' reinvention of the New Deal project, however, had deeply altered the significance of FDR's New Deal initiatives. The image accompanying the "security with freedom" campaign was not Roosevelt but Lincoln, and Belli's economic rights were in many respects no more than updated versions of the nineteenth-century common-law baseline of negative liberties in a new twentieth-century guise. Guaranteeing economic security, Pound cracked with casual racism, was like "attempting what the colored preacher aptly called unscrewing the inscrutable": it simply couldn't be done. "Freedom from want and freedom from fear," he told a Los Angeles gathering in honor of Bill of Rights Week in 1949, were the kinds of "lavish promises" that were "easily made" but impossible to fulfill. The promises of the welfare state, in Pound's description, were the dangerous propaganda of "Marxian doctrine."[88]

Although Pound insisted in his introduction to Belli's *Modern Trials* that the "sporting theory of justice" had passed "from the greater part of the land," the opposite was closer to the truth.

Pound's partnership with Belli in *Modern Trials* marked the rehabilitation of the adversarial common-law trial and its sporting theory as a mechanism for the administration of justice. Belli described the ideal trial lawyer as "a kicker, a passer, a runner, and a man who could back up the line and surreptitiously slip into the backfield." The trial lawyer was a competitor in the "juridical decathlon" of the courtroom. Here was the sporting theory taken to new heights. Indeed, Belli insisted, the trial lawyer was a "forensic gladiator," a "knightly champion" of the individual against the insurance company dragons.[89]

Belli and the NACCA thus raised no challenge to the administration of justice by hired-gun agents in the adversary system. To the contrary, lawyers' market motives were the underpinnings of the tort system they had begun to create. With Belli's idea of "the adequate award" as their "Rosetta stone," the plaintiffs' bar promised to be "The Equalizers," providing through entrepreneurial lawyering what the administrative state would have done through bureaucracy. The trial lawyers claimed merely that both sides in the contest should have hired guns. The "scales of justice," as Belli loved to remind his audiences, had been "loaded against" the little guy, but thanks to the trial bar both sides could have "equal representation before the courts, commissions, legislatures, and before the public generally." Here in the basic charter of ATLA was Belli's gladiator model writ large. "Our sword," announced the editor of the NACCA's newsletter in 1957, "is the quest for justice." In a sense, the plaintiffs' bar had rejected sociological transformation in favor of raising the stakes of the adversary process. "The trial table in a personal injury lawsuit, circa 1957," one observer noted, "is no place for the faint of heart. It is not a penny ante game; the pots are sweet and the ribbon-clerks must stand aside."[90]

Yet for all the talk of economic security, Belli conceded in his less bombastic moments that personal injury awards were in fact "not necessarily 'fair' or 'adequate'"; they were merely a "market" price for what entrepreneurial plaintiffs' lawyers had made into a "marketable commodity." Like the "placing of a price tag on a rug or a house or a horse or a violin," what Belli called the "dollar price tags" on personal injury "reduced the subject to the language and reasoning of the marketplace."[91]

What drove the market in personal injury lawsuits was not always so much the interests of the plaintiffs' bar's clients, though this was surely important at least some of the time. In an unusual moment of candor, Belli admitted that lawyers opposed administrative compensation schemes at least in part because they did "not relish the prospect of losing 75 per cent of their business in one fell swoop." The livelihood of the entrepreneurial torts bar animated plaintiffs' lawyers' opposition to administrative compensation schemes. Trial lawyers fought hard, and often successfully, to preserve the tort system with its unlimited damages, its juries, its "adequate awards," and its contingency fees, against all administrative challengers.[92]

The "adequate award" served as the trial lawyers' badge of modern economic freedom through the common-law courts, establishing the security and dignity promised by Roosevelt with the freedom so long associated with the common law. Here in the adequate award was protection for the little man, without an army of new civil service bureaucrats or a massive public bureaucracy. But *The Adequate Award* was also the name of Belli's luxury yacht.[93]

*
*
*

By the early and mid-1960s, the NACCA's campaign to promote Anglo-American courts and the civil jury against administrative alternatives had proven remarkably successful. Notwithstanding considerable confidence among many observers that no-fault commissions would displace the common-law courts in important fields like automobile injuries, no state in the nation ultimately enacted comprehensive no-fault automobile injury legislation. Even in states in which the insurance industry supported administrative compensation proposals, the NACCA managed to hold off the threat of administration. More than once, the powerful mid-twentieth-century American labor movement threw its weight behind no-fault automobile injury legislation at the state level and in Congress. Every time, opposition by the trial lawyers successfully prevented significant inroads on the domain of the common law. And when the trial lawyers needed to trigger government action rather than merely obstruct it, they proved they could do that, too. In 1965, the plaintiffs' bar campaign to reject the Warsaw Convention finally succeeded when President Lyndon Johnson gave notice that the United States would formally denounce it because of its limits on liability.[94]

Among other things, the plaintiffs' bar had managed to reestablish the courts as an important forum for economic regulation. Since Pound's days in Nebraska, progressive observers of American law such as his colleague Edward Ross had sharply criticized courts as poorly suited to engage in the regulation of economic activity. Courts had been the bane of progressive reform, and Franklin Roosevelt's 1937 plan to pack the Supreme Court with justices friendlier to New Deal legislation seemed to usher in what political scientist Robert McCloskey would later call "the end of economic supervision" by the Supreme Court, a retreat the lower courts would surely follow. In subsequent decades, as historians have long observed, the courts would again assert their authority in areas such as race discrimination and civil liberties. And yet in the 1940s and 1950s, even as Thurgood Marshall and organizations like the NAACP Legal Defense and Education Fund were mapping out strategies for reinvigorating the power of the courts, the trial bar identified courts not only as a source of new norms in the areas of civil rights and civil liberties, but also as an institution for a new kind of regulatory activity that adapted New Deal notions to the institutions of the common law. Indeed, no sooner did the plaintiffs' bar turn back to the courts than they began to reassert the kinds of claims that had made the business lobbies infamous in the years before the New Deal. Where once business interests had invoked the Constitution and the courts to strike down regulatory legislation, now the plaintiffs' bar turned to constitutions—especially state constitutions—and the courts to strike down legislation that limited tort liability.[95]

Yet to say that Belli and Pound managed to limit the spread of public administration into the field of personal injury law is not to say that they stanched the rise of administration per se. To be sure, Belli and Pound championed the virtues of the common-law jury trial and of the individualized justice that the common law could provide. Leading trial lawyers spoke far and wide of the deep personal trust that marked the relationship of lawyer and client. As against administrative compensation schemes that would "standardize the amount of damages," Belli insisted that the appropriate measure of damages must take "into account the individual's situation." He added that "each person's loss is personal to him or her alone, and this must be considered in determining the amount of damages he or she deserves." But for all their talk of the value of individualized adjudications, civil juries, and the common-law trial system, Belli and ATLA, with Pound as their comrade-in-arms, were themselves agents of that system's transformation. Sometimes unwittingly, and sometimes quite self-consciously, Belli and the trial lawyers helped not to recreate the system of juries and common-law adjudication, but rather to invent a massive, sprawling, and distinctively American system of private administration for the administration of claims made by tort plaintiffs.[96]

Private administration in the tort system predated the

NACCA and ATLA, to be sure. Wherever large organizations such as railroads and manufacturing corporations caused widespread injuries, and wherever insurance companies provided liability insurance, claims departments arose to process and routinize victims' tort claims. In turn, groups of plaintiffs' agents sprung up as intermediaries between injured potential claimants and the organizations with which their claims would be lodged. In nineteenth-century manufacturing centers, informal worker representatives approached employers on behalf of injured workers, often taking a fee both from the injured employee, for whom the representative procured a payment, and from the employer, for whom the representative provided peace against potentially time-consuming litigation and a disgruntled workforce. As early as the 1890s, lawyers in places like upstate New York (where Roscoe Pound's father had practiced only a few decades before) began to package hundreds, and sometimes even thousands, of claims for settlement with the public utilities whose telegraph and telephone lines and railroad rights-of-way caused damage to neighboring property owners. At the turn of the twentieth century, claims brokers in Texas set up claims shops in which they purchased and brokered as many as 60 percent of the tort claims made against railroads in areas such as San Antonio. (Further east, a Philadelphia lawyer named Samuel Evans Maires had begun to do essentially the same thing just a few years earlier.) In New York City in the 1910s, the legendary Abraham Gatner "developed a system for eliminating the waste involved in handling accidents" by setting up a "well-organized ambulance chasing office" with field officers, central managers, and a clerical staff. And by the 1920s, investigations of personal injury practice in leading urban areas found that personal injury claims were being directed into the "hands of relatively few lawyers," most of whom seemed to have refined the claims process into something that resembled "a business" more than the practice of law in the courts.[97]

Belli and the midcentury trial lawyers, however, turned the

claims practices of earlier generations of plaintiffs' representatives into big business. Between 1950 and 1959, as the NACCA hit its stride, the total expenditures in the American tort system increased threefold. By the end of the twentieth century, the costs of the tort system as a share of gross domestic product reached 2.3 percent, almost twice as great a share as the next leading industrialized nation state (Italy), and almost four times as great as the United Kingdom.[98]

As the tort system grew, a newly specialized modern plaintiffs' bar brought the techniques of modern business administration to the business of modern tort law. Inspired by the private administrative efficiencies of Henry Ford's assembly lines and Frederick Winslow Taylor's rationally engineered bureaucracies, Belli and the fledgling ATLA worked to replicate on the plaintiffs' side the defense-side systems of claims administration that had long minimized the costs of claims resolution for insurers, railroads, and other repeat players. Increasingly sophisticated referral networks arose within the plaintiffs' bar, for example, that allowed nonspecialists to send cases along to specialists while retaining a share of the fee. At the same time, plaintiffs'-side law firms grew and chose to specialize rather than diversify their practices. The result was a sharply increased concentration of claims in the hands of a small number of specialist plaintiffs' firms. In Chicago in the 1950s, for example, one-third of all firms on the defense and plaintiffs' sides handled "something like 90 percent of the cases." In New York City, less than 2 percent of the plaintiffs' bar handled almost 13 percent of personal injury claims; 5 percent of plaintiffs' lawyers conducted 22.5 percent of the personal injuries trials, while on the defense side, 5 percent of the lawyers conducted 24.8 percent of all trials. The trial numbers typically understated the specialization. Leading personal injury lawyers regularly handled between 750 and 1,000 cases each year; many lawyers averaged "more than 500 cases a year." The new generation of specialist lawyers in Texas and in Illinois typically had between 100 and 150 personal injury cases on their docket at any one time.[99]

Specialist claims administrators on both sides developed an array of shortcuts and bargaining conventions for the streamlined, stereotyped resolution of the claims that entered the system. Where the common law entailed cumbersome and slow inquiries into the facts of a particular case, private administrative schemes operated by plaintiffs' lawyers and insurance company claims adjusters aimed to produce what sociologist H. Laurence Ross called in his classic 1970 study of the subject "a collectively satisfactory return" on the run of claims they resolved. In areas like automobile accidents, in which the number of claims was massive and in which the underlying factual scenarios were relatively repetitive, claims adjusters and plaintiffs' representatives developed rules of thumb and bargaining conventions for the efficient processing of the claims, resolving questions of liability by reference to categories such as "rear-enders, red-light cases, stop sign cases, and the like." Defense lawyers reduced accident investigations to a few "simple but valuable calculations" designed to get to the right result over the run of the cases without costly inquiries into the circumstances of particular claims. As one Philadelphia study in 1953 found, the parties to settlement negotiations made only "superficial" investigations into claims; their aim was "speed in settlement."[100]

Perhaps the most important shortcuts of all were the ones developed to arrive at claims values. In the American law of torts, the damages to be awarded in any given case were (as they remain in the early twenty-first century) enormously open ended. What, after all, was an arm, or a leg, or a bad back worth? Economic loss might be measured with relatively concrete measures such as wage loss and medical bills (in practice, economic damages were often quite malleable). But with respect to open-ended injuries such as pain and suffering, the common law provided virtually no guidance to judges and juries or to the lawyers and claims adjusters who sought to settle such cases in the shadow of the law.[101]

And so claims adjusters and plaintiffs' lawyers alike employed "yardsticks" or bargaining conventions of one sort or another to arrive at damages determinations. The "three times three" rule (in which pain and suffering damages equaled three times a plaintiff's economic damages) governed in some jurisdictions and among some adjusters and lawyers. Elsewhere, plaintiffs' lawyers followed the complex "Sindell Formula," created by NACCA lawyers at the Cleveland firm of Sindell & Sindell. Chicago lawyers in the 1950s and 1960s created formal tables for the valuation of back and neck injuries, tables they continuously revised by reference to jury verdicts in the relevant area. In complex, multiparty accident disputes, bargaining conventions such as "the rule of thirds" split settlements among plaintiffs' lawyer, claimant, and third parties such as the claimant's own insurer. Like the rules of thumb employed for liability determinations, such "going rates" organized the settlement market, enabling "attorneys and insurance companies to do business in personal injury cases on a sound actuarial basis much like life expectancy tables." Formulas offered a speedy and efficient way to get to a number that would resolve the litigation. That such formulas were simply the way things worked surely helped lawyers sell such settlements to their clients. For insurers, formulas and rules of thumb provided a set of hard-and-fast rules by which they limited the discretion of their often poorly paid claims adjusters.[102]

Belli's greatest contribution to the tort system may have been his work gathering and systematizing data on claims values. By collecting plaintiffs'-side information about settlement values in his article "The Adequate Award" and in regular updates, Belli did for plaintiffs what institutional position and scale had done almost automatically for repeat-play defendants and insurers. The *NACCA Law Journal* similarly took up the publication of settlement and verdict value information for dissemination to NACCA member readers. And in 1959, Belli published *Modern Damages,* a massive three-volume collection of damages and settlement values for every conceivable kind of injury. For the plaintiffs' bar, reviewers said, it was "a Golconda of information, comparable to Bowditch's Practical Navigator," a veritable "vade mecum" for the plaintiffs' bar.[103] Here at last was the kind of information, collected in one place, that could provide plaintiffs' agents with the same kinds of settlement value information that their counterparts in the insurance companies had long had.

Armed with rules of thumb, damages formulas, and Belli's collection of common-law damages awards, plaintiffs' lawyers in the middle of the twentieth century were able—at least in certain areas of the tort system, such as automobile accidents— to provide injury victims with a relatively effective system of compensation. What the contingency fee plaintiffs' bar had accomplished was to create a privately administered system of social insurance for automobile-injury victims. For most claimants, entrance into the lawyer's stable of claimants meant taking a place in what functioned as a kind of aggregate compensation system in which the risks of litigation were spread across the pool of claimants. The system in which they made their claims was a "part-recovery-most-of-the-time matter." Almost two-thirds of all claims in automobile-injury cases, for example, produced payments of some sort, and one 1950s study found that over 80 percent of claims made with the help of a lawyer produced payments equal to or greater than the claimant's out-of-pocket expenses before lawyer fees. The overwhelming majority of automobile claims, moreover, were resolved within one year, a figure that increased to more than 80 percent when the defendant was an insurance company. Indeed, by the mid-1960s, automobile accident liability payments were being made through the tort settlement system almost as speedily as through the no-fault compensation systems whose advocates had promised to bring an end to the delays of the common law. Much like the automobile administrative compensation systems, in other words, the ostensibly individualized common law of torts had become a system for the aggregate resolution of personal injury claims—a system that socialized the risks of the activities out of which it arose.[104]

Specialist plaintiffs'-side bargaining agents who knew the shortcuts, the heuristics, and the rules of thumb seemed to have made the settlement process considerably more efficient. In Chicago, for example, insurers found that for precisely these reasons, the repeat-play plaintiffs'-lawyer specialist was "an easier man to deal with than a general practitioner."[105]

Indeed, the decentralized, privately administered tort system offered a number of advantages over its public competitors. Benefit schedules in legislatively created administrative compensation systems such as workmen's compensation became notoriously out of date in the middle years of the twentieth century. Inflation ate away at legislative ceilings on benefits that had been reasonable when they were enacted in the 1910s. Compensation in the tort system, by contrast, was dynamic rather than static. As plaintiffs' lawyer Joseph Sindell (creator of the Sindell Formula) observed, the settlement values in tort law's system of private administration were always subject to what he called "trial balloon" adjudication, in which the values being used in the settlement process could be recalibrated to respond to changes in the judgment value of the claims in question. As one defense lawyer put it in 1962, "jury verdicts change to conform with conditions and attitudes that change with the times." The "tables" used in settling tort claims were "continuously being revised to reflect these changes."[106]

For all its virtues, however, the tort system was also deeply flawed. As a mechanism for compensating injuries, the tort system worked much better for small and standard injuries than for more severe or idiosyncratic ones. The more severe or unusual the injury, the longer the time it took to reach a settlement and the lower the ratio of damages or settlement value to actual injury. Indeed, the routinized settlement process into which run-of-the-mill cases were directed was especially ill suited to deal with high-value cases arising out of exceptionally severe injuries. Such cases were far more likely to involve expensive and time-consuming trials. Thousands upon thousands of routine automobile accidents each year resolved themselves into well-ordered patterns. But idiosyncratic tort claims could be enormously cumbersome to resolve. Moreover, even in the routine cases the tort system was highly susceptible to individualized irrationality. Payments in individual cases could be powerfully affected by everything from the charisma or attractiveness of the victim to the quality of the legal representation the victim received.[107]

Most troubling were the extraordinary administrative costs that the tort settlement system entailed. The paradox of the modern tort system Belli had helped to create was that its great virtue and its chief flaw were one and the same: the reliance on precisely the private initiative and profit motive that Pound had faulted early in his career. Contingent-fee legal services for tort plaintiffs—combined with personal injury lawyers' interest in their reputation for achieving high-value settlements and awards for their clients—helped to align the interests of plaintiffs and their lawyers, turning the private initiative of lawyer–claims administrators to work for injury victims. Contingent fees, moreover, often helped to turn the plaintiffs' lawyers into effective gatekeepers, keeping weak claims out of the system. But private initiative was nonetheless extraordinarily costly and brought with it persistent gaps between private interests and the public good. It was the contingent fee, after all, that had financed Belli's aptly named yacht. And though the administrative streamlining of the tort settlement process brought down the administrative costs of the system during the 1960s, these costs continued throughout the twentieth century and into the twenty-first to make up about one-half of the total cost of the tort system. Of the approximately $5.4 billion expended on the tort system in 1960, less than $3 billion went to compensate injury victims. The rest was eaten up by administrative expenses such as defendants' and insurers' claims processing costs and plaintiffs' representatives' contingent fees.[108]

Regardless of the relative merits of public and private administrative systems, the ironies of private administration were powerful. The trial lawyers had effectively recreated what they had purported to oppose: administration, though under private auspices and by a different name. For all the money going into the tort system, an increasingly tiny slice of tort claims—less than one percent, by most accounts—produced the trial and the individually tailored determination of damages that Belli and his colleagues in ATLA purported to champion. In the civil justice system that Belli and ATLA helped to create, the overwhelming majority of tort lawsuits—between 70 and 90 percent of all tort claim filings—settled. Indeed, studies of the tort system suggest that somewhere between 60 and 99 percent of tort claims, depending on local negotiating norms, did not even produce a lawsuit, but were instead resolved by plaintiffs' lawyers and insurance company claims adjusters according to rules of thumb and settlement-value formulas. To be sure, these conventions and going rates were efficient ways to resolve injury claims. But their efficiency lay precisely in the abandonment of the individualized approach championed by the tort bar in its fight against public administration.[109]

There was no better evidence of the convergence of the common-law system on the administrative structure of public compensation schemes than Belli's three-volume *Modern Damages*. For all its power to even up the sides, *Modern Damages*—the plaintiffs' bar's "register of the true value of serious injury cases in the marketplace," as Stuart Speiser called it—made apparent just how closely the torts process could resemble the very administrative compensation systems that the plaintiffs' bar so vociferously opposed. Here in Belli's *Modern Damages* were compensation grids derived from the tort settlement process that were almost identical to those created by administrative workmen's compensation schemes. Belli tabulated and listed values by "parts of the body"—"arms"; "arms—amputation of one arm"; "back and spine"; "blood"; "body functions"; "brain"; "breast and chest"; "ears—disfigurement"; "eyes—impairment of vision"; and so on, for hundreds of pages. He listed values for cases involving injuries to the "body as a whole" as well as "amputations—both arms"; "amputations—both feet"; "amputations—both hands"; "amputations—both legs"; "amputations—multiple involving different limbs." *Modern Damages* converted all of these injuries into settlement values for the private administrative system that operated in the shadow of tort law.[110]

Belli the gladiator seemed successfully to have rehabilitated Pound's long-reviled "sporting theory of justice." Yet what Belli and his colleagues in ATLA managed to accomplish was the creation of a private administrative state, whose extravagant costs and often intangible benefits were as hotly controversial as Belli himself. Pound's compromise with the sporting theory had not held off the erosion of his prized common-law jury trials or his prized individualized adjudications. It had merely changed the mechanism of their displacement, substituting private administration for the public administration Pound had come to revile.[111]

*
*
*

Melvin Belli became a member of the U.S. Supreme Court bar on the same day in April 1937 on which the Court upheld the National Labor Relations Act in the case of the *National Labor*

Relations Board v. Jones & Laughlin Steel Corporation. Belli never did much work before the Supreme Court. But he was never one to let practicality get in the way of an opportunity to burnish his reputation, and Supreme Court bar membership was effectively open to any member of a state bar in good standing.[112]

As Belli sat in the Supreme Court building listening to the justices read their decision in *Jones & Laughlin,* he was watching a transformative moment in the New Deal state. The Wagner Act, as the labor relations statute was known, authorized a massive federal reorganization of American labor markets under a sprawling new administrative agency known as the National Labor Relations Board. Critics of the New Deal saw the Wagner Act as socialism, pure and simple. And though their fears proved to be exaggerated, the act powerfully shaped the trajectory of American labor law for the next half-century. Where late nineteenth and early twentieth-century courts had played enormously influential roles in overseeing struggles between labor and management, the administrative apparatus of the NLRB became one of the most important regulatory institutions in the mid-twentieth-century American economy.

The Supreme Court's decision in *Jones & Laughlin* to uphold the Wagner Act signaled a new era for the United States. The courts, it seemed, would no longer rigorously police the constitutional limits on the power of the federal government and the states to replace the common law with comprehensive regulatory systems. Nor, it seemed, would courts reject (as they once had) the delegation of broad powers by Congress to administrative agencies such as the NLRB. The administrative state, in short, seemed poised to replace the common-law courts in what political scientist Stephen Skowronek has influentially called the "state of courts and parties" that the United States had inherited from the nineteenth century.[113]

Yet from the very day *Jones & Laughlin* was decided, and indeed from within the Supreme Court chambers themselves, Belli and the trial lawyers charted a new course for the courts. Under the auspices of Belli, Pound, and the trial bar, courts reemerged as powerful players in the creation of American public policy even in precisely the areas that the New Deal state seemed most likely to shift toward administration and legislation. Just under the radar of the New Deal state's publicly administered programs, the trial bar created a vast, sprawling, largely invisible, and distinctly American system for the regulation of personal injury. That system has not produced any public accounting of its performance. The statistics of its operations are notoriously unreliable and difficult to compile. Its chroniclers (themselves relatively obscure) call the tort settlement system an "invisible law" for the administration of tort claims. Indeed, Roscoe Pound's biographers have omitted his relationship with Belli from Pound's life story, apparently regarding it as insignificant. The Harvard Law School simply omitted Pound's correspondence with the trial lawyers from its otherwise comprehensive microfilm of the Roscoe Pound Papers, effectively excising ATLA's beginnings from the most comprehensive record of Pound's life.[114]

And yet for all its invisibility—and partly *because of* its invisibility—the privately administered American tort settlement system has proven remarkably resilient in the decades since Belli and Pound helped to found it. In a sense, the contest between tort and administration in the United States was not a fair fight. As Pound learned, the common law and the courts had developed powerful constituencies committed to their perpetuation. With Pound's help, the trial lawyer constituency effectively mobilized nationalist sentiments on behalf of legal institutions that at once defined American nationhood and created opportunities for private brokers and intermediaries such as the lawyers of the plaintiffs' bar. Belli, Pound, and the trial lawyers had made the traditions of the nation-state and its legal institutions into powerful rallying cries in the fight against public administrative institutions.

By 1957, four years after Pound had formally joined in its efforts, the NACCA—soon to become ATLA—was the second largest bar association in the United States. In the 1960s, its annual conventions regularly featured warm opening greetings from presidents of the United States and their attorneys general. (Automobile accidents, Lyndon Johnson told an approving ATLA audience in 1966, were second only to the Vietnam War among the problems facing the nation.) By the mid-1960s, ATLA's formation and successes prompted political scientists to consider whether interest-group-driven litigation in the courts might be as much of a threat to American democratic processes as the capture of administrative agencies by regulated industries seemed to be. In the 1970s, Melvin Belli's fifth wife (and not his last) would take up a position inside the administration of President Jimmy Carter.[115] And by the end of the twentieth century, the legal profession contributed more than any other industry to the finances of one of America's two major political parties. In the short space of half a century, the Democratic Party—the party of Franklin Roosevelt, the New Deal, and public administration—had come to rely on the organization of Melvin Belli and private administration as a virtually indispensable ally. It was, and is, a relationship as startling as the one between the King of Torts and the Dean of Harvard.

Epilogue:
Law and the National Frame

As long as nation-states persist, debate will surely continue over whether they are a constructive means for organizing human social life. For every powerful account of nationalism's long-standing destructive power, or of the nation-state's new shortcomings in a global age, there is an equally powerful defense of nationhood as the foundation of modern democracy and as the basis for modern constitutionalisms with their laudable norms of equality and freedom.[1]

In the United States, a nation that is now stronger than any the world has ever seen, we have barely even begun to make sense of the phenomenon of nationhood. And yet at the beginning of the twenty-first century, the problem of American nationhood animates many of the most pressing questions in American law. In the U.S. Supreme Court, for example, patriot and cosmopolitan justices wage a battle over the legitimacy of legal norms from outside the American national experience for interpreting the U.S. Constitution. Justice Antonin Scalia has pronounced that "the views of other nations . . . cannot be imposed upon Americans." ("We must never forget," Justice Scalia contends, "that it is a Constitution for the United States of America that we are expounding.") A majority of the Supreme Court, by contrast, has repeatedly held that transnational and foreign norms are in fact relevant to the elaboration of ostensibly domestic principles of American law in areas such as the death penalty and the law of privacy. In the contest over international and foreign legal norms, we can see traces of the contests over the nation that run through American constitutionalism, from the haunted visions of James

Wilson to the comparative constitutionalism of Elias Hill, from Crystal Eastman's cosmopolitan energies to the nativist efforts of Melvin Belli and Roscoe Pound.[2]

Perhaps because of American nationhood's legal and constitutional foundations, the United States often seems exceptionally reluctant to participate in the multilateral creation of international legal norms. The United States at the end of the twentieth century and the beginning of the twenty-first has distinguished itself for refusing to participate in international agreements. It has withdrawn from parts of the jurisdiction of the International Court of Justice. It has renounced the Kyoto Protocols on environmental emissions and global warming. It refuses to accede to an International Criminal Court. It even chronically declines to pay its dues at the United Nations.[3]

Indeed, even when the United States purports to agree to be governed by international legal norms, the question of whether legal norms of any kind—domestic or international—constrain the United States from pursuing its national interests has moved front and center. As I write this, debate rages over whether national self-interest justifies torture and near-torture in interrogations, and whether national defense decisions by the President, including decisions to spy on American citizens, are ever subject to legal or constitutional constraint. Controversy storms over whether national self-interest justifies ostensibly lawless offshore zones that are within the "jurisdiction and control" of the United States but outside its "ultimate sovereignty" and thus (by some accounts) outside the reach of its courts. Supreme Court citations to international and foreign law notwithstanding, American law often seems exceptionally resistant to outside influence.[4]

In early twenty-first-century encounters between law and American nationhood, we are witnessing the unfolding of a process of national and legal formation more than two centuries old. Since James Wilson first dreamed of the nation as a timeless pyramid in the 1780s, the legal commitments that created the legal entity known as the United States have given rise to imagined identities, aspirational ideals, entrenched institutions, and vested interests. In the intervening two centuries, a nation greater than the sum of its legal parts, and in many respects independent of them, has been erected on the legal foundations of the U.S. Constitution. This is what Lincoln understood in 1861 when he suspended the writ of habeas corpus lest "all the laws, but one" were "to go unexecuted, and the government itself to go to pieces." And this is what Justice Robert Jackson understood in 1949 when he warned that the Constitution was not a "suicide pact" for the nation. The United States is a nation based in law, but one that has developed a vital (if at times Frankenstein-like) independence from its constitutive legal commitments.[5]

Among the most remarkable features of American nationhood has been its capaciousness and variety, its capacity to animate widely disparate and often starkly opposed political and legal ideals and interests. James Madison and James Wilson may have had deeply divergent visions for the United States in 1787 and 1788, but both of their visions fit within the big tent of American constitutionalism. If Klansman Rufus Bratton was an American nationalist, so too, in his own way, was the emigrationist Elias Hill when he dreamed of a "United States of Africa." World War I may have ushered in a wave of nationalist fervor, but Crystal Eastman and the early American Civil Liberties Union were able deftly to turn national symbols to the defense of wartime dissenters. Indeed, even as Eastman purported to reject the nation-state as an organizing model for human affairs, the categories of the nation—and of American nationhood in particular—animated her thinking. It was, after all, a "United States of the World" for which she argued, one that drew on the traditions of her own nation even as she sought to transcend them. And by the same token, nationhood could be invoked both in support of an economic Bill of Rights, as Franklin Roosevelt had sought to do in his national social programs in the New Deal, and in favor of the common law, as Melvin Belli and Roscoe Pound succeeded in doing during the 1950s.[6]

This capaciousness in American nationhood—its big tent—has often led observers to mistake widespread (though not universal) embrace of a shared set of national symbols for consensus about the character and meaning of national ideals and institutions. As we saw in the introduction, this was Louis Hartz's error, as it has been the error of countless observers of the American experience before and after him. The four case studies here suggest that there has been sharp disagreement over the content of American nationhood, disagreement that began with the very different visions of the founding generation and persists right up into the present day. There have, in short, been many American nationhoods, and the chapters in this book have only begun to make sense of them.

Yet if American nationhood has not proven to be Hartz's ideological straightjacket, if there have been many American nationhoods, its tent has not been so large as to accommodate all values, interests, or institutions. American nationhoods have been many and varied, but they have not been unbounded. The history of American nationhood has been one not only of variety and contingency, but also of limits and constraints. James Wilson's dream of a nation of laws that would aspire to a perfection outside of the forces of time badly misread the character of the pluralist, lawyer-friendly institutions created by the Constitution he himself had helped to write. The South Carolina freedpeople's struggle for citizenship in Reconstruction ran headlong into the limits and backward-looking instincts of the nation's courts. Crystal Eastman's internationalist critiques of the nation-state were virtually impossible to articulate from within the American national tradition, though the civil liberties campaign that emerged from those critiques was. And the common-law institutions of American nationhood and their attendant ideologies provided people such as Melvin Belli and Roscoe Pound with powerful resources in the contest between the common law and the administrative state.

In each of these instances, American nationhood bounded the contingency of American legal history and its openness to global influences, channeling extranational movements such as internationalism into intranational programs such as civil liberties. Nationhood has put an often barely discernible frame on the legal and political life of the United States, making certain ways of life easier and some political movements more difficult, facilitating the pursuit of particular interests and obstructing the advancement of others.[7]

Consider once again, for example, the contests at the beginning of the twenty-first century that appear outwardly as battles between patriots and cosmopolitans in the U.S. Supreme Court. In one sense, these contests are not between patriots and cosmopolitans at all, but rather merely contests among competing patriots, working within long-standing traditions of American nationhood. Justice Scalia takes up the tradition of American distinctiveness and exceptionalism (its "separate and equal" station, as the Declaration of Independence put it), on the one hand, while the Court's majority takes up the tradition of American universalism (the self-evident truths of all men) on the other.[8] Here and elsewhere, we can see the dynamic of American nationhood at work almost every day in the United States's basic operations, sometimes for good (as when national self-interest drives the United States to root out readily observable race discrimination), and sometimes for ill (as when the United States renders detainees to a foreign state that engages in torture). In each such instance, American nationhood has licensed and sustained a wide array of political and legal practices while subtly bounding the universe of possibilities.[9]

These are the seductions and the limits of American nationhood, and this is the power and the tragedy of the national frame. Even as the United States provides one of the world's most effective mechanisms for mobilizing highly laudable ideals, it has placed significant boundaries—often virtually invisible ones—on their achievement.

Notes

Acknowledgments

Index

ℕotes

INTRODUCTION

1. On nationalism as an "imagined community," see Benedict Anderson's influential *Imagined Communities: Reflections on the Origin and Spread of Nationalism* (Verso, rev. ed., 1991).

2. James Crawford, *The Creation of States in International Law* (Clarendon Press, 1979) (defined by the norms and conventions); Mark W. Janis, *An Introduction to International Law* 185–87 (Aspen Publishers, 4th ed., 2003) (international law definition of a state); Arthur Nussbaum, *A Concise History of the Law of Nations* 135–37 (Macmillan, 1947) and David Armitage, "The Declaration of Independence and International Law," 59 *Wm. & Mary Q.* 39, 55 (2002) (from "law of nations" to "international law"); Sarah H. Cleveland, "Powers Inherent in Sovereignty: Indians, Aliens, Territories, and the Nineteenth Century," 81 *Texas Law Review* 1 (2002).

3. E.g., Hans Kohn, *American Nationalism: An Interpretive Essay* 8–9 (Macmillan, 1957) (distinctively based in law); see also George P. Fletcher, *Our Secret Constitution: How Lincoln Redefined American Democracy* (Oxford University Press, 2001); Liah Greenfeld, *Nationalism: Five Roads to Modernity* 400 (Harvard University Press, 1992); Anatol Lieven, *America Right or Wrong: An Anatomy of American Nationalism* (Oxford University Press, 2004); Michael Lind, *The Next American Nation: The New Nationalism and the Fourth American Revolution* 3 (Free Press, 1995); Jed Rubenfeld, *Freedom and Time: A Theory of Constitutional Self-Government* 80, 158 (Yale University Press, 2001).

4. Rogers Brubaker, *Citizenship and Nationhood in France and Germany* (Harvard University Press, 1992); Hartmutt Lehmann and Hermann Wellenreuther, eds., *German and American Nationalism: A Comparative Perspective* (Berg, 1999); David A. Bell, *The Cult of the Nation in France: Inventing Nationalism, 1680–1800,* pp. 3–15 (Harvard University Press, 2001); Anderson, *Imagined Communities,* 52–65. On the legal beginnings of American nationhood in the British Empire, see Mary Sarah Bilder, *The*

Transatlantic Constitution: Colonial Legal Culture and the Empire (Harvard University Press, 2004); Daniel J. Hulsebosch, *Constituting Empire: New York and the Transformation of Constitutionalism in the Atlantic World, 1664–1830* (University of North Carolina Press, 2005); Ellen Holmes Pearson, "Revising Custom, Embracing Choice," in Eliga H. Gould and Peter S. Onuf, eds., *Empire and Nation: The American Revolution in the Atlantic World* (Johns Hopkins University Press, 2005). On American constitutionalism as the constitution of a people bound across time, see Bruce A. Ackerman, *We the People: Foundations* (Belknap / Harvard University Press, 1991); Rubenfeld, *Freedom and Time.* One form of American nationalism that has claimed to be a tradition of shared descent was the Confederacy during the Civil War. See James M. McPherson, "Was Blood Thicker than Water? Ethnic and Civil Nationalism in the American Civil War," 143 *Proc. Am. Phil. Soc'y* 102, 102–03 (1999). The terms "ethnocultural fact" and "political fact" are drawn from Brubaker, *Citizenship and Nationhood,* p. 4.

5. Armitage, "Declaration of Independence and International Law"; Kohn, *American Nationalism,* 31–32; Michael Walzer, *What It Means to Be an American: Essays on the American Experience* 23–49 (Marsilio Publishers, 1996); Randolph Bourne, "Trans-National America," in Carl Resek, ed., *War and the Intellectuals: Essays by Randolph Bourne, 1915–1919,* pp. 107–23 (Harper & Row, 1964); see also Greenfeld, *Nationalism,* 397–484; Lieven, *America Right or Wrong;* Ian Dyck, "Local Attachments, National Identities, and World Citizenship in the Thought of Thomas Paine," 35 *History Workshop Journal* 117 (1993); Rob Kroes, "America and the European Sense of History," 86 *J. Am. Hist.* 1135 (1999); Mae Ngai, "'The Unlovely Residue of Outworn Prejudices': The Hart-Cellar Act and the Politics of Immigration Reform, 1945–1965," in Michael Kazin and Joseph A. McCartin, eds., *Americanism: New Perspectives on the History of an Ideal* 108–27 (University of North Carolina Press, 2006); Minxin Pei, "The Paradoxes of American Nationalism," *Foreign Policy* 31–37 (May–June 2003); Robert H. Wiebe, *Who We Are: A History of Popular Nationalism* 94 (Princeton University Press, 2002).

6. Louis Hartz, *The Liberal Tradition in America: An Interpretation of American Political Thought since the Revolution* 9 (Harcourt, Brace, 1955); see also Kohn, *American Nationalism,* 13; Samuel Huntington, *American Politics: The Promise of Disharmony* 25 (Harvard University Press, 1981); Lieven, *America Right or Wrong;* Seymour Martin Lipset, *American Exceptionalism: A Double-Edged Sword* (Norton, 1996); Seymour Martin Lipset,

Continental Divide: The Values and Institutions of the United States and Canada (Routledge, 1990); Peter Novick, *That Noble Dream: The Objectivity Question and the American Historical Profession* (Cambridge University Press, 1988).

7. Sean Wilentz, "Against Exceptionalism: Class Consciousness and the American Labor Movement, 1790–1920," 26 *International Labor and Working Class History* 1–24 (1984); Rogers M. Smith, "Beyond Tocqueville, Myrdal, and Hartz: The Multiple Traditions in America," 87 *Am. Pol. Sci. Rev.* 549 (1993); Karen Orren, *Belated Feudalism: Labor, the Law, and Liberal Development in the United States* (Cambridge University Press, 1992).

8. Charles Bright and Michael Geyer, "Where in the World Is America? The History of the United States in the Global Age," in Thomas Bender, ed., *Rethinking American History in a Global Age* 63, 65 (University of California Press, 2002) ("leaky containers"); Prasenjit Duara, *Rescuing History from the Nation: Questioning Narratives of Modern China* (University of Chicago Press, 1995); Linda Basch, Nina Glick Schiller, and Christina Sztanton Blanc, *Nations Unbound: Transnational Projects, Postcolonial Predicaments, and Deterritorialized Nation-States* (Routledge, 1994); David Thelen, "The Nation and Beyond: Transnational Perspectives on United States History," 86 *J. Am. Hist.* 965–75 (1999). For a sharp critique of the excesses of the postnationalist historical move, see Ron Robin, "The Exhaustion of Enclosures: A Critique of Internationalization," in Bender, *Rethinking American History,* 367–80.

9. For a recent account emphasizing both porousness and boundedness in American history, see Thomas Bender, *A Nation among Nations: America's Place in World History* (Hill and Wang, 2006).

10. It is worth noting that, as David Bell has recently observed in his study of ancien régime France, nationality as an *identity* is often very different from nationalism as a *political ideology.* See Bell, *Cult of the Nation in France.* Here I follow the political theory literature and subsume these two often different phenomena under the term *nationalism,* by which I mean to refer to the constellation of ideas (identitarian or ideological) that privilege connections to a national community. See, for example, David Miller, *On Nationality* (Oxford University Press, 1995). On the sentimental dimensions of American nationhood, see Kazin and McCartin, *Americanism.*

11. Publius [Alexander Hamilton], Federalist No. 16, in *The Federalist Papers* 151, 154 (Isaac Kramnick, ed., Penguin, 1987).

12. Rogers Brubaker, *Nationalism Reframed: Nationhood and the Na-*

tional Question in the New Europe 178 (Cambridge University Press, 1996); see also Rogers Brubaker, "Myths and Misconceptions in the Study of Nationalism," in John A. Hall, ed., *The State of the Nation: Ernest Gellner and the Theory of Nationalism* 272–306 (Cambridge University Press, 1998). On the many uses and forms of nationalism in the United States, see Gary Gerstle, *American Crucible: Race and Nation in the Twentieth Century* (Princeton University Press, 2001); Gary Gerstle, *Working-Class Americanism: The Politics of Labor in a Textile City, 1914–1960* (Cambridge University Press, 1989); Cecilia Elizabeth O'Leary, *To Die For: The Paradox of American Patriotism* (Princeton University Press, 1999).

13. On "rooted cosmpolitanism," see Bruce A. Ackerman, "Rooted Cosmopolitanism," 104 *Ethics* 516–35 (1994); Mitchell Cohen, "Rooted Cosmopolitanism," 39 *Dissent* 478–83 (Fall 1992); Kwame Anthony Appiah, *The Ethics of Identity* 213–72 (Princeton University Press, 2005); Bonnie Honig, *Democracy and the Foreigner* 98–104 (Princeton University Press, 2001); Julie Kristeva, *Nations without Nationalism* 32 (Leon S. Roudiez, trans., Columbia University Press, 1993); Kok-Chor Tan, *Justice without Borders: Cosmopolitanism, Nationalism, and Patriotism* (Cambridge University Press, 2004).

14. For the classic examples of the social history view, see Lawrence M. Friedman, *A History of American Law* (Touchstone Books, 3d ed., 2005); Lawrence M. Friedman and Jack Ladinsky, "Social Change and the Law of Industrial Accidents," 67 *Colum. L. Rev.* 50 (1967). For the classic analysis of the social history approach and the law-and-society framework, see Robert W. Gordon, "Critical Legal Histories," 36 *Stanford Law Review* 57 (1984). See also Charles F. Sabel and Jonathan Zeitlin, "Historical Alternatives to Mass Production: Politics, Markets, and Technology in Nineteenth-Century Industrialization," 108 *Past and Present* 133 (1985); John Fabian Witt, *The Accidental Republic: Crippled Workingmen, Destitute Widows, and the Remaking of American Law* (Harvard University Press, 2004).

15. Important steps in the direction of integrating the category of the nation into the history of American law include Carol Anderson, *Eyes Off the Prize: The United Nations and the African-American Struggle for Human Rights, 1944–1955* (Cambridge University Press, 2003); Mary L. Dudziak, *Cold War Civil Rights: Race and the Image of American Democracy* (Princeton University Press, 2000); David C. Hendrickson, *Peace Pact: The Lost World of the American Founding* (University Press of Kansas, 2003); Hulsebosch, *Constituting Empire;* Ira Katznelson and Martin Shefter, eds., *Shaped by War and Trade: International Influences on American Political Development*

(Princeton University Press, 2002); Mae M. Ngai, *Impossible Subjects: Illegal Aliens and the Making of Modern America* (University of Chicago Press, 2004); Christina Duffy Burnett, "Untied States: American Expansion and Territorial Deannexation," 72 *U. Chi. L. Rev.* 797 (2005).

In one dimension, turning to the nation-state would take the form of following the lead of two decades of political science scholarship that has effectively brought the state back into the explanation of political history. The classics here are Peter B. Evans, Dietrich Rueschemeyer, and Theda Skocpol, eds., *Bringing the State Back In* (Cambridge University Press, 1983); Theda Skocpol, *Protecting Soldiers and Mothers: The Political Origins of Social Policy in the United States* (Belknap / Harvard University Press, 1992); Stephen Skowronek, *Building a New American State: The Expansion of National Administrative Capacities, 1877–1920* (Cambridge University Press, 1982). Those who would develop the nation-state as a category for the study of the history of American law will inevitably have to start with William E. Forbath's classic, *Law and the Shaping of the American Labor Movement* (Harvard University Press, 1991).

16. For some of the many varieties of liberal or civic nationalism, see Hannah Arendt, *The Origins of Totalitarianism* 267–302 (Harcourt, 1976); Gerstle, *American Crucible*, 3–13, 365–74; David A. Hollinger, *Postethnic America: Beyond Multiculturalism* (Basic Books, rev. ed., 2000); Michael Ignatieff, *Blood and Belonging: Journeys into the New Nationalism* 6–7 (Farrar, Straus, and Giroux, 1993); Will Kymlicka, *Politics in the Vernacular: Nationalism, Multiculturalism, and Citizenship* (Oxford University Press, 2001); Lind, *The Next American Nation;* Miller, *On Nationality;* Rogers M. Smith, *Civic Ideals: Conflicting Visions of Citizenship in U.S. History* (Yale University Press, 1997); Yael Tamir, *Liberal Nationalism* (Princeton University Press, 1992); Walzer, *What It Means to Be an American,* 8–12; Thomas Nagel, "The Problem of Global Justice," 33 *Phil. & Pub. Aff.* 113 (2005). On rooted or democratic cosmopolitanisms, see the references in note 12 above.

17. On the historically constructed character of national identities, see Jeremy Waldron, "Minority Cultures and the Cosmopolitan Alternative," 25 *U. Mich. J. L. Reform* 751, 781 (1992).

1. THE PYRAMID AND THE MACHINE

1. *Pennsylvania Gazette,* June 2, 1779 ("monopolizers and forestallers"); "Philadelphia Society One Hundred Years Ago, or, The Reign of

Continental Money," 3 *Pennsylvania Magazine of History and Biography* 361, 383–94 (1879) (raised prices); "A Proclamation," *Pennsylvania Gazette,* Jan. 20, 1779 (bread and other necessities); "Memorial of the First Company of Philadelphia Militia Artillery, 1779," 7 *Pennsylvania Archives* 392, 393–94 (Samuel Hazard, ed., 1853); John K. Alexander, "The Fort Wilson Incident of 1779: A Case Study of the Revolutionary Crowd," 31 *Wm. & Mary Q.* 589, 594, 601 (1974).

2. "Philadelphia Society One Hundred Years Ago," 389; "The Attack on Fort Wilson, Oct. 4, 1779," 5 *Pennsylvania Magazine of History and Biography* 475 (1881); Charles Page Smith, *James Wilson: Founding Father, 1742–1798* (University of North Carolina Press, 1956); Charles J. Stillé, *The Life and Times of John Dickinson, 1732–1808,* p. 21 (Philadelphia: Historical Society of Pennsylvania, 1891); I. G. Doolittle, "Sir William Blackstone and His 'Commentaries on the Laws of England' (1765–9): A Biographical Approach," 3 *Oxford J. Legal Studs.* 99 (1983); William Blake Odgers, "Sir William Blackstone," 27 *Yale L. J.* 599, 601–03 (1918); George W. Carey, "James Wilson's Political Thought and the Constitutional Convention," 17 *Political Science Reviewer* 49, 80 (1987); Lance Banning, *The Sacred Fire of Liberty: James Madison and the Founding of the Federal Republic* 144 (Cornell University Press, 1995); Max Farrand, *The Framing of the Constitution of the United States* 21 (Yale University Press, 1913).

3. "To the Citizens of Pennsylvania," *Pennsylvania Gazette,* Dec. 15, 1779; Smith, *James Wilson,* 83, 119–23, 132; Charles H. Lincoln, *The Revolutionary Movement in Pennsylvania, 1760–1776,* pp. 261–62 (Philadelphia University, 1901); Alexander, "Fort Wilson Incident," 590; Robert L. Brunhouse, *The Counter-Revolution in Pennsylvania, 1776–1790,* pp. 9, 27–38 (Octagon Books, 1971).

4. "The Attack on Fort Wilson," 475; "Philip Hagner's Narrative," in 2 *Life and Correspondence of Joseph Reed* 426 (William B. Reed, ed., Philadelphia: Lindsay and Blakiston, 1847); Alexander, "Fort Wilson Incident," 605–6.

5. Richard B. Morris, "'We the People of the United States': The Bicentennial of a People's Revolution," 82 *Am. Hist. Rev.* 1, 8 (1977); "Philadelphia Society One Hundred Years Ago," 391–92; "The Attack on Fort Wilson," 476; "Narrative of M'Lane," in 2 *Life and Correspondence of Joseph Reed,* 150, 152; "Philip Hagner's Narrative," 427; "The Fort Wilson Riot. Statement of Charles Wilson Peale," in 2 *Life and Correspondence of Joseph Reed,* 423, 425; Alexander, "Fort Wilson Incident," 589, 606.

6. J. R. Pole, "Reflections on American Law and the American Revolution," 50 *Wm. & Mary Q.* 123, 153 (1993).

7. David A. Bell, *Lawyers and Citizens: The Making of a Political Elite in Old Regime France* (Oxford University Press, 1994); Michael P. Fitzsimmons, *The Parisian Order of Barristers and the French Revolution* 39–40 (Harvard University Press, 1987); Eugene Huskey, *Russian Lawyers and the Soviet State: The Origins and Development of the Soviet Bar, 1917–1939*, pp. 34–79 (Princeton University Press, 1986); Zigurds L. Zile, ed., *Ideas and Forces in Soviet Legal History* 95–96, 172–73 (Oxford University Press, 1992); Richard B. Morris, "Legalism versus Revolutionary Doctrine in New England," 4 *New England Q.* 195, 195 (1931); John M. Murrin, "The Legal Transformation: The Bench and the Bar of Eighteenth-Century Massachusetts," in Stanley Katz, ed., *Colonial America: Essays in Politics and Social Development* 415, 442 (Little, Brown, 1971); John M. Murrin, "Anglicizing an American Colony" (Ph.D. diss., Yale University, 1966); see also Milton M. Klein, "New York Lawyers and the Coming of the American Revolution," in Leo Hershkowitz and Milton M. Klein, eds., *Courts and Law in Early New York* 88–101 (Kennikat Press, 1978); Peter Charles Hoffer, "Custom as Law," 50 *Wm. & Mary Q.* 160, 160 (1993); Bruce H. Mann, "Legal Reform and the Revolution," in Jack P. Greene and J. R. Pole, eds., *The Blackwell Encyclopedia of the American Revolution* 437–42 (Blackwell Reference, 1991).

8. Gordon S. Wood, "A Note on Mobs in the American Revolution," 23 *Wm. & Mary Q.* 635, 639–42 (1966); Pauline Maier, "Popular Uprisings and Civil Authority in Eighteenth-Century America," 27 *Wm. & Mary Q.* 3, 29–35 (1970); Gordon S. Wood, *The Creation of the American Republic, 1776–1787*, p. 608 (University of North Carolina Press, 1969); Publius [James Madison], Federalist No. 10, in James Madison, Alexander Hamilton, and John Jay, *The Federalist Papers* 122, 124 (Isaac Kramnick, ed., Penguin, 1987 [1788]).

9. Alexander, "Fort Wilson Incident," 607.

10. J. G. A. Pocock, *The Machiavellian Moment: Florentine Political Thought and the Atlantic Republican Tradition* 328 (Princeton University Press, 1975); see also J. G. A. Pocock, "Civic Humanism and Its Role in Anglo-American Thought," in J. G. A. Pocock, *Politics, Language, and Time: Essays on Political Thought and History* 80, 100 (Atheneum, 1971).

11. Ira Katznelson and Kenneth Prewitt, "Constitutionalism, Class, and the Limits of Choice in U.S. Foreign Policy," in Richard Fagen, ed.,

Capitalism and the State in U.S.–Latin American Relations 30–31 (Stanford University Press, 1979); Dietrich Rueschemeyer, "Comparing Legal Professions Cross-Nationally: From a Professions-Centered to a State-Centered Approach," 11 *Am. Bar Foundation Research J.* 415, 436 (1986).

12. Smith, *James Wilson,* 3–17; John Clive and Bernard Bailyn, "England's Cultural Provinces: Scotland and America," 11 *Wm. & Mary Q.* 200, 206 (1954); Robert Annan to Bird Wilson, May 16, 1805, Rush Papers, Library Company of Philadelphia Collection, Historical Society of Pennsylvania, Philadelphia; see also James Buchan, *Crowded with Genius—The Scottish Enlightenment: Edinburgh's Moment of the Mind* 4 (HarperCollins, 2003); David Lieberman, "The Legal Needs of a Commercial Society: The Jurisprudence of Lord Kames," in Istvan Hont and Michael Ignatieff, eds., *Wealth and Virtue: The Shaping of Political Economy in the Scottish Enlightenment* 203–34 (Cambridge University Press, 1983).

13. Paul Wood, "Science in the Scottish Enlightenment," in Alexander Broadie, ed., *The Cambridge Companion to the Scottish Enlightenment* 94, 99–100 (Cambridge University Press, 2003); Buchan, *Crowded with Genius,* 1; Smith, *James Wilson,* 17–19; Mark David Hall, *The Political and Legal Philosophy of James Wilson, 1742–1798,* pp. 8–9 (University of Missouri Press, 1997).

14. Richard B. Sher, "Introduction: Scottish-American Cultural Studies, Past and Present," in Richard B. Sher and Jeffrey R. Smitten, eds., *Scotland and America in the Age of Enlightenment* 1, 8 ("the 'flood'") (Princeton University Press, 1990); Smith, *James Wilson,* 20–21; Gary Wills, *Inventing America: Jefferson's Declaration of Independence* 176–80 (Houghton Mifflin, 2002); Samuel Fleischacker, "The Impact on America: Scottish Philosophy and the American Founding," in Broadie, *Cambridge Companion to the Scottish Enlightenment,* 316, 317–18; David Fate Norton, "Francis Hutcheson in America," 154 *Studies on Voltaire and the Eighteenth Century* 1547, 1551–68 (1976).

15. Annan to Wilson, May 16, 1805, Rush Papers; Norton, "Francis Hutcheson in America," 1553; Smith, *James Wilson,* 24–31.

16. Review of *The American Jurist* (vol. 1), in 30 *North American Review* 418, 418 (1829); Charles Warren, *A History of the American Bar* 4, 41–42, 44 (Little, Brown, 1911); Lawrence M. Friedman, *A History of American Law* 94–102 (Simon & Schuster, 2nd ed., 1985); Peter Charles Hoffer, *Law and People in Colonial America* 35–45, 46–47, 94 (Johns Hopkins University Press, rev. ed., 1998); Cornelia Hughes Dayton, *Women before the*

Bar: Gender, Law, and Society in Connecticut, 1639–1789, p. 27 (University of North Carolina Press, 1995); Bruce H. Mann, *Neighbors and Strangers: Law and Community in Early Connecticut* 93–94 (University of North Carolina Press, 1987); A. G. Roeber, *Faithful Magistrates and Republican Lawyers: Creators of Virginia Legal Culture, 1680–1810,* p. 48 (University of North Carolina Press, 1981); George Lee Haskins, *Law and Authority in Early Massachusetts: A Study in Tradition and Design* 117–18 (Macmillan, 1960); David Thomas Konig, *Law and Society in Puritan Massachusetts: Essex County, 1629–1692,* p. 114 (University of North Carolina Press, 1979); Susie M. Ames, ed., *County Court Records of Accomack-Northampton, Virginia, 1632–1640,* p. xv (American Historical Association, 1954); Julius Goebel Jr., "King's Law and Local Custom in Seventeenth-Century New England," 31 *Colum. L. Rev.* 416 (1931); Morris, "Legalism versus Revolutionary Doctrine," 199; Murrin, "Legal Transformation," 420.

17. *Note-Book Kept by Thomas Lechford Esq., Lawyer in Boston, Massachusetts Bay* . . . (Cambridge: John Wilson & Son, 1885); Gerard W. Gawalt, *The Promise of Power: The Emergence of the Legal Profession in Massachusetts, 1760–1840,* pp. 16, 20 (Greenwood Press, 1979) ("live upon the sins"); Murrin, "Legal Transformation," 432; Philanthropos, *To the Freeholders and Freemen of the City and County of New-York* (printed by John Holt, February 19, 1768) (Evans 11040); N.A., *The Art of Pleading: An Imitation of Part of Horace's Poetry* 7 (James Parker, 1751); John Locke, "The Fundamental Constitutions of Carolina," in *Locke: Political Essays* 160, 174 (art. 64/70) (Mark Goldie, ed., Cambridge University Press, 1997); Anton-Hermann Chroust, 1 *The Rise of the Legal Profession in America* 170 (University of Oklahoma Press, 1965); Warren, *History of the American Bar,* 43–44; John Adams, Diary (Jan. 3, 1759), in 2 *The Works of John Adams* 58 & n. (Charles Francis Adams, ed., Little, Brown, 1851–65).

18. Gabriel Thomas, *An Account of Pennsylvania and West Jersey* 43 (Cyrus Townsend Brady, ed., Burrows Brothers, 1903 [1698]); Chroust, 1 *Rise of the Legal Profession,* 211; Warren, *History of the American Bar,* 101, 104, 107.

19. Lyle v. Richards, 9 Serg. & Rawle 322 (Pa. 1823) (Tilghman, C. J.); Eben Moglen, "Considering Zenger: Partisan Politics and the Legal Profession in Provincial New York," 94 *Colum. L. Rev.* 1495, 1523 (1994).

20. John Hill Martin, *Martin's Bench and Bar of Philadelphia* 18 (Philadelphia: Rees Welsh & Co., 1883); Warren, *History of the American Bar,* 101.

21. Murrin, "Legal Transformation," 438–39, 442; Chroust, 1 *Rise of*

the Legal Profession, 33, 101–3, 181–83; Warren, *History of the American Bar,* 142; Stephen Botein, "The Legal Profession in Colonial North America," in Wilfrid Prest, ed., *Lawyers in Early Modern Europe and America* 129, 135 (Holmes & Meier, 1981); Mann, *Neighbors and Strangers,* 101–36; Bruce H. Mann, "The Evolutionary Revolution," 50 *Wm. & Mary Q.* 168, 173 (1993); Pole, "Reflections on American Law," 135, 146–48; also Moglen, "Considering Zenger"; Morris, "Legalism versus Revolutionary Doctrine," 203; William Blackstone, 3 *Commentaries on the Laws of England* 180–84 (Clarendon Press, 1768); Julius Goebel Jr. and T. Raymond Naughton, *Law Enforcement in Colonial New York: A Study in Criminal Procedure, 1664–1776,* p. 59 (Commonwealth Fund, 1944).

22. Warren, *History of the American Bar,* 109–10; Chroust, 1 *Rise of the Legal Profession,* 229–31 ("unrivaled excellence"); Martin, *Martin's Bench and Bar,* 18; E. Alfred Jones, *American Members of the Inns of Court,* xxviii–xxix (Saint Catherine Press, 1924); Roscoe Pound, *The Lawyer from Antiquity to Modern Times* 161 (West Pub. Co., 1953).

23. Jackson Turner Main, *The Social Structure of Revolutionary America* 101, 103, 146, 192 (Princeton University Press, 1965); Catherine Snell Crary, "The American Dream: John Tabor Kempe's Rise from Poverty to Riches," reprinted in Hershkowitz and Klein, *Courts and Law in Early New York,* 75; also Klein, "New York Lawyers and the Coming of the American Revolution," 91.

24. Practice Book (October 1767), vol. 4, pp. 176–200, James Wilson Papers, Historical Society of Pennsylvania, Philadelphia; Geoffrey Seed, *James Wilson* 5 (KTO Press, 1978).

25. Bruce H. Mann, *Republic of Debtors: Bankruptcy in the Age of American Independence* (Harvard University Press, 2002); Charles Royster, *The Fabulous History of the Dismal Swamp Company: A Story of George Washington's Times* 362–64, 371–72, 385 (Borzoi Books, 1999); Ethel E. Rasmussen, "Democratic Environment—Aristocratic Aspirations," 90 *Pennsylvania Magazine of History and Biography* 155, 179–81 (1966); Business Correspondence, pp. 1–115, vol. 5, James Wilson Papers; Wilson to "Gentlemen," Jan. 16, 1785, pp. 21ff., vol. 3, James Wilson Papers; Smith, *James Wilson,* 159–68; Paul Demund Evans, *The Holland Land Company* 31 (Buffalo Historical Society, 1924); Shaw Livermore, *Early American Land Companies: Their Influence on Corporate Development* 110n, 153–54, 208 (Oxford University Press, 1939).

26. Edward Gibbon, 1 *The History of the Decline and Fall of the Roman*

Empire, ch. 3, p. 103 (David Womersley, ed., Penguin, 1994 [1776]); T. C. Smout, "Where Had the Scottish Economy Got to by the Third Quarter of the Eighteenth Century?" in Hunt and Ignatieff, *Wealth and Virtue,* 45–72; Pocock, *Machiavellian Moment,* 49–80; Istvan Hunt and Michael Ignatieff, "Needs and Justice in the Wealth of Nations: An Introductory Essay," in Hunt and Ignatieff, *Wealth and Virtue,* 1–44; John Robertson, "The Scottish Enlightenment at the Limits of the Civic Tradition," in id., pp. 137–78; J. G. A. Pocock, "Cambridge Paradigms and Scotch Philosophers," in id., pp. 235–52; J. G. A. Pocock, "Civic Humanism and its Role in Anglo-American Thought," in *Politics, Language, and Time* 80, 101–2 (Atheneum, 1971); Samuel Fleischacker, "Adam Smith's Reception among the American Founders, 1776–1790," 59 *Wm. & Mary Q.* 897, 916–17 (2002); Daniel Walker Howe, "Why the Scottish Enlightenment Was Useful to the Framers of the American Constitution," 31 *Comparative Studies in Society and History* 572, 574 (1989); J. G. A. Pocock, "Gibbon's *Decline and Fall* and the World View of the Late Enlightenment," 10 *Eighteenth-Century Studies* 287 (1977).

27. J. G. A. Pocock, "Machiavelli, Harrington, and English Political Ideologies in the Eighteenth Century," 22 *Wm. & Mary Q.* 549, 582 (1965); David Hume, "On Commerce," in David Hume, *Political Essays* 98–99, 100 (Knud Haakonssen, ed., Cambridge University Press, 1994 [1741]); David Hume, "Of the Independence of Parliament," in id., p. 24; Adam Smith, *The Theory of Moral Sentiments* 70 (Prometheus Books, 2000 [1759]); Albert O. Hirschman, *The Passions and the Interests: Political Arguments for Capitalism before Its Triumph* 7–66 (Princeton University Press, 1977).

28. Francis Hutcheson, *An Inquiry Concerning Beauty, Order, Harmony, Design* 25 (Peter Kivy, ed., Martinus Nijhoff, 1973); John Locke, *An Essay Concerning Human Understanding* 72, 89 (A. D. Woozley, ed., New American Library, 1964 [1689]); Francis Hutcheson, *An Essay on the Nature and Conduct of the Passions and Affections,* xvii (Dublin: S. Powell, 1728), reprinted in 2 *Collected Works of Francis Hutcheson* (Bernhard Fabian, ed., Georg Olms Verlag, 1990); [Henry Home, Lord Kames], *Historical Law-Tracts* 2 (Edinburgh: A. Kincaid, 2nd ed., 1761); [Henry Home, Lord Kames], *Principles of Equity* 18, 20, 32 (Edinburgh: A. Millar & A. Kincaid, 2nd ed., 1767).

29. Hutcheson, *Essay on the Nature and Conduct of the Passions,* 7, 14; Francis Hutcheson, *A Short Introduction to Moral Philosophy in Three*

Books . . . 54 (R. Foulis, 1747), reprinted in 4 *Collected Works of Francis Hutcheson;* also Smith, *Theory of Moral Sentiments,* 63–64; Wills, *Inventing America,* 195–96.

30. Quotations come in order from pp. 201–4, 133, 136, 134, 134–35 of 1 *The Works of James Wilson* (Robert Green McCloskey, ed., Harvard University Press, 1967). See also Thomas Reid, *An Inquiry into the Human Mind on the Principles of Common Sense* (Derek R. Brookes, ed., Edinburgh University Press, 1997 [1764]); William Shakespeare, *Hamlet,* act 2, scene 2 (Tucker Brooke and Jack Randall Crawford, eds., Yale University Press, 1947).

31. Quotations from (in order) pp. 238, 136, and 145 of 1 *Works of James Wilson.* See also "James Wilson's Charge to the Grand Jury," 2 *Documentary History of the Supreme Court of the United States* 396, 401 (Maeva Marcus et al., eds., Columbia University Press, 1988) (hereinafter *DHSCUS*).

32. Adam Smith, *The Wealth of Nations,* bk. 4, ch. 8, pt. 3, p. 646, and bk. 3, ch. 4, p. 449 (Edwin Cannan, ed., Modern Library 2000 [1776]).

33. 2 *Works of James Wilson,* 835, 836; James Wilson, *On the Improvement and Settlement of Lands in the United States: An Essay by the Late James Wilson . . .* 11, 13–14 (Research Bulletin of the Free Library of Philadelphia, 1946). A handwritten copy appears as "Prospectus of an Association for the Promotion of Immigration from Europe," in vol. 2 of the James Wilson Papers, Historical Society of Pennsylvania, pp. 41–50.

34. Wilson, *On the Improvement and Settlement,* 15, 30–31.

35. 1 *Works of James Wilson,* 232, 238; Publius [Alexander Hamilton], Federalist No. 15, *Federalist Papers,* 145, 146; Wilson letter [to Dutch investors], March 12, 1785, in vol. 3, pp. 21–30, James Wilson Papers, Historical Society of Pennsylvania; Wilson, *On the Improvement and Settlement,* 24.

36. Hannah Arendt, *On Revolution* 142 (Viking Press, 1963).

37. Morris, quoted in Arthur Meier Schlesinger, "Political Mobs and the American Revolution," 99 *Proc. Am. Phil. Soc'y* 244, 249 (1955); Smith, quoted in Klein, "New York Lawyers and the Coming of the American Revolution," 97, and Richard B. Morris, "Class Struggle and the American Revolution," 19 *Wm. & Mary Q.* 3, 6 (1962); Gerry, quoted in Merrill Jensen, "The American People and the American Revolution," 57 *J. Am. Hist.* 5, 31 (1970). On the Declaration, see Robert M. Weir, "Who Shall Rule at Home," 6 *J. Interdisc. Hist.* 679, 695 (1976).

38. Gary B. Nash, *Urban Crucible: The Northern Seaports and the Origins of the American Revolution* 94–95, 169–83, 196 (Harvard University Press, 1979); Gary B. Nash, "The Transformation of Urban Politics, 1700–1765," 60 *J. Am. Hist.* 605 (1973); Douglas Greenberg, "The Middle Colonies in Recent American Historiography," 36 *Wm. & Mary Q.* 396, 408 (1979); Richard Maxwell Brown, "Violence and the American Revolution," in Stephen G. Kurtz and James H. Hutson, eds., *Essays on the American Revolution* 81, 97 (University of North Carolina Press, 1973).

39. Gary B. Nash, "Poverty and Poor Relief in Pre-Revolutionary Philadelphia," 33 *Wm. & Mary Q.* 3, 6–9 (1976); Gary B. Nash, "Up from the Bottom in Franklin's Philadelphia," 77 *Past and Present* 57, 82 (1977) ("great and overgrown"); Jensen, "American People and the American Revolution," 30 ("enormous proportion").

40. Edmund S. Morgan and Helen M. Morgan, *The Stamp Act Crisis: Prologue to Revolution* 168–79 (University of North Carolina Press, 1953); Thomas C. Grey, "Origins of the Unwritten Constitution: Fundamental Law in American Revolutionary Thought," 30 *Stan. L. Rev.* 843, 879–81 (1978); Warren, *History of the American Bar,* 124 (quoting *Life and Correspondence of James Iredell* without page no.); James P. Whittenburg, "Planters, Merchants, and Lawyers: Social Change and the Origins of the North Carolina Regulation," 34 *Wm. & Mary Q.* 215, 237–38 (1977); *Liberty and Property, without Oppression* (n.p. [1769]) (Evans 41951); Frank B. Ward, "The American Revolution and the Legal Profession in New Jersey" 45, 64–65 (A.B. thesis, Princeton University, 1966); Chroust, 2 *Rise of the Legal Profession,* 26–27; Paul A. Gilje, *Rioting in America* 43–45 (Indiana University Press, 1996).

41. Klein, "New York Lawyers and the Coming of the American Revolution," 91; Murrin, "Legal Transformation," 443; Murrin, "Anglicizing an American Colony," app. D, pp. 311–13; Chroust, 2 *Rise of the Legal Profession,* 6–7, 11; Lorenzo Sabine, 1 *Biographical Sketches of the Loyalists of the American Revolution* 59–60 (Kennikat Press, 1966 [1864]), quoted in Chroust, 2 *Rise of the Legal Profession,* 11 n.25; Pound, *Lawyer from Antiquity to Modern Times,* 174. In the colonial population as a whole, historians estimate some 400,000 loyalists out of a population of 2.5 million people. See Robert McCluer Calhoon, *The Loyalists in Revolutionary America, 1760–1781,* p. ix (Harcourt Brace Jovanovich, 1973).

42. Joseph Moreau Gottschalk, "The Loyalists of Philadelphia" 13, 39, 63–78 (M.A. thesis, University of Virginia, 1929); William Montgomery

Meigs, *The Life of Charles Jared Ingersoll* 20 (J. B. Lippincott, 1897); Ernest H. Baldwin, "Joseph Galloway, The Loyalist Politician," 26 *Pennsylvania Magazine of History and Biography* 161, 289, 321 (1902); Robert R. Bell, *The Philadelphia Lawyer: A History, 1735–1945*, p. 77 (Associated University Press, 1992).

43. Horace Binney, "Leaders of the Old Bar of Philadelphia," reprinted in Law Association of Philadelphia, *Addresses Delivered March 13, 1902 . . . to Commemorate the Centennial Celebration of the Law Association . . .* 113–15, 121, 123–29 (Sign of the Ivy Leaf, 1906); Horace Binney, "Life of Chief Justice Tilghman," *American Law Magazine*, Apr. 1843, p. 1; James T. Mitchell, "Historical Address," in Law Association of Philadelphia, *Addresses*, 13, 45; T. I. Wharton, "A Memoir of William Rawle," in Law Association of Philadelphia, *Addresses*, 240, 245–46; Thomas R. Meehan, "Courts, Cases, and Counselors in Revolutionary and Post-Revolutionary Pennsylvania," 91 *Pennsylvania Magazine of History and Biography* 3, 4 (1967).

44. Meehan, "Courts, Cases, and Counselors," 5, 14–16, 17–23, 28 ("an agreement"); see also Brunhouse, *Counter-Revolution in Pennsylvania*, 36–37; 1 *The Pennsylvania State Trials: Containing the Impeachment, Trial, and Acquittal of Francis Hopkinson and John Nicholson, Esquires . . .* (Philadelphia: Francis Bailey, 1795); Baldwin, "Joseph Galloway," 321; Chroust, 2 *Rise of the Legal Profession*, 26–27; [Jesse B. Higgins], *Sampson against the Philistines, or, the Reformation of Lawsuits . . .* 12 (Philadelphia: B. Graves, 2nd ed., 1805) ("enmity"); Gary B. Nash, "The Philadelphia Bar and Bench, 1800–1861," 7 *Comparative Studies in Society and History* 203, 212 (1965) ("eminent lawyers").

45. Carl Becker, Book Review, 79 *The Nation* 146 (1904), reviewing Burton Alva Konkle, *The Life and Times of Thomas Smith, 1745–1809* (Campion & Co., 1904) ("critical situation"); John Dickinson, "Letters from a Farmer in Pennsylvania" (1768), in Forrest McDonald, ed., *Empire and Nation* 19 & n. (Prentice-Hall 1962); Joseph Reed to Earl of Dartmouth, Dec. 27, 1773, in 1 *Life and Correspondence of Joseph Reed* 54, 55 (William B. Reed, ed., Philadelphia: Lindsay & Blakiston, 1847).

46. Bell, *Philadelphia Lawyer*, 80; see also Morris, "Legalism versus Revolutionary Doctrine," 207 (Massachusetts); Ward, "American Revolution and the Legal Profession in New Jersey"; Robert A. Ferguson, *Law and Letters in American Culture* 59–66 (Harvard University Press, 1984). Of the men who served in the Continental Congress, 42 percent (144 of 339) were lawyers.

47. 1 *Works of James Wilson,* 354.

48. James Wilson to Robert Morris, Jan. 14, 1777, in 6 *Letters of Delegates to Congress* 104 (Paul H. Smith, ed., Library of Congress, 1976–2000); James Wilson to George Washington, Apr. 21, 1789, in 1 *DHSCUS,* [Part 2] 612, 612–13; James Wilson to William Bingham, Aug. 24, 1791, in 1 *Works of James Wilson,* 59–64; James Wilson to George Washington, Dec. 31, 1791, in 4 *DHSCUS,* 571–73.

49. "James Wilson's Appointment as Associate Justice in 1789," in 1 *DHSCUS,* 44, 48; George Washington to James Wilson, Jan. 23, 1792, in 9 *Papers of George Washington: Presidential Series* 501 (W. W. Abbot, ed., University Press of Virginia, 1983–); 1 *Works of James Wilson,* 64.

50. "James Wilson's Charge to the Grand Jury," May 23, 1791, in 2 *DHSCUS,* 166, 191–92.

51. 1 *The Records of the Federal Convention of 1787,* pp. 48, 49, 57 (Max Farrand, ed., Yale University Press, 1911). Compare Thomas Reid's *Inquiry into the Human Mind,* 210, which describes common sense as "built upon a broad foundation."

52. 2 *Documentary History of the Ratification of the Constitution: Ratification of the Constitution by the States—Pennsylvania* 574, 580 (Merrill Jensen, ed., State Historical Society of Wisconsin, 1976) (hereinafter *DHRC*) (comments of James Wilson, Dec. 11, 1787); James Wilson, "Speech on Choosing the Members of the Senate by Electors; Delivered on 31st December, 1789, in the Convention of Pennsylvania," in 2 *Works of James Wilson,* 781, 785; 1 *Works of James Wilson,* 315, 403.

53. Hutcheson, *Inquiry Concerning Beauty,* 41; Reid, *Inquiry into the Human Mind,* 210; Hutcheson, *A Short Introduction to Moral Philosophy,* 300–301.

54. William Wistanley, *The New Help to Discourse: or Wit and Mirth Intermixt with More Serious Matter . . .* 68–69 (Boston: Reprinted by J. Franklin, 1722) (Evans 2408); John Adams, *The Flowers of Ancient History; Comprehending on a New Plan, the Most Remarkable and Interesting Events, as Well as Characters of Antiquity . . .* 20–21 (Philadelphia: Jacob Johnson & Co., 1795) (Evans 28149) (compare Abbé Millot [Claude Francois Xavier], *Elements of General History* 45–51 (Worcester, Mass.: Isaiah Thomas, 1789)); [Sir William Temple], "An Essay upon the Original and Nature of Government" 45, 83–84, in [Sir William Temple], *Miscellanea* (London: A. M. & R. R. for Edw. Gellibrand, 1680); Smith, *James Wilson,* 276; see also [Francis Bacon], *Letters, Memoirs, Parliamentary Affairs, State Papers, &c. with some Curious Pieces in Law and Philosophy Publish'd from the Origi-*

nals of the Lord Chancellor Bacon 425 (Robert Stephens, ed., London: Olive Payne, 1736); Josiah Woodward, *Fair Warnings to a Careless World, or, The Serious Practice of Religion* . . . 47 (Boston: Gamaliel Rogers, 1729); James Bruce, *An Interesting Narrative of the Travels of James Bruce, Esq. into Abyssinia* . . . 33–34 (New York: Reprinted for Berry & Rogers, 1790).

55. Blackstone, 3 *Commentaries,* 320 (see also 1, 153); Robert Willman, "Blackstone and the 'Theoretical Perfection' of English Law in the Reign of Charles II," 26 *Historical Journal* 39, 44 (1983); James Hervey, "Reflections on a Flower-Garden," in James Hervey, 1 *Meditations and Contemplations: In Two Volumes* . . . 156–57 (8th ed., Daniel Fowle, 1750) (Evans 6516); Adams, *Flowers of Ancient History,* 20–21; Samuel Johnson, *Rasselas, Prince of Abissinia* 81 (Greenfield, Mass.: Thomas Dickman, 1795).

56. James Stevens Curl, *Egyptomania: The Egyptian Revival, A Recurring Theme in the History of Taste* 79–109 (Manchester University Press, 1994); Jean-Marcel Humbert, Michael Pantazzi, and Christiane Ziegler, *Egyptomania: Egypt in Western Art, 1730–1930,* pp. 36–199 (National Gallery of Canada, 1994).

57. "The Honest Politician," *Pennsylvania Gazette,* Dec. 22, 1779; William Hillhouse, *A Dissertation, in Answer to a Late Lecture on the Political State of America* 15 (New Haven: T. & S. Green, 1789); Philip Freneau, "The Pyramids of Egypt: A Dialogue," in *The Poems of Philip Freneau, Written Chiefly during the Late War* 13–17 (Philadelphia: Francis Bailey, 1786 [1770]); Thomas Jefferson, "Catalogue of Paintings &c at Monticello," in Susan Stein, *The Worlds of Thomas Jefferson at Monticello* 434–36 (Harry N. Abrams, 1993); Worthington Chauncey Ford, ed., 12 *Journals of the Continental Congress, 1774–1789,* p. 339 (U.S. Government Printing Office, 1914); Richard S. Patterson and Richardson Dougall, *The Eagle and the Shield: A History of the Great Seal of the United States* 66–67 (U.S. Government Printing Office, 1976).

58. Daniel J. Boorstin, "Afterlives of the Great Pyramids," *Wilson Quarterly* 130–39 (Summer 1992); Humbert et al., *Egyptomania,* 43.

59. Zur Shalev, "Measurer of All Things: John Greaves (1602–1652), the Great Pyramid, and Early Modern Metrology," 63 *Journal of the History of Ideas* 555, 568, 573 (2002); Witold Kula, *Measures and Men* 90–101 (R. Szreter, trans., Princeton University Press, 1986); H. Arthur Klein, *The World of Measurements: Masterpieces, Mysteries, and Muddles of Metrology* (Simon & Schuster, 1974); Daniel J. Boorstin, *The Mysterious Science of*

the Law 39–40 (Harvard University Press, 1941); John Greaves, *Pyramidographia, or A Description of the Pyramids in Aegypt* preface (unpaginated), 94 (London: George Badger, 1646).

60. Boorstin, "Afterlives," 132–33; 1 *An Universal History from the Earliest Account of Time to the Present: Compiled from Original Authors; and Illustrated with Maps, Cuts, Notes, Chronological and Other Tables,* xl–xlv, 210–12, 407 (Dublin: Edward Bate, 1744); Jonathan Edwards, *Sermons, on the Following Subjects* . . . 8–9 (Hartford: Hudson and Goodwin, 1780) (Evans 16767); see also *Universal History,* p. 212 (same estimate).

61. Greaves, *Pyramidographia,* 45, 58; 1 *Works of James Wilson,* 129–30; Patterson and Dougall, *Eagle and the Shield,* 26; Robert A. Ferguson, *Reading the Early Republic* 172–97 (Harvard University Press, 2004) ("Finding Rome in America").

62. Blackstone quotations (in order) are from the *Commentaries,* vol. 1, pp. 5, 31, and 271, and vol. 4, p. 436; see also Charles Viner, *A General Abridgment of Law and Equity Alphabetically Digested under Proper Titles* . . . (Aldershot: Printed for the author, 1748), table of contents; David Lieberman, *The Province of Legislation Determined: Legal Theory in Eighteenth-Century Britain* 29–67 (Cambridge University Press, 1989); Michael Lobban, "Blackstone and the Science of Law," 30 *Historical Journal* 311 (1987); S. F. C. Milsom, "The Nature of Blackstone's Achievement," 1 *Oxford J. Legal Studs.* 1 (1981).

63. Doolittle, "Blackstone . . . a Biographical Approach," 110; "Commonplace Book, 1766," pp. 1–20, in vol. 4, James Wilson Papers, Historical Society of Pennsylvania.

64. Lieberman, *Province of Legislation Determined,* 86–87; Jeremy Bentham, *A Comment on the Commentaries and A Fragment on Government* (J. H. Burns and H. L. A. Hart, eds., University of London Athlone Press, 1977); 1 *Works of James Wilson,* 103, 114, 81; "Considerations on the Nature and Extent of the Legislative Authority of the British Parliament," in 2 *Works of James Wilson,* 721, 723, 726; see [Kames,] *Historical Law-Tracts,* p. ix; see also Barbara A. Black, "The Constitution of Empire: the Case for the Colonists," 124 *U. Pa. L. Rev.* 1157, 1178 (1976). On Wilson's complicated relationship to Blackstone, see Stephen A. Conrad, "James Wilson's 'Assimilation of the Common-Law Mind,'" 84 *Nw. U. L. Rev.* 186 (1989); John V. Jezierski, "Parliament or People: James Wilson and Blackstone on the Nature and Location of Sovereignty," 32 *Journal of the History of Ideas* 95 (1971).

65. 1 *Records of the Federal Convention,* 379–80, 93; 2 *DHRC,* 488 ("If this is meant by a natural aristocracy . . . can it be objectionable, that men should be employed that are most noted for their virtue and talents?"); Curl, *Egyptomania,* 79–83.

66. Quotations (in order) are from 1 *Works of James Wilson,* 141, 132–33, 334; see also 2 *DHSCUS,* 415, 356.

67. 2 *DHRC,* 568; J. G. A. Pocock, "Modes of Political and Historical Time in Early Eighteenth-Century England," in J. G. A. Pocock, *Virtue, Commerce, and History: Essays on Political Thought and History, Chiefly in the Eighteenth Century* 91, 92 (Cambridge University Press, 1985); 2 *DHRC,* 339, 342. Compare Hume: "Almost all the governments, which exist at present, or of which there remains any record in story, have been founded originally, either on usurpation or conquest, or both, without any pretense of a fair consent, or voluntary subjection of the people." David Hume, "Of the Original Contract," in *Political Essays* (Haakonssen, ed.), 186, 189–90. It is worth noting here Wilson's belief that the use of metaphor could transmit truth to the heart where reason might only render truth "evident to the understanding." 1 *Works of James Wilson,* 101; see also Stephen A. Conrad, "Metaphor and Imagination in James Wilson's Theory of Federal Union," 13 *Law & Social Inq.* 1 (1988).

68. Smith, *James Wilson,* 301; 1 *Records of the Federal Convention,* 413; 1 *Works of James Wilson,* 354, 129–30; 2 *DHRC,* 584; 1 *Works of James Wilson,* 71, 145; 2 *DHRC,* 584.

69. Jack N. Rakove, *Original Meanings: Politics and Ideas in the Making of the Constitution* 143 (Knopf, 1996); John Montgomery to James Wilson, March 2, 1788, in 2 *DHRC,* 701–6; Gawalt, *Promise of Power,* 20 ("live upon the sins"); Grant Gilmore, *The Ages of American Law* 111 (Yale University Press, 1977).

70. 2 *DHRC,* 362; 1 *Records of the Federal Convention,* 605.

71. 2 *Works of James Wilson,* 446; Ferguson, *Law and Letters,* 65; 1 *Works of James Wilson,* 69–70; 2 *DHRC,* 492, 524–25; 1 *Works of James Wilson,* 125; Stephen Skowronek, *Building a New American State: The Expansion of National Administrative Capacities, 1877–1920,* pp. 39–46 (Cambridge University Press, 1982) ("the state of courts and parties"); Rueschemeyer, "Comparing Legal Professions Cross-Nationally," 436.

72. John Adams to James Warren, April 22, 1776, in 3 *Letters of Delegates to Congress, 1774–1789,* p. 569 (Paul H. Smith et al., eds., U.S. Government Printing Office, 1976–); John Adams to Moses Gill, June 10, 1775, in 1 *Letters of Delegates to Congress,* 466; "New York, January 27,"

Pennsylvania Gazette, Feb. 3, 1790; 2 *DHRC*, 136–37; see also M. A. Stewart, "Religion and Rational Theology," in Broadie, *Cambridge Companion to the Scottish Enlightenment*, 31, 39 (Hume); Smith, *Theory of Moral Sentiments*, 464; George Berkeley, *A Treatise Concerning the Principles of Human Knowledge* 398 (Colin Murray Turbayne, ed., Bobbs-Merrill, 1970 [1710]); Blackstone, 1 *Commentaries*, 153.

73. Gilbert Tennent, *Twenty-Three Sermons upon the Chief End of Man* 204 (Philadelphia: William Bradford, 1744) (Evans 5500); R. Watson, *An Apology for the Bible* 63 (Boston: Manning & Loring, 1796) (Evans 31565); 10 *Works of John Adams*, 283; Benjamin Rush, "Of the Mode of Education Proper in a Republic," in Benjamin Rush, *Essays: Literary, Moral, and Philosophical* 6, 14–15 (Thomas & Samuel F. Bradford, 1798).

74. "At the Instance of Benjamin Franklin: A Brief History of the Library Company of Philadelphia," available at http://www.librarycompany.org/instance.htm; Leo Marx, *The Machine in the Garden: Technology and the Pastoral Ideal in America* 161 (Oxford University Press, 1964); Wills, *Inventing America*, 100–101; Tench Coxe, *View of the United States of America in a Series of Papers . . .* 35 (Philadelphia: Printed for William Hall and Wrigley & Berriman, 1794); "Report on Weights and Measures," in 16 *The Papers of Thomas Jefferson* 602–75 (Julian P. Boyd, ed., Princeton University Press, 1961); Wills, *Inventing America*, 105–10.

75. Marx, *Machine in the Garden*, 162; Wills, *Inventing America*, 95; see also John F. Kasson, *Civilizing the Machine: Technology and Republican Values in America, 1776–1900*, pp. 3–36 (Grossman, 1976).

76. Charles Pettit to James Hutchinson, Dec. 18, 1785, in 23 *Letters of Delegates to Congress*, 68; Smith, *Theory of Moral Sentiments*, 464.

77. [John Stevens], *Observations on Government Including Some Animadversions on Mr. Adams's Defence of the Constitutions . . . by a Farmer, of New Jersey* 31–32 (New York: W. Ross, 1787) (Evans 20465); 2 *The Debates in the Several State Conventions, on the Adoption of the Federal Constitution* 188 (Jonathan Elliot, ed., Washington: Printed for the editor, 1836) (hereinafter *Elliot's Debates*) (Jan. 4, 1788); [Anon.], *Prophetic Conjectures on the French Revolution . . .* 55 (Baltimore: John Havel, 1794) (Evans 47190); 3 *Records of the Federal Convention*, 292 (comments of Luther Martin); 4 *Elliot's Debates*, 309 (comments of Rawlins Lowndes); 2 *Elliot's Debates*, 264 (comments of Alexander Hamilton).

78. Richard Price, *Observations on the Nature of Civil Liberty . . .* 5 (Philadelphia: Reprinted by John Dunlap, 1776) (Evans 15030); William Cobbett, *A Little Plain English, Addressed to the People of the United States,*

on the *Treaty, Negociated with his Brittanic Majesty* . . . 66 (Philadelphia: Thomas Bradford, 1796) (Evans 30214) ("mere machine"); Jonathan Edwards, *A Dissertation Concerning Liberty and Necessity* . . . 56 (Worcester, Mass.: Leonard Worcester, 1797) (Evans 32073); "An Address to the Public," *Pennsylvania Gazette,* Nov. 25, 1789; *Journal of William Maclay, United States Senator from Pennsylvania, 1789–1791,* p. 321 (Edgar S. Maclay, ed., New York: D. Appleton & Co., 1890) ("mere political machine"); Samuel Osgood to Stephen Higginson, Feb. 2, 1784, in 21 *Letters of Delegates of Congress,* 323, 329; *Journal of William Maclay,* 108; John Adams to the President of Congress, Dec. 28, 1780, in 10 *Papers of John Adams* 442 (Robert J. Taylor et al., eds., Belknap / Harvard University Press, 1996). See Madison's concern that if "the machine [of the Congress] will be enlarged . . . the fewer, and often the more secret, will be the springs by which its motions are directed." Publius [Madison], Federalist No. 58, *Federalist Papers,* 347, 351. Madison expressed a similar anxiety about the machine-constitution when he warned against "multiplying the parts of the machine" of state. Banning, *Sacred Fire of Liberty,* 61. But Madison also invoked the Newtonian model, as when he argued that a congressional negative over state laws was required to "controul the centrifugal tendency of the States; which, without it, will continually fly out of their proper orbits and destroy the order & harmony of the political system." 1 *Records of the Federal Convention,* 165.

79. John Adams, *A Defence of the Constitutions of Government of the United States of America* 323 (Hall and Sellers, 1787); J. G. A. Pocock, *The Ancient Constitution and the Feudal Law: A Study of English Historical Thought in the Seventeenth Century* 144 (Cambridge University Press, 1957); Wood, *Creation of the American Republic,* 587–92, 606–15.

80. [Stevens], *Observations on Government,* 27; 1 *Records of the Federal Convention,* 135; see also Publius [James Madison], Federalist No. 10, *Federalist Papers,* 123–24. Douglass Adair famously suggested that in this respect, framers such as Madison went past Hume, for whom the most important factions tended to be what he would have called factions of "principle," to focus on commercial faction. Douglass Adair, "'That Politics May Be Reduced to a Science': David Hume, James Madison, and the Tenth Federalist," 20 *Huntington Library Q.* 343 (1957). Larry Kramer, "Madison's Audience," 112 *Harv. L. Rev.* 611 (1999), calls into question the extent to which Madison's pluralist arguments gained a receptive hearing.

81. Letter by Andrew Ellicott, *Pennsylvania Gazette,* Apr. 30, 1788; [James Madison], Federalist No. 37, in id., 241, 246 (also in *Federalist Pa-*

pers, 247, 252); *Debates, Resolutions, and Other Proceedings of the Convention of the Commonwealth of Massachusetts* 133 (Boston: Adams and Nourse, 1788) (Evans 21242).

82. 1 *Records of the Federal Convention,* 254, 151, 380, 141, 132; 2 *Works of James Wilson,* 552; see also Stephen A. Conrad, "Polite Foundation: Citizenship and Common Sense in James Wilson's Republican Theory," 1984 *Sup. Ct. Rev.* 359 (1984); Conrad, "Metaphor and Imagination," 11–13.

83. David Hume, "Of the Independency of Parliament," in *Political Essays* (Haakonssen, ed.), 24; 1 *Records of the Federal Convention,* 381 (comment of Hamilton), 135 (comment of Madison), 306 (Hamilton); David Hume, "Of the Origin of Justice and Property," in *David Hume's Political Essays* 28, 35 (Charles W. Hendel, ed., Bobbs-Merrill, 1953); [James Madison], Federalist No. 51, *Federalist Papers,* 318, 318–20; Hume, "That Politics May be Reduced to a Science," in *Political Essays* (Haakonssen, ed.), 12, 5; see also Daniel Walker Howe, "The Political Psychology of *The Federalist,*" 44 *Wm. & Mary Q.* 485 (1987); Jack N. Rakove, "The Madisonian Theory of Rights," *31 Wm. & Mary L. Rev.* 245, 252–53 (1989); Jack N. Rakove, "The Madisonian Moment," 55 *U. Chi. L. Rev.* 473 (1988).

84. Wood, *Creation of the American Republic,* 606.

85. Charles W. Anderson, "How to Make a Good Society," in Karol Edward Soltan and Stephen L. Elkin, eds., *The Constitution of Good Societies* 103, 113 (Pennsylvania State University Press, 1996).

86. Pocock, "Modes of Political and Historical Time," 92.

87. David Hume, "On the Idea of the Perfect Commonwealth," in *Political Essays* (Haakonssen, ed.), 221, 233; "Oration Delivered on the Fourth of July 1788, at the Procession Formed at Philadelphia," in 2 *Works of James Wilson,* 779–80.

88. Rakove, *Original Meanings,* 145–46; Smith, *James Wilson,* 303. In the Federal Convention, Wilson's interventions (especially in late May and early June) were often remarkably ill timed. He himself was "not prepared" with a practical suggestion for how the convention might adopt his recommendation for direct election of the Senate (1 *Records of the Federal Convention,* 52), and his abrupt proposal for a unitary executive was met with silence ("a considerable pause ensuing," id., 65). His nationalization language was so strong that he was quickly at pains to reassure delegates that he did not mean to abolish the states (id., 137, 153). And from the middle of June until the Great Compromise, Wilson repeatedly (and clumsily) threatened walkouts by the large states (id., 179–83, 482). In the Pennsylvania ratify-

ing convention, Wilson's often overwrought erudition came in for heavy mockery. 2 *DHRC,* 571 n.1.

89. Robert Green McCloskey, "Introduction," to 1 *Works of James Wilson,* 37; Burton Alva Konkle, *James Wilson and the Constitution: The Opening Address in the Official Series of Events Known as the James Wilson Memorial, Delivered before the Law Academy of Philadelphia on November 14, 1906* (The Academy, 1907); Edmund Randolph to George Washington, Jan. 21, 1792, in 4 *DHSCUS,* 575 (Blackstone used "Herculean" to describe codification proposals in England at Blackstone, 3 *Commentaries,* 267); Bell, *Philadelphia Lawyer,* 71 ("entirely met"); Andrew C. McLaughlin, "James Wilson in the Philadelphia Convention," 12 *Pol. Sci. Q.* 1, 20 (1897); John Adams to Abigail Adams, March 5, 1796, in 1 *DHSCUS,* 842; see also 1 *DHSCUS,* 631.

90. *Federal Gazette,* Mar. 9, 1789, in 1 *DHSCUS,* 609; General Anthony Wayne to James Wilson, May 20, 1789, in 1 *DHSCUS,* 619–20; Smith, *James Wilson,* 305; McCloskey, "Introduction," 30; *Federal Gazette* (Boston), June 10, 1793, in 2 *DHSCUS,* 406; John Quincy Adams to Thomas Boylston Adams, June 23, 1793, in 2 *DHSCUS,* 408–10; Bell, *Philadelphia Lawyer,* 71.

91. *General Advertiser,* Apr. 20, 1792, in 6 *DHSCUS,* 54; 6 *DHSCUS,* 280–89, 282 n.50; "Moultrie v. Georgia," 5 *DHSCUS,* 496, 505–6; *Aurora* (Philadelphia), Feb. 16, 1795, in 5 *DHSCUS,* 506; "Presentment of the Grand Jury of Chatham County, Georgia," Oct. 21, 1796, in 5 *DHSCUS,* 554.

92. John F. Manning, "The Eleventh Amendment and the Reading of Precise Constitutional Texts," 113 *Yale L. J.* 1663, 1673–1680 (2004).

93. *Dunlap's Daily Advertiser,* Feb. 18, 1793, in 5 *DHSCUS,* 217, 219; Chisholm v. Georgia, 2 U.S. 419, 453, 464, 453–54, 460, 459, 462 (1793) (Wilson, J.).

94. *Federal Gazette,* Mar. 9, 1789, 1 *DHSCUS,* 609 ("genius . . . precedent"); Smith, *James Wilson,* 358, 298 ("too rarefied . . . visionary theorist"; "bewildering eloquence . . . ambition"); *Chisholm,* 2 U.S. at 454 ("pernicious"); Edmund Pendleton to Nathan Pendleton, Aug. 10, 1793, in 5 *DHSCUS,* 232–33 ("looks in vain"); Smith, *James Wilson,* 358 ("monarchy men"; "confiscated property"; "immediately issue").

95. Seed, *James Wilson,* 10; Mann, *Republic of Debtors,* 187–88; George Palmer to James Wilson, April 27, 1780, in vol. 5, pp. 1–10, James Wilson Papers; Peter Galen to James Wilson, Sept. 22, 1787, vol. 5, pp. 41–50, James Wilson Papers; Smith, *James Wilson,* 298. On Wilson's ever-mount-

ing debts, see generally vol. 5 of the manuscript Wilson Papers at the Historical Society of Pennsylvania ("Business Correspondence"). Wilson's critics were not entirely off base in this regard. Throughout the 1780s, Wilson and his partners used an elaborate system of local agents and political contacts to circumvent regulations that aimed to reserve western lands for farmers rather than speculators (pp. 11–20 of vol. 5, James Wilson Papers); see also Evans, *Holland Land Company*, 109–10. In 1794, Henry Drinker claimed that Wilson himself—"in his exalted station"—was going into land offices to search out defects in the land titles of competing speculators. David W. Maxey, "The Translation of James Wilson," *Journal of the Supreme Court Historical Society* 29, 30 (1990).

96. Benjamin Rush to John Adams, Apr. 22, 1789, in 1 *DHSCUS*, 613–14; John Adams to Benjamin Rush, May 17, 1789, in 1 *DHSCUS*, 619; John Adams to Abigail Adams, Mar. 5, 1796, in 1 *DHSCUS*, 842; Audit Committee Report, May 31, 1790, in vol. 5, pp. 51–60, James Wilson Papers; "Report of the Committee to Whom Was Referred . . . the Memorial of the Illinois and Wabash Land Company, by James Wilson, Their President . . . Published by Order of the House of Representatives," in vol. 2, pp. 112–20, James Wilson Papers; Smith, *James Wilson*, 369; William Rawle to James Wilson, June 19, 1792, vol. 3, pp. 31–40, James Wilson Papers; George Washington to Henry Lee Jr., Sept. 8, 1797, 1 *The Papers of George Washington, Retirement Series* 341–42 (Dorothy Twohig et al., eds., University Press of Virginia, 1999); Royster, *Fabulous History*, 384.

97. "Mort" to James Wilson, Mar. 4, 1795, and Robert A. Farmar to James Wilson, July 16, 1795, pp. 91–100, vol. 5, James Wilson Papers; Wilson, "On the Improvement and Settlement," 13; Smith, *James Wilson*, 369–74.

98. Smith, *James Wilson*, 397; G. K. Taylor to Wilson, Jan. 30, 1796, pp. 101–110, vol. 5, James Wilson Papers; Smith, *James Wilson*, 383; Mann, *Republic of Debtors*, 100–101; Robert Morris to John Nicholson, Dec. 8, 1796, microformed on *Papers of Robert Morris, Private Letterbook*, Reel 10, vol. 2, Columbia University; Smith, *James Wilson*, 380; Maxey, "Translation of James Wilson," 30.

99. 3 *DHSCUS*, 152 n.20. On Wilson's 1796 imprisonment, see also the hint from Robert Morris's correspondence in Barbara Ann Chernow, "Robert Morris: Land Speculator, 1790–1801," p. 214 (Ph.D. diss., Columbia University, 1974); 3 *DHSCUS*, 132–33, 137, 146, 152, 491; "Land for Sale," and George Peter to James Wilson, Dec. 29, 1796, vol. 5, pp. 101–110, James Wilson Papers; Smith, *James Wilson*, 382–87.

100. 3 *DHSCUS,* 492; James Wilson to Joseph Thomas, Esq., Raleigh, Dec. 2, 1797, pp. 101–110, vol. 5, James Wilson Papers (also reprinted in 3 *DHSCUS,* 231–32); James Wilson to Joseph Thomas, May 12, 1798, in 3 *DHSCUS,* 265–67.

101. Thomas Blount to John Gray Blount, Feb. 16, 1798, in 3 *DHSCUS,* 242; Thomas Blount to John Gray Blount, Feb. 26, 1798, in 3 *DHSCUS,* 243 n.6; James Wilson to Bird Wilson, Apr. 21, 1798, in 3 *DHSCUS,* 254–55; Pierce Butler to Samuel Wallis, June 14, 1798, in 3 *DHSCUS,* 267–68; Hannah Wilson to Bird Wilson, Sept. 1, 1998, in 3 *DHSCUS,* 289; James Wilson to Bird Wilson, Burlington, Sept. 6, 1797, and James Wilson to Bird Wilson, Raleigh, Dec. 17, 1797, pp. 101–110, vol. 5, James Wilson Papers; James Wilson to Bird Wilson, Aug. 4, 1798, in 3 *DHSCUS,* 282; Samuel Johnston to James Iredell, July 28, 1798, in 1 *DHSCUS,* 859–61; James Iredell to Hannah Iredell, Aug. 6, 1798, in 3 *DHSCUS,* 283; Hannah Wilson to Bird Wilson, July 28, 1798, in 3 *DHSCUS,* 281; James Iredell to Sarah Gray, Aug. 25, 1798, in 1 *DHSCUS,* 861; Jacob Rush to Benjamin Rush, Sept. 8, 1798, in 1 *DHSCUS,* 862.

102. Benjamin Rush, *The Autobiography of Benjamin Rush, His "Travels Through Life" together with His Commonplace Book for 1789–1813,* p. 237 (George W. Corner, ed., Princeton University Press, 1948); Thomas Jefferson to Robert Skipwith, Aug. 3, 1771, in 1 *Papers of Thomas Jefferson,* 76–77; Wills, *Inventing America,* 189.

103. George Fisher, *The American Instructor: Or, Young Man's Best Companion* 303 (B. Franklin & D. Hall, 10th ed., 1753) (Evans 7120); Hervey, 1 *Meditations and Contemplations,* 96; Voltaire, "Apis," in *The Philosophical Dictionary, for the Pocket, Translated from the French Edition, Corrected by the Author* 10–11 (Catskill, N.Y.: T. & M. Croswel, 1796) (Evans 31518); Johnson, *Rasselas,* 89; Greaves, *Pyramidographia,* 17. By the early nineteenth century, English commentators were critiquing the previous generation's vogue for the tyrranical pyramids as "the very climax of absurdity." Curl, *Egyptomania,* 110.

104. Pocock, "Modes of Political and Historical Time," 92–93.

2. ELIAS HILL'S EXODUS

1. June Moore to William Coppinger, Oct. 13, 1871, reel 109, *Records of the American Colonization Society* (Library of Congress Photo-duplication Service, 1971) (hereinafter *RACS*); United States Department

of Agriculture, *Soil Survey: York County South Carolina,* series 1961, no. 17 (Apr. 1965); Oscar M. Lieber, *Report of the Survey of South Carolina: First Annual Report to the General Assembly of South Carolina* 112 (Columbia, S.C.: R. W. Gibbes, 2nd ed., 1858); Douglas Summers Brown, *A City without Cobwebs: A History of Rock Hill, South Carolina* 80–82 (University of South Carolina Press, 1953); A. M. Grist, "Bethesda and Sardis Church History," *Yorkville Enquirer,* Dec. 19 and 22, 1933, reprinted in *The Quarterly: York County, South Carolina,* vol. 15, no. 5 (York County Geological and Historical Society, June 2003); "History of the Union Baptist Church" (typescript, n.d.), Liberia Connections Folder, Historical Center of York County, York, South Carolina; Manuscript Census Records, York County, South Carolina, Eighth Census of the United States, 1860, Schedule 1, p. 83.

2. June Moore to William Coppinger, Oct. 22, 1871, reel 109, *RACS* (sent ahead); June Moore to William Coppinger, Oct. 16, 1871, and John Wallace to William Coppinger, Feb. 22, 1872, reel 109, *RACS* (Uncle Elias); "Departure of Our Fall Expedition," *African Repository,* Dec. 1871, pp. 353, 354 (ferried from place to place).

3. George P. Rawick, ed., 10 *The American Slave: A Composite Autobiography: Arkansas Narratives (Part 6),* pp. 187, 188 (Greenwood Publishing Co., 1972) (Works Progress Administration interview with Ervin E. Smith) (Confederate troops); Lacy K. Ford Jr., *Origins of Southern Radicalism: The South Carolina Upcountry, 1800–1860,* p. 236 (Oxford University Press, 1988) (Main Street); Taylor Branch, *Parting the Waters: America during the King Years, 1954–1963,* pp. 415–16 (Simon & Schuster, 1988) (Freedom Ride); Charlotte, Columbia, and Augusta R.R. to William Coppinger, Dec. 20, 1871, reel 109, *RACS* (train car); Thomas S. Malcom to William McLain, Sep. 20, 1871, reel 108, *RACS* (double-decked barque); A. Alexander to William Coppinger, Nov. 6, 1871, reel 109, *RACS.*

4. Steven Hahn, *A Nation under Our Feet: Black Political Struggles in the Rural South from Slavery to the Great Migration* 467 (Harvard University Press, 2003) ("grassroots emigrationism"); see also Nell Irvin Painter, *Exodusters: Black Migration to Kansas after Reconstruction* (Norton, 1976); William Cohen, *At Freedom's Edge: Black Mobility and the Southern Quest for Racial Control, 1861–1915* (Louisiana State University Press, 1991); David E. Bernstein, *Only One Place of Redress: African Americans, Labor Regulations, and the Courts from Reconstruction to the New Deal* 10–27 (Duke University Press, 2001); Robert G. Athearn, *In Search of Canaan: Black Migration to Kansas, 1879–80* (Regents Press of Kansas, 1978).

5. Albert O. Hirschman, *Exit, Voice, and Loyalty: Responses to Decline in Firms, Organizations, and States* (Harvard University Press, 1970).

6. Manuscript Census Records, York County, South Carolina, Eighth Census of the United States, 1860, Schedule 1, p. 83; Samuel Brooks Mendenhall, "A Compilation of York County Post Offices" (typescript, Ebenezer, South Carolina, 1960) and Hart Collection, RG-6, Harvey–Hill, Notebook 18 (William D. Hill), Historical Center of York County, York, South Carolina; "Will of William Hill, State of South Carolina," York County Public Library, Rock Hill Branch, Local History Room; A. M. Grist, "Just A-Rolling along the Way," *Yorkville Enquirer*, Oct. 31, 1933 (wet nurse; local lore); James M. McPherson, *Crossroads of Freedom: Antietam* (Oxford University Press, 2002) (lost dispatch); Hal Bridges, *Lee's Maverick General: Daniel Harvey Hill* 273–76 (McGraw-Hill Book Co., 1961).

7. Marina Wikramanayake, *A World in Shadow: The Free Black in Antebellum South Carolina* 13 (University of South Carolina Press, 1973) (house slaves more likely to be freed); Ira Berlin, *Slaves without Masters: The Free Negro in the Antebellum South* 150 (Pantheon, 1974) (same); Orville Vernon Burton, *In My Father's House Are Many Mansions: Family and Community in Edgefield, South Carolina* 399 n.54 (University of North Carolina Press, 1985) (majority of upcountry free blacks were mulattos); Manuscript Census Report for 1860, South Carolina, York County, Schedule 1, p. 83 ("mulatto"); A. M. Grist, "Just A-Rolling Along," *Yorkville Enquirer*, Oct. 27, 1933 (Dorcas's great-grandson); Grist, "Just A-Rolling along the Way" (freed in 1861).

8. 5 *Testimony Taken by the Joint Select Committee to Inquire into the Condition of Affairs in the Late Insurrectionary States (South Carolina)* 1406 (U.S. Government Printing Office, 1872) (hereinafter *KKK Testimony*) (described his father); Hart Collection, RG-6, Harvey–Hill, Notebook 18, Historical Center of York County (Andrew Hill).

9. "An Act to Restrain the Emancipation of Slaves, and to Prevent Free Persons of Color from Entering into This State," Dec. 20, 1820, in Thomas Cooper and David J. McCord, eds., 7 *The Statutes at Large of South Carolina* 459 (Columbia, S.C.: A. S. Johnson, 1840); Burton, *In My Father's House* 203 (seldom did so); South Carolina Department of Archives and History, General Assembly Records and Petitions, in Legislative Papers, available at http://www.archivesindex.sc.gov (never granted such a waiver); Manuscript Census Records, York County, South Carolina, Eighth Census of the United States, 1860, Schedule 1, p. 83.

10. "Afflicted," *African Repository,* Sept. 1871, p. 281 ("afflicted"); Grist, "Just A-Rolling along the Way," ("something like rheumatism"); Bridges, *Lee's Maverick General,* 16 (young Daniel Harvey); "Letter from Elias Hill," *African Repository,* July 1872, p. 222 ("never afterward"); 5 *KKK Testimony,* 1412 ("the size of a man's wrist"); "Departure of Our Fall Expedition," *African Repository,* Dec. 1871, pp. 353, 354 ("legs now resemble. . ."); "Letter from Elias Hill," *African Repository,* July 1872, p. 222 ("presented the appearance"; "could not help himself"); "Afflicted," *African Repository,* Sept. 1871, p. 281 ("utterly unable"); 5 *KKK Testimony,* p. 1477 ("turn over"); "Afflicted," p. 281 ("scribbling").

11. "Departure of Our Fall Expedition," pp. 353, 354 ("remarkable character"); "Afflicted," p. 281 ("most remarkable"; "massive"); "Letter from Elias Hill," *African Repository,* July 1872, p. 222 ("finely developed"); 5 *KKK Testimony,* 1406 (education); "Afflicted," p. 281 ("conned from the Bible"; "all York County"); Grist, "Just A-Rolling along the Way," ("far above the average").

12. Grist, "Just A-Rolling along the Way"; 7 *Statutes at Large of South Carolina,* 413 (1740 prohibition on teaching slaves); see also 7 *Statutes at Large of South Carolina,* 468 (same in 1834).

13. Joseph C. Kennedy, *Population of the United States in 1860, Compiled from the Original Returns of the Eighth Census* 451 (U.S. Government Printing Office, 1864) (demographics); Wikramanayake, *World in Shadow,* 22, app. A3 (regional demographics). Only 1,362 blacks lived as free in 1860 in the nine upcountry counties that would become the focus of the federal Klan trials eleven years later. Living alongside some 100,852 black slaves, free blacks in these nine Piedmont counties made up 1.3 percent of the black population, as compared to 2.4 percent of the black population statewide. See Kennedy, *Population . . . in 1860* [*Eighth Census*], 448–53.

14. Wikramanayake, *World in Shadow,* 27 (close proximity); Berlin, *Slaves without Masters,* 251, 259 ("tucked away"; "isolated cottages").

15. "An Act for the Better Ordering and Governing Negroes and Other Slaves in This Province" (May 10, 1740), in 7 *Statutes at Large of South Carolina,* 398 ("every negro"); Wikramanayake, *World in Shadow,* 54–55 (certificate; testimony); "An Act Respecting Slaves, Free Negroes, Mulattoes and Mestizoes. . . ," in 7 *Statutes at Large of South Carolina,* 441 (gather together); 7 *Statutes at Large of South Carolina,* 440–41 ("assemblies"); "An Act to Amend the Laws in Relation to Slaves and Free Persons of Color" (Dec. 17, 1834), in 7 *Statutes at Large of South Carolina,* 368 (schools);

Wikramanayake, *World in Shadow*, 151 (white guardian); 7 *Statutes at Large of South Carolina*, 402 (without juries); Wikramanayake, *World in Shadow*, 63–66 (same); 7 *Statutes at Large of South Carolina*, 405 (self-defense).

16. 7 *Statutes at Large of South Carolina*, 433 (immigration from West Indies), 450 (seized into slavery); Wikramanayake, *World in Shadow*, 19 (panoply of new laws); 7 *Statutes at Large of South Carolina*, 459 (total ban on immigration), 461 (tax; "suffered to return").

17. 7 *Statutes at Large of South Carolina*, 443 ("livelihood"), 459 ("by act"); Berlin, *Slaves without Masters*, 144 ("fully emancipated"); Wikramanayake, *World in Shadow*, 37–43 (same); "Act to Prevent the Emancipation of Slaves of 1841," in 11 *The Statutes at Large of South Carolina*, 154 (Columbia, S.C.: Republican Printing Co., 1873) (voiding the trusts); Berlin, *Slaves without Masters*, 145 ("evasions"); Wikramanayake, *World in Shadow*, 22 (dramatically slowing).

18. James M. Banner Jr., "The Problem of South Carolina," in Stanley Elkins and Eric McKitrick, eds., *The Hofstadter Aegis* 60 (Knopf, 1974) ("no other state"); Ford, *Origins of Southern Radicalism*, 101 (highest ratio of slaves); Richard Hofstadter, "John C. Calhoun: The Marx of the Master Class," in Richard Hofstadter, *The American Political Tradition and the Men Who Made It* 87–118 (Knopf, 1948); Drew Gilpin Faust, *James Henry Hammond and the Old South: A Design for Mastery* (Louisiana State University Press, 1982); Daniel Webster, [Second] Reply to Hayne, in Edwin P. Whipple, ed., *The Great Speeches and Orations of Daniel Webster* 227 (Little, Brown, 1895); William W. Freehling, *Prelude to Civil War: The Nullification Crisis in South Carolina, 1816–1836* (Harper & Row, 1966); John Barnwell, *Love of Order: South Carolina's First Secession Crisis* (University of North Carolina Press, 1982); Steven A. Channing, *Crisis of Fear: Secession in South Carolina* (Simon & Schuster, 1970); John Amasa May and Joan Reynolds Faunt, *South Carolina Secedes* (University of South Carolina Press, 1960).

19. John Niven, *John C. Calhoun and the Price of Union* (Louisiana State University Press, 1988); Faust, *James Henry Hammond;* Burton, *In My Father's House*, 94–95 (Preston Brooks); Francis Butler Simkins, *Pitchfork Ben Tillman* (Louisiana State University Press, 1944); Nadine Cohodas, *Strom Thurmond and the Politics of Southern Change* (Simon & Schuster, 1993).

20. Samuel N. Thomas, "History of York County," in Samuel N. Thomas, *Historical Properties of York County, South Carolina* (York County

Historical Commission, 1995); C. Vann Woodward, ed., *Mary Chesnut's Civil War* 715, 760, 764, 771 (Yale University Press, 1981) (sought refuge); Joel Williamson, *After Slavery: The Negro in South Carolina during Reconstruction, 1861–1877,* p. 5 (University of North Carolina Press, 1965) (blacks migrated); Julie Saville, *The Work of Reconstruction: From Slave to Wage Laborer in South Carolina, 1860–1870,* pp. 30–31 (Cambridge University Press, 1994); William C. Davis, *An Honorable Defeat: The Last Days of the Confederate Government* 206 (Harcourt, 2001) (Jefferson Davis); Nora Marshall Davis, "Jefferson Davis's Route from Richmond, Virginia, to Irwinville, Georgia, April 2–May 10, 1865," in *Proceedings of the South Carolina Historical Association, 1941,* pp. 11–20 (1941) (same). In Fairfield County, at the southern end of the Piedmont, the 1860 census recorded only 1,578 white males between 15 and 60 years of age in 1860. Yet during the war, the county sent an astounding 2,000 men to fight in the Confederate Army. See Fitz Hugh Master, *History of Fairfield County, South Carolina, from "Before the White Man Came" to 1942,* p. 125 (Columbia, S.C.: State Commercial Printing Co., 1946); Jerry L. West, *The Reconstruction Ku Klux Klan in York County, South Carolina, 1865–1877,* p. 130 (Jefferson, N.C.: McFarland & Co., 2002) (model for the dashing hero); Raymond A. Cook, *Thomas Dixon* 19–31 (Twayne Publishers, 1974). Dixon dedicated *The Clansman* to his uncle, Colonel Leroy McAfee, a leader along with Bratton of the York County Klan.

21. Ford, *Origins of Southern Radicalism,* 257 (middling wealth of upcountry farmers); Stephanie McCurry, *Masters of Small Worlds: Yeoman Households, Gender Relations, and the Political Culture of the Antebellum South Carolina Low Country* 53 (Oxford University Press, 1995) (same); Faust, *James Henry Hammond,* 36 ("truest prudence"); Ford, *Origins of Southern Radicalism,* 360–364 ("independent, enfranchised, and free" and Trescot); McCurry, *Masters of Small Worlds,* 282 (Thompson). On the slaveholders' republicanism of upcountry whites, see generally Faust, *James Henry Hammond,* 40, 134; McCurry, *Masters of Small Worlds;* Steven Hahn, *The Roots of Southern Populism: Yeoman Farmers and the Transformation of the Georgia Upcountry, 1850–1890* (Oxford University Press, 1983); Burton, *In My Father's House,* 102–3; Steven Hahn, "The 'Unmaking' of the Southern Yeomanry: The Transformation of the Georgia Upcountry," in Steven Hahn and Jonathan Prude, eds., *The Countryside in the Age of Capitalist Transformation* 179–203 (University of North Carolina Press, 1985); Stephen Hahn, "The Yeomanry of the Nonplantation South: Upper

Piedmont Georgia, 1850–1860," in Orville Vernon Burton and Robert C. McMath Jr., eds., *Class, Conflict, and Consensus: Antebellum Southern Community Studies* 29–56 (Greenwood Press, 1982); Lacy K. Ford, "Republican Ideology in a Slave Society: The Political Economy of John C. Calhoun," 54 *J. Southern Hist.* 405–24 (1988); Stephanie McCurry, "The Two Faces of Republicanism: Gender and Proslavery Politics in Antebellum South Carolina," 78 *J. Am. Hist.* 1245–64 (1992).

22. Don E. Fehrenbacher, *The Dred Scott Case: Its Significance in American Law and Politics* 64–73 (Oxford University Press, 1978) (from ad hoc to the Missouri Compromise); "Rights of Free Virginia Negroes," 1 U.S. Op. Atty. Gen. 506–9 (Nov. 7, 1821); "Pre-Emption Rights of Colored Persons," 4 U.S. Op. Atty. Gen. 147–48 (March 15, 1843); Bowers v. Newman, 2 McMul. 472, 27 S.C.L. 472 (S.C.Err. 1842) (O'Neall, J., dissenting); White v. Tax Collector of Kershaw, 3 Rich. 136, 37 S.C.L. 136 (S.C. App. L. 1846) ("three classes").

23. Dred Scott v. Sandford, 60 U.S. (19 How.) 393 (1857); Fehrenbacher, *Dred Scott Case,* 357 ("only people on the face of the earth," italics omitted). The best textual reading of the three-fifths clause, which allocated congressional representation in race-neutral language "by adding to the whole Number of free Persons . . . three fifths of all other Persons," suggested the contrary. Taney never once mentioned the three-fifths clause in his opinion.

24. Fehrenbacher, *Dred Scott Case,* 417–38 (little controversy); Roy Basler, ed., 2 *The Collected Works of Abraham Lincoln* 177, 179 (Rutgers University Press, 1953); *Dred Scott,* 60 U.S. (19 How.) at 407; Wilson Jeremiah Moses, ed., *Classical Black Nationalism: From the American Revolution to Marcus Garvey* 110, 112 (New York University Press, 1996) ("shall we fly").

25. Sanford Levinson, *Constitutional Faith* 3 (Princeton University Press, 1988) ("American citizenship").

26. Hirschman, *Exit, Voice, and Loyalty,* 76; William Lloyd Garrison, "Resolution Adopted by the Antislavery Society," Jan. 27, 1843, quoted in Walter M. Merrill, *Against Wind and Tide: A Biography of Wm. Lloyd Garrison* 205 (Harvard University Press, 1963); James Henry Hammond to Hon. R. F. Simpson (Nov. 22, 1860), in Carol Bleser, ed., *The Hammonds of Redcliffe* 89–90 (Oxford University Press, 1981).

27. William Goodell, *The American Slave Code* 364 (New York: American and Foreign Anti-Slavery Society, 1852). On the capacity of the Constitution to contain political argument in the United States, see Louis Hartz,

The Liberal Tradition in America (Harcourt, Brace, 1955); Gordon S. Wood, *The Creation of the American Republic, 1776–1787*, pp. 562–64 (Norton, 1969).

28. William S. McFeely, *Frederick Douglass* 329–32 (Norton, 1991) (Egypt and Haiti).

29. John W. Blassingame, ed., 4 *The Frederick Douglass Papers* 240–41 (Yale University Press, 1979) ("grandest aggregations" to "instructive and useful"); 3 *Douglass Papers,* 574 ("costly transportation"), 507 ("bail out the ocean"), 574 ("missionaries to the moon"); 4 *Douglass Papers,* 526 ("abandonment"), 529 ("solemnly bound"), 526 ("expedient" to "still to be settled"), 526 ("utter impracticability"); McFeely, *Frederick Douglass,* 371 ("loyalty enough"; "love our country"); 3 *Douglass Papers,* 508 ("destiny").

30. "The Colored Convention," *Yorkville Enquirer,* Oct. 26, 1871; *Address in the Convention of the Colored People of the Southern States, Begun to Be Holden in the City of Columbia, South Carolina, on Wednesday, the Eighteenth Day of October 1871,* Library of Congress Printed Ephemera Collection, portfolio 173, folder 23.

31. Herbert Aptheker, "Maroons within the Present Limits of the United States," 24 *J. Negro Hist.* 167 (1939); Barbara Klamon Kopytoff, "The Early Political Development of Jamaican Maroon Societies," 35 *Wm. & Mary Q.* 287 (1978); Claude A. Clegg III, *The Price of Liberty: African Americans and the Making of Liberia* 22–23 (University of North Carolina Press, 2004) (small groups of blacks); Wilson Jeremiah Moses, "Introduction," in Moses, ed., *Classical Black Nationalism,* 7–9 (same); Sheldon H. Harris, *Paul Cuffe: Black America and the African Return* (Simon & Schuster, 1972); Lamont D. Thomas, *Rise to Be a People: A Biography of Paul Cuffe* (University of Illinois Press, 1986); P. J. Staudenraus, *The African Colonization Movement, 1816–1865,* p. 84 (Columbia University Press, 1961) (Haytien Emigration Society); J. B. Taylor, *Biography of Elder Lott Cary, Late Missionary to Africa* (Baltimore: Armstrong & Berry, 1837).

32. Wilson Jeremiah Moses, *The Golden Age of Black Nationalism, 1850–1925* (Oxford University Press, 1978); David Walker, "An Appeal in Four Articles" (1830), reprinted in Moses, ed., *Classical Black Nationalism,* 76 (pyramids); Alexander Crummell, *Destiny and Race: Selected Writings, 1840–1898* (Wilson Jeremiah Moses, ed., University of Massachusetts Press, 1992); Cyril E. Griffith, *The African Dream: Martin R. Delany and the Emergence of Pan-African Thought* 103–4 (Pennsylvania State University Press, 1975) (proud African civilization). On the uses of the Psalms passage,

see Robin D. G. Kelley, "How the West Was One: The African Diaspora and the Re-Mapping of U.S. History," in Thomas Bender, ed., *Rethinking American History in a Global Age* 123, 125 (University of California Press, 2002), and the scholarship cited therein.

33. On the origins of the American Colonization Society, see Clegg, *Price of Liberty,* 29–52; Lamin Sanneh, *Abolitionists Abroad: American Blacks and the Making of Modern West Africa* 190–221 (Harvard University Press, 1999); Tom W. Shick, *Behold the Promised Land: A History of Afro-American Settler Society in Nineteenth-Century Liberia* 5–7 (Johns Hopkins University Press, 1980); Staudenraus, *African Colonization Movement,* 12–58; Douglas R. Egerton, "'Its Origin Is Not a Little Curious': A New Look at the American Colonization Society," 5 *J. Early Republic* 463, 466 (1985); Monday B. Abasiattai, "The Search for Independence: New World Blacks in Sierra Leone and Liberia, 1787–1847," 23 *J. Black Studies* 107 (1992); Howard Temperley, "African-American Aspirations and the Settlement of Liberia," 21 *Slavery and Abolition: A Journal of Slave and Post-Slave Studies* 67 (2000); Frankie Hutton, "Economic Considerations in the American Colonization Society's Early Effort to Emigrate Free Blacks to Liberia, 1816–1836," 68 *J. Negro Hist.* 376 (1983). *Report of Naval Committee on Establishing a Line of Mail Steamships to the Western Coast of Africa. . . .* 42 (Washington: Gideon & Co., 1850) ("father of the Constitution"); "Emigrants Sent by the American Colonization Society," *African Repository,* April 1875, p. 55 (almost 10,000); James Forten to Paul Cuffee (Jan. 25, 1817), in Jonathan H. Bracey Jr. et al., eds., *Black Nationalism in America* 45–46 (Bobbs-Merrill, 1970) (increasing reluctance); Kwando M. Kinshasa, *Emigration versus Assimilation: The Debate in the African American Press, 1827–1861,* pp. 177–89 (Jefferson, N.C.: McFarland & Co., 1988) (denouncing); William Lloyd Garrison, *Thoughts on African Colonization: or, An Impartial Exhibition of the Doctrines, Principles and Purposes of the American Colonization Society . . .* 74 (Boston: Garrison & Knapp, 1832) (white southern supporters); Josiah Priest, *Bible Defence of Slavery; and Origin, Fortunes, and History of the Negro Race* 496 (Glasgow, Ky.: W. S. Brown, 1852) ("removal").

34. Bracey et al., eds., *Black Nationalism in America,* 67–120; Wilson Jeremiah Moses, ed., *Liberian Dreams: Back-to-Africa Narratives from the 1850s* (Pennsylvania State University Press, 1998); James Theodore Holly and J. Dennis Harris, eds., *Black Separatism and the Caribbean, 1860* (University of Michigan Press, 1970); Elliott P. Skinner, *African Americans and U.S. Policy toward Africa, 1850–1924,* pp. 47–49 (Howard University Press,

1992) (emigration conventions); Howard Holman Bell, *A Survey of the Negro Convention Movement, 1830–1861* (Arno Press, 1969) (same); Moses, *Golden Age of Black Nationalism,* 18 (Blyden); Crummell, *Destiny and Race;* Moses, *Golden Age of Black Nationalism,* 35 (Delany, Garnet); Clegg, *Price of Liberty,* 172 (Canada); "Emigrants Sent by the American Colonization Society," *African Repository,* April 1875, p. 55 (1850s Liberia emigration); William Seraile, "Afro-American Emigration to Haiti during the American Civil War," 35 *The Americas* 185–200 (1978) (Haiti).

35. Toyin Falola, "Introduction," in Martin R. Delany, *The Condition, Elevation, Emigration, and Destiny of the Colored People of the United States and Official Report of the Niger Valley Exploring Party* 10 (Toyin Falola, ed., Humanity Books, 2004) ("intensest emodiment"); Delany, *Conditon, Elevation,* 173–74 ("to imagine"), 172 ("we can have"), 221 ("Poles in Russia"); Delany, "Condition, Elevation," in Moses, ed., *Classical Black Nationalism,* 124 (nation-state status); *Dred Scott,* 60 U.S. at 403–4 ("associated together"; "like the subjects"). On Delany, see also Griffith, *African Dream;* Victor Ullman, *Martin R. Delany: The Beginnings of Black Nationalism* (Beacon Press, 1971); Nell Irvin Painter, "Martin R. Delany: Elitism and Black Nationalism," in Leon Litwack and August Meier, eds., *Black Leaders of the Nineteenth Century* 149 (University of Illinois Press, 1991). On the long tradition of black thought about citizenship in the United States, see Robin D. G. Kelley, "'But a Local Phase of a World Problem': Black History's Global Vision, 1883–1950," 86 *J. Am. Hist.* 1045, 1048–49 (1999) and the sources cited therein.

36. Delany, *Conditon, Elevation* (Falola, ed.), 224 (Greek independence), 221–22 ("the claims"); Edward Wilmot Blyden, "The Call of Providence to the Descendants of Africa in America," in Moses, ed., *Classical Black Nationalism,* 195 ("African nationality"); Seraile, "Afro-American Emigration to Haiti," 187 ("seek elsewhere"), 188 ("colored nation"); Delany, *Conditon, Elevation* (Falola, ed.), 247–48 ("all colored men").

37. Edward Blyden, "The Call of Providence to the Descendants of Africa in America," in Moses, ed., *Classical Black Nationalism,* 204 ("framers"); Delany, *Conditon, Elevation* (Falola, ed.), 185 ("pitiful dependency"); Charles Henry Huberich, 1 *The Political and Legislative History of Liberia* 829 (New York: Central Book Co., 1947) (Liberian Declaration of Independence).

38. Constitution of the Republic of Liberia (1847), art. 1, §1 ("equally free"), art. V, §13 ("great object"; "none but persons of color"), in

Huberich, 2 *Political and Legislative History of Liberia,* 853, 863, 865 ("not synonymous"); "Fifty-Sixth Annual Meeting: Proceedings of the Fifty-Sixth Annual Meeting of the American Colonization Society" [January 21, 1873], reel 290, *RACS* ("black man's country"). The Liberian Constitution of 1847 was modeled largely on the U.S. Constitution. Its early drafts were prepared by a white American lawyer, Simon Greenleaf. The racially exclusive citizenship provision was added to Greenleaf's draft by black Americo-Liberians. Greenleaf's letters at the Harvard Law Library shed fascinating light on the early drafting process. Many thanks to Fred Konefsky at the University of Buffalo for bringing these letters to my attention.

39. *Congressional Globe,* 37th Cong., 2d sess., p. 1806 (April 24, 1862) (Senator Davis), p. 1815 (April 24, 1862) (Senator Saulsbury).

40. Id., pp. 2504–5 (June 2, 1862) (Rep. Biddle), pp. 1773–76 (April 23, 1862) (Senator Sumner), pp. 2534–35 (June 3, 1862) (Rep. John Crittenden).

41. U.S. Const., amends. 13, 14, 15; Eric Foner, *Reconstruction: America's Unfinished Revolution, 1863–1877,* pp. 239–61, 271–80 (Harper & Row, 1988) (proposal and ratification of Thirteenth, Fouteenth, and Fifteenth Amendments); Bernard Schwartz, ed., 1 *Statutory History of the United States: Civil Rights* 23 (Chelsea House Publishers, 1970) ("obliterate"); "An Act to Protect All Persons in the United States in Their Civil Rights, and Furnish the Means of Their Vindication," 14 Statutes at Large 27 (1866) (Civil Rights Act).

42. "A Remarkable Man for Liberia," *African Repository,* Sept. 1871, pp. 280, 281 ("clear"); "Departure of Our Fall Expedition," *African Repository,* Dec. 1871, pp. 353, 354 ("unusual power"); "A Remarkable Man for Liberia," pp. 280, 281 ("leader"); Grist, "Just A-Rolling along the Way," ("heard a long distance").

43. 5 *KKK Testimony,* 1408 ("license to preach"); 13 *The Statutes at Large of South Carolina, Containing the Acts from December 1861 to December 1866,* pp. 269, 279 (Columbia, S.C.: Republican Printing Co., 1875) (licensing requirements); "Educational Statistics," in *Reports and Resolutions of the General Assembly of the State of South Carolina at the Regular Session, 1869–70,* pp. 421, 463–64 (Columbia, S.C.: Republican Printing Co., 1870) (one-room schoolhouse); *Reports and Resolutions of the General Assembly of the State of South Carolina at the Regular Session, 1870–71,* p. 225 (Republican Printing Co., 1871) (same); Rawick, ed., 10 *The American Slave,* 187–89 (Works Progress Administration interview with Ervin

E. Smith) ("only colored teacher"); 5 *KKK Testimony,* 1408 (president of Union League council). There were seven teachers in York County in 1871 described as "colored" by the state government, but Hill also appears to have taught in schools across the North Carolina border in Mecklenberg County, where he may well have been the only black teacher. *Reports and Resolutions of the General Assembly of the State of South Carolina at the Regular Session, 1871–72,* p. 89 (Columbia, S.C.: Republican Printing Co., 1872).

44. Francis A. Walker, 1 *Statistics of the Population of the United States . . . Compiled from the Original Returns of the Ninth Census (June 1, 1870),* table 2, p. 60 (U.S. Government Printing Office, 1872); Eric Foner, *Freedom's Lawmakers: A Directory of Black Officeholders during Reconstruction,* p. xiv (Oxford University Press, 1993) (black officeholding); Thomas C. Holt, *Black over White: Negro Political Leadership in South Carolina during Reconstruction* 97 (University of Illinois Press, 1977) (state General Assembly majorities).

45. Ullman, *Martin R. Delany,* 311 ("rally"), 315 (Redpath); Saville, *The Work of Reconstruction,* 164 (Turner). Louisiana, Mississippi, and South Carolina all had black majority populations in 1870, but in Louisiana blacks outnumbered whites by a mere one-half of one percent. Mississippi blacks outnumbered the state's whites by a more significant margin—there were some 60,000 more blacks than whites in the state in 1870. See 1 *Statistics of the Population of the United States,* table 2.

46. Holt, *Black over White,* 95 ("African dominion"); see also 3 *KKK Testimony,* 483 ("final catastrophe").

47. Compare Allen W. Trelease, *White Terror: The Ku Klux Klan Conspiracy and Southern Reconstruction* 71 (Harper & Row, 1971), with 5 *KKK Testimony,* 1372 (first appearance of Klan in S.C.); Michael C. Scoggins, *A Brief History of Historic Brattonsville* (York County Culture and Heritage Commission, 2003); *The Patriot* (Columbia/Tristar Studios, 2000); Jerry L. West, *The Reconstruction Ku Klux Klan in York County, South Carolina, 1865–1877,* pp. 126–30 (Jefferson, N.C.: McFarland & Co., 2002) (Bratton in the Klan).

48. Brown, *City without Cobwebs,* 81–82; Trelease, *White Terror,* 362 ("no other Southern county"); 5 *KKK Testimony,* 1391 (between three and twelve); Trelease, *White Terror,* 363 (forty-five); West, *Reconstruction Ku Klux Klan,* 41 ("nearly every white man"). Compare West, *Reconstruction Ku Klux Klan,* 41 (less than 1,400 Klan members), with Trelease, *White Ter-*

ror, 363 (1,800 Klan members). Today, at the opening of the twenty-first century, historical markers honoring the founders of Rock Hill, South Carolina, single out for special distinction the same Scotch-Irish families that provided the leaders of the local Klan. In the 1950s, Bratton's York home would be razed to make way for an auto parts store.

49. Faust, *James Henry Hammond,* 44 (quoting *Columbia Southern Times,* Jan. 29, 1830) ("constitution of '89"); *Report of the Joint Select Committee to Inquire into the Condition of Affairs in the Late Insurrectionary States* 25 (U.S. Government Printing Office, 1872) (hereinafter *KKK Report*) ("as bequeathed to us"); 3 *KKK Testimony,* 23 ("restoration"); *KKK Report,* 25 (opposition to Reconstruction Amendments); *Proceedings in the Ku Klux Trials at Columbia, S.C., in the United States Circuit Court, November Term, 1871,* pp. 589–90 (Columbia, S.C.: Republican Printing Co., 1872) (hereinafter *Proceedings in the KK Trials*) ("freedom of the African race"), 589 ("slavery as it existed"); Trelease, *White Terror,* p. xlv (slave patrols); see also West, *Reconstruction Ku Klux Klan,* 35 (same); *KKK Report,* 233 ("recover").

50. Trelease, *White Terror,* 362 ("climax"), 349 ("most conspicuous"); 3 *KKK Testimony,* 2, 11, *KKK Report,* 35 ("hundreds of persons"); Trelease, *White Terror,* 365 (600 incidents and 11 murders); *Proceedings in the KK Trials,* 504–6 (Tom Roundtree).

51. *Proceedings in the KK Trials,* 288–89, 339 ("promised him"; "carry on"); West, *Reconstruction Ku Klux Klan,* 123 ("if ever"); *Proceedings in the KK Trials,* 348 ("damned").

52. *Proceedings in the KK Trials,* 371 (Governor Scott); "Report of the Adjutant and Inspector General of the State of South Carolina, November, 1870," in *Reports and Resolutions of the General Assembly of the State of South Carolina at the Regular Session, 1870–71,* p. 597 (Columbia, S.C.: Republican Printing Co., 1871) (same); *Proceedings in the KK Trials,* 234 ("going to kill Williams"), 246 (Briar Patch); Scoggins, *Brief History of Historic Brattonsville,* 12 (Harriet Rainey).

53. [M. S. Carroll,] "The Jim Williams Raid: First Person Reminiscence c. 1924," R610, box 2, folder 2, Galloway Papers, R610, Historical Center of York County, South Carolina.

54. 3 *KKK Testimony,* 33 ("terrified"); Herbert Shapiro, "The Ku Klux Klan during Reconstruction: The South Carolina Episode," 49 *J. Negro Hist.* 34, 47 (1964) ("out of their wits"); 3 *KKK Testimony,* 37 ("never reach there"), 76 ("very next"); *Proceedings in the KK Trials,* 775–76 ("leading

men"); 3 *KKK Testimony,* 79 (Newberry County). See also "Intimidating Witnesses," *Yorkville Enquirer,* Jan. 4, 1872.

55. *Proceedings in the KK Trials,* 444 ("voice is hushed"); West, *Reconstruction Ku Klux Klan,* 69 ("silenced his court"); *Proceedings in the KK Trials,* 701 ("voices shall be shut up").

56. West, *Reconstruction Ku Klux Klan,* 80 (within a week; "a town in war"); *KKK Report,* 1 ("a condition of affairs"); "An Act to Enforce the Provisions of the Fourteenth Amendment to the Constitution of the United States" (April 20, 1871), 17 Stat. 13 (1871); *KKK Report,* 2 (heard evidence); "By the President of the United States of America: A Proclamation," 7 *A Compilation of the Messages and Papers of the Presidents* 135–36 (U.S. Government Printing Office, 1896–1899); "Proclamation," in 7 *A Compilation of the Messages and Papers,* 136–38 (habeas corpus); Richard Zuczek, *State of Rebellion: Reconstruction in South Carolina* 98 (University of South Carolina Press, 1996) (472 arrests).

57. Foner, *Reconstruction,* 457–59 (South Carolina as focal point); Kermit L. Hall, "Political Power and Constitutional Legitimacy: The South Carolina Ku Klux Klan Trials, 1871–1872," 33 *Emory L. J.* 921, 936 (1984) (biggest trials); Trelease, *White Terror,* 399 (200 defendants in Mississippi by September 1871); "Report of Major Merrill—Presentments by the Grand Jury," in 5 *KKK Testimony,* 1599 (500 defendants, 80 indictments).

58. William L. Barney, "Johnson, Reverdy," http://www.anb.org/articles/04/04–00571.html, *American National Biography Online,* Feb. 2000, access date Jan. 8, 2005; *Congressional Globe,* 39th Cong., 1st sess., 3029 (June 8, 1866) ("insult to th[e] states"); Bruce Tap, "Stanbery, Henry," http://www.anb.org/articles/04/04–00939.html, *American National Biography Online,* Feb. 2000, access date Jan. 8, 2005; Lou Falkner Williams, *The Great South Carolina Ku Klux Klan Trials, 1871–1872,* p. 53 (University of Georgia Press, 1996) (Wade Hampton); Francis B. Simkins, "The Ku Klux Klan in South Carolina, 1868–1871," 12 *J. Negro Hist.* 606, 643 (1927) ($10,000); *Proceedings in the KK Trials,* 187 (contributions poured in); "Affairs in York," *Yorkville Enquirer,* Oct. 19, 1871 (oversee the prosecution).

59. "An Act to Enforce the Right of Citizens of the United States to Vote in the Several States of This Union" (May 31, 1870), 16 Stat. 140 (1870); Ku Klux Klan Act, 17 Stat. 13 (1871); *Proceedings in the KK Trials,* 825–35 (indictments); L. Williams, *South Carolina Ku Klux Klan Trials,* 62–76.

60. Akhil Reed Amar, *The Bill of Rights: Creation and Reconstruction* 3–133 (Yale University Press, 1998); Akhil Reed Amar, "The Bill of Rights and the Fourteenth Amendment," 101 *Yale L. J.* 1193, 1198–1215 (1992); *Proceedings in the KK Trials*, 15–34, 68–88.

61. *Proceedings in the KK Trials*, 62 ("manifestly"), 147 ("same restriction"), 63 ("lodged discretion").

62. *Proceedings in the KK Trials*, 432 ("that Constitution"); *Dred Scott*, 60 U.S. at 407 ("at the time of the Declaration"); *Proceedings in the KK Trials*, 380, 35 ("in its purity"), 432 ("ancient Constitution").

63. *KKK Report*, 509 (53 witnesses).

64. William Coppinger to William McLain, Sept. 18, 1871, reel 108, *RACS* ("jet black"); 5 *KKK Testimony*, 1409, 1413 (Moore carries Hill), 1405 (tell "on who whipped him"), 1477 (helping with Merrill's investigation).

65. 5 *KKK Testimony*, 1406–7; Easter Hill's name appears in "List of Emigrants for Liberia," *African Repository*, Dec. 1871, pp. 355, 356, and in the Manuscript Census Report for 1880, South Carolina Enumeration District 168, Supervisor District 1, p. 13.

66. 5 *KKK Testimony*, 1407–8; also John B. Carwile, *Reminiscences of Newberry: Embracing Important Occurrences, Brief Biographies of Prominent Citizens and Historical Sketches of Churches; to Which Is Appended an Historical Account of Newberry College* 39–40 (Charleston, S.C.: Walker, Evans, & Cogswell Co., 1890) (clocks in the upcountry).

67. *KKK Report*, 517, 526, 509 ("persons of the very lowest grade"); 5 *KKK Testimony*, 1415 (Van Trump–Hill exchange).

68. *Proceedings in the KK Trials*, 763 (jurors watching other cases).

69. L. Williams, *South Carolina Ku Klux Klan Trials*, 58 (black juries); *Operations of the Department of Justice . . . 1872*, p. 11 (U.S. Government Printing Office, 1873) (conviction statistics); L. Williams, *South Carolina Ku Klux Klan Trials*, 122–23 (same). There are minor discrepancies in the statistical reporting.

70. George Fisher, "The Jury's Rise as Lie Detector," 107 *Yale L. J.* 575, 680 (1997) (criminal defendants incompetent to testify); John Fabian Witt, "Making the Fifth," 77 *Tex. L. Rev.* 825 (1999) (same); "State Items," *Yorkville Enquirer*, Oct. 26, 1871 ("oath of the accused"); Act of Mar. 16, 1878, ch. 37, 20 Stat. 30 (1878) (authorizing testimony of criminal defendants in federal court); Lynn Willoughby, *The "Good Town" Does Well: Rock Hill, S.C., 1852–2002*, p. 51 (Orangeburg, S.C.: Rock Hill Sesquicentennial, 2002) ("pall over everything"); "A Gloomy Prospect," *Yorkville En-*

quirer, Oct. 26, 1871 ("now more gloomy"); also "The Military Arrests," *Yorkville Enquirer,* Oct. 26, 1871 (same); Foner, *Reconstruction,* 458–59 ("broken"). In state criminal prosecutions, criminal defendants could testify beginning in 1866. See Fisher, "The Jury's Rise as Lie Detector," 669.

71. 5 *KKK Testimony,* 1413 ("changed right around"; "at night"); Foner, *Reconstruction,* 459 (2,000 whites); *Operations of the Department of Justice . . . 1872,* p. 10 (same); "A Gloomy Prospect," *Yorkville Enquirer,* Oct. 23, 1871 (same); "From Union County," *Yorkville Enquirer,* Oct. 19, 1871 ("our best young men"); 5 *KKK Testimony,* 1372 (pukes to Canada); West, *Reconstruction Ku Klux Klan,* 128 and 190 n.6 (Rufus Bratton); L. Williams, *South Carolina Ku Klux Klan Trials,* 105 (same).

72. *Proceedings in the KK Trials,* 575–76 (settlement meeting), 357 (Bratton), 356–57, 371 (Moore), 357 (Williams); "Public Meeting at Clay Hill," *Yorkville Enquirer,* Feb. 16, 1871 (nighttime meetings and white assurances).

73. "The Union Outrage," *Yorkville Enquirer,* Feb. 23, 1871 ("black gowns"); *Proceedings in the KK Trials,* 673 ("raiding and shooting"); 5 *KKK Testimony,* 1407–8, 1409 (Moore and Hill).

74. 5 *KKK Testimony,* 1410 ("called a meeting"; "pledged themselves"; "white neighbors"; "every one of them"; "take their pledges"), 1411 ("lost hope").

75. Elias Hill to Rev. William Coppinger, Apr. 14, 1871, reel 108, *RACS* ("all colored here"; "hundreds & thousands"); 5 *KKK Testimony,* 1410 ("to live in this country peaceably"); Hill to Coppinger, Apr. 14, 1871 ("for Good"; "now dispised"); 5 *KKK Testimony,* 1411 ("the reason"); "More Attempts at Robbery," *Yorkville Enquirer,* Sept. 7, 1871 (Cathcart). The 21/ 31 figure was calculated by comparing names in the testimony taken by the Joint Select Committee in South Carolina (*KKK Testimony,* vols. 3–5) and names in the transcripts of the Klan trials of 1871 (*Proceedings in the KK Trials*) with the names of the Clay Hill emigrants in "List of Emigrants for Liberia," *African Repository,* Dec. 1871, pp. 355–60.

76. 5 *KKK Testimony,* 1412 ("Western states"); Edward W. Blyden, "Visit to Arthington," *African Repository,* Apr. 1889, pp. 44, 46 ("lazy and unenterprising").

77. Elias Hill to William Coppinger, April 3, 1871, reel 108, *RACS* (crude script); "Remarkable Man for Liberia," *African Repository,* Sept. 1871, p. 281 ("conned"); 5 *KKK Testimony,* 1412 ("greater encouragement"; "only refuge").

78. Eric Foner, *Nothing but Freedom: Emancipation and Its Legacy* (Lou-

isiana State University Press, 1983); "Fifty-Fifth Annual Report of the American Colonization Society, Presented January 16, 1872," *African Repository,* Feb. 1872, pp. 33ff. (25 acres); William Coppinger to Elias Hill, April 6, 1871, reel 213, *RACS* ("every drop").

79. Faust, *James Henry Hammond,* 157 (close relative); Sterling Stuckey, *Slave Culture: Nationalist Theory and the Foundations of Black America* (Oxford University Press, 1987); Margaret B. DesChamps, "Antislavery Presbyterians in the Carolina Piedmont," *Proceedings of the South Carolina Historical Association* 6, 10–11 (South Carolina Historical Association, 1954) (upcountry ministers); Burton, *In My Father's House,* 399 n.54 (one-way passages); Louise Pettus, *The Waxhaws* 95 (Regal Graphics, 1993) (neighboring Lancaster County), on file in the "Liberia Connections" Folder, Historical Center of York County. Hill's local paper, the *Yorkville Enquirer,* regularly reported on the shipment to Liberia of illegally enslaved Africans seized by the U.S. Navy (so-called recaptives). The *Enquirer* viewed Liberia and indeed the navy's attempts to enforce the ban on the slave trade with great disdain. "Those Africans," *Yorkville Enquirer,* Sept. 16, 1858; "The Slaver," *Yorkville Enquirer,* Sept. 23, 1858; see also "The Case of the Slaver Echo," *Yorkville Enquirer,* Sept. 30, 1858.

80. Exodus 39:10 and 28:17 (Sardis); "Letter from Rev. Elias Hill" (Jan. 3, 1872), *African Repository,* Apr. 1872, p. 116 (quoting Romans 10:1); "Letter from Rev. Elias Hill" (Feb. 15, 1872), *African Repository,* July 1872, p. 222 (quoting Psalms 68:31); 5 *KKK Testimony,* 1412 (father from Africa); Elias Hill to Rev. William Coppinger, Apr. 14, 1871, reel 108, *RACS* ("long cherished desire"; "dying"); John Wallace to William Coppinger, Dec. 25, 1871, reel 109, *RACS* ("our native land"); "Letter from Mr. Scott Mason" (April 12, 1872), *African Repository,* July 1872, pp. 222–23 ("until he sets his foot"); "A Remarkable Man for Liberia," *African Repository,* Sept. 1871, pp. 280–82 ("nowhere else" and "enthusiast"); "Letter from Rev. Elias Hill" (Feb. 15, 1872), *African Repository,* July 1872, p. 222 ("duty"). On the uses of the Psalms passage, see Kelley, "How the West Was One," 123, 125, and the scholarship cited therein.

81. *African Repository* quoted in Hahn, *Nation under Our Feet,* 321 ("calls upon it"); "Want to Go to Liberia," *African Repository,* May 1871, p. 129 (thousands of freedpeople); Executive Committee Minutes, Washington, D.C., Jan. 11, 1872, reel 294, *RACS* ("some twelve hundred"); "Fifty-Fifth Annual Report," *African Repository,* Feb. 1872, pp. 33ff. ("between two and three thousand applicants").

82. Brison Hydes [?] to William Coppinger, Dec. 4, 1871, reel 109, *RACS* ("whole colored tribe"); "From North Carolina," *African Repository,* May 1871, p. 131 ("increasing spirit"); "Fifty-Fifth Annual Report," *African Repository,* Feb. 1872, pp. 33ff. (Decatur); [R. B.?] Thomas to M. W. Moore, Feb. 7, 1872, reel 109 (Mobile), "Emigration Applications, 1856–1889," reel 314 (Selma), Moses McDonald to John H. B. Latrobe, March 5, 1872, reel 109 (Brunswick), Enoch Parker to William Coppinger, Nov. 20, 1872, reel 110 (Pulaski), Enoch Parker to William Coppinger, Nov. 25, 1872, reel 110 ("in a fever"), Jacob McKinney to McLain, Oct. 28, 1871, reel 109 ("citizens of the United States"), all in *RACS.*

83. Elias Hill to William Coppinger, June 15, 1871, reel 108 ("hundreds & more"), J. D. Currence to William Coppinger, Nov. 19, 1871, reel 109 ("favorable newes"), Nelson Davies to William Coppinger, Dec. 25, 1871, reel 109 ("as soon as"), John Wallace to William Coppinger, Jan. 5, 1872, reel 109 (40 emigrants), S. Reaves to William Coppinger, Sept. 20, 1873, reel 111 ("the people at this place"), all in *RACS;* "Fifty-Fifth Annual Report of the American Colonization Society, Presented January 16, 1872," *African Repository,* Feb. 1872, pp. 33 ff. ("great change"; "most remarkable"; "more numerous"); John Wallace to William Coppinger, Dec. 25, 1871, reel 109, *RACS* ("we are down").

84. Providence Washington Insurance Co. to Jonathan H. B. Latrobe, Oct. 31, 1871, reel 109, *RACS* (Chicago fire); State Board of Agriculture of South Carolina [Harry Hammond], *South Carolina Resources and Population, Institutions and Industries* 158 (Walker, Evans & Cogswell, 1883) (cotton season); Rev. [Shmell?] McKinny to William McLain, Jan. 10, 1872, reel 109 (crop timing, end-of-season shortfalls), Elias Hill to William Coppinger, June 15, 1871, reel 108 ("they all pray"), John Wallace to William Coppinger, April 7, 1872, reel 110 (end-of-season shortfall), Nelson Thompson to William Coppinger, Oct. 13, 1872, reel 109 (rental year), John Wallace to William Coppinger, Feb. 12, 1872, reel 109 (assets such as hogs, cows, and horses), all in *RACS.* On the Colonization Society's financial difficulties, see Clegg, *Price of Liberty,* 256.

85. June Moore to William Coppinger, Oct. 22, 171, reel 109 ("som black folks"), William Coppinger to Elias Hill, July 29, 1871, reel 213 ("planters"), June Moore to William Coppinger, Oct. 27, 1871, reel 109 ("white folk"), all in *RACS.*

86. Elias Hill to William Coppinger, Apr. 14, 1871, reel 108, *RACS* ("one hundredth"); Walker, 1 *Statistics of the Population of the United States*

. . . *Ninth Census,* 5; "Emigrants Sent by the American Colonization Society," *African Repository,* Apr. 1875, p. 55 (annual emigration numbers).

87. Elias Hill to Rev. William Coppinger, Apr. 14, 1871, reel 108, *RACS* ("well to do"); "Gone to Liberia," *Yorkville Enquirer,* Nov. 2, 1871 ("most industrious"); Manuscript Census Report for 1870, York County, South Carolina (23 percent); William Coppinger to William McLain, Sept. 18, 1871, reel 108, and William Coppinger to Executive Committee, Oct. 6, 1871, reel 294, *RACS* (land sales); "Report of the Comptroller General to the General Assembly of the State of South Carolina, November, 1870," in *Reports and Resolutions of the General Assembly of the State of South Carolina at the Regular Session, 1870–71,* p. 225 (Columbia, S.C.: Republican Printing Co., 1871) (school payments); "Sale of Goods from the Estate of Cynthia Smith, Free Person of Color," RG 10, Galloway Papers, Box 2, Folder 12 ("Free Persons of Color"), Historical Center of York County (estate-auction records). It also may have been important that the 1871 cotton growing season had been a dry one in York County. As a result, the cotton was probably out of the ground early that year. "The Drought and Its Lessons," *Yorkville Enquirer,* Sept. 7, 1871.

88. Elias Hill to William Coppinger, June 15, 1871, reel 108 ($81.50 in June), June Moore to William Coppinger, Oct. 27, 1871, reel 109 ($80 in October), June Moore to William Coppinger, Oct. 11, 1871, reel 109 (same), William Coppinger to William McLain, Sept. 18, 1871, reel 108 (preference to Clay Hill company), William Coppinger to Elias Hill, Apr. 17, 1871, reel 213 (same), William Coppinger to William McLain, Nov. 3, 1871, reel 109 ($900 in cash), William Coppinger to William McLain, Sept. 23, 1871, reel 108 (train fares), all in *RACS.* The group from Georgia that joined the Clay Hill company passage to Liberia similarly had funds at its disposal—almost $2,000 in certificates of deposit. William Coppinger to William McLain, Sept. 22, 1871, reel 108, *RACS.*

89. "Letter from Rev. Elias Hill" (Jan. 3, 1872), *African Repository,* Apr. 1872, p. 116; "From Liberia: Letter from Rev. Elias Hill" (Jan. 3, 1872), *Yorkville Enquirer,* Feb. 22, 1872 ("swift gales. . ."; Grand Cape Mount); Rev. Chas. W. Thomas, *Adventures and Observations on the West Coast of Africa, and Its Islands . . .* 113 (New York: Derby & Jackson, 1860) (Cape Mesurado); Alfred Brockenbrough Williams, *The Liberian Exodus: An Account of the Voyage of the First Emigrants in the Bark "Azor," and Their Reception at Monrovia . . .* 28 (Charleston, S.C.: News and Courier Book Presses, 1878) (Jenkins's coffee trees).

90. "Letter from Rev. Elias Hill," (Jan. 3, 1872), *African Repository*, Apr. 1872, p. 116 (December 16 sermon); "Letters from Henry W. Dennis, Esq." (Dec. 21, 1871), *African Repository*, Mar. 1872, p. 94 (exploring Arthington); A. Williams, *Liberian Exodus*, 47 (twenty-five miles); Elias Hill to William Coppinger, Feb. 16, 1872, reel 162, *RACS* (school and church); "Letters from Henry W. Dennis, Esq." (Dec. 21, 1871), *African Repository*, Mar. 1872, p. 95 (small frame house); "Fifty-Fifth Annual Report," *African Repository*, Feb. 1872, pp. 33ff. (same); "Letter from Rev. Elias Hill" (Feb. 15, 1872), *African Repository*, July 1872, p. 222 (Hill's arrival in Arthington; sermon); "Letters from Henry W. Dennis, Esq." (Dec. 21, 1871), *African Repository*, Mar. 1872, p. 95 (same).

91. John Wallace to William Coppinger, Feb. 12, 1872, reel 109, *RACS* ("well pleased"; "all glad"); see also "Letter from Elias Hill," *Yorkville Enquirer*, Feb. 22, 1872; June Moore and Solomon Hill to William Coppinger, [May 21?] 1872, reel 162, *RACS* ("well satisfied"); Solomon Hill to William Coppinger, Sept. 7, 1873, reel 162, *RACS* ("beter sadisfide"); "Letter from Liberia," *Yorkville Enquirer*, Aug. 6, 1874 (edited version of same); June Moore and Solomon Hill to William Coppinger, [May 21?] 1872, reel 162, *RACS* ("bey somebody"); June Moore to William Coppinger, July 10, 1876, reel 163, *RACS* ("only sorry").

92. *Proceedings in the KK Trials*, 91–92 (circuit court ruling); L. Williams, *Great South Carolina Ku Klux Klan Trials*, 71–76.

93. *Operations of the Department of Justice . . . 1872*, pp. 26, 36 (1,200 cases); L. Williams, *Great South Carolina Ku Klux Klan Trials*, 110–11 (trial backlog); West, *Reconstruction Ku Klux Klan*, 116–17 (same); Robert J. Kaczorowski, *The Politics of Judicial Interpretation: The Federal Courts, Department of Justice and Civil Rights, 1866–1876*, pp. 109–10 (Oceana Publications, 1985) ("only as far" and April suspension); L. Williams, *Great South Carolina Ku Klux Klan Trials*, 125, 174 n.33 (clemency); *Proceedings in the KK Trials*, 768 (Samuel G. Brown); West, *Reconstruction Ku Klux Klan*, 154 (Brown's release). Grant had begun to pardon the Klan defendants as early as January 1873. West, *Reconstruction Ku Klux Klan*, 143–44; "Arrests," *Yorkville Enquirer*, Feb. 12, 1874 (Robert M. Steele, probably Max Steele). As Major Merrill observed, the Klan trials had ultimately failed to extinguish either "the dissatisfaction of the white leaders with the results of the war" or "their determination to nullify these as far as possible." Zuczek, *State of Rebellion*, 106. For decades, historians interpreted the Klan trials in South Carolina as a resounding victory for the federal government's

efforts to protect freedpeople's rights: e.g., Foner, *Reconstruction,* 457–59; Trelease, *White Terror,* 418; see also Mark Wiener, *Black Trials: Citizenship from the Beginnings of Slavery to the End of Caste* 183–213 (Knopf, 2004). More recent accounts are more skeptical: e.g., L. Williams, *Great South Carolina Ku Klux Klan Trials;* West, *Reconstruction Ku Klux Klan;* Richard Zuczek, "The Federal Government's Attack on the Ku Klux Klan: A Reassessment," 97 *South Carolina Historical Magazine* 47–64 (1996).

94. United States v. Avery, 80 U.S. (13 Wall.) 250 (1872). The date of the decision is from Kaczorowski, *Politics of Judicial Interpretation,* 130.

95. *The Slaughterhouse Cases,* 83 U.S. (16 Wall.) 36, 67 (1873); Ronald M. Labbé and Jonathan Lurie, *The Slaughterhouse Cases: Regulation, Reconstruction, and the Fourteenth Amendment* 136–241 (University Press of Kansas, 2003) (delayed decision).

96. Kaczorowski, *Politics of Judicial Interpretation,* 143 (on the Court's "masterful political stratagem" in the *Slaughterhouse Cases*); *Slaughterhouse Cases,* 83 U.S. (16 Wall.) at 73 ("distinction between"), 76 ("protection by the government") (quoting Corfield v. Coryell, 6 F. Cas. 546, 551–52 (C.C.E.D. Pa. 1823) (Bushrod Washington, J.)), 79 ("seat of government"; "high seas"; "navigable waters"), 78 ("left to the State").

97. *Slaughterhouse Cases,* 83 U.S. at 94 (Field, J., dissenting), 51–52 (argument of John A. Campbell for the plaintiff butchers); Charles L. Black Jr., *A New Birth of Freedom: Human Rights, Named and Unnamed* 72 (Grosset/Putnam, 1997) ("shade of Calhoun"); *Proceedings in the KK Trials,* 380, 432–35 (Corbin); *KKK Report,* 25 ("constitutional liberty"); see generally William E. Forbath, "Lincoln, the Declaration, and the 'Grisly, Undying Corpse of States' Rights': History, Memory, and Imagination in the Constitution of a Southern Liberal," 92 *Georgetown L. J.* 709, 745–47 (2004).

98. United States v. Cruikshank, 92 U.S. (2 Otto) 542 (1875); United States v. Reese, 92 U.S. (2 Otto) 214 (1875); Foner, *Reconstruction,* 564–87.

99. C. Vann Woodward, *Reunion and Reaction: The Compromise of 1877 and the End of Reconstruction* (Little, Brown, 1951); Vincent P. DeSantis, "Rutherford B. Hayes and the Removal of the Troops and the End of Reconstruction," in J. Morgan Kousser and James M. McPherson, eds., *Region, Race, and Reconstruction: Essays in Honor of C. Vann Woodward* 417–50 (Oxford University Press, 1982); Zuczek, *State of Rebellion,* 190–93; Francis Butler Simkins and Robert Hilliard Woody, *South Carolina during Reconstruction* 514–41 (University of North Carolina Press, 1932);

George Brown Tindall, *South Carolina Negroes, 1877–1900*, pp. 14–16 (University of South Carolina Press, 1952).

100. 2 *KKK Testimony*, p. 1263 (opposition to constitutionality of Reconstruction amendments); Foner, *Reconstruction*, pp. 574–75 (Red Shirts); Simkins and Woody, *South Carolina during Reconstruction*, p. 499 (same); Kuczek, *State of Rebellion*, pp. 170, 192–201 (same); Willoughby, *The Good Town*, pp. 53–55 (Rock Hill parade); George P. Rawick, ed., 10 *The American Slave: A Composite Autobiography: Arkansas Narratives (Part 6)*, pp. 187–89 (Greenwood Publishing Co., 1972) ("Bloody Town").

101. Victor Ullman, *Martin R. Delany*, 501–5 (Liberian Exodus Co.); George A. Devlin, *South Carolina and Black Migration, 1865–1940*, p. 90 (Garland Publishing, 1989) (65,000 registrants); "Liberia and the Exodus Movement," *African Repository*, July 1878, p. 75 (150,000 interested); see also "The Departure of the Azor," *African Repository*, July 1878, p. 77; Clegg, *Price of Liberty*, 259; Cohen, *At Freedom's Edge*, 158–60; Tindall, *South Carolina Negroes*, 153–61; Hahn, *Nation under Our Feet*, 360 (half a million); George B. Tindall, "The Liberian Exodus of 1878," 53 *South Carolina Historical Magazine* 133, 145 (1952) ("no more than dogs"; "our mouths shut").

102. Clegg, *Price of Liberty*, 69, 159–60 (mortality rates); Antonio McDaniel, *Swing Low, Sweet Chariot: The Mortality Cost of Colonizing Liberia in the Nineteenth Century* 88–105 (University of Chicago Press, 1995) (same); American Colonization Society, "Information about Going to Liberia" (American Colonization Society [1877?]), Butler Library Rare Books Department, Columbia University (3 percent); Elias Hill to William Coppinger, Feb. 16, 1872, reel 162, *RACS* ("acclimating fever"; "portion"; "chills"); "Letter from Mr. Scott Mason" (April 12, 1872), *African Repository*, July 1872, pp. 222–23 (died).

103. June Moore and Solomon Hill to William Coppinger, [May?] 21, 1872, reel 162 ("great meney"; one-third; "wanting to goe back"); "Letter from Mr. Scott Mason" (April 12, 1872), *African Repository*, July 1872, pp. 222–23 ("preparing to return" and wait at the harbor); June Moore to William Coppinger, [May 21?] 1872, reel 162, *RACS* (everyone who was able to); "Returned from Liberia," *Yorkville Enquirer*, Nov. 28, 1872 (in Boston); A. M. Grist, "Bethesda and Sardis Church History," *Yorkville Enquirer*, Dec. 19 and 22, 1933, reprinted in the *The Quarterly: York County, South Carolina*, vol. 15, no. 5 (York County Geological and Historical Society, June 2003) (thirty-six; names of returnees); History of the Union Bap-

tist Church (typescript, n.d.), Liberia Connections Folder, Historical Center of York County (returnees).

104. "From Liberia: Letter from Rev. Elias Hill" (Jan. 3, 1872), *Yorkville Enquirer*, Feb. 22, 1872 ("governmental affairs"); William McLain to William Coppinger, Oct. 19, 1871, Oct. 30, 1871, and Nov. 3, 1871, reel 109, *RACS* (had said nothing); William McLain to William Coppinger, Nov. 3, 1871, reel 109, *RACS* (civil war); "From Liberia: Letter from Rev. Elias Hill" (Jan. 3, 1872), *Yorkville Enquirer*, Feb. 22, 1872 ("President, Attorney-General"). On the Roye affair, see C. Abayomi Cassell, *Liberia: History of the First African Republic* 277–80 (Fountainhead Publishers, 1970); Joseph Saye Guannu, *A Short History of the First Liberian Republic* 9–12 (Exposition Press of Florida, 1985); Huberich, 2 *Political and Legislative History of Liberia*, 1132–33; Charles S. Johnson, *Bitter Canaan: The Story of the Negro Republic* 98–101 (Transaction Books, 1987); J. Gus Liebenow, *Liberia: The Quest for Democracy* 17, 90 (Indiana University Press, 1987); Thomas W. Livingston, "The Exportation of American Higher Education to West Africa: Liberia College, 1850–1900," 45 *J. Negro Education* 246, 257 (1976). The Colonization Society continued its pattern of misleadingly positive descriptions of Liberia even after Hill wrote back with reports of the governmental upheaval. Compare "From Liberia: Letter from Rev. Elias Hill" (Jan. 3, 1872), *Yorkville Enquirer*, Feb. 22, 1872, with the *African Repository* account of same letter.

105. Liebenow, *Liberia: The Quest for Democracy*, 22–23; Santosh C. Saha, "Agriculture in Liberia during the Nineteenth Century: Americo-Liberians' Contribution," 22 *Canadian J. African Studs.* 224–25 (1988); M. B. Akpan, "Liberia and the Universal Negro Improvement Association: The Background to the Abortion of Garvey's Scheme for African Colonization," 14 *J. African Hist.* 105, 112 (1973); Howard W. French, *A Continent for the Taking: The Tragedy and Hope of Africa* 107 (Knopf, 2004) (failed state).

106. "From Liberia: Letter from Rev. Elias Hill" (Jan. 3, 1872), *Yorkville Enquirer*, Feb. 22, 1872 ("rich and well-to-do," "work . . . at low wages"); James Fairhead et al., eds., *African-American Explorations in West Africa: Four Nineteenth-Century Diaries* 18–21 (Indiana University Press, 2003) (ethnic discrimination and coerced native labor); A. Williams, *Liberian Exodus* 45–46 (slave labor already in the 1870s); Akpan, "Liberia and the Universal Negro Improvement Association," 105 (Ferdinand Po); I. K. Sundiata, *Black Scandal: America and the Liberian Labor Crisis, 1929–1936*

(Institute for the Study of Human Issues, 1980) (Firestone); Frank Chalk, "The Anatomy of an Investment: Firestone's 1927 Loan to Liberia," 1 *Canadian J. African Studs.* 12–32 (1967) (same); I. K. Sundiata, "Prelude to a Scandal: Liberia and Fernando Po, 1880–1930," 15 *J. African Hist.* 97–112 (1974) (Ferdinand Po and League of Nations); Frank Chalk, "Du Bois and Garvey Confront Liberia: Two Incidents of the Coolidge Years," 1 *Canadian J. African Studs.* 135–42 (1967) (same).

107. A. Williams, *Liberian Exodus*, 47 ("flourishing settlement"), 41 ("mad on the subject"); June Moore to William Coppinger, July 10, 1876, reel 163, *RACS* ("9,000 coffee trees"); Edward W. Blyden, "Visit to Arthington," *African Repository*, April 1889, pp. 44, 45 ("leading men"); Cassell, *Liberia: History of the First African Republic,* 339 (Hill & Moore); Blyden, "Visit to Arthington," 45 ("architect"; "beginning"); "A York Negro in Liberia," *Rock Hill Herald,* Dec. 11, 1884, in Liberia Connections Folder, Historical Center of York County (Philadelphia coffee trader); Max Belcher, *A Land and Life Remembered: Americo-Liberian Folk Architecture* 22 (University of Georgia Press, 1988) ($100,000 annually), 23 (Solomon Hill's Monrovia mansion). June Moore oversaw the school in Arthington until at least 1881 (see June Moore to American Colonization Society, June 9, 1881, reel 164, *RACS*); he died in 1898 (see Cassell, *Liberia: History of the First African Republic,* 379).

108. A. Williams, *Liberian Exodus,* 44 ("wealthier planters"; "Southern planter"); Katherine Olukemi Bankole, "The Use of Electronic Information Technology in Historical Research on African Diaspora Studies and the emigration to Liberia, 1827–1901," 27 *Liberian Studies J.* 40, 45 (2001) (rumors; President Roberts); Edward W. Blyden to William Coppinger, Dec. 2, 1871, reel 162, *RACS* (coup to preserve ethnic exploitation); A. Williams, *Liberian Exodus,* 45–46 (coerced labor); Temperley, "African-American Aspirations and Liberia," 86–87 ("segregation in Alabama"). On ethnic discrimination in Liberia, see M. B. Akpan, "Black Imperialism: Americo-Liberian Rule over the African Peoples of Liberia, 1841–1964," 7 *Canadian J. African Studs.* 217–36 (1973); Livingston, "Exportation of Higher Education to West Africa," 246, 249–50; Svend E. Holsoe, "A Study of Relations between Settlers and Indigenous Peoples in Western Liberia, 1821–1847," 4 *African Historical Studies* 331–62 (1971); Augustine Konneh, "Citizenship at the Margins: Status, Ambiguity, and the Mandingo of Liberia," 39 *African Studies Review* 141–54 (1996).

109. Nicholas Lemann, *The Promised Land: The Great Migration and*

How It Changed America 6 (Knopf, 1991) (Great Migration statistics); Hahn, *Nation under Our Feet*, 465–67 (same); George M. Fredrickson, *Black Liberation: A Comparative History of Black Ideologies in the United States and South Africa* 160 (Oxford University Press, 1995) (Marcus Garvey); Painter, *Exodusters*, 184, 256 (Kansas numbers); Hahn, *Nation under Our Feet*, 334–35 (same); August Meier, *Negro Thought in America, 1880–1915*, p. 288 n.1 (University of Michigan Press, 1963) (emigration used for both migration and emigration); Hahn, *Nation under Our Feet*, 466–67 ("striking resemblances"). On the Great Migration, see James R. Grossman, *Land of Hope: Chicago, Black Southerners, and the Great Migration* (University of Chicago Press, 1989); Peter Gottlieb, *Making Their Own Way: Southern Blacks' Migration to Pittsburgh, 1916–1930* (University of Illinois Press, 1987); Neil Fligstein, *Going North: Migration of Blacks and Whites from the South, 1900–1950* (Academic Press, 1981).

110. R. T. Greener, "The Emigration of Colored Citizens from the Southern States," 11 *Journal of Social Science* 22, 30 (May 1880); Richard T. Greener, "The Negro Will Migrate," 139 *North American Review* 88 (1884); James Oakes, *Slavery and Freedom: An Interpretation of the Old South* 169–74 (Norton, 1990) (fugitive slaves).

111. Michael J. Klarman, *From Jim Crow to Civil Rights: The Supreme Court and the Struggle for Racial Equality* 100 (Oxford University Press, 2004) ("extralegal force"); Gerald Rosenberg, *The Hollow Hope: Can Courts Bring About Social Change?* 157, 159 (University of Chicago Press, 1991) ("the current of history"). Critics of the idea that legal change brought about the successes of the civil rights movement are on more solid ground when their critique is of the effectiveness of *courts* rather than the effectiveness of *law*. Courts, as the Clay Hill freedpeople knew all too well, are not the only sources of law.

112. "A Remarkable Man for Liberia," *African Repository*, Sept. 1871, pp. 280–82 ("loved the United States"; "a United States of Africa").

113. Hirschman, *Exit, Voice, and Loyalty*, 78 (loyalty serves the role of "keeping exit at bay"); McFeely, *Frederick Douglass*, 371 ("loyalty enough"); H. W. Dennis to William Coppinger, Dec. 14, 1871, reel 162, *RACS* (John Marshall). For a similar interpretation of the distinction between American emigrants to Liberia and the Old Testament exodus, see Howard Temperley, "African-American Aspirations and the Settlement of Liberia," 21 *Slavery and Abolition: A Journal of Slave and Post-Slave Studies* 67, 77 (2000).

3. INTERNATIONALISTS IN THE NATION-STATE

1. Thomas L. Haskell, "The Curious Persistence of Rights Talk in the 'Age of Interpretation,'" in David Thelen, ed., *The Constitution and American Life* 324, 328–29 (Cornell University Press, 1988); Jeremy Waldron, "Nonsense upon Stilts? A Reply," in Jeremy Waldron, ed., *"Nonsense upon Stilts": Bentham, Burke, and Marx on the Rights of Man* 151–209 (Methuen, 1987).

2. Abrams v. United States, 250 U.S. 616, 630 (1919) (Holmes, J., dissenting) ("fighting faiths"); David M. Kennedy, *Over Here: The First World War and American Society* 50 (Oxford University Press, 1980) ("individualistic tradition"); David M. Rabban, *Free Speech in Its Forgotten Years* 3 (Cambridge University Press, 1997) ("early Victorian platitudes"); Randolph S. Bourne, "The War and the Intellectuals," in Carl Resek, ed., *War and the Intellectuals: Collected Essays, 1915–1919*, pp. 3, 11 (Harper & Row, 1964); Raymond B. Fosdick, "Liberty in America," *Outlook*, Feb. 2, 1916, pp. 282, 285; Ernest Hemingway, *A Farewell to Arms* 196 (Charles Scribner's Sons, 1929); see also Paul Fussell, *The Great War and Modern Memory* 21 (Oxford University Press, 1975) (describing Hemingway's disillusionment). For an especially elegant version of the pragmatist solution to the puzzle, see Louis Menand, *The Metaphysical Club: A Story of Ideas in America* (Farrar, Straus, and Giroux, 2001).

3. Samuel P. Huntington, *American Politics: The Promise of Disharmony* 85 (Harvard University Press, 1981); Michael Kent Curtis, *Free Speech, "The People's Darling Privilege": Struggles for Freedom of Expression in American History* 389–94 (Duke University Press, 2000); Donald Johnson, *The Challenge to American Freedoms: World War I and the Rise of the American Civil Liberties Union*, pp. vii–ix (University of Kentucky Press, 1963); Kennedy, *Over Here*, 72–92; Paul L. Murphy, *World War I and the Origin of Civil Liberties in the United States* 26–30 (Norton, 1979); Samuel Walker, *In Defense of American Liberties: A History of the ACLU* 11–47 (Southern Illinois University Press, 2nd ed., 1999); Robert E. Cushman, "The Repercussions of Foreign Affairs on the American Tradition of Civil Liberty," 92 *Proc. Am. Phil. Soc'y* 257 (1948); Michael J. Klarman, "Rethinking the Civil Rights and Civil Liberties Revolutions," 82 *Va. L. Rev.* 1, 34–38 (1996); Michael Les Benedict, "Victorian Moralism and Civil Liberty in the Nineteenth-Century United States," in Donald G. Nieman, ed., *The Constitution, Law, and American Life: Critical Aspects of the Nineteenth-*

Century Experience 91, 109 (University of Georgia Press, 1992) ("terribly dismal").

4. Letter from William English Walling to L. Hollingsworth Wood (Jan. 7, 1918), microformed on reel 1, vol. 3, *American Civil Liberties Union Archives: The Roger Baldwin Years, 1917–1950* (Scholarly Resources, 1995) [hereinafter *ACLU Archives*] (Lincoln's "limitations"); see generally Mark E. Neely Jr., *The Fate of Liberty: Abraham Lincoln and Civil Liberties* (Oxford University Press, 1991) (describing Lincoln's wartime speech policies); Geoffrey R. Stone, *Perilous Times: Free Speech in Wartime from the Sedition Act of 1798 to the War on Terror* 108–19 (W. W. Norton & Co., 2004) (same); Murphy, *World War I and the Origin of Civil Liberties,* 9 (quoting Henry Steele Commanger). James Madison to Thomas Jefferson (Oct. 17, 1788), in Jack N. Rakove, ed., *James Madison: Writings* 418, 420 (Library of America, 1999). On nineteenth-century restraints on speech and other expressive activity, see Curtis, *Free Speech,* 9; Russel B. Nye, *Fettered Freedom: Civil Liberties and the Slavery Controversy, 1830–1860* (Michigan State University Press, 1949); Rabban, *Free Speech in Its Forgotten Years;* John W. Wertheimer, "Free Speech Fights: The Roots of Modern Free-Expression Litigation in the United States" 51–67 (Ph.D. diss., Princeton University, 1992).

5. Max Eastman, *Enjoyment of Living* 1 (Harper, 1948) ("center of gravity").

6. Joan D. Hedrick, *Harriet Beecher Stowe: A Life,* p. vii (Oxford University Press, 1994) ("little woman"); Max Eastman, *Heroes I Have Known* 1–15 (Simon & Schuster, 1942); Blanche Wiesen Cook, "Introduction," in Blanche Wiesen Cook, ed., *Crystal Eastman on Women and Revolution* 1, 4 (Oxford University Press, 1978); Sylvia A. Law, "Crystal Eastman: NYU Law Graduate," 66 *NYU L. Rev.* 1963 (1991).

7. M. Eastman, *Heroes I Have Known,* 8–9 ("feminist principles"); Crystal Eastman, "Mother-Worship," in Cook, ed., *Women and Revolution,* 41, 45, 43 ("boys' work and girls' work" and "Woman"), and in Blanche Wiesen Cook, ed., *Toward the Great Change: Crystal and Max Eastman on Feminism, Antimilitarism, and Revolution* 193, 196 (Garland Publishing, 1976) (same); Cook, "Introduction," *Women and Revolution,* 9; Blanche Wiesen Cook, "Introduction," in Cook, ed., *Toward the Great Change,* 15, 17 ("be an individual"; "loss of yourself"; "conformity with the crowd").

8. David Brion Davis, *The Problem of Slavery in the Age of Revolution 1770–1823,* p. 275 (Cornell University Press, 1975) (alternative forms of

labor exploitation); Hedrick, *Harriet Beecher Stowe,* 328–31 (Florida plantation); Richard Wightman Fox, *Trials of Intimacy: Love and Loss in the Beecher-Tilton Scandal* (University of Chicago Press, 1999) (apparent affair); Sylvia A. Law, "Crystal Eastman: Organizer for Women's Rights, Peace, and Civil Liberties in the 1910s," 28 *Valparaiso U. L. Rev.* 1305, 1310 (1994) (not a single state); M. Eastman, *Enjoyment of Living,* 330 ("the 'old regime'").

9. Thomas L. Haskell, *The Emergence of Professional Social Science: The American Social Science Association and the Nineteenth-Century Crisis of Authority* 24–47 (University of Illinois Press, 1977); James T. Kloppenberg, *Uncertain Victory: Social Democracy and Progressivism in European and American Thought, 1870–1920,* pp. 107–14 (Oxford University Press, 1986); Dorothy Ross, *The Origins of American Social Science* pp. xiii–xxii (Cambridge University Press, 1991); Morton G. White, *Social Thought in America: The Revolt against Formalism* 47–58 (Viking Press, 1949); Annis Ford Eastman to Catherine Crystal Eastman (July 16, 1903), box 5, folder 132, Crystal Eastman Papers, Schlesinger Library, Radcliffe Institute for Advanced Study, Harvard University (hereinafter Crystal Eastman Papers); Academic Transcript of Catherine Crystal Eastman (June 8, 1904), Columbia University, Office of the Registrar.

10. Ross, *Origins of American Social Science,* 107 ("socialistic ideal"), 106–22 (marginalist economics).

11. F. H. Hankins, "Franklin Henry Giddings, 1855–1931: Some Aspects of His Sociological Theory," 37 *Am. J. Soc.* 349, 359 (1931) ("chance and probability"); Franklin H. Giddings, "The Concepts and Methods of Sociology," 10 *Am. J. Soc.* 161, 161 (1904) ("aggregations"); also Franklin H. Giddings, *Studies in the Theory of Human Society* 144–53 (Macmillan Co., 1922) (same); F. H. Giddings, "Social Self-Control," 24 *Pol. Sci. Q.* 569, 574, 579, 581 (1909) ("standardization and discipline"; "variations from itself"); also Clarence H. Northcott, "The Sociological Theories of Franklin H. Giddings," 24 *Am. J. Soc.* 1, 12 (1918) (same).

12. Giddings, "Concepts and Methods of Sociology," 161 ("social pressure"; "restrictions on liberty"); Franklin H. Giddings, "Book Review," 17 *Pol. Sci. Q.* 704, 706 (1902) ("riotous use"); Franklin H. Giddings, "The Measurement of Social Pressure," 11 *Publications Am. Stat. Ass'n* 56, 56 (1908) ("legal forms"; "increasing inequality"); Franklin H. Giddings, "Government or Human Evolution: Individualism and Collectivism by Edmond Kelly," 17 *Pol. Sci. Q.* 704, 706 (1902) ("utopian collectivism"); Franklin

H. Giddings, "The Natural Rate of Wages," 2 *Pol. Sci. Q.* 620, 621 (1887) ("middle view"; difficult to strike); Giddings, "Social Self-Control," 588 ("general welfare" . . . "supremely important"); also Franklin H. Giddings, "A Theory of Social Causation," *Publications Am. Econ. Ass'n* (3rd ser., vol. 5), May 1904, pp. 139, 167–68 (same); Franklin H. Giddings and Agnes Mathilde Wergeland, "The Ethics of Socialism," 1 *Int'l J. Ethics* 239, 240–41 (1891) (old nostrums).

13. Letters from Annis Ford Eastman to Catherine Crystal Eastman, May 1904, box 5, folder 139, Crystal Eastman Papers (bad exam experience).

14. Bradwell v. Illinois, 83 U.S. (16 Wall.) 130, 141 (1872) (Bradley, J., concurring); 4 Bureau of the Census, Dep't of Commerce, *Thirteenth Census of the United States Taken in the Year 1910: Population 1910, Occupational Statistics* 54, 136–37 (1914) (133 women lawyers); Virginia G. Drachman, *Sisters in Law: Women Lawyers in Modern American History* 2, 252 (Harvard University Press, 1998) (percentages in the professions). Bradwell never sought admission after 1873, but she was admitted to practice in 1890 when the Illinois Supreme Court (on its own motion) reversed itself and approved her original 1869 application. Susan Gluck Mezey, "Myra Colby Bradwell," http://www.anb.org/articles/11/11–00095.html, *American National Biography Online*, Feb. 2000.

15. Drachman, *Sisters in Law,* 256; Law, "Crystal Eastman, NYU Law Graduate," 1977; Crystal Eastman to Max Eastman (Nov. 28, 1904) ("even more wild"); Crystal Eastman to Annis Ford Eastman (Dec. 17, 1906); Crystal Eastman to Annis Ford Eastman (Apr. 18, 1907); Crystal Eastman to Annis Ford Eastman (June 8, 1907), all in box 6, Crystal Eastman Papers.

16. Crystal Eastman to Annis Ford Eastman (Oct. 10, 1907) ("a good practice"); Crystal Eastman to Max Eastman (Oct. 17, 1907) ("tingling"); Crystal Eastman to Annis Ford Eastman (Oct. 16, 1907) ("every chance of winning"); see also Crystal Eastman to Annis Ford Eastman (Apr. 21, 1908); Crystal Eastman to Max Eastman (Oct. 17, 1911) (Hillquit and Alger); Crystal Eastman to Max Eastman (Oct. 4, 1911) (same), all in box 6, Crystal Eastman Papers.

17. John Fabian Witt, *The Accidental Republic: Crippled Workingmen, Destitute Widows, and the Remaking of American Law* 126–31, 143–44 (Harvard University Press, 2004) (Pittsburgh Survey); Crystal Eastman to Annis Ford Eastman (Sept. 21, 1907), box 6, Crystal Eastman Papers

("strange to say" . . . "interesting to me sociologically"); Crystal Eastman, *Work-Accidents and the Law* (Russell Sage, 1910).

18. Witt, *Accidental Republic,* 22–42.

19. Id., 43–70.

20. Daniel T. Rodgers, *Atlantic Crossings: Social Politics in a Progressive Age* 211–66 (Harvard University Press, 1998) (western European nations); Crystal Eastman, "The American Way of Distributing Industrial Accident Losses: A Criticism," *Publications Am. Econ. Ass'n* (3rd ser.), Apr. 1909, 119 ("national economy"), 126 ("American system"); Emory S. Bogardus, "The Relation of Fatigue to Industrial Accidents," 17 *Am. J. Soc.* 206, 208 (1911) ("each year . . . as surely as"); Crystal Eastman, "The Three Essentials for Accident Prevention," in Cook, ed., *Women and Revolution,* 280, 281–82 ("good stuff"; "start a revolution"); C. Eastman, *Work-Accidents and the Law,* 218 ("justice between individuals"; "distribution of the loss").

21. Crystal Eastman to Max Eastman (Mar. 24, 1909), box 6, Crystal Eastman Papers ("book of fame"); Annis Ford Eastman to Crystal Eastman (May 3, 1909), box 5, folder 159, Crystal Eastman Papers (appointment); Crystal Eastman to Annis Ford Eastman (Mar. 28, 1908) (appointment), and Crystal Eastman to Max Eastman (June 15, 1909) (appointment), both box 6, Crystal Eastman Papers; Crystal Eastman to J. Mayhew Wainwright (Nov. 13, 1909), box 6, folder July–Dec. 1909, J. Mayhew Wainwright Papers, New-York Historical Society; "The Reminiscences of John Spargo" 174 (1957), Columbia University, Oral History Research Office; Memorandum on Division of Work on Report (n.d.), box 6, folder 1909–1912, J. Mayhew Wainwright Papers, New-York Historical Society.

22. Crystal Eastman, "Work-Accidents and Employers' Liability," in Cook, ed., *Women and Revolution,* 269, 278–79 ("originally intended"); Ives v. South Buffalo Ry., 94 N.E. 431, 439–48 (N.Y. 1911) (employers' property rights); Witt, *Accidental Republic,* 152–86 (rights tradition).

23. Witt, *Accidental Republic,* 180–84 (set off a search); Wainwright Commission Staff to J. Mayhew Wainwright (Jan. 30, 1911), box 6, folder 1911, J. Mayhew Wainwright Papers, New-York Historical Society (break off her work); Crystal Eastman to Max Eastman, Feb. 6, 1911, box 6, Crystal Eastman Papers (beginning to dread).

24. Leon Stein, *The Triangle Fire* 117, 213 (William Greider, ed., Cornell University Press, 2001 [Lippincott, 1962]); David von Drehle, *Triangle: The Fire That Changed America* 3 (Atlantic Monthly Press, 2003); Crystal Eastman to Max Eastman (Apr. 3, 1911), box 6, Crystal Eastman Papers

("sank into my soul"); C. Eastman, "Work-Accidents and Employers' Liability," in Cook, ed., *Women and Revolution,* 281 ("benevolent talk . . . revolution").

25. Crystal Eastman, "Suffragists Ten Years After," in Cook, ed., *Women and Revolution,* 132–35; Crystal Eastman to Max Eastman (n.d. [1913?]; and Mar. 29, 1913), box 6, Crystal Eastman Papers.

26. Lillian D. Wald, *Windows on Henry Street* 286 (Little, Brown, 1934) ("intense hush"; "muffled drums"); "Protesting Women March in Mourning," *New York Times,* Aug. 30, 1914, p. 11 ("robed in black . . . not as nations"); C. Roland Marchand, *The American Peace Movement and Social Reform, 1898–1918,* pp. 182–84 (Princeton University Press, 1972).

27. On American antiwar organizations during World War I, see Charles Chatfield, *For Peace and Justice: Pacifism in America, 1914–1941* (University of Tennessee Press, 1971); Charles DeBenedetti, *Origins of the Modern American Peace Movement, 1915–1929* (KTO Press, 1978); Marchand, *American Peace Movement,* 148, 206–7, 256, 358. Alan Dawley's *Changing the World: American Progressives in War and Revolution* (Princeton University Press, 2003), is uneven and unfortunately marred by a number of errors, but is nonetheless valuable.

28. Nathaniel Berman, "'But the Alternative Is Despair': European Nationalism and the Modernist Renewal of International Law," 106 *Harv. L. Rev.* 1792, 1798 (1993) ("international legal modernism").

29. Franklin H. Giddings, "The Heart of Mr. Spencer's Ethics," 14 *Int'l J. Ethics* 496, 499 (1904) ("communication"); Franklin H. Giddings, "Imperialism?" 13 *Pol. Sci. Q.* 585, 596 (1898) (closer contact); Sondra R. Herman, *Eleven against War: Studies in American Internationalist Thought, 1898–1921,* pp. 10–21 (Hoover Institution Press, 1969); Warren F. Kuehl, *Seeking World Order: The United States and International Organization to 1920,* p. 87 (Vanderbilt University Press, 1969); Gerald J. Mangone, *A Short History of International Organization* 93–97 (McGraw-Hill, 1954); David S. Patterson, *Toward a Warless World: The Travail of the American Peace Movement, 1887–1914,* pp. 11–12 (Indiana University Press, 1976).

30. Arthur Nussbaum, *A Concise History of the Law of Nations* 196 (rev. ed., Macmillan, 1954) (16,000 treaties); Calvin DeArmond Davis, *The United States and the First Hague Peace Conference* 146–61 (Cornell University Press, 1962); Calvin DeArmond Davis, *The United States and the Second Hague Peace Conference* 289–302 (Duke University Press, 1975); Mangone, *Short History of International Organization,* 127 ("peaceful relations").

31. Martti Koskenniemi, *The Gentle Civilizer of Nations: The Rise and Fall of International Law, 1870–1960*, pp. 4, 13, 12–19 (Cambridge University Press, 2002) ("professional self-awareness," *l'esprit d'inernationalité*).

32. Kuehl, *Seeking World Order*, 41–43 (Lake Mohonk); American Conference on International Arbitration, *The American Conference on International Arbitration Held in Washington, D.C., April 22 and 23, 1896* (New York: Baker & Taylor, 1896); American Conference on International Arbitration, *The Second American Conference on International Arbitration Held in Washington, D.C., January 12, 1904* (Washington, D.C.: Gibson Bros., 1904); Marchand, *American Peace Movement*, 39 (American Society for International Law); American Association for International Conciliation, *Publisher's Introduction to Official Documents Looking toward Peace* (American Association for International Conciliation, 1917); Buffalo Peace and Arbitration Society, *First Report of the Executive Committee and Treasurer* (Buffalo Peace and Arbitration Society, 1911); Chicago Peace Society, *Report of the Chicago Peace Society, 1912* (Chicago Peace Society, 1913); Jay William Hudson, *What Is the New Internationalism?* (Massachusetts Peace Society, 1915); New York Peace Society, *Officers, Constitution* (New York Peace Society, 1908); James Brown Scott, "Judicial Proceedings as a Substitute for War or International Self-Redress," *Maryland Q.*, Feb. 1910, p. 1; American School Citizenship League, *An Eleven Year Survey of the Activities of the School Peace League from 1908 to 1919*, p. 11 (American School Citizenship League, 1919); Larry L. Fabian, *Andrew Carnegie's Peace Endowment: The Tycoon, the President, and Their Bargain of 1910*, p. 1 (Carnegie Endowment for International Peace, 1985).

33. Marchand, *American Peace Movement*, 23 ("veritable flood"); Davis, *Second Hague Peace Conference*, 19 ("new internationalism"); Convention for the Pacific Settlement of International Disputes (Hague I) (July 29, 1899), 32 *Statutes at Large* 1779 (U.S. Government Printing Office, 1899); Nicholas Murray Butler, *The International Mind: An Argument for the Judicial Settlement of International Disputes* (Charles Scribner's Sons, 1912).

34. Hamilton Holt, "A League of Peace," in John Whiteclay Chambers, ed., *The Eagle and the Dove: The American Peace Movement and United States Foreign Policy, 1900–1922*, pp. 17, 18 (2nd ed., Garland Publishing, 1991) (new "Magna Charta"); William McKinley, "First Inaugural Address" (March 4, 1897), reprinted in *Inaugural Addresses of the Presidents of the United States from George Washington, 1789, to George Bush, 1989*, pp. 193, 200 (U.S. Government Printing Office, 1989) ("moral influence"); James L. Tryon, "A Permanent Court of International Justice," 22 *Yale L. J.* 203, 203

(1913) ("substituting law"); M. A. Stobart, *Women and War* 18 (World Peace Foundation Pamphlet Series, vol. 3, no. 2, 1913) ("spiritual evolution"); Louis P. Lochner, *Internationalism among Universities* 12 (World Peace Foundation Pamphlet Series, vol. 3, no. 7, 1913) ("bond of union"); William Howard Taft, "World Peace and the General Arbitration Treaties," in Chambers, ed., *The Eagle and the Dove*, 21, 22 ("a court of nations"); Hudson, *What Is the New Internationalism?* 3 ("never before"); Carnegie Endowment for International Peace, *Carnegie Endowment Year Book for 1911*, p. 3 (1912) ("discarded as disgraceful"). The analogy of the abolition of war to the abolition of slavery was commonly made. See, e.g., Walter L. Fisher, "Preparations for Peace," S. Doc. No. 64–323 (1916); John Hay and Elihu Root, *Instructions to the American Delegates to the Hague Conferences, 1899 and 1907*, p. 9 (World Peace Foundation Pamphlet Series, vol. 3, no. 4, 1913). McKinley, "First Inaugural Address," in *Inaugural Addresses*, 200 ("reason and peace"); Elihu Root, "The Function of Private Codification (April 27, 1911)," reprinted in *Addresses on International Subjects, by Elihu Root* 57, 69 (Robert Bacon and James Brown Scott, eds., Harvard University Press, 1916); Elihu Root, *Panama Canal Tolls* 27 (World Peace Foundation Pamphlet Series, vol. 3, no. 3, 1913); Elihu Root, "The Hague Peace Conferences (April 15, 1907)," in *Addresses on International Subjects, by Elihu Root*, 129, 144, 134.

35. Herman, *Eleven against War*, 22–54; 2 Philip C. Jessup, *Elihu Root* 3–136 (Archon Books, 1964 [Dodd, Mead & Co., 1938]).

36. Elihu Root, "Nobel Peace Prize Address" (scheduled for Sept. 8, 1914, not delivered due to war), in *Addresses on International Subjects, by Elihu Root*, 153, 157 ("independence of nations"); Elihu Root, "The Relations between International Tribunals of Arbitration and the Jurisdiction of National Courts (April 23, 1909)," in *Addresses on International Subjects, by Elihu Root*, 33, 34 ("mutually exclusive sovereignties" and "parliament of man"); Elihu Root, "The Causes of War (Feb. 26, 1909)," in *Miscellaneous Addresses, by Elihu Root* 275, 277 (Robert Bacon and James Brown Scott, eds., Harvard University Press, 1917) ("responsible positions").

37. Root, "Relations Between International Tribunals," in *Addresses on International Subjects, by Elihu Root*, 35–36. On the private law analogy, see Martti Koskenniemi, *From Apology to Utopia: The Structure of International Legal Argument* 68–73 (Finnish Lawyers' Pub. Co., 1989); David Kennedy, "International Law and the Nineteenth Century: A History of an Illusion," 17 *Quinnipiac L. Rev.* 99, 113 (1997).

38. John Dewey, "Introduction," in Jane Addams, *Peace and Bread in Time of War,* p. xv (anniversary ed., King's Crown Press, 1945).

39. Jane Addams, "The Revolt against War," in Jane Addams et al., *Women at the Hague: The International Peace Congress of 1915,* pp. 69, 72 (Mary Jo Deegan, ed., Humanity Books, 2003) ("nationalistic words . . . abstractions"); Addams, *Peace and Bread in Time of War,* 52 ("transcended national boundaries . . . national suspicions"); also Addams, "The Revolt against War," in *Women at the Hague,* 72; Max Eastman, "What Is Patriotism and What Shall We Do with It?" in Cook, ed., *Toward the Great Change,* 239, 246–47 ("artificial unit[s]"); also S. L. Fridenberg, *An Appeal for International Union, Dedicated to the Commonwealth* 3 (S. L. Fridenberg, 1915); Norman Thomas[?], Untitled Partial Typescript (circa Oct. 1916) ("awaken[ing] suspicion"), and Norman Thomas to Dr. Laidlaw (Mar. 15, 1917), both in Norman Thomas Papers, New York Public Library (hereinafter Norman Thomas Papers); M. Eastman, "What Is Patriotism," in Cook, ed., *Toward the Great Change,* 246–47 ("international union . . . national union").

40. Norman Thomas to Members of the Fellowship of Reconciliation 3 (Apr. 23, 1917), Norman Thomas Papers ("children of God"); "3,000 Would Rather Die Than Fight," *New York Journal,* Sept. 4, 1917, *ACLU Archives,* reel 6, vol. 46 (socialist and communist); "The Psychological Examination of Conscientious Objectors" (n.d. [Dec. 1918?]), Norman Thomas Papers (socialist and communist); Walter L. Fisher, Preparations for Peace, S. Doc. No. 64–323 (1916) (federal system); "Refuses to Serve in Draft Army," *Boston Advertiser,* Aug. 31, 1917, *ACLU Archives,* reel 1, vol. 4 ("only principle").

41. Speech by Amos Pinchot, American Union Against Militarism (n.d.), reel 1, American Union Against Militarism Papers (Scholarly Resources, 2001), Swarthmore College Peace Collection (hereinafter AUAM Papers) ("aggressive spirit" . . . "mutual recognition").

42. Alice Thacher Post, "A Statement on Preparedness," Address before the Preliminary Meeting of the Woman's Peace Party at the Hotel McAlpin, New York (Nov. 19, 1915), reel 101, folder 1.1, Lillian D. Wald Papers, Columbia University (hereinafter Wald Papers) ("clearing-house"); Civil Liberties Bureau, American Union Against Militarism, Proposed Announcement for the Press (circa fall 1917), reel 1, AUAM Papers ("work against militarism").

43. Lillian D. Wald to Amos Pinchot (March 13, 1917), reel 7, folder

8.1, Wald Papers ("wonderful secretary"); also Marchand, *American Peace Movement,* 240–43; Crystal Eastman, "A Platform of Real Preparedness," in Cook, ed., *Women and Revolution,* 241, 246 ("energy and genius"); American Union Against Militarism, Statement to the Press (n.d.), reel 1, AUAM Papers ("ideal of internationalism"); American Union Against Militarism, Statement Concerning the Anti-Militarism Committee (n.d.), reel 1, AUAM Papers ("World Peace"); American Union Against Militarism, "Development" (typescript circa Sept.–Oct. 1917), reel 1, AUAM Papers ("democratic federation"); also Charles T. Hallinan to Lillian D. Wald (Jan. 11, 1915 [1916?]), reel 102, folder 2.2, Wald Papers; David Starr Jordan to Lillian D. Wald (Mar. 6, 1917), reel 3, folder 4.5, Wald Papers; Statement of Commission for Enduring Peace, *Hearing on H.R. 6921 and H.J. Res. 32 before the House Comm. on Foreign Affairs, 64th Cong.* 9–10 (1916) ("unnationalism").

44. H. A. Overstreet, "The Next Step in International Control," *Four Lights,* Apr. 7, 1917 ("already internationalized"; slavery example).

45. American Union Against Militarism, Statement Concerning the Anti-Militarism Committee ("personal work"); Kennedy, *Over Here,* 34–36 (private advocacy); Lillian D. Wald to Newton Baker (June 20, 1917), reel 1, folder 1.2, Wald Papers (same); Letter from Lillian D. Wald to Emily Balch (May 23, 1917), reel 1, folder 1.3, Wald Papers (same).

46. Lillian D. Wald to Crystal Eastman (Aug. 26, 1917), reel 1, AUAM Papers ("impulsive radicalism"); Marchand, *American Peace Movement,* 219, 243 ("greatly help"); Chatfield, *For Peace and Justice,* 23 (American Union campaigns); American Union Against Militarism, Anti-Preparedness Committee Typescript (n.d.), reel 1, AUAM Papers (same); Letter from Crystal Eastman to Lillian D. Wald (May 29, 1916), reel 102, folder 2.3, Wald Papers ("people acting directly"); also Thomas J. Knock, *To End All Wars: Woodrow Wilson and the Quest for a New World Order* 63 (Oxford University Press, 1992); Crystal Eastman to Lillian D. Wald (May 27, 1916), reel 102, folder 2.3, Wald Papers.

47. Annis Ford Eastman, "Women's Relation to Good Citizenship" (n.d.), unpublished manuscript, box 4, folder 86, Crystal Eastman Papers; An Act in Reference to the Expatriation of Citizens and Their Protection Abroad, 34 *Statutes at Large* 1228, 1228–29 (1907); MacKenzie v. Hare, 239 U.S. 299, 301 (1915) (upholding 1907 statute); Candice Lewis Bredbenner, *A Nationality of Her Own: Women, Marriage, and the Law of Citizenship* 45–112 (University of California Press, 1998); Marchand,

American Peace Movement, 194–208; Nancy F. Cott, "Justice for All? Marriage and Deprivation of Citizenship in the United States," in Austin Sarat and Thomas R. Kearns, eds., *Justice and Injustice in Law and Legal Theory* 77, 87–89 (University of Michigan Press, 1996); Virginia Sapiro, "Women, Citizenship, and Nationality: Immigration and Naturalization Policies in the United States," 13 *Politics & Soc'y* 1, 10–11 (1984). In 1922, the Cable Act authorized certain women who lost their citizenship under the 1907 legislation to seek renaturalization, but there is no evidence that Eastman took advantage of the opportunity. The Cable Act (which was prompted by women voters newly enfranchised by the Nineteenth Amendment in 1920) did not automatically restore what the 1907 statute had taken away. Act Relative to the Naturalization and Citizenship of Married Women, ch. 411, §4, 42 Stat. 1021 (1922).

48. On the relationships between gender and internationalism in the late nineteenth and early twentieth centuries, see Harriet Hyman Alonso, *Peace as a Women's Issue: A History of the U.S. Movement for International Peace and Women's Rights* (Syracuse University Press, 1993); Gail Bederman, *Manliness and Civilization: A Cultural History of Gender and Race in the United States, 1880–1917* (University of Chicago Press, 1995); Kristin L. Hoganson, *Fighting for American Manhood: How Gender Politics Provoked the Spanish-American and Philippine-American Wars* (Yale University Press, 1998); Kristin Hoganson, "'As Badly Off as Filipinos'": U.S. Women's Suffragists and the Imperial Issue at the Turn of the Twentieth Century," *J. Women's Hist.* 9 (Summer 2001); Judith Papachristou, "American Women and Foreign Policy, 1898–1905," 14 *Diplomatic Hist.* 493 (1990); and Floya Anthias and Nira Yuval-Davis, "Introduction," in Floya Anthias and Nira Yuval-Davis, eds., *Woman—Nation—State* 6–11 (Macmillan, 1989).

49. Edna Kenton, "Bounded on the North, South, East, and West," *Four Lights,* Jan. 27, 1917 ("long ago . . . neighbors and friends"); "To George Washington and Patrick Henry: Greetings!" *Four Lights,* Mar. 10, 1917 ("destroy geography"). Eastman and the Woman's Peace Party were not completely utopian on this point: "there will still be numerous independent sovereign nations" after the war was finished, they conceded; but at the very least the war's end could bring into being international structures to mediate the militarist rivalries that had brought on the war. A. D., "Friendly Relations Commissions," *Four Lights,* Apr. 7, 1917.

50. Louis Henkin, *International Law: Politics and Values* 8–10 (M. Nijhoff, 1995) ("relic"); also Stephen D. Krasner, *Sovereignty: Organized*

Hypocrisy (Princeton University Press, 1999); Addams, "Revolt against War," in *Women at the Hague,* 73–74 ("violent loyalty"); Norman Thomas to Alfred T. Carton (Sept. 7, 1917), Norman Thomas Papers ("metaphysical entity"). For the point that claims of national attachment and obligation should be treated as skeptically as claims of natural individual rights, see Jeremy Waldron, "Minority Cultures and the Cosmopolitan Alternative," 25 *U. Mich. J. L. Reform* 751, 781 (1992).

51. American Union, "Development" ("after war was declared"); Addams, *Peace and Bread in Time of War,* 107 ("all the activities"); Crystal Eastman, Typescript (June 14, 1917), reel 1, AUAM papers ("not blocking"); Elihu Root, *Address in Chicago* 3, 5 (Sept. 14, 1917) (National Security League, Patriotism through Education Series No. 17, 1917) ("question of peace or war . . . succeed in the war"); also Elihu Root, "Foreign Affairs, 1913–1916 (Feb. 15, 1916)," in *Addresses on International Subjects, by Elihu Root,* 427, 427–28. H. C. Peterson and Gilbert C. Fite, *Opponents of War, 1917–1918,* p. 79 (University of Wisconsin Press, 1957) (quoting Vance); "They Who Play with Fire," *Grand Rapids Press,* May 31, 1917 ("treason"); also "Christian Pacifists Are Given Cold Shoulder," *Long Beach Telegram,* Sept. 7, 1917, both on reel 4, vol. 29, *ACLU Archives;* "Speaking of Conscientious Objectors," *Army and Navy News,* Sept. 6, 1917, reel 6, vol. 47, *ACLU Archives.* On the culture of obligation in World War I America, see Christopher Joseph Capozzola, "Uncle Sam Wants You: Political Obligations in World War I America" 284–351 (Ph.D. diss., Columbia University, 2002).

52. Harley Notter, *The Origins of the Foreign Policy of Woodrow Wilson* 264 (Johns Hopkins Press, 1937) (Princeton and American Peace Society); John Milton Cooper Jr., *The Warrior and the Priest: Woodrow Wilson and Theodore Roosevelt* 273, 275 (Belknap Press of Harvard University Press, 1983) ("neutral in fact"; "association of nations"); also Ruhl J. Bartlett, *The League to Enforce Peace* 34 (University of North Carolina Press, 1944); 37 *The Papers of Woodrow Wilson* 115 (Arthur S. Link, ed., Princeton University Press, 1966–1994) ("joint effort"); 36 *Papers of Woodrow Wilson,* 645 ("band themselves together"); 40 *Papers of Woodrow Wilson,* 534 (Fourteen Points).

53. 36 *Papers of Woodrow Wilson,* 45 ("equality of rights . . . military preparation"); Knock, *To End All Wars,* 162 ("over the heads"), 11–12, 114–15; also Laurence W. Martin, "Woodrow Wilson's Appeals to the People of Europe," 74 *Pol. Sci. Q.* 498, 499 (1959); 41 *Papers of Woodrow Wil-*

son, 55 ("people of the countries"); Crystal Eastman, "Editorial," in Cook, ed., *Women and Revolution,* 291 ("international union").

54. 41 *Papers of Woodrow Wilson,* 520–27 ("vindication of right," "we shall be satisfied," "nations great and small," "free peoples").

55. Arthur S. Link, "That Cobb Interview," 72 *J. Am. Hist.* 7, 11–12 (1985) ("illiberalism at home"; "would not survive"); Cooper, *Warrior and the Priest,* 330 ("very unwise").

56. *To Punish Espionage and Interference with Neutrality: Hearings on S. 8148 Before the House Committee on the Judiciary, 64th Congress* (1917) (debated legislation); American Union Against Militarism, Bulletins (Feb. 1917), reel 101, folder 1.1, Wald Papers (same); An Act to Authorize the President to Increase Temporarily the Military Establishment, 40 Stat. 76 (1917); Espionage Act of 1917, 40 Stat. 217, 230; 40 Stat. 411 (1917); Act of May 16, 1918, 40 Stat. 553 (amending the Espionage Act); Eldridge Foster Dowell, *A History of Criminal Syndicalism Legislation in the United States* 147 (Johns Hopkins Press, 1939); Cecilia Elizabeth O'Leary, *To Die For: The Paradox of American Patriotism* 220–45 (Princeton University Press, 1999); Peterson and Fite, *Opponents of War,* 18, 213–14; William Henry Thomas Jr., "The United States Department of Justice and Dissent during the First World War" (Ph.D. diss., University of Iowa, 2002).

57. Murphy, *World War I and the Origin of Civil Liberties,* 98 ("reign of terror"), 95 ("God have mercy"); Peterson and Fite, *Opponents of War,* 115 ("God have mercy"); Harry N. Scheiber, *The Wilson Administration and Civil Liberties, 1917–1921,* pp. 30, 63 (Cornell University Press, 1960) (more than 2,000 prosecutions; *Leader* and *Nation* episodes); Masses Publ'g Co. v. Patten, 244 F. 535, 537 (S.D.N.Y. 1917); Max Eastman, *Love and Revolution: My Journey through an Epoch* 61 (Random House, 1964); Rabban, *Free Speech in Its Forgotten Years,* 261–66.

58. Peterson and Fite, *Opponents of War,* 18 (private vigilantes); Geo. H. Greenfield, "Democracy's Battle," p. 6 (n.d.), and National Civil Liberties Bureau, Press Statement (July 1917), both on reel 4, *ACLU Archives* (private vigilantes); Capozzola, "Uncle Sam Wants You," 26–81 (quasi-private patriotism); Cooper, *Warrior and the Priest,* 331 ("weaklings"); Kennedy, *Over Here,* 61–66 (CPI); Stephen Vaughn, *Holding Fast the Inner Lines: Democracy, Nationalism, and the Committee on Public Information* (University of North Carolina Press, 1980) (same); Henry Litchfield West, *University Military Training as a Permanent Principle of National Defense* 3 (National Security League, 1918) ("everything or nothing"); also

Alfred M. Brooks, *Converted and Secret Americans* 5 (National Security League, Patriotism through Education Series No. 30, 1918); S. Stanwood Menken, *A Concept of National Service* 2 (National Security League, Patriotism through Education Series No. 27, 1918) ("unconditional traitors"); Knock, *To End All Wars,* 169 ("professional internationalists"); Peterson and Fite, *Opponents of War,* 148–49 ("in effect, traitorous"); Chatfield, *For Peace and Justice,* 4 ("Treason's Twilight Zone").

59. American Union Against Militarism, "Development" ("logical, courageous"; "extreme patriots . . . federal penitentiary"); American Union Against Militarism, Memorandum of Organization, p. 2 (circa Apr. 1917), Norman Thomas Papers ("impracticable"); John Morton Blum, *Woodrow Wilson and the Politics of Morality* 144 (Little, Brown, 1956) ("turned his back").

60. John Haynes Holmes, *I Speak for Myself: The Autobiography of John Haynes Holmes* 189 (Harper, 1959) ("But lo"). American Union Against Militarism, Memorandum of Organization, p. 2 ("anti-conscription campaign"); "Development" ("prevent and oppose"; "general abrogation"); Minutes of the Meeting (June 4, 1917) ("logical consequence"); Minutes of the Meeting (June 15, 1917), all on reel 1, AUAM Papers.

61. Proposed Announcement for the Press, reel 1, AUAM Papers ("during war time" and "chief war work"); Letter from Crystal Eastman to Lillian D. Wald (June 18, 1917), reel 102, folder 2.4, Wald Papers ("Civil Liberties Bureau"); American Union Against Militarism, Minutes of the Meeting (June 4, 1917) (same); American Union Against Militarism, Minutes of the Executive Committee Meeting (June 25, 1917), reel 1, AUAM Papers (same).

62. Murphy, *World War I and the Origin of Civil Liberties,* 9 (British National Council and "first time"); also Marvin Swartz, *The Union of Democratic Control in British Politics during the First World War* 51 (Clarendon Press, 1971) (same).

63. Wesley Newcomb Hohfeld, "Fundamental Legal Conceptions as Applied in Judicial Reasoning," 26 *Yale L. J.* 710 (1917); Wesley Newcomb Hohfeld, "Some Fundamental Legal Conceptions as Applied in Judicial Reasoning," 23 *Yale L. J.* 16 (1913); Joseph William Singer, "The Legal Rights Debate in Analytical Jurisprudence from Betham to Hohfeld," 1982 *Wisc. L. Rev.* 975, 1057–58.

64. Norman Thomas to Roger Nash Baldwin (Sept. 7, 1917), reel 4, AUAM Papers ("never commend democracy"); Cook, "Introduction," in

Cook, ed., *Women & Revolution*, 20; Woman's Peace Party of New York City, "Our War Record: A Plea for Tolerance," in Chambers, ed., *The Eagle and the Dove*, 128 ("full free and continuous"); also American Union Against Militarism, "Seven Congressmen on Preparedness" and "A Challenge Accepted" (n.d.), both on reel 1, AUAM Papers; National Civil Liberties Bureau, "Who Has Been Imprisoned under the Espionage Act?", handbill, reel 15, folder 14, Wald Papers. On the political theory of democracy and international peace, see Michael W. Doyle, "Kant, Liberal Legacies, and Foreign Affairs," (parts 1 & 2), 12 *Phil. & Pub. Aff.* 205, 323 (1983).

65. Oswald G. Villard, Typescript (n.d.), reel 102, folder 2.4, Wald Papers (strategic tool); 1 *Revolutionary Radicalism: Its History, Purpose, and Tactics, . . . The Report of the Joint Legislative Committee . . . In the Senate of the State of New York, Part I . . .*, p. 1088 (J. B. Lyon Co., 1920) ("good lot of flags").

66. "The Reminiscences of Roger Nash Baldwin" 158 (1961), Columbia University, Oral History Research Office ("first associate"); American Union Against Militarism, Secretary's Recommendations (n.d. [fall 1917?]), reel 1, AUAM Papers ("actual testing").

67. M. Eastman, *Enjoyment of Living*, 45–49 (scarlet fever); Wainwright Commission Staff to J. Mayhew Wainwright (Jan. 30, 1911), J. Mayhew Wainwright Papers, New-York Historical Society (employers' liability commission); Crystal Eastman to Lillian D. Wald (Apr. 11, 1916), reel 102, folder 2.3, Wald Papers ("strictly in bed"); Max Eastman to Lillian D. Wald (n.d. [1928?]), reel 3, folder 4.2, Wald Papers ("chronic disease"); Crystal Eastman to Roger Nash Baldwin (Mar. 23, 1921), reel 24, vol. 68, *ACLU Archives* ("too tired").

68. Marchand, *American Peace Movement*, 255 n.80 ("crazy to get back"; "nothing left"); Crystal Eastman to Lillian D. Wald (n.d.), reel 102, folder 2.3, Wald Papers ("in a great many respects"); also Crystal Eastman to Lillian D. Wald (circa Apr. 1917), reel 102, folder 2.4, Wald Papers; Crystal Eastman to Lillian D. Wald (n.d.), reel 102, folder 2.4, Wald Papers (Atlantic City); Crystal Eastman to Lillian D. Wald (Apr. 11 [1917?]), reel 102, folder 2.3, Wald Papers (Atlantic City).

69. David S. Tanenhaus, *Juvenile Justice in the Making* (Oxford University Press, 2004); Michael Willrich, *City of Courts: Socializing Justice in Progressive Era Chicago* (Cambridge University Press, 2003); "Reminiscences of Roger Nash Baldwin," p. 27 ("professional standards" and "judicial interfer-

ence"); Bernard Flexner and Roger N. Baldwin, *Juvenile Courts and Probation* (Century Co., 1914).

70. "Reminiscences of Roger Nash Baldwin," p. 55 ("uneasy"); Robert C. Cottrell, *Roger Nash Baldwin and the American Civil Liberties Union* 1–60 (Columbia University Press, 2000) (Baldwin's background); Peggy Lamson, *Roger Baldwin: Founder of American Civil Liberties Union* 278 (Houghton Mifflin, 1976) ("downright silly"). Even in the 1920s, Baldwin would become involved in international causes, such as opposition to imperialism in India and elsewhere. Baldwin usually approached these international causes outside of his official capacity as the leader of U.S. civil liberties organizations like the ACLU. Moreover, by the early 1920s (and for much of the rest of his life) his international interests were thoroughly caught up in the early Cold War contests between the Soviet Union and the United States—contests in which Baldwin sympathized with the Soviets until his switch to vigorous anticommunism by the end of the 1930s. Cottrell, *Roger Nash Baldwin,* 169–98, 262–63.

71. Crystal Eastman to Emily Balch (June 14, 1917), in Cook, ed., *Toward the Great Change,* 271 ("a party of opposition"); Crystal Eastman to Lillian D. Wald (Sept. 25, 1917), reel 102, folder 2.4, Wald Papers ("work for Civil Liberties"); Norman Thomas to Lillian D. Wald (Aug. 27, 1917), Norman Thomas Papers ("political obstruction"); Letter to Mr. Evans (Mar. 20, 1917), Norman Thomas Papers ("against hysterical legislation"); Kennedy, *Over Here,* 35–36 (resignation); Catherine Crystal Eastman to Lillian D. Wald (Sept. 25, 1917), reel 102, folder 2.4, Wald Papers (resignation); Lillian D. Wald to Roger N. Baldwin (Oct. 12, 1917), reel 10, folder 1.8, Wald Papers (resignation).

72. "Reminiscences of Roger Nash Baldwin," pp. 60–61 (raid and seizure); "Urges Indictments for Seditious Talk," *New York Times,* Sept. 5, 1917, p. 4 ("foreigners"; "soap-box orators"); M. Eastman, *Love and Revolution,* 92–99, 118–24 (not once but twice); Cottrell, *Roger Nash Baldwin,* 83–90 (convicted and sentenced).

73. Telegram from E. F. Alexander to Roger N. Baldwin (Nov. 1, 1917) (Herbert Bigelow); Press Release, National Civil Liberties Bureau (Nov. 7, 1917) (Herbert Bigelow); "They Who Play with Fire," *Grand Rapids Press,* May 1917 ("seditious"), all on reel 4, *ACLU Archives;* Statement to the *New York Tribune* by the Civil Liberties Bureau of the American Union Against Militarism (Sept. 27, 1917), reel 102, folder 2.4, Wald Papers ("enemies within"); Theodore Roosevelt, "Speech at Springfield, Illinois (Aug. 26,

1918)," in Chambers, ed., *The Eagle and the Dove,* 127 ("German autocracy"); also Knock, *To End All Wars,* 169; Elihu Root, "The Conditions and Possibilities Remaining for International Law after the War (April 27, 1921)," in Robert Bacon and James Brown Scott, eds., *Men and Policies: Addresses by Elihu Root* 427, 432 (Harvard University Press, 1925) ("responsibilities of nations").

74. Norman Thomas et al. to Lillian D. Wald (Jan. 19, 1920), reel 10, folder 12.4, Wald Papers ("new direction"); Roger N. Baldwin to Lawrence G. Brooks (Sept. 24, 1917), reel 4, *ACLU Archives* ("German names"); "Worldwide Anarchist Plot," *New York Times,* Dec. 26, 1917, p. 1; Peterson and Fite, *Opponents of War,* 253 ("into one pot"); Richard Polenberg, *Fighting Faiths: The Abrams Case, the Supreme Court, and Free Speech* 155–71, 195–96 (Viking, 1987) (Palmer Raids and Lusk Committee); Kennedy, *Over Here,* 87 (Wilson); Scheiber, *Wilson Administration and Civil Liberties,* 57 (peacetime extension); "Miss Wald's War Attitude," *New York Post,* Jan. 25, 1919, reel 6, *ACLU Archives* (Lillian Wald).

75. Crystal Eastman and Roger Baldwin to American Union Locals, Affiliated Organizations, Correspondents, and Members (Aug. 31, 1917), reel 102, folder 2.4, Wald Papers (130th anniversary); Roger N. Baldwin to Lawrence G. Brooks (Sept. 24, 1917), reel 4, *ACLU Archives* ("highest authority in the country"); Roger N. Baldwin to Adolph Germer (Dec. 10, 1917), reel 1, vol. 3, *ACLU Archives* ("legal defense"); John L. Metzen to Civil Liberties Bureau (Aug. 9, 1917), reel 4, vol. 32, *ACLU Archives* ("patriots in the true sense"); American Union Against Militarism, Proposed Announcement for the Press (n.d., [fall 1917?]), reel 1, AUAM Papers ("believe ourselves to be patriots"); Norman Thomas to Lillian D. Wald (August 27, 1917), Norman Thomas Papers ("cause of civil liberties"); Crystal Eastman to Editor of the *New York Tribune* (Aug. 28, 1917), reel 1, folder 1.6, Wald Papers ("no more patriotic duty"; "ancient American liberties").

76. National Civil Liberties Bureau to Friends (Jan. 5, 1918), reel 1, vol. 3, *ACLU Archives* ("highest type"); also Walker, *In Defense of American Liberties,* 53.

77. George W. Egerton, *Great Britain and the Creation of the League of Nations: Strategy, Politics, and International Organization, 1914–1919,* pp. 138–40 (University of North Carolina Press, 1978) (Paris Peace Conference); Knock, *To End All Wars,* 194–245 (same); Margaret O. MacMillan, *Peacemakers: The Paris Conference of 1919 and Its Attempt to End War* 94–98 (J. Murray, 2001) (same); Addams, *Peace and Bread,* 152–77 (Zurich Con-

ference); DeBenedetti, *Origins of the Modern American Peace Movement,*
91–92 (Zurich Conference); Herman, *Eleven against War,* 147 (Zurich
Conference); The Covenant of the League of Nations, preamble (League of
Nations, 1924).

78. Albert De Silver to B. N. Langdon-Davies (June 6, 1919) ("international conference"); B. N. Langdon-Davies to Albert De Silver (June 30,
1919) (Eastman and Fuller); Arthur Ponsonby (n.d.) ("enlightened and
democratic"); also Walter Fuller to Albert De Silver (Aug. 5, 1919); B. N.
Langon-Davies to Mr. Furnas (Aug. 27, 1919) ("wider internationalism"),
all on reel 9, vol. 73, *ACLU Archives;* Albert De Silver to Lillian D. Wald
(Oct. 2, 1919), reel 15, Wald Papers (Conference program).

79. Zachariah Chafee Jr. to Albert De Silver (Oct. 8, 1919); Albert De
Silver to Felix Frankfurter (Oct. 7, 1919); Albert De Silver to Roscoe Pound
(Oct. 7, 1919); Franklin H. Giddings to Albert De Silver (Oct. 7, 1919), all
on reel 9, vol. 73, *ACLU Archives.*

80. Cooper, *Warrior and the Priest,* 340–45 (Wilson struggled).

81. Kennedy, *Over Here,* 359–62 (Wilson struggled); Knock, *To End
All Wars,* 246–76 (Wilson struggled); Conference on the Anglo-American
Tradition of Liberty, Verbatim Report (New York, N.Y., Oct. 1919),
pp. 522 ("old assumptions"; "Middle Ages"); 554 ("not national"); 523
("territorial basis"); 554 ("nationalistic segregation"); 575 (impracticality
quickly apparent); 554, 563 (protonationalists versus internationalists); 564
("between nationalism and internationalism"); 563 ("unnecessary bog");
575 ("wreck"); 583–84 (mess of differences); all on reel 9, vol. 73, *ACLU
Archives.*

82. Norman Thomas et al. to Lillian D. Wald (Jan. 19, 1920), reel 10,
folder 12.4, Wald Papers (Baldwin reorganized as ACLU; "American constitutional rights"; "trade unionism"); Roger N. Baldwin, "The Fight for Civil
Liberty during the War" 1 (1920), unpublished manuscript, reel 14, vol.
108, *ACLU Archives* ("antiwar organization"); also American Civil Liberties
Union, Questionnaire on Condition of Civil Liberty (Feb. 1921), reel 24,
vol. 169, *ACLU Archives;* Walker, *In Defense of American Liberties,* 130–33
(purge of communists).

83. Fussell, *Great War and Modern Memory,* 21 (the ironic and the
modernist); Jay Winter, *Sites of Memory, Sites of Mourning: The Great War in
European Cultural History* 9, 18 (Cambridge University Press, 1995) ("traditional languages").

84. Holmes, *I Speak for Myself,* 189 ("surrender the idealism"); Crystal

Eastman, "The Socialist Party Convention," in Cook, ed., *Toward the Great Change,* 436, 439 ("proof against a strain"), 437 ("practical value"; "capitalist state"); Crystal Eastman, "Now We Can Begin," in Cook, ed., *Toward the Great Change,* 75, 78 ("feminist sons").

85. On the history of the twentieth-century human rights movement, see Rosemary Foot, *Rights beyond Borders: The Global Community and the Struggle over Human Rights in China* 29–59 (Oxford University Press, 2000); Mary Ann Glendon, *A World Made New: Eleanor Roosevelt and the Universal Declaration of Human Rights* (Random House, 2001); Paul Gordon Lauren, *The Evolution of International Human Rights: Visions Seen* 159, 166–232 (University of Pennsylvania Press, 2nd ed., 2003); A. W. Brian Simpson, *Human Rights and the End of Empire: Britain and the Genesis of the European Convention* (Oxford University Press, 2001); Kenneth Cmiel, "The Emergence of Human Rights in the United States," 86 *J. Am. Hist.* 1231–50 (1999); Kenneth Cmiel, "The Recent History of Human Rights," 109 *Am. Hist. Rev.* 117–35 (2004).

4. THE KING AND THE DEAN

1. Jack Jones, "Educator Cautions Lawyers on Ethics," *Daily Oklahoman,* Dec. 5, 1957, p. 1, reel 59, folder 3, Roscoe Pound Papers, Harvard Law Library Special Collections (hereinafter Pound Papers) (on Pound's reputation); *KAPA Koments: Official Publication of Kansas Association of Plaintiffs' Attorneys,* vol. 2, no. 1, February 1954, n.p., folder 1, box 146, Pound Papers (same); Edward A. Purcell Jr., *The Crisis of Democratic Theory: Scientific Naturalism and The Problem of Value* 85 (University of Kentucky Press, 1973) (same); N. E. H. Hull, *Roscoe Pound and Karl Llewellyn: Searching for an American Jurisprudence* 81–85 (University of Chicago Press, 1997); Peter L. Strauss, "The Place of Agencies in Government: Separation of Powers and the Fourth Branch," 84 *Colum. L. Rev.* 573 (1984).

2. Robert Wallace, "The King of Torts," *Life Magazine,* Oct. 18, 1954, pp. 71–82; Melvin M. Belli, *Blood Money: Ready for the Plaintiff* 10 (Grosset and Dunlap, 1956) ("Barnum"); Melvin M. Belli Sr. with John Carlova, *Belli for Your Malpractice Defense,* p. ix (Medical Economics Books, 2nd ed., 1989) (Jolly Roger); Melvin M. Belli with Robert Blair Kaiser, *My Life on Trial: An Autobiography* 242 (William Morrow, 1976) (same); "Melvin Belli Dies at 88," *New York Times,* July 11, 1996, p. B13 ("border-town bordello"); Stuart M. Speiser, *Lawyers and the American Dream* 229–

30 (M. Evans and Co., 1993) (Mickey Cohen); *The Rolling Stones Gimme Shelter* (Maysles Films, 1970) (rock and roll); Renata Adler, "Screen: Blunt Philosophy with Dual Exhausts and a Clear Logic," *New York Times,* May 30, 1968, p. 21 (reviewing *Wild in the Streets,* featuring Melvin Belli); "Metro Will Film Baseball Comedy," *New York Times,* Oct. 12, 1950, p. 52 (Belli produces *Tokyo File 212);* "Tax Bill Irritates Many Executives, Who Call Liquid Lunches a Myth," *Wall Street Journal,* Aug. 3, 1982, p. 35 ("show a little class"); George Gent, "TV: A Fleeting Look at Trial Lawyers," *New York Times,* May 1, 1968, p. 95; Jon R. Waltz, "Dallas Justice," 74 *Yale L. J.* 581, 586 (1965); Gordon B. Baldwin, "The Trial of Jack Ruby," 18 *Stan. L. Rev.* 765, 767 (1966); Colin Evans, *Super Lawyers: America's Courtroom Celebrities* 25 (Visible Ink Press, 1997).

3. Belli, *My Life on Trial,* 182 ("policeman's billy"); Melvin M. Belli, 1 *The Law Revolt: A Summary of Trends in Modern Criminal and Civil Law* 1060 (Trial Lawyers Service Co., 1968) (same); Melvin M. Belli to Roscoe Pound (Dec. 3, 1962), folder 37–7, series 3, Pound Papers (same); Belli, *My Life on Trial,* 182 ("strawberry blond" and "discoursed on Henry VIII"); Robert Wallace, *Life and Limb: An Account of the Career of Melvin M. Belli, Personal-Injury Trial Lawyer* 245 (Doubleday and Co., 1955) ("Swedish massage-parlor").

4. Robert A. Kagan, *Adversarial Legalism: The American Way of Law* (Harvard University Press, 2001); Thomas F. Burke, *Lawyers, Lawsuits, and Legal Rights: The Battle over Litigation in American Society* (University of California Press, 2002); Sean Farhang, "The Litigation State: Public Regulation and Private Lawsuits in the American Separation of Powers System" (typescript, Columbia University, 2004); Robert C. Lieberman, "Private Power and American Bureaucracy: The EEOC and Civil Rights Enforcement," paper presented at the American Political Development Colloquium, University of Virginia (March 18, 2005); Robert A. Kagan, "Adversarial Legalism and American Government," in Marc K. Landy and Martin A. Levin, eds., *The New Politics of Public Policy* 88–117 (Johns Hopkins University Press, 1995); Robert A. Kagan and Lee Axelrod, "Adversarial Legalism: An International Perspective," in Pietro S. Nivola, ed., *Comparative Disadvantages? Social Regulations and the Global Economy* 146– 202 (Brookings Institution Press, 1997); Steven Kelman, *Regulating America, Regulating Sweden: A Comparative Study of Occupational Safety and Health Policy* 228–37 (MIT Press, 1981); Herbert Jacob et al., eds., *Courts, Law, and Politics in Comparative Perspective* (Yale University Press, 1996);

W. Kip Viscusi, ed., *Regulation through Litigation* (Brookings Institution Press, 2002).

5. Daniel T. Rodgers, *Atlantic Crossings: Social Politics in a Progressive Age* 4 (Harvard University Press, 1998); Peter Flora et al., 1 *State, Economy, and Society in Western Europe, 1815–1975,* pp. 193–243 (Macmillan, 1983); Edward D. Berkowitz and Kim McQuaid, *Creating the Welfare State: The Political Economy of Twentieth-Century Reform* (University Press of Kansas, rev. ed., 1992); John C. Coffee Jr., "Understanding the Plaintiffs' Attorney: The Implications of Economic Theory for Private Enforcement of Law through Class and Derivative Actions," 86 *Colum. L. Rev.* 669, 669 (1986); Jacob S. Hacker, *The Divided Welfare State: The Battle over Public and Private Social Benefits in the United States* (Cambridge University Press, 2002); John Fabian Witt, *The Accidental Republic: Crippled Workingmen, Destitute Widows, and the Remaking of American Law* (Harvard University Press, 2004); David Beito, *From Mutual Aid to Welfare State: Fraternal Societies and Social Services, 1890–1967* (University of North Carolina Press, 2000); William E. Forbath, "The Long Life of Liberal America: Law and State-Building in the U.S. and England," 24 *Law and History Review* 179, 182 (2006); Ellis W. Hawley, "Social Policy and the Liberal State in Twentieth-Century America," in Donald T. Critchlow and Ellis W. Hawley, eds., *Federal Social Policy: The Historical Dimension* 117–39 (Pennsylvania State University Press, 1988); Brian Balogh, "Reorganizing the Organizational Synthesis: Federal-Professional Relations in Modern America," 5 *Studs. in Am. Pol. Dev.* 119–72 (1991); Brian Balogh, "Associative Action: The State in Late Nineteenth-Century America," paper presented at Columbia University Institutions Workshop (April 4, 2002); Christopher Howard, *The Hidden Welfare State: Tax Expenditures and Social Policy in the United States* (Princeton University Press, 1997); Sanford M. Jacoby, *Modern Manors: Welfare Capitalism since the New Deal* (Princeton University Press, 1997); Jennifer Klein, *For All These Rights: Business, Labor, and the Shaping of America's Public–Private Welfare State* (Princeton University Press, 2003); James A. Wooten, *The Employee Retirement Income Security Act of 1974: A Political History* (University of California Press, 2004); Ariela R. Dubler, "In the Shadow of Marriage: Single Women and the Legal Construction of the Family and the State," 112 *Yale L. J.* 1641 (2003).

6. Rowland Evans and Robert Novak, "America's Most Powerful Lobby," *Reader's Digest,* April 1994, p. 131.

7. David Vogel, *National Styles of Regulation: Environmental Policy in*

Great Britain and the United States 278–79 (Cornell University Press, 1986) (pluralist and fractured government); George Tsebelis, *Veto Players: How Political Institutions Work* (Princeton University Press, 2002).

8. *U.S. Tort Costs: 2004 Update, Trends, and Findings on the Cost of the U.S. Tort System* (Tillinghast Towers-Perrin, 2004) ($250 billion); Alan Brinkley, *The End of Reform: New Deal Liberalism in Recession and War* (Knopf, 1995).

9. Neb. Const., art. 1, §21 (1875); David Wigdor, *Roscoe Pound: Philosopher of Law* 3–9 (Greenwood Press, 1974).

10. Hull, *Roscoe Pound and Karl Llewellyn*, 47–48.

11. Id., 49; Wigdor, *Roscoe Pound*, 66

12. Hull, *Roscoe Pound and Karl Llewellyn*, 39–40; Wigdor, *Roscoe Pound*, 36–46 (pressure from his father), 70–71 (case against Bryan; corporate clients).

13. Hull, *Roscoe Pound and Karl Llewellyn*, 49; Wigdor, *Roscoe Pound*, 103.

14. Dorothy Ross, *The Origins of American Social Science* 180 (Cambridge University Press, 1991) (Ross at Stanford); Edward Alsworth Ross, "Social Control," 1 *Am. J. Soc.* 513, 522 (1896) (Darwinian evolution); Edward Alsworth Ross, "Social Control II: Law and Public Opinion," 1 *Am. J. Soc.* 753, 759 (1896) ("corner stone"; "ponderous and slow-moving").

15. Edward A. Ross, *The Principles of Sociology* (Century Co., 1921) ("prince"); Wigdor, *Roscoe Pound*, 112 (helped to forge).

16. Roscoe Pound, "The Growth of Administrative Justice," 2 *Wisc. L. Rev.* 325 (1924) ("throughout the English speaking world"; administrative bodies being strengthened); Roscoe Pound, "The Spirit of the Common Law," 18 *Green Bag* 17, 19 (1906) ("commissions and boards"); Roscoe Pound, "The Administration of Justice in the Modern City," 26 *Harv. L. Rev.* 302, 323 (1913) ("public utilities . . . administrative prevention"); Roscoe Pound, "The Common Law and Legislation," 21 *Harv. L. Rev.* 383, 406–7 (1908) ("sociological laboratory"); see also Roscoe Pound, "The Administrative Application of Legal Standards," in *Report of the Forty-Second Annual Meeting of the American Bar Association Held at Boston, Massachusetts, September 3, 4, 5, 1919*, pp. 445, 448 (Lord Baltimore Press, 1919).

17. Lawrence M. Friedman, *A History of American Law* 329–40 (Simon & Schuster, 3rd ed., 2005); Morton Keller, *The Life Insurance Enterprise, 1885–1910*, pp. 194–213 (Harvard University Press, 1963); James W. Ely, *Railroads and American Law* 71–104 (University of Press of Kansas, 2001); Gabriel Kolko, *Railroads and Regulation, 1877–1916* (Princeton University

Press, 1965); Thomas K. McCraw, *Prophets of Regulation* (Harvard University Press, 1984); Stephen Skowronek, *Building a New American State: The Expansion of National Administrative Capacities, 1877–1920* (Cambridge University Press, 1982); James Harvey Young, *Pure Food: Securing the Federal Pure Food and Drugs Act of 1906* (Princeton University Press, 1989); Martin J. Sklar, *The Corporate Reconstruction of American Capitalism, 1890–1916*, pp. 324–32 (Cambridge University Press, 1988) (Federal Trade Commission); Linda Gordon, *Pitied but Not Entitled: Single Mothers and the History of Welfare, 1890–1935* (Free Press, 1994) (mothers' pensions); Theda Skocpol, *Protecting Soldiers and Mothers: The Political Origins of Social Policy in the United States* (Harvard University Press, 1992) (same); David S. Tanenhaus, *Juvenile Justice in the Making* (Oxford University Press, 2004); Michael Willrich, *City of Courts: Socializing Justice in Progressive Era Chicago* 208–40 (Cambridge University Press, 2003); Witt, *Accidental Republic,* 126–51.

18. Roscoe Pound, "Justice According to Law (II)," 14 *Colum. L. Rev.* 1, 22 (1914) ("common-law polity"); Alexis de Tocqueville, *Democracy in America,* vol. 1, part 2, ch. 8, p. 270 (trans. George Lawrence, ed. J. P. Mayer, Harper and Row, 1966); Roscoe Pound, "The Limits of Effective Legal Action," 3 *Am. Bar Ass'n J.* 56, 68–69 (1917) ("individual initiative"); also Pound, "Spirit of the Common Law," 25. On the nineteenth-century American state and the role of courts, see William J. Novak, *The People's Welfare: Law and Regulation in Nineteenth-Century America* 19–50 (University of North Carolina Press, 1996); Morton J. Horwitz, *The Transformation of American Law, 1780–1860* (Harvard University Press, 1977); Morton J. Horwitz, *The Transformation of American Law, 1870–1960: The Crisis of Legal Orthodoxy* (Oxford University Press, 1992); Skowronek, *Building a New American State,* 39–46.

19. Pound, "Limits of Effective Legal Action," 66 (elaborate evidentiary rules), 68–69 ("set the law in motion"), 57 ("not equal to the task"); see also Pound, "Administration of Justice in the Modern City," 309.

20. Roscoe Pound, "The Causes of Popular Dissatisfaction with the Administration of Justice," 14 *Am. L. Rev.* 445, 445 (1906); also Roscoe Pound, "Legislation as a Social Function," 18 *Am. J. Soc.* 755, 768 (1913); Pound, "Social and Legal Justice," in *Proceedings of the Thirtieth Annual Meeting of the Missouri Bar Association Held at St. Louis, Missouri, September 26–27–28, 1912,* p. 110 (Kansas City: F. P. Burnap Stationery and Printing Co., 1913).

21. Pound, "Causes of Dissatisfaction," 447 ("sporting theory"), 448

("incidents of private litigation"); Pound, "Do We Need a Philosophy of Law?" 5 *Colum. L. Rev.* 339, 347 (1905) ("a fair fist fight"; "best pluck" (quoting Manson, 8 *Law Quarterly Rev.* 161)).

22. Pound, "Causes of Dissatisfaction," 447 ("individual is supposed"); Pound, "Do We Need a Philosophy of Law," 347 ("conspicuous advantage"); Roscoe Pound, "Liberty of Contract," 18 *Yale L. J.* 454, 454 (1908) ("much of the discussion," quoting Ross), 457 ("purely juristic notions"), 463 ("theoretical equality"); Pound, "Social and Legal Justice," 113 ("mere juggling," quoting Ely).

23. Pound, "Social and Legal Justice," 112 ("not merely fair play between individuals," quoting Commons), 117 ("legal idea of justice," citing Lester Ward), 118 ("mass of mankind"; "free road"), 119 ("watchword . . . full moral life"); Roscoe Pound, "The Need of a Sociological Jurisprudence," 19 *Green Bag* 607, 613–14 (1907) ("standard of justice"); Wigdor, *Roscoe Pound,* 213–14 ("social interests").

24. Pound, "Need of a Sociological Jurisprudence," 609 ("already well-marked"); Roscoe Pound, "The Courts and Legislation," 7 *Am. Pol. Sci. Rev.* 361, 374 (1913) ("fundamental conceptions"); Wigdor, *Roscoe Pound,* 137 ("legal order of nature"); Pound, "Social and Legal Justice," 121 ("grave reproach"); Roscoe Pound, [Untitled Note], 27 *Harv. L. Rev.* 731, 732 (1914) ("no bar to the reception of ideas"), 734 ("law lectures of James Wilson"). For Pound favoring foreign sources, see also Wigdor, *Roscoe Pound,* 203; Roscoe Pound, "The Influence of French Law in America," 3 *Ill. L. Rev.* 354 (1909).

25. Wigdor, *Roscoe Pound,* 138, 201–2, 141, 143, 195–97; Willrich, *City of Courts,* 107–8 (Chicago reform efforts and Juvenile Court); Hammer v. Dagenhart, 247 U.S. 251 (1918).

26. *Rules of Civil Procedure for the District Courts of the United States, with Notes as Prepared under the Direction of the Advisory Committee and Proceedings of the Institute on Federal Rules, Cleveland, Ohio, July 21, 22, 23, 1938* (American Bar Association, 1938); Brief for the State of Oregon (Brandeis Brief), Muller v. Oregon, 208 U.S. 412; Purcell, *Crisis of Democratic Theory,* 76–77; Wigdor, *Roscoe Pound,* 201 (Frankfurter to Learned Hand, 1913); A. Leo Levin and Russell R. Wheeler, "Epilogue," in A. Leo Levin and Russell R. Wheeler, eds., *The Pound Conference: Perspectives on Justice in the Future* 289, 290 (West Publishing, 1979) (draw on Pound's ideas); James M. Landis, "Constitutional Limitations on the Congressional Power of Investigation," 40 *Harv. L. Rev.* 153, 205 (1926) (same); James M.

Landis, "A Note on Statutory Interpretation," 43 *Harv. L. Rev.* 886 (1930) (same).

27. Roscoe Pound, "Mechanical Jurisprudence," 8 *Colum. L. Rev.* 605, 609 (1908); also Wigdor, *Roscoe Pound.*

28. William R. Roalfe, *John Henry Wigmore: Scholar and Reformer* (Northwestern University Press, 1977); William Twining, *Theories of Evidence: Bentham and Wigmore* 171 (Weidenfeld and Nicolson, 1985); John C. Hutcheson Jr., "Dean Wigmore's Contribution to Judging as Administration," 29 *Ill. L. Rev.* 413, 415–16 (1934); Wigdor, *Roscoe Pound,* 254 (Harvard deanship); Richard Warner, "Roscoe Pound," in *American National Biography Online* (February 2000), accessed Aug. 27, 2005 (death of Grace Pound); Hull, *Karl Llewellyn and Roscoe Pound,* 173–222 (sharp differences); Horwitz, *Transformation, 1870–1960* (same); Purcell, *Crisis of Democratic Theory,* 85 (same); Roscoe Pound, "The Call for a Realist Jurisprudence," 44 *Harv. L. Rev.* 697 (1931), 711 ("polemics"), 705 ("dogmatic rejections"); see also Roscoe Pound, "The Future of the Common Law," 7 *U. Cincinnati L. Rev.* 343, 360 (1933).

29. Hull, *Roscoe Pound and Karl Llewellyn,* 47 and n.41 (Willa Cather); William Kunsler, "Dean of Harvard Law," *New York Times,* Nov. 28, 1948, p. BR42. The Willa Cather essay was printed in 1894 in a University of Nebraska student newspaper. It did not name Pound, but that Pound was its subject was sufficiently clear to cause the Pound family to break off relations with Cather. See James Woodress, *Willa Cather: Her Life and Art* 63 (Pegasus, 1970).

30. Hull, *Roscoe Pound and Karl Llewellyn,* 60 ("to please them").

31. Wigdor, *Roscoe Pound,* 233 ("creative period"), 250 (Hitler); Charles A. Beard, "Germany Up to Her Old Tricks," *New Republic,* Oct. 24, 1934, pp. 299–300 (Pound and Nazi Germany); "One of the Happenings," *New Republic,* Sep. 26, 1934, p. 170 (same).

32. Pound, "Need of a Sociological Jurisprudence," 613–14 ("human wants"); Franklin D. Roosevelt, "Campaign Address on Progressive Government at the Commonwealth Club," in 1 *The Public Papers and Addresses of Franklin D. Roosevelt* 742, 752–56 (Random House, 1938); Witt, *Accidental Republic,* 198–200 ("security"); David M. Kennedy, *Freedom from Fear: The American People in Depression and War, 1929–1945,* pp. 99–100 (Oxford University Press, 1999) (same); Elizabeth Borgwardt, *A New Deal for the World: America's Vision for Human Rights* 20 (Harvard University Press, 2005) ("freedom from want"); Cass R. Sunstein, *The Second Bill of*

Rights: FDR's Unfinished Revolution and Why We Need It More Than Ever (Basic Books, 2004) ("second Bill of Rights").

33. "Report of the Special Committee on Administrative Law," 63 *Annual Report of the American Bar Association* 331, 346–51 (1938), 340 ("Marxian idea"), 346–48 (caprice and prejudice), 349 (dangerously combined), 350 ("yield[ed] to political pressure"), 350–51 ("perfunctory routine"); Wigdor, *Roscoe Pound,* 273–74 ("avowed dictatorship").

34. "Roscoe Pound Raps Welfare Fallacy," *Los Angeles Times,* Apr. 15, 1950, p. 7 ("charitably minded pickpocket"); "Ex Law Dean Reports on Unions' Immunities," *Los Angeles Times,* May 20, 1957, p. 13; Roscoe Pound, "Union Immunity," *Wall Street Journal,* July 22, 1957, p. 10 (odious privileges); Roscoe Pound, "The Rule of Law and the Modern Welfare State," 7 *Vand. L. Rev.* 1, 29 (1953) (inimical to the rule of law); "Threats to Rights of Man Assessed," *Los Angeles Times,* Dec. 10, 1949, p. A7 (relief from poverty); "Pound Denounces a Welfare State," *New York Times,* Feb. 8, 1950, p. 29 ("service state"); Wigdor, *Roscoe Pound,* 278 (opposed Eisenhower).

35. "China Policy Group Invites Full Inquiry," *Washington Post,* Apr. 24, 1950, p. 4 (angry fringe); Arthur G. McDowell to Roscoe Pound (Oct. 10, 1962), folders 133–1 to 133–4, Series 7, Miscellany, Pound Papers (vice-chairman); Lisa McGirr, *Suburban Warriors: The Origins of the New American Right* 78–79, 218–23 (Princeton University Press, 2001) (John Birch Society); Arthur G. McDowell to Roscoe Pound (May 2, 1961) (John Birch Society; Council Against Communist Aggression); Arthur G. McDowell to Roscoe Pound (Dec. 26, 1962) (same); Roscoe Pound to Arthur G. McDowell (Dec. 30, 1952) ("veritable chamber"); Roscoe Pound to Arthur G. McDowell, Nov. 26, 1951 ("lawless high-handedness"); all in folders 133–1 to 133–4, Series 7, Miscellany, Pound Papers.

36. Richard Hofstadter, *The Paranoid Style in American Politics and Other Essays* (Knopf, 1965); see also Alan Brinkley, "The Problem of American Conservatism," 99 *Am. Hist. Rev.* 409 (1994).

37. Belli, *My Life on Trial,* 19 ("self-reliant young men").

38. Belli, *My Life on Trial,* 19 (first woman pharmacist), 26–27 (Leonie Belli), 29, 35 (Caesar Belli); Albert Averbach and Melvin M. Belli, eds., 1 *Tort and Medical Yearbook,* p. xii (Bobbs-Merrill, 1961) ("pioneer family"); Melvin M. Belli Sr. and Mel Krantzler with Christopher Taylor, *Divorcing* 1–4 (St. Martin's Press, 1988) (moralizing strictures).

39. Gerald Gunther, *Learned Hand: The Man and the Judge* 146 (Knopf, 1994) ("sickness and death"); Belli, *My Life on Trial,* 37–39 (high school principal; "knew I'd be a lawyer"); Wallace, *Life and Limb,* 52 ("attacked by a bottle").

40. Belli, *My Life on Trial,* 88–93 (interest in personal injury cases; Bryant trial). Belli later reported that the verdict in the Bryant case was $31,883.25 (Belli, *My Life on Trial,* 93), but the appellate decision affirming the verdict clearly states that it was $27,500. See Bryant v. Market Street Ry Co., 158 P.2d 18 (Cal. App.), aff'd 163 P.2d 33 (Cal. App. 1945). The difference may be accounted for by pre- and postjudgment interest.

41. William Flynn, "Ruby's Lawyer Has Reputation as Courtroom Barrymore," *Washington Post,* Jan. 20, 1964, p. A4 (part lawyer, part actor; "Even a Rolls"; and velvet briefcase); Wallace, *Life and Limb,* 12 (standard courtroom outfit); Speiser, *Lawyers and the American Dream,* 221 ("Congress gaiters"); Seymour Korman, "Sparks Are Expected to Fly at Trial of Jack Ruby," *Chicago Tribune,* Jan. 23, 1964, p. W12; Evans, *Super Lawyers,* 19.

42. Wallace, *Life and Limb,* 12–15, 119 (butcher paper episode; 682-pound client); Evans, *Super Lawyers,* 24 (breast enhancement); "Fan Lays Claim to Willie Mays unless Giants Pay Judgment," *New York Times,* Feb. 8, 1962, p. 50.

43. Escola v. Coca-Cola Bottling Co., 150 P.2d 436 (Cal. 1944); Gerber v. Farber, 129 P.2d 485 (Cal. App. 1942) (regularly lost).

44. Melvin M. Belli, 1 *Modern Trials,* p. vi (Bobbs-Merrill, 1954) (Traynor as Belli's teacher). On the *Escola* case, see Mark Geistfeld, "*Escola v. Coca-Cola Bottling Co.:* Strict Products Liability Unbound," in Robert L. Rabin and Stephen D. Sugarman, eds., *Torts Stories* 229–58 (Foundation Press, 2003).

45. Geistfeld, "*Escola v. Coca-Cola,*" 252–58; Robert L. Rabin, "Tort Law in Transition: Tracing the Patterns of Sociolegal Change," 23 *Valparaiso L. Rev.* 1 (1988); Gary T. Schwartz, "The Beginning and the Possible End of the Rise of Modern American Tort Law," 26 *Ga. L. Rev.* 601 (1992); G. Edward White, *Tort Law in America: An Intellectual History* 197–207 (Oxford University Press, 1981).

46. Belli, 2 *Law Revolt,* 558 (tort lawyers could remake the law); Belli, *My Life on Trial,* 209 ("winds of change"); Melvin M. Belli, *"Ready for the Plaintiff!" A Story of Personal Injury Law* 6 (Henry Holt, 1956) ("gladiator for sale"); Wallace E. Sedgwick, Book Review (reviewing *Modern*

Trials), 8 *Stan. L. Rev.* 535, 536 (1956) ("total war"); Melvin M. Belli, "Pre-Trial: Aid to the New Advocacy," 43 *Cornell L. Q.* 34, 38 (1957) ("sparks of conflict"); Melvin M. Belli, *The Modern Trial Lawyer: An Address by Melvin Belli at the Convention of International Academy of Trial Lawyers, November 23, 1956*, p. 18 (same); 1 Melvin M. Belli, *The Law Revolution—Criminal Law* 282 (Sherbourne Press, 1968) ("we must serve well"); Belli, *Ready for the Plaintiff,* 6 ("greatest social benefit").

47. Wallace, *Life and Limb,* 125 ("commodity to sell," internal quotation marks omitted); Belli, *My Life on Trial,* 88 ("economic system").

48. Marc Galanter, "Why the Haves Come Out Ahead: Speculations on the Limits of Legal Change," 9 *Law & Soc'y Rev.* 95 (1974) (one-shotters and repeat players); Belli, *My Life on Trial,* 88 ("poor man").

49. Lartigue v. R. J. Reynolds, 317 F.2d 19 (5th Cir. 1963); Hudson v. R. J. Reynolds Tobacco Co., 314 F.2d 776 (5th Cir. 1963); Belli, *My Life on Trial,* 221–22 (tobacco cases); Melvin M. Belli, 1 *Modern Damages* 30 (Bobbs-Merrill, 1959); Melvin M. Belli, *Belli Files: Reflections on the Wayward Law* 219 (Prentice-Hall, 1983) (improve image); Richard S. Jacobson and Jeffrey R. White, *David v. Goliath: ATLA and the Fight for Everyday Justice* 1–22 (Association of Trial Lawyers of America, 2004) (sharing information and coordinating legislative efforts among plaintiffs' lawyers); Rita Jameson, "ATLA," *Trial,* July 1980, p. 56 (same).

50. Samuel Horovitz, "Editorial: NACCA and Its Objectives," 10 *NACCA L. J.* 17, 21 (1952).

51. *KAPA Koments: Official Publication of Kansas Association of Plaintiffs' Attorneys,* vol. 2, no. 1, February 1954, n.p., folder 1, box 146, Pound Papers ("Sam the Vacationer"); Jacobson and White, *David v. Goliath,* 17 ("Billy Graham"); Ernest W. Bogusch, "Samuel Horovitz—60 Years Old," *NACCA Newsletter,* Nov. 1957, p. 2, reel 59, folder 3, Pound Papers ("sprang like wildfire"); Jacobson and White, *David v. Goliath,* 13, 23 (35 lawyers to 300); Jameson, "ATLA," 56 (5,000 lawyers to 7,000 to 22,000); Joseph Bear, "NACCA Conventions," 6 *NACCA L. J.* 212, 213 (1950); also Jacobson and White, *David v. Goliath,* 72 (estimating 600 at the 1950 convention); "NACCA Convention, Transcript, and New Officers," 14 *NACCA L. J.* 355 (1954) (1,200 at 1954 convention). On the NACCA's phenomenal growth, see Edward B. Rood, "The Big Push (1961–1966)," *Trial,* July–August 1971, pp. 24–25, 44.

52. Jacobson and White, *David v. Goliath,* 21 ("legal ecstasy"); Belli, *My Life on Trial,* 128–29 (Belli joined); Wallace, *Life and Limb,* 79 ("Belli

they have in mind"); Belli, *Ready for the Plaintiff,* 10; Belli, *My Life on Trial,* 134 (barnstormed); Stuart M. Speiser, *Lawsuit* 266 (Horizon Press, 1980); Laurence S. Locke, "NACCA Convention and Officers," 4 *NACCA L. J.* 311, 313 (1949).

53. Jacobson and White, *David v. Goliath,* 22, 163–64.

54. Id., 64 ("we need legislation"; "we need a lobby"); Belli, *Ready for the Plaintiff,* 10 (same); Wallace, *Life and Limb,* 79 (encouraged lawyers to lobby); J. Harold Land, "NACCA Convention," 5 *NACCA L. J.* 236, 237 (1950) (conventions organized to bring in judges); Samuel Horovitz, "Editorial: NACCA and Its Objectives," 10 *NACCA L. J.* 17, 28 (1952) (same); Einer R. Elhauge, "Does Interest Group Theory Justify More Intrusive Judicial Review?" 101 *Yale L. J.* 31 (1991) (judge-made law susceptible).

55. Speiser, *Lawsuit,* 342 ("real weapon"); Paula Stone to NACCA Member (n.d.), reel 58, Pound Papers (mailing list); Lester Velie, "And Then—Sudden Ruin," *Nation's Business,* June 1952, p. 29 ("postgraduate school"); also Alfred S. Julien, "The Vice-Prez Sez," *NACCA Newsletter,* Nov. 1957, p. 2, reel 59, folder 3, Pound Papers ("the greatest post graduate educational force this country has ever seen"); Lou Ashe, "In the Beginning . . . Belli," *Trial,* July–August 1971, p. 21 ("lawyers' school"); George Fuermann, *Houston: Land of the Big Rich* 69–70 (Doubleday and Co., 1951) ("Houston's Riviera"; "tragic imitation"); "NACCA Convention and Meetings," 10 *NACCA L. J.* 284 (1952) (Belli Seminars); Belli to Roscoe Pound (n.d. [1962?]), folder 37–7, series 3, Pound Papers (8:30 A.M. to midnight); Ernest W. Bogusch, "NACCA Convention, Branches, and Meetings," 11 *NACCA L. J.* 244, 244 (1953) ("famous pre-Convention courses").

56. Jacobson and White, *David v. Goliath,* 20, 93 (Belli Seminars; Julien's files); Wallace, *Life and Limb,* 79, 125–26 (Belli Seminars); Speiser, *Lawsuit,* 342 ("rogues gallery").

57. "Verdicts or Awards Exceeding $50,000," 1 *NACCA L. J.* 99 (1948) ("meagre verdicts"); Belli, *My Life on Trial,* 134 ("if awards were low").

58. Melvin M. Belli, "The Adequate Award," 39 *Cal. L. Rev.* 1 (1951), 4 (baseball players and racehorses), 6–8 (inflation), 5 ("appallingly inadequate"), 3 ("restorative"); see also Melvin M. Belli Sr., *The More Adequate Award: A Collection of More Adequate Awards to February 1952* (Belli, Ashe, and Pinney, 1952).

59. Lester Velie, "And Then—Sudden Ruin," *Nation's Business,* June 1952, p. 29 (ominous upward trend); Robert P. Hobson, "NACCA—As Viewed by Defense Counsel," *Kentucky State Bar Journal,* Sept. 1956, folder 3, box 146, Pound Papers (same); Raymond G. Schultz, "Investment Income and Casualty Insurance Profits," 26 *Journal of Insurance* 33 (1959) (same); Charles P. Hall Jr., "Special Risk Health Insurance," 31 *J. Risk & Insurance* 63 (1964) (same); Louis L. Jaffe, "Damages for Personal Injury: The Impact of Insurance," 18 *Law & Contemp. Probs.* 219, 222 (1953) (NACCA and rising verdicts); Clement E. Vose, "Interest Groups, Judicial Review, and Local Government," 19 *Western Pol. Q.* 85, 96 (1966) (same); Belli, *Ready for the Plaintiff,* 11 ("Belli and his cohorts"); *U.S. Tort Costs: 2004 Update, Trends and Findings on the Cost of the U.S. Tort System* 13 (Tillinghast Towers-Perrin, 2004) (http://www.towersperrin.com/tillinghast/publications/reports/Tort_2004?Tort.pdf) (total costs).

60. Jacobson and White, *David v. Goliath,* 97–98 nn.32–58 (ATLA members as counsel), 114 (landowners); "Reform Pressed in Injury Cases," *New York Times,* Jan. 4, 1959, p. 119 (charitable hospitals); Jacobson and White, *David v. Goliath,* 126 (emotional injury), 135–36 (crashworthiness), 136, 275–76 (Nader, ATLA, and Corvair); Ralph Nader, *Unsafe at Any Speed: The Designed-In Dangers of the American Automobile* (Grossman, 1965).

61. Speiser, *Lawyers and the American Dream,* 235 ("greatest coup"); also Richard S. Jacobson, "Groans, Growth, and Maturity," *Trial,* July–August 1971, pp. 26, 29 ("greatest achievement"); Belli, *My Life on Trial,* 133 (Harvard address); Melvin Belli to Roscoe Pound (Dec. 3, 1962), folder 37–7, series 3, Pound Papers (Harvard address); Samuel B. Horovitz, "Editorial: NACCA and the Spirit of Public Service," 9 *NACCA L. J.* 17, 18 (1952) (Pound in Los Angeles); Roscoe Pound, "The Development of Legal Liability," 10 *NACCA L. J.* 186, 197 (1952) (Pound in Houston); Ernest W. Bogusch, "Sam Horovitz—Sixty Years Old," *NACCA Newsletter,* Nov. 1957, p. 2, reel 59, folder 3, Pound Papers ("fortuitous day"); Samuel B. Horovitz, "Editorial: Our New Editor-in-Chief, Dean Roscoe Pound," 12 *NACCA L. J.* 19 (1953) ("foremost legal scholar").

62. See Letters in folder 2, box 146 (much needed additional income); and Roscoe Pound to Arthur G. McDowell (Dec. 19, 1961), folders 133–1 to 133–4, Series 7, Miscellany (Harvard pension), both in Pound Papers; Hull, *Roscoe Pound and Karl Llewellyn,* 41–42 n.26 (pension); Richard Warner, "Roscoe Pound," in *American National Biography Online* (February

2000), accessed Aug. 27, 2005 (no children); Wigdor, *Roscoe Pound,* 252–53 ("nuttier and nuttier"); Roscoe Pound to Samuel B. Horovitz (Apr. 16, 1963), reel 58 ("embarrassing"); also Samuel B. Horovitz to Roscoe Pound (Apr. 17, 1963), reel 58, both in Pound Papers.

    63. Samuel Stern to Roscoe Pound (Feb. 25, 1960), folder 3 (Socrates); Thomas Lambert to Roscoe Pound (Sept. 6, 1961), folder 5 ("Hercules"); both in box 146, Pound Papers.

    64. Melvin Belli to Roscoe Pound (Sept. 11, 1954), folder 37–7, series 3 (Belli and Pound); Melvin Belli to Roscoe Pound (June 27, 1957), folder 37–7, series 3 (same); Samuel B. Horovitz to Boston Gas Co. (Oct. 9, 1956), folder 3, box 146 (lunches); Samuel B. Horovitz to Roscoe Pound (June 17, 1960), folder 2, box 146 (same); Samuel B. Horovitz to Roscoe Pound (June 1, 1961), folder 5, box 146 (same); K. Howard Drake to Horovitz (June 26, 1963), reel 58 (same); Samuel B. Horovitz to Roscoe Pound (July 30, 1963), reel 58 (same); Ernest W. Bogusch to Roscoe Pound, Sept. 18, 1959, folder 3, box 146 ("see you Saturday"); Roscoe Pound to Melvin Belli (July 22, 1959), folder 37–7, series 3 (wife died Jan. 22, 1959), all in Pound Papers; "Mrs. Roscoe Pound," *New York Times,* Jan. 23, 1959, p. 26 (obituary); Samuel B. Horovitz to Roscoe Pound (Apr. 6, 1961), folder 1, box 146, Pound Papers (sister died); "Dr. Louise Pound," *New York Times,* June 28, 1958, p. 69 (obituary); Samuel B. Horovitz to Edward B. Hanley (Nov. 15, 1960), folder 5, box 146 ("The Game"); Roscoe Pound to Mrs. Samuel Horovitz (Sep. 7, 1960), folder 5, box 146 (dinner); Samuel B. Horovitz to Roscoe Pound (Oct. 30, 1962), reel 58 (scrapbook); Samuel B. Horovitz to Roscoe Pound (Aug. 23, 1960), folder 4, box 146 (sister in Nebraska); Samuel B. Horovitz to Dr. Leo Cass (June 18, 1963), reel 58 (health insurance and medical care); Watertown Office of Selectmen to Roscoe Pound c/o Samuel B. Horovitz (Oct. 25, 1962), reel 58 (correspondence and mail); all in Pound Papers.

    65. Samuel Horovitz, "Editorial: NACCA's Fifth Anniversary," 7 *NACCA L. J.* 13 (1951) (grants to law faculty); Mark DeWolf Howe, "Rights of Maritime Workers," 5 *NACCA L. J.* 146 (1950), 6 *NACCA L. J.* 131 (1950); Stefan A. Riesenfeld, "Basic Problems in the Administration of Workmen's Compensation," 8 *NACCA L. J.* 21 (1951); Stefan A. Riesenfeld, "Forty Years of Workmen's Compensation," 7 *NACCA L. J.* 15, 23 (1951); Wex S. Malone, "Damage Suits and the Contagious Principle of Workmen's Compensation," 9 *NACCA L.J.* 20 (1952); Ernst W. Bogusch, "NACCA Convention, Branches, and Meetings," 13 *NACCA L. J.* 295,

299 (1954) ("every field of legal endeavor"); Belli, *Blood Money*, 174 ("about as shady").

66. A. Leo Levin and Russell R. Wheeler, *The Pound Conference: Perspectives on Justice in the Future* 111 (West Publishing Co., 1979) (comments of Erwin Griswold) ("weren't too happy"). Roscoe Pound to Ben C. Cohen (Aug. 16, 1955) (foundation grant); Roscoe Pound to William G. Cloon (Aug. 12, 1955) (same), both in folder 2, box 146, Pound Papers. "Scholar Wins Award," *New York Times,* June 1, 1955, p. 35 (same).

67. Fred Brady, "Dean's Old Residence Now Medico-Legal Forum," *Boston Sunday Herald,* Sept. 29, 1957, p. 38, folder 2, box 146 (ties growing stronger); Roscoe Pound to Melvin M. Belli (August 8, 1958), folder 37–7, series 3 (extraordinarily energetic); Samuel Horovitz to Roscoe Pound (Sept. 27, 1956), folder 1, box 146 (Pound traveling and writing for NACCA); List of Paid Registrants for NACCA European Trip, Mar. 18, 1957, folder 2, box 146; "Claim Lawyers Plan Two-Day Meeting Here," newspaper clipping, folder 2, box 146; John J. O'Connor Jr. to Roscoe Pound (May 13, 1958), and John J. O'Connor Jr. to Samuel B. Horovitz (May 1, 1958), folder 2, box 146 (Pound traveling and writing for NACCA); William G. Cloon to Roscoe Pound (May 8, 1958), folder 2, box 146 (May 24, 1958 address by Pound at the Pound Foundation); "Roscoe Pound Speaks Here" [newspaper clipping from *Chicago Sun Times*], n.d. [1958?], reel 59, folder 3; Jack Jones, "Educator Cautions Lawyers on Ethics," *Daily Oklahoman,* Dec. 5, 1957, reel 59, folder 3; E. M. Nichols to Roscoe Pound (July 1, 1961), and Roscoe Pound to E. M. Nichols (July 6, 1961), folder 5, box 146 (lobbying for judges); Samuel B. Horovitz to Roscoe Pound (May 15, 1963), reel 58 (same); Roscoe Pound to David Blackshear (Feb. 16, 1954), folder 1, box 146 (indefatigable); Roscoe Pound to Samuel B. Horovitz (Mar. 1, 1960), folder 3, box 146 (ethics charges); Charles C. Steadman to Roscoe Pound (Mar. 3, 1960), folder 3, box 146 (same); also Roscoe Pound to David Sindell (July 27, 1961), and David Sindell to Roscoe Pound (July 31, 1961), folder 5, box 146; all in Pound Papers; Roscoe Pound, "Introduction," in Melvin M. Belli, *Modern Trials* p. xiii (Bobbs-Merrill, 1954) ("indispensable"); Roscoe Pound to Melvin M. Belli (May 20, 1954), folder 37–7, series 3 ("monumental work"), Pound Papers.

68. Roscoe Pound to Melvin M. Belli (Mar. 21, 1962), folder 37–7, series 3 ("Dear Belli"); Van H. Pinney to Roscoe Pound (Feb. 1, 1955), folder 37–7, series 3 (Belli and tobacco suits); also Roscoe Pound to Samuel Stern

(Nov. 13, 1956), folder 2, box 146 (same); Benjamin Marcus to Roscoe Pound (Jan. 4, 1960), folder 3, box 146 (citing Pound's correspondence to courts); Benjamin Marcus to Roscoe Pound (Dec. 22, 1959), telegram, folder 4, box 146 (same); all in Pound Papers.

69. Telegram from David Blackshear to Roscoe Pound (Feb. 22, 1954) (NACCA opponents in Louisiana); Orville Richardson to Roscoe Pound (Mar. 11, 1954) (NACCA opponents in Missouri); Roscoe Pound to Orville Richardson (Mar. 8, 1954) (Missouri); William G. Cloon to Roscoe Pound (Aug. 9, 1955) (NACCA opponents in Michigan); A. E. Papale to David Blackshear (Feb. 22, 1954) ("Father of American Jurisprudence"); all in folder 1, box 146, Pound Papers. "NACCA Convention, Transcript, and New Officers," 14 *NACCA L. J.* 355, 356–57 (1954) (speaker and honoree); also Jacobson and White, *David v. Goliath,* 85 (same); David Blackshear to Roscoe Pound (March 5, 1954), folder 1, box 146 (keys to the city); *KAPA Koments: Official Publication of Kansas Association of Plaintiffs' Attorneys,* vol. 2, no. 1, February 1954, n.p., folder 1, box 146 (Pound's picture); *The Advocate: Publication of the West Virginia Trial Lawyers' Association,* Christmas Issue 1962, p. 3, reel 58 (honorary member); all in Pound Papers.

70. Roscoe Pound–NACCA Foundation Balance Sheet, Dec. 3, 1957 ($25,000); "Roscoe Pound Home, Library Are Opened in Watertown," newspaper clipping, n.d.; Board of Trustees of the Roscoe Pound–NACCA Foundation to Editor (Oct. 15, 1956); all in reel 59, folder 3, Pound Papers.

71. Samuel B. Horovitz to Roscoe Pound (May 22, 1956), folder 3, box 146 (utilities); Samuel B. Horovitz to Colonial Coal Co., May 2, 1956, folder 3, box 146 (same); Samuel B. Horovitz to Boston Edison Co. (Oct. 1, 1956), folder 3, box 146 (same); Samuel B. Horovitz to Boston Gas Co. (Oct. 9, 1956), folder 3, box 146 (same); Melvin M. Belli to Roscoe Pound (Feb. 15, 1962), folder 377, series 3 (editorial board); John Wm. Riley, "Dean Pound, Almost Ninety, Late for Party—Working," *Boston Sunday Globe,* Oct. 23, 1960, reel 59, folder 3 (state Supreme Court justices); "Birthday Party," *Boston Herald,* n.d. [fall 1957], reel 59, folder 3; *Boston Sunday Herald* clipping, n.d. [fall 1958], folder 3, box 146 (eighty-eighth birthday, 1958); Roscoe Pound to Thomas Lambert (Oct. 17, 1959), folder 3, box 146; Fred Brady, "Dean Pound Lauded on Ninetieth Birthday," *Boston Herald,* Oct. 21, 1960, folder 4, box 146 (Supreme Court justices); "Dean Pound's Ninetieth Birthday Tomorrow," *Boston Globe,* Friday, Oct.

21, 1960, folder 4, box 146; "Law World Honors Roscoe Pound at Ninety," newspaper clipping [fall 1960], reel 59, folder 3; Samuel B. Horovitz to Governor John A. Volpe (Nov. 5, 1962), reel 58, Roscoe Pound Papers; see also "200 Honor Dean Pound of Harvard," *Boston Sunday Herald,* May 5, 1963, reel 58; "Roscoe Pound Home, Library Are Opened in Watertown," newspaper clipping, n.d., reel 59, folder 3 (Fleming James); Lucy B. Pound to Friend (Nov. 25, 1957), reel 59, folder 3 (same); Leo S. Karlin to Roscoe Pound (Jan. 28, 1961), folder 1, box 146 (honorary chairman); NACCA Bar Association, Proposed Program as Part of Fifteenth Annual Convention (typescript, July 16–22, 1961, Statler Hilton Hotel, Boston, Massachusetts), folder 5, box 146 (Justice Clark); also Samuel B. Horovitz to Roscoe Pound (June 23, 1963), reel 58 (same); Tom C. Clark to Samuel B. Horovitz (Nov. 27, 1962), reel 58 (Clark's chambers); Samuel B. Horovitz to NACCA (Sep. 27, 1962), reel 58 (same); all in Pound Papers.

72. "Adjudication or Administration?" ms. 1964; Lillian McLaughlin, "Cites Need: 'One World' Schooling," newspaper clipping, folder 1, box 146 (common law bulwark); Roscoe Pound, "The Development of Constitutional Guarantees of Liberty," [address given at Wabash College, 1945], p. 8 ("administrative machinery"); Roscoe Pound to Melvin M. Belli (Oct. 15, 1956), folder 37–7, series 3 ("client caretakers"); all three in Pound Papers. Also Pound, "Introduction," in Belli, *Modern Trials,* pp. xiii–xiv (office lawyers); Fred Brady, "Dean's Old Residence Now Medico-Legal Forum," *Boston Sunday Herald,* Sept. 29, 1957, p. 38, folder 2, box 146, Pound Papers ("uncompromising and inveterate"; "communism or the millennium"); also Roscoe Pound, "The Reader's Digest Article," 15 *NACCA L. J.* 21, 23–28 (1955) (same); Laurence S. Locke, "NACCA Convention and Officers," 4 *NACCA L. J.* 311, 312 (1949) ("tough-minded"); Orville Richardson, "Should Contingent Fee Contracts in Personal Injury Cases Be Subject to Judicial Control?" ms., folder 4, box 146, Pound Papers ("secondary position"); 4 *NACCA L.J.* 312 ("tough minded"); also "The National Board of Trial Advocacy," *Trial,* July 1980, p. 62.

73. Samuel B. Horovitz, "Editorial: The Injured Workers' Plight," 2 *NACCA L. J.* 11, 16 (1948) (opposing expansion of workmen's compensation); 2 *NACCA L. J.* 214–15 (erosion by inflation); Locke, "NACCA Convention and Officers," 4 *NACCA L. J.* 312, 314 (central pillars and proposals); Samuel B. Horovitz, "Workmen's Compensation and the Claimant," 287 *Annals of the American Academy of Political and Social Science* 53, 60 (1953) (central pillars); also Samuel B. Horovitz, "Editorial: The American

Bar Association Resolution to Abolish the FELA and the Jones Act," 5 *NACCA L. J.* 11 (1950); Jacobson and White, *David v. Goliath,* 14, 15, 64.

74. Witt, *The Accidental Republic,* 194–95; Jonathan Simon, "Driving Governmentality: Automobile Accidents, Insurance, and the Challenge to Social Order in the Inter-War Years, 1919–1941," 4 *Conn. Insurance L. J.* 521–588 (1998); Guido Calabresi, *The Costs of Accidents: A Legal and Economic Analysis* 3–16 (Yale University Press, 1970); Robert E. Keeton and Jeffrey O'Connell, *Basic Protection for the Traffic Victim: A Blueprint for Reforming Automobile Insurance* (Little, Brown, 1965).

75. Richard M. Heins, "Compensating the Automobile Accident Victim," 24 *J. Risk & Insurance* 73, 75 (1957) (automobile compensation proposals); P. S. Atiyah, "American Tort Law in Crisis," 7 *Oxford Journal of Legal Studies* 279–301 (1987) (midcentury observers).

76. Rita Jameson, "ATLA," *Trial,* July 1980, pp. 56, 59 ("civil jury system"); Roscoe Pound, "Administrative Law: Its Growth, Procedure, and Significance," 7 *U. Pitt. L. Rev.* 269, 274–75 (1941) ("higher plane"); see also Roscoe Pound, "The Economic Interpretation and the Law of Torts," 53 *Harv. L. Rev.* 365, 385 (1940); "Tort or Liability" ms., p. 19, Pound Papers ("grossly inadequate"); also Roscoe Pound, "The Development of Legal Liability," 10 *NACCA L. J.* 186, 197 (1952); Associated Press, "Roscoe Pound Criticizes Court Setup," *Providence Sunday Journal,* July 24, 1960, folder 4, box 146; Gerald Jonas, "Work Is First for Harvard's Law Expert," *Boston Sunday Herald,* Oct. 22, 1960, reel 59, folder 3 (against encroachments on the jurisdiction of the common law); NACCA Fourteenth Annual Convention Program, San Francisco, California, Jack Tar Hotel, July 22–28, 1960—Honolulu, July 28–August 5, folder 4, box 146 (opposing incursions on "traditional concepts of justice"); Samuel B. Horovitz to Roscoe Pound (Aug. 23, 1960), folder 4, box 146; Samuel B. Horovitz to Roscoe Pound (Aug. 25, 1960), folder 4, box 146; Roscoe Pound, "Personal Injury: A Social or a Legal Problem?" ms., reel 58; Roscoe Pound to Arne Fougner (Sept. 9, 1960), folder 5, box 146 (arbitrary schedules), all in Pound Papers; "Criticism of Workmen's Compensation Rising from Industry, Labor," *Wall Street Journal,* May 4, 1961, p. 1; Jacobson and White, *David v. Goliath,* 41–42.

77. "Pound Criticizes Opinion on Public Paying Losses," *Los Angeles Times,* Mar. 17, 1950, p. A2 ("involuntary Good Samaritan"); Roscoe Pound, "The Problem of the Exploding Bottle," 40 *BU L. Rev.* 167 (1960) ("exceptionally able").

78. Untitled speech beginning "More than a decade ago," ms. 1961, Pound Papers ("agitation"); Roscoe Pound, "Reparation and Prevention in the Law of Today," 12 *NACCA L. J.* 197, 198 ("individual liberty . . . welfare or service state"); also Jacobson and White, *David v. Goliath,* 186; Wallace, *Life and Limb,* 215 ("assembly line justice"); also Belli, *Blood Money,* 120–26 (same); Jameson, "ATLA," pp. 56, 59 ("euthanasia"). "NACCA: Rumor and Reflection," *Congressional Record,* 85th Cong., 1st sess. (comments of the Hon. Herbert Zelenko, Jan. 22, 1957), p. 3, folder 2, box 146 ("from the side"); "Automobile Commission Is Not Sound, Local Attorney States," *Los Angeles Metropolitan News,* Sep. 14, 1959, folder 2, box 146; B. Nathaniel Richter to Samuel B. Horovitz (June 10, 1959), folder 3, box 146 (against administration); Lou Ashe to Roscoe Pound (Jan. 28, 1960), folder 3, box 146; Roscoe Pound to Lou Ashe (Jan. 25, 1960), folder 3, box 146; Arne Fougner to Roscoe Pound (Aug. 2, 1960), folder 5, box 146; NACCA Fourteenth Annual Convention Program, San Francisco, California, Jack Tar Hotel, July 22–28, 1960—Honolulu, July 28–August 5, folder 4, box 146; all in Pound Papers. Belli later misdescribed himself as having supported no-fault administrative compensation systems. See Belli, *My Life on Trial,* 158.

79. "The Rise of the Service State and Its Consequences" ms., p. 3, Pound Papers ("pedigree"; "grown up with"); "Report of the Special Committee on Administrative Law," in 63 *Annual Report of the American Bar Association* 331, 340–43 (Lord Baltimore Press, 1938) ("Marxian claim"; "only administrative ordinances"; French lawyers); also "Reception Fetes Dr. Pound for Free China Aid," *Los Angeles Times,* May 1, 1952, p. A3 (Soviet law); Wigdor, *Roscoe Pound,* 273–74 ("Duce or Fuhrer"); Roscoe Pound to Arthur G. McDowell, Esq. (June 18, 1952), folders 133–1 to 133–4, Series 7, Miscellany, Pound Papers ("high road"). On American nationalism and the limits of the New Deal administrative state, see Alice Kessler-Harris, "In The Nation's Image: The Gendered Limits of Social Citizenship in the Depression Era," 86 *J. Am. Hist.* 1251 (1999), and Aaron Friedberg, "American Antistatism and the Founding of the Cold War State," in Ira Katznelson and Martin Shefter, eds., *Shaped by War and Trade: International Influences on American Political Development* (Princeton University Press, 2002).

80. Roscoe Pound, "The Future of the Common Law," 7 *U. Cincinnati L. Rev.* 343 (1933), 355 ("precious inheritance"), 358–59 ("frame of mind"; "supremacy of law"); "Threats to Rights of Man Assessed," *Los Angeles*

Times, Dec. 10, 1949, p. A7 (highest point); Roscoe Pound, "Justice According to Law (II)," 14 *Colum. L. Rev.* 1, 22 ("Oriental justice"); Roscoe Pound, "The Judicial Office Today," 25 *Am. Bar Ass'n J.* 731, 735 (1939) ("ideas of public law"; "profound effect"); also Roscoe Pound, *Administrative Law: Its Growth, Procedure, and Significance* 132 (University of Pittsburgh Press, 1942); "General Johnson Cracks Down on Roosevelt," *Chicago Daily Tribune,* Sept. 17, 1937, p. 2; Roscoe Pound, "Changing Law in a Changing World" ms., pp. 1 ("complete giving up"), 3 ("Anglo-American"; "American allegiance"); Roscoe Pound, "The American Idea of Government" ms., p. 14 ("exotic theories . . . from Continental Europe"); also Roscoe Pound, "The Rise of the Service State and Its Consequences" ms., pp. 9–10; all in Pound Papers.

81. Melvin Belli, "Japanese Law," 11 *Hastings L. J.* 130, 149 (1959) ("national character"); Roscoe Pound, "What Is the Common Law?" 4 *U. Chi. L. Rev.* 176, 186 (1936) ("universal"; "English-speaking peoples"); Melvin M. Belli and Danny R. Jones, *Belli Looks at Life and Law in Russia* 73 (Bobbs-Merrill, 1963) ("great heritage"; "legal cement"); Belli, *Ready for the Plaintiff,* 5 ("true American"); Belli, *Blood Money,* 268 ("Blackstone . . . Mansfield"); Melvin M. Belli Sr. and Allen P. Wilkinson, *Everybody's Guide to the Law,* p. xiii (Harcourt Brace, 1986) ("best legal system").

82. Belli and Wilkinson, *Everybody's Guide to the Law,* p. xix ("twelve ordinary citizens"; "above all"); Belli, *Blood Money,* 240 ("faces"), 247 ("best system"); Melvin M. Belli, "The Modern Trial Lawyer," in Albert Averbach and Melvin M. Belli, eds., 2 *Tort and Medical Yearbook,* 1, 3 (Bobbs, Merrill, 1962) ("Stalin's calendar pronouncement"), 19 ("Big Brother"); Stefan A. Riesenfeld, "Forty Years of Workmen's Compensation," 7 *NACCA L. J.* 15, 23 (1951) ("red-shift").

83. Stuart M. Speiser, "Warsaw Convention and the American Lawyer," *Harvard Law Record,* Oct. 8 and 15, 1959; Roscoe Pound to W. C. Hannemann (Nov. 9, 1961); both in folder 1, box 147, Pound Papers.

84. Roscoe Pound, "The Idea of a Universal Law," 1 *UCLA L. Rev.* 7, 8–9 (1953) ("name of law"). Also Roscoe Pound, "The Future of American Law" ms., p. 14; Roscoe Pound, "The Rise of the Service State and Its Consequences" ms., p. 3; Roscoe Pound to Thomas Lambert (Sept. 7, 1961), folder 5, box 146; Roscoe Pound to Melvin M. Belli (Aug. 15, 1955), folder 37–7, series 3 (Belli in Asia); all in Pound Papers. Belli, "Modern Trial Lawyer," in Averbach and Belli, eds., 2 *Tort and Medical Yearbook,* 5 ("common law jury"; "free trial bar"); Melvin M. Belli Sr., *The Use of Demonstrative Ev-*

idence in Achieving "the More Adequate Award" 3 (Law Offices of Belli, Ashe, and Pinney, 1951) ("government such as the Soviet"). Samuel B. Horovitz to Roscoe Pound (Aug. 1, 1961); Samuel B. Horovitz to Cullen M. Ward (Aug. 28, 1961); Roscoe Pound to Professor M. J. Sethna (Aug. 11, 1961) ("had a wonderful time" lecturing in Calcutta); Samuel B. Horovitz to Roscoe Pound, (Oct. 5, 1961); all in folder 1, box 147, Pound Papers. K. Howard Drake to Samuel B. Horovitz (June 26, 1963); Samuel B. Horovitz to Friend, n.d. (scrawled note to Pound, Apr. 25, 1963); both in reel 58, Pound Papers. David R. Francis, "Roscoe Pound: Man of the Law," *Christian Science Monitor,* Oct. 22, 1960; "Law World Honors Roscoe Pound at Ninety," newspaper clipping [fall 1960] ("great super-government"); "Dean Pound Sees Universal Law without Superstate," newspaper clipping [fall 1957?], all in reel 59, folder 3, Pound Papers; Roscoe Pound to Arthur Larson, May 26, 1959, Duke University World Law Center folder; Roscoe Pound, "Personal Injury: A Social or a Legal Problem?" ms., reel 58; both in Pound Papers.

85. Belli, *My Life on Trial,* 62–68 (Belli in the NRA); Roscoe Pound, "The Rule of Law and the Modern Social Welfare State," 7 *Vand. L. Rev.* 1, 13 (1953) ("social service state . . . general security"); Melvin M. Belli, *The Modern Trial Lawyer: An Address by Melvin Belli at the Convention of International Academy of Trial Lawyers, November 23, 1956,* p. 18 (1956) ("social security"); Belli, *The More Adequate Award,* 9; Belli, *The Use of Demonstrative Evidence,* 10 ("pain and suffering").

86. Belli, "Adequate Award," 4 ("economic freedom. . . from capital"); also Belli, *The More Adequate Award,* 10 (same); Belli, *Blood Money,* 63 ("right of dignity").

87. Roscoe Pound, "Tort or Liability" ms., p. 21, Pound Papers ("life and limb . . . free individual"). Belli, *The Use of Demonstrative Evidence,* 1 ("were it not"); *KAPA Koments: Official Publication of Kansas Association of Plaintiffs' Attorneys,* vol. 2, no. 1, February 1954, n.p., folder 1, box 146, Pound Papers ("security with freedom").

88. *KAPA Koments: Official Publication of Kansas Association of Plaintiffs' Attorneys,* vol. 2, no. 1, February 1954, n.p., folder 1, box 146 (Lincoln); Roscoe Pound, "The Rise of the Service State and Its Consequences" ms., p. 6 ("colored preacher"); both in Pound Papers. "Threats to Rights of Man Assessed," *Los Angeles Times,* Dec. 10, 1949, p. A7 ("lavish promises"); "Pound Denounces a Welfare State," *New York Times,* Feb. 8, 1950, p. 29 ("Marxian doctrine").

89. Pound, "Introduction," in Belli, 1 *Modern Trials,* p. xix ("sporting

theory"); Melvin M. Belli, "The Modern Trial Lawyer," in Averbach and Belli, eds., 2 *Tort and Medical Yearbook,* 1, 3 ("a kicker, a passer"; "juridical decathlon"); Belli, *Ready for the Plaintiff,* 6 ("forensic gladiator"); also Jerome H. Spingarn, "Wanted: Compensation," *New York Times,* Feb. 10, 1957, p. 256; Sedgwick, Book Review, 536 ("knightly champion" and dragons).

90. Speiser, *Lawyers and the American Dream,* 222 ("Rosetta stone"; "The Equalizers"); Belli, *Blood Money,* 6 ("scales of justice . . . loaded"); Samuel B. Horovitz, "Editorial: NACCA and Its Objectives," 10 *NACCA L. J.* 17, 18–19 (1952) ("equal representation"); Thomas F. Lambert Jr., "From the Editor's Scratchpad," *NACCA Newsletter,* Nov. 1957, reel 59, folder 3, Pound Papers ("Our sword"); John H. Thornton Jr., "Book Review," 43 *Va. L. Rev.* 483, 483 (1957) ("not a penny ante game"); Pound, "Judicial Trial or Administrative Investigation?" ms. pp. 5, 10 13; see also Pound, "Adjudication or Administration?" ms. p. 6; both in Pound Papers.

91. Melvin M. Belli, *Modern Trials: Abridged Edition* 234 (Bobbs-Merrill, 1963) ("not necessarily . . . market price"); Belli, 1 *Modern Damages,* 62 ("price tag"), 63 ("dollar price . . . marketplace").

92. Belli, *Blood Money,* 122 ("do not relish").

93. Evans, *Super Lawyers,* 25 (yacht).

94. Robert E. Keeton and Jeffrey O'Connell, "Alternative Paths Toward Nonfault Automobile Insurance," 71 *Colum. L. Rev.* 241, 244 (1971); David R. Klock, "No-Fault Motor Vehicle Insurance, 40 *J. Risk & Insurance* 272, 273 (1973); 49 U.S.C.A. §40105 (West Publishing Co., 2005) (Warsaw Convention notice of denunciation). The next year, after the International Air Transport Association increased the cap on damages still further (by almost 500 percent), the United States withdrew its notice of denunciation.

95. Peter J. Irons, *A People's History of the Supreme Court* 333–35 (Penguin Books, 1999); Ira Katznelson and Bruce Pietrykowski, "Rebuilding the American State: Evidence from the 1940s," 5 *Studs. in Am. Pol. Dev.* 301, 336–37 (1991); John Hart Ely, *Democracy and Distrust: A Theory of Judicial Review* 73–77 (Harvard University Press, 1980); Robert G. McCloskey, *The American Supreme Court* 123 (University of Chicago Press, 2nd ed., rev. Sanford Levinson, 1994); Alan Brinkley, *The End of Reform: New Deal Liberalism in Recession and War* 154–74 (Random House, 1995); Mark V. Tushnet, *The NAACP's Legal Strategy against Segregated Education, 1925–1950* (University of North Carolina Press, 1987); Risa Lauren

Goluboff, "Let Economic Equality Take Care of Itself: the NAACP, Labor Litigation, and the Making of Civil Rights in the 1940s," 52 *UCLA L. Rev.* 1393 (2005); John G. Fleming, *The American Tort Process* 68–100 (Oxford University Press, 1988) (constitutionality); John Fabian Witt, "The Long History of State Constitutions and American Tort Law," 36 *Rutgers L. J.* 1159 (2005).

96. Joseph Schneider, "Accident Litigation: The Common Man Sues," 287 *Annals of the American Academy of Political and Social Science* 69, 69 (1953) (personal trust and individualized representation); George E. Allen, "The Role of a Plaintiff Lawyer in Personal Injury Litigation," 41 *Va. L. Rev.* 827 (1955) (same); Belli and Wilkinson, *Everybody's Guide to the Law,* p. xx ("standardize the amount . . . deserves").

97. Samuel Issacharoff and John Fabian Witt, "The Inevitability of Aggregate Settlement: An Institutional Account of American Tort Law," 57 *Vand. L. Rev.* 1571, 1590–96 (2004) (worker representatives); In re Clark, 77 N.E. 1 (N.Y. 1906) (upstate lawyers); Marc Shukaitis, "A Market in Personal Injury Tort Claims," 16 *J. Legal Stud.* 329, 343 (1987) (Texas claims shops); also Samuel R. Gross, "We Could Pass a Law: What Would Happen if Contingent Legal Fees Were Banned?" 47 *DePaul L. Rev.* 321, 328 (1998) (same); Maires's Case, 7 Pa. D. 297 (Pa. Common Pleas, 1898) (Philadelphia lawyer); Robert Monaghan, "The Liability Claim Racket," 3 *Law & Contemp. Probs.* 491, 493–96 (1936) (Abraham Gatner); Isidor J. Kresel, "Ambulance Chasing, Its Evils and Remedies Therefor," in *New York State Bar Association Proceedings of the Fifty-Second Annual Meeting* 323, 328 (Argus Co., 1929) ("relatively few . . . business"); also *Report to Appellate Division, First Judicial Department, by Mr. Justice Wasservogel* 4 (M. B. Brown Printing and Binding Co., 1928) (same).

98. *U.S. Tort Costs: 2004 Update,* 13; *Tort Cost Trends: An International Perspective* 14 (Tillinghast, 1992).

99. Edward A. Purcell Jr., "The Action Was outside the Courts: Consumer Injuries and the Uses of Contract in the United States, 1897–1945," in Willibald Steinmetz, ed., *Private Law and Social Inequality in the Industrial Age* 505, 512 (Oxford University Press, 2000) (insurer claims practices); Stephen C. Yeazell, "*Brown,* the Civil Rights Movement, and the Silent Litigation Revolution," 57 *Vand. L. Rev.* 1975, 1991–92, 1995–96 (2004) (plaintiffs' firm size and referral networks); Stephen C. Yeazell, "Re-Financing Civil Litigation," 51 *DePaul L. Rev.* 183, 197–211 (2001) (firm size); Herbert M. Kritzer, "From Litigators of Ordinary Cases to Litigators

of Extraordinary Cases," 51 *DePaul L. Rev.* 219, 228–29 (2001) (firm size); Jonathan R. Laing, "Lawyers Specializing in Personal Injury Suits Find Business Is Good," *Wall Street Journal,* Aug. 2, 1972, p. 1 (referral networks); Herbert M. Kritzer, *Risks, Reputations, and Rewards: Contingency Fee Legal Practice in the United States* 58–61 (Stanford University Press, 2004) (referral networks); also Sara Parikh, "Professionalism and Its Discontents: A Study of Social Networks in the Plaintiffs' Personal Injury Bar" 60 (Ph.D. diss., University of Chicago, 2001) (Illinois referral networks); John P. Heinz et al., "The Changing Character of Lawyers' Work: Chicago in 1975 and 1995," 32 *Law & Soc'y Rev.* 751, 761 (1998) (increased specialization); "FELA Specialists," 2 *For the Defense* 70 (1961) (railroad worker claims concentration); Hans Zeisel, Harry Kalven, and Bernard Buchholz, *Delay in Court* 193 (Little, Brown, 1959) (Chicago); Maurice Rosenberg and Michael I. Sovern, "Delay and the Dynamics of Personal Injury Litigation," 59 *Colum. L. Rev.* 1115, 1166–67 (1959) (New York City); *Report to Appellate Division, First Judicial Department, by Mr. Justice Wasservogel,* 5 ("more than 500 cases"); Stephen Daniels and Joanne Martin, "'It's Darwinism—Survival of the Fittest': How Markets and Reputations Shape the Ways in Which Plaintiffs' Lawyers Obtain Clients," 21 *Law & Policy* 377, 381 (1999) (Texas); Parikh, "Professionalism and Its Discontents," 37 (Illinois).

100. Mark Geistfeld, "Placing a Price on Pain and Suffering," 83 *Cal. L. Rev.* 773 (1995) (bargaining conventions); H. Laurence Ross, *Settled out of Court: The Social Process of Insurance Claims Adjustment* (Aldine Publishing Co., 2nd ed., 1980); Issacharoff and Witt, "Inevitability of Aggregate Settlement," 1605 ("collectively satisfactory"; "rear-enders"; "simple . . . calculations"); John F. Adams, "Survey of the Economic-Financial Consequences of Personal Injuries Resulting from Automobile Accidents in the City of Philadelphia, 1953," in *Economics and Business Bulletin of the School of Business and Public Administration,* Temple University, March 1955, p. 72 ("superficial . . . speed"); Herbert M. Kritzer, *The Justice Broker: Lawyers and Ordinary Litigation* 100–101, 105 (Oxford University Press, 1990) (little legal research; average of twenty hours per case); Herbert M. Kritzer, "A Comparative Perspective on Settlement and Bargaining in Personal Injury Cases," 14 *Law & Social Inq.* 167, 168 n.6 (1989) (little back-and-forth); Richard E. Miller and Austin Sarat, "Grievances, Claims and Disputes: Assessing the Adversary Culture," 15 *Law & Soc'y Rev.* 542, 545 (1981) (instant settlement agreements); Kritzer, *Risks, Reputations, and Rewards,* 177

(settlement negotiations not done in person); Jason Scott Johnson and Joel Waldfogel, "Does Repeat Play Elicit Cooperation? Evidence from Federal Civil Litigation," 31 *J. Legal Stud.* 39 (2002) (speedy resolution by repeat players); Ronald Gilson and Robert H. Mnookin, "Disputing through Agents: Cooperation between Lawyers in Litigation," 94 *Colum. L. Rev.* 509 (1994) (bargaining efficiencies between repeat players).

    101. Catherine M. Sharkey, "Unintended Consequences of Medical Malpractice Damages Caps," 80 *NYU L. Rev.* 391 (2005) (economic damages malleable).

    102. Issacharoff and Witt, "Inevitability of Aggregate Settlement," 1606 (yardsticks; "three times three"; Sindell Formula); Philip J. Hermann, "Predicting Verdicts," *Insurance L. J.*, Aug. 1962, pp. 505, 513–15 (Chicago tables), 516 ("like life expectancy tables"); Tom Baker, "Blood Money, New Money, and the Moral Economy of Tort Law in Action," 35 *Law & Soc'y Rev.* 275, 304 (2001) ("rule of thirds"); Stephen Daniels and Joanne Martin, "'We Live on the Edge of Extinction All the Time': Entrepreneurs, Innovation, and the Plaintiffs' Bar in the Wake of Tort Reform," in Jerry Van Hoy, ed., *Legal Professions: Work, Structure, and Organization* 157 (Elsevier Science, 2001) ("going rates"); Issacharoff and Witt, "Inevitability of Aggregate Settlement," 1604–5 (limited discretion). Kritzer doubts that juries use consistent formulae to calculate noneconomic damages. Herbert M. Kritzer, "Contingent Free Lawyers," 23 *Law & Social Inq.* 795, 817–18 (1998).

    103. Joseph Bear, "NACCA Conventions," 6 *NACCA L. J.* 212, 214 (1950) (Belli teaching settlement practices); also "Tentative program for NACCA Convention," 7 *NACCA L. J.* 236 (1951) (same); Belli, *The More Adequate Award* (updates); "Verdicts or Awards Exceeding $50,000," 1 *NACCA L. J.* 99 (1948) (settlement and verdict values); Belli, *Modern Damages;* Joseph W. Bishop, Book Review, 69 *Yale L. J.* 925, 929 (1960) ("Golconda . . . vade mecum").

    104. Marc A. Franklin, Robert H. Chanin, and Irving Mark, "Accidents, Money, and the Law," 61 *Colum. L. Rev.* 1, 35 (1961) ("part-recovery"); Adams, "Survey of the Economic-Financial Consequences of Personal Injuries," 46; see also Miller and Sarat, "Grievances, Claims and Disputes," 563; Mark J. Browne and Joan T. Schmit, "Patterns in Personal Automobile Third Party Bodily Injury Litigation, 1977–1997," (Sept. 7, 2004), p. 9, http://ssrn.com/abstract=588481 (70 percent of cases resolved within one year); James S. Kakalik and Nicholas M. Pace, *Costs and Compensation Paid*

in Tort Litigation (RAND: Institute for Civil Justice, 1986); Michael J. Saks, "Do We Really Know Anything about the Behavior of the Tort Litigation System—and Why Not," 140 *U. Pa. L. Rev.* 1147, 1222 (1992); Issacharoff and Witt, "Inevitability of Aggregate Settlement," 1614–15 (as speedy as no-fault); Kritzer, *Risks, Reputations, and Rewards,* 16 (risk-sharing features of tort claims system); Jerry van Hoy, "Markets and Contingency: How Client Markets Influence the Work of Plaintiffs' Personal Injury Lawyers," 6 *Int'l J. of the Legal Profession* 345, 358–59 (1999). The aggregate character of tort claims settlement practices was especially clear in bulk or package settlements that became common wherever repeat-play plaintiffs agents and defense agents came together. See Comment, "Settlement of Personal Injury Cases in the Chicago Area," 47 *Nw. U. L. Rev.* 895, 905 (1953); "New York Supreme Court Adopts Important Rules," 15 *Am. Bar Ass'n J.* 448 (1929); "Contingent Fee Accident Litigation in Philadelphia," 15 *Am Bar Ass'n* J. 2 (1929); "Report of the Committee of Censors," in *Massachusetts Law Quarterly Supplement to Volume 14,* Nov. 1928, p. 47; Howard M. Erichson, "Informal Aggregation: Procedural and Ethical Implications of Coordination Among Counsel in Related Lawsuits," 50 *Duke L.J.* 381, 388 n.7 (2000); Jack B. Weinstein, *Individual Justice in Mass Tort Litigation: The Effect of Class Actions, Consolidations, and Other Multiparty Devices* 74 (Northwestern University Press, 1995); Ross, *Settled Out of Court,* 143.

105. Ross, *Settled Out of Court,* 166–67 (shortcuts; rules of thumb); Comment, "Settlement of Personal Injury Cases in the Chicago Area," 904–905 and n.48 (1953) ("easier man to deal with"); also "Address of Vice-President J. Scofield Rowe," in *Third Convention, International Association of Casualty and Surety Underwriters* 55, 60 (1913) (plaintiffs' lawyers are the "lubricant" of the system).

106. *Report of the National Commission on State Workmen's Compensation Laws* 13–14 (U.S. Government Printing Office, 1972) (low benefits); Melvin Belli, ed., *Trial and Tort Trends through 1955,* p. 307 (Central Book Co., 1956) ("trial balloon"); Philip J. Hermann, "Predicting Verdicts in Personal Injury Cases," *Insurance L. J.,* Aug. 1962, pp. 505, 515 ("change with the times"; "continuously being revised").

107. Rosenberg and Sovern, "Delay and the Dynamics of Personal Injury Litigation," 1135 (8.6 percent of cases producing payments of greater than $10,000 go to trial, whereas 2.9 percent of all cases producing payments go to trial); Young B. Smith, "Compensation for Automobile Acci-

dents," 32 *Colum. L. Rev.* 785, 796 (far more likely); also George L. Priest and Benjamin Klein, "The Selection of Disputes for Litigation," 13 *J. Legal Stud.* 1 (1984) (unusual or extreme cases go to trial); Kent D. Syverud, "ADR and the Decline of the American Civil Jury," 44 *UCLA L. Rev.* 1935, 1943 (1997) (same); Randall R. Bovbjerg et al., "Valuing Life and Limb in Tort: Scheduling Pain and Suffering," 83 *Nw. U. L. Rev.* 908 (1989) (rationality in the aggregate); Adams, "Survey of the Economic-Financial Consequences of Personal Injuries," 88 (quality of legal representation).

108. David Wilkins, "Who Should Regulate Lawyers?" 105 *Harv. L. Rev.* 799, 820 (1992) (one-shot–repeat-play problem in lawyer-client relationship); Robert H. Mnookin, "Negotiation, Settlement, and the Contingent Fee," 47 *DePaul L. Rev.* 363 (1998) (irrationalities of market in contingent-fee legal services); Kritzer, *Risks, Reputations, and Rewards,* 188–89 (lawyer earnings); Eric Helland and Alexander Tabarrok, "Contingency Fees, Settlement Delay, and Low-Quality Litigation: Empirical Evidence from Two Datasets," 19 *J. Law, Econ., & Organ.* 517 (2003) (gatekeepers); Herbert M. Kritzer, "Contingency Fee Lawyers as Gatekeepers in the Civil Justice System," 81 *Judicature* 22 (July–August 1997) (gatekeepers); *U.S. Tort Costs: 2004 Update,* 7 (administrative costs declining over time), 13 ($5.4 billion in 1960).

109. Insurance Research Council, *Injuries in Auto Accidents* 74 (Insurance Research Council, June 1999) (more than 90 percent of filings produce pretrial settlements; less than one percent of claims produce a filing); Saks, "Do We Really Know Anything about the Behavior of the Tort Litigation System," 1212–13 (settlement rates); Miller and Sarat, "Grievances, Claims, and Disputes," 542 (higher proportion of tort cases settle); Herbert M. Kritzer, "Adjudication to Settlement: Shading in the Gray," 70 *Judicature* 161 (1986); Adams, "A Survey of the Economic-Financial Consequences of Personal Injuries," 64–65 (Philadelphia 1953: only 412 of 144,600 claims involve the filing of suits); Rosenberg and Sovern, "Delay and the Dynamics of Personal Injury Litigation," 1163 (sixty claims without lawsuits for every forty lawsuits).

110. Speiser, *Lawsuit,* 262 ("true value"); Belli, 2 *Modern Damages,* pp. v–xi.

111. Cf. In re Bridgestone / Firestone Inc., 288 F.3d 1012, 1020 (7th Cir. 2002) (Easterbrook, J.) (comparing a mass tort class action to the use of "Gosplan or another central planner," who "*may* hit on the price of wheat" but only by "serendipity").

112. NLRB v. Jones & Laughlin Steel Corp. 301 U.S. 1 (1937).

113. Stephen Skowronek, *Building a New American State: The Expansion of National Administrative Capacities, 1877–1920* (Cambridge University Press, 1982).

114. Jacobson and White, *David v. Goliath,* 20 ("invisible law"). The Special Collections Department of the Harvard Law Library microfilmed the NACCA boxes of the Pound Papers in response to my interest in them after I completed this research, two decades after the rest of the Pound collection was filmed.

115. Perry Nichols to Samuel B. Horovitz, Oct. 16, 1956, reel 59, folder 3 (second largest); "Justice Clark Seeks NACCA Support," *PI&E Bulletin,* reel 58 (presidents and attorneys general), both in Pound Papers; "What's News," *Wall Street Journal,* Feb. 3, 1966, p. 1 (Lyndon Johnson); Clement E. Vose, "Interest Groups, Judicial Review, and Local Government," 19 *Western Pol. Q.* 85, 96 (1966) (litigation as democratic threat); Richard A. Watson et al., "Bar Politics, Judicial Selection, and the Representation of Social Interests," 61 *Am. Pol. Sci. Rev.* 54 (1967) (same); Melvin M. Belli Sr. and Mel Krantzler with Christopher Taylor, *Divorcing* 9–10 (St. Martin's Press, 1988) (Jimmy Carter).

EPILOGUE

1. On the destructive potential of nation-states, see for example the recent account by Mark Mazower, *Salonica, City of Ghosts: Christians, Muslims, and Jews, 1430–1950* (Knopf, 2005), and the classic account by Elie Kedouri, *Nationalism* (Blackwell Publishers, 4th ed., 1960). For an argument against the nation-state as a necessary feature of liberal constitutionalism, see Joshua Cohen and Charles Sabel, "Extra Rempublicam Nulla Justitia?" 34 *Phil. & Pub. Aff.* 147 (2006); and, for the limits of the nation-state as a mechanism for regulation, see Joshua Cohen and Charles F. Sabel, "Administrative Law and Global Politics: A Possibility for Democracy?" *NYU Journal of International Law and Politics* (forthcoming 2006). For defenses of the nation-state as necessary for liberal constitutionalism and democratic self-government, see Jed Rubenfeld, "The Two World Orders," *Wilson Quarterly,* vol. 27, no. 4 (Autumn 2003), pp. 22–36; Jeremy A. Rabkin, *Law without Nations: Why Constitutional Government Requires Sovereign States* (Princeton University Press, 2005); Thomas Nagel, "The Problem of Global Justice," 33 *Phil. & Pub. Aff.* 113 (2005); and the classic account by Hannah Arendt, *The Origins of Totalitarianism* 267–302 (Harcourt, 1976).

2. Thompson v. Oklahoma, 487 U.S. 815, 869 n.4 (1988) (Scalia, J.,

dissenting); also Knight v. Florida, 528 U.S. 990 (1999) (Thomas, J., concurring in denial of certiorari); *Thompson,* 487 U.S. at 831 n.34 (comparative practice on juvenile death penalty); Atkins v. Virginia, 536 U.S. 304, 316 n.21 (2002) (comparative practice on death penalty for the mentally retarded); Lawrence v. Texas, 539 U.S. 558, 576–77 (2003) (comparative practice on same-sex sodomy); Roper v. Simmons, 125 S. Ct. 1183, 1198–1200 (2005) (comparative practice on juvenile death penalty); also *Roper,* 125 S. Ct. at 1215–16 (O'Connor, J., concurring).

3. Charles Lane, "U.S. Quits Pact Used in Capital Cases," *Washington Post,* March 10, 2005, p. A1; Andrew C. Revkin, "Bush Shift Could Doom Air Pact, Some Say," *New York Times,* March 17, 2001, p. 7; Neil A. Lewis, "U.S. Is Set to Renounce Its Role in Pact for World Tribunal," *New York Times,* May 5, 2002, p. 18; Lizette Alvarez, "Senate Ends Bitter Dispute with the U.N. on Dues," *New York Times,* Feb. 8, 2001, p. 9.

4. "Standards of Conduct for Interrogation under 18 U.S.C. §§2340–2340A: Memorandum for Alberto R. Gonzales, Counsel for the President," in Karen J. Greenberg and Joshua L. Dratel, eds., *The Torture Papers: The Road to Abu Ghraib* 172–217 (Cambridge University Press, 2005); Rasul v. Bush, 542 U.S. 466 (2004); "Possible Habeas Jurisdiction over Aliens Held in Guantanamo Bay, Cuba: Memorandum from Patrick F. Philbin and John C. Yoo to William J. Haynes II," in Greenberg and Dratel, eds., *Torture Papers,* 29–37; Gary Jeffrey Jacobsohn, "The Permeability of Constitutional Borders," 82 *Tex. L. Rev.* 1763, 1814 (2004); Paul W. Kahn, "Speaking Law to Power: Popular Sovereignty, Human Rights, and the New International Order," 1 *Chicago Journal of International Law* 1, 3 (2000); Jed Rubenfeld, "The Two World Orders," *Wilson Quarterly,* vol. 27, no. 4 (Autumn 2003), pp. 22–36. For a trenchant critique of the resistance thesis, see Judith Resnik, "Law's Migration: American Exceptionalism, Silent Dialogues, and Federalism's Multiple Ports of Entry," 115 *Yale L. J.* 1564 (2006).

5. William H. Rehnquist, *All the Laws but One: Civil Liberties in Wartime* 38 (Knopf, 1998); Terminiello v. City of Chicago, 337 U.S. 1, 37 (1949) (Jackson, J., dissenting).

6. "A Remarkable Man for Liberia," *African Repository,* Sept. 1871, pp. 280–82 ("a United States of Africa"); "To George Washington and Patrick Henry: Greetings!" *Four Lights,* Mar. 10, 1917, New York Public Library ("United States of the World"). On the many ways in which the ideology of Americanism has been invoked, see Michael Kazin and Joseph A. McCartin, eds., *Americanism: New Perspectives on the History of an Ideal* (University of North Carolina Press, 2006).

7. On the significance of American nationhood in shaping historical experience, see Thomas Bender, *A Nation among Nations: America's Place in World History* 248–49, 289–94 (Hill and Wang, 2006).

8. For the interpretation of the Supreme Court controversy as a controversy among competing forms of patriotism, see Sarah H. Cleveland, "Is There Room for the World in Our Courts?" *Washington Post,* March 20, 2005, p. B4.

9. Mary L. Dudziak, *Cold War Civil Rights: Race and the Image of American Democracy* (Princeton University Press, 2000); The Committee on International Human Rights and the Center for Human Rights and Global Justice, *Torture by Proxy: International and Domestic Law Applicable to "Extraordinary Renditions"* (Association of the Bar of the City of New York, 2004).

Acknowledgments

This book has benefited greatly from the generosity of students, colleagues, and friends. Faculty workshops in the cosmopolitan setting of Columbia Law School provided genial debuts for these essays. The hospitality of a Harrington Faculty Fellowship at the University of Texas Law School and a visiting professorship at Harvard Law School provided the opportunity to research and draft Parts Two and Four of the book. Ken Abraham, Stuart Banner, Barbara Black, Christina Burnett, Ken Cmiel, David Brion Davis, Ariela Dubler, David Engstrom, Cindy Estlund, Robert Ferguson, George Fletcher, Eric Foner, Willy Forbath, Katherine Franke, Barbara Fried, Barry Friedman, Glenda Gilmore, Bob Gordon, Tom Grey, Dan Hulsebosch, Sam Issacharoff, Fred Konefsky, Mark Mazower, Gillian Metzger, John Mikhail, Bill Nelson, Gerry Neumann, Richard Primus, John Reid, Chuck Sabel, Peter Schuck, Cathy Sharkey, Herb Sloan, David Stebenne, Robert Steinfeld, Peter Strauss, Susan Sturm, Jeremy Waldron, and Liz Wolff, among many others, provided helpful comments on parts or all of the manuscript. Faculty workshops, colloquia, and panels at the American Society for Legal History, Brooklyn Law School, the Law and Society Association, New York University, Ohio State University, Stanford University, UCLA, the University of Kyoto, the University of Pennsylvania, the University of Texas, the University of Tokyo, the University of Virginia, and Yale University helped to hone the arguments. Librarians and archivists at Columbia's Diamond Law Library, the New York Public Library, the Historical Society of Pennsylvania, the Historical Center of York County (South Carolina), Princeton's Seeley G. Mudd Manuscript Library, the Columbia

Rare Book and Manuscript Library, and the Harvard Law School Library Special Collections made the book possible. Research by Elizabeth Edmondson, Kristin Flower, and Nick Sydow at Harvard, and Michael Grunfeld, Mollie Marr, Alexander Michaels, Tony O'Rourke, Sarah Seo, Alex Swartz, and Lisa Zeidner at Columbia helped me track down innumerable hard-to-find sources. Max Belcher and Blanche Wiesen Cook generously helped to secure images for reproduction in the book, as did Jeffrey White at the Association of Trial Lawyers of America and Verlon Stone at the Liberian Collections Project of Indiana University. An early version of Part Three of the book was published in volume 54 of the *Duke Law Journal*.

Annie Murphy Paul's love sustained this book, and her editorial savvy improved it beyond measure. Theodore Paul Witt has come along to grace its final stages with good humor and a beautiful smile.

Index

Abolition, 159, 161, 162

Abrams v. United States, 157, 158

Act of Union, between England and Scotland, 22–23

Adams, John (founding father), 26, 62, 63, 66, 71, 72, 76

Adams, John (children's book author), 50

Adams, John Quincy, 72

Addams, Jane, 173, 174, 179, 180, 186–187, 188, 203, 227

"Adequate Award, The," 244, 270

Adger, John B., 131

Administration, 209–210, 211, 213–217, 221–223, 226–229, 231–234, 239–240, 242, 246, 247, 252–262, 264–266, 272, 274, 276–278, 282; continental Europe and, 213, 226–227, 253, 256–257; welfare state and, 213, 232, 256, 262; examples of, 221–222; rise of, 221–222, 231–232, 252–254, 256, 260, 275–276; corporate law and, 252–253; arguments in favor of, 254; automobile accidents and, 254, 255, 256, 259, 265, 269, 271–272, 273, 278; no-fault compensation systems and, 254, 258–259, 261, 265, 272; limited liability and, 259, 265, 266. *See also* Belli-Pound-NACCA relationship; Private administration; Sociological jurisprudence; Warsaw Convention

AFL-CIO, 253

Africa, emigration to, 106. *See also* Liberia; Sierra Leone

African Methodist Episcopal Church, 114

Age of skepticism, 159

Akerman, Amos, 120, 121, 122

Alger, George W., 166

Alison, Francis, 24

Allen, James, 42

Allison's Creek, 85, 126

Al-Qaeda, 3

American Bar Association, 212, 223–224, 225, 227, 228, 230, 232, 253

American Civil Liberties Union, 160, 197, 205–206, 207–208, 281, 350n70. *See also* Baldwin, Roger; National Civil Liberties Bureau

American Colonization Society, 86, 105–106, 110, 113, 143; Liberia and, 105, 108–109; emigration to Liberia, 105, 106, 131–133, 134–137, 138, 140, 146; difficulty financing passage to Liberia, 135–136; misinformation regarding Liberia, 146–147, 332n104

American Conference for Democracy and Terms of Peace, 173

American Conference on International Arbitration, 176

American Defense Society, 192

American League to Limit Armaments, 173

American legal institutions, 209, 213–217, 221–230, 232, 234, 238–239, 242, 246, 252–266,

American legal institutions (*continued*) 276–277; federalism, 209, 215; jury trial, 209, 215, 222, 223, 224, 238, 255, 256, 258, 260, 261, 263, 264, 265, 266, 274, 281, 282; common law courts and judges, 213–217, 221, 223, 226, 227, 232, 233, 261, 264–266, 276, 277; social policy functions through, 213–217, 222, 237–239, 265–266, 277–278; bicameral legislatures, 215; separation of powers, 215; private initiative and, 222–223, 224, 227, 238–239, 254, 273, 277. *See also* Belli-Pound-NACCA relationship

American Neutral Conference Committee, 173

American Peace Society, 188

American Protective League, 192

American Revolution, 15, 16, 20; treatment of lawyers in, 18, 19; fate of lawyers in, 38–39; response of lawyers to, 41–44

American Rights League, 192

American School Peace League, 176

American Trial Lawyers Association. *See* Association of Trial Lawyers of America

American Union Against Militarism, 160, 173, 181–182, 183–184, 185, 187, 188–189, 192–198, 199–201; Civil Liberties Bureau of, 194–197, 200–201; Truth About Preparedness Campaign, 200. *See also* American Civil Liberties Union; National Civil Liberties Bureau

Ames, James Barr, 219

Anderson, Charles, 69

Anglicization, and colonial lawyers, 27–29

Anglo-American Tradition of Liberty Conference, 203–205

Annan, Robert, 23–24

Antietam, 89

Appomattox, Lee's surrender at, 97, 137

Arendt, Hannah, 38–39

Arkansas (state), 87

Arnold, Benedict, 83

Arthington, Liberia, 139, 146, 148, 149, 150, 154, 333n107; success of settlement, 149–150; coerced labor in, 150

Articles of Confederation, 47

Ashe, Lou, 256

Association of Trial Lawyers of America (ATLA), 214, 215, 242, 244, 245–246, 255, 263, 266, 267, 268, 274, 275, 278. *See also* National Association of Claimants' Counsel of America; Private administration; Trial lawyers

ATLA. *See* Association of Trial Lawyers of America

ATLA Exchange, 244

Automobile accidents. *See* Administration; Tort law

Avery, James T., 117, 142

Avery, U.S. v., 142

Bacon, Francis, 58

Bailyn, Bernard, 23

Baker, Newton, 183–184, 200

Baldwin, Roger, 160, 194–195, 196–199, 200, 201–203, 205, 206, 207, 350n70. *See also* American Civil Liberties Union; American Union Against Militarism; Eastman, Crystal; National Civil Liberties Bureau

Barry, J. L., 125–126
Beard, Charles, 231
Beecher, Henry Ward, 161, 162
Beecher, Lyman, 161
Beecher, Thomas, 161
Belli, Caesar Arthur, 234–235
Belli, Leonie Mouron, 234–235
Belli, Melvin Mouron, 9, 211, 256, 270, 271, 274, 275–276, 278, 280, 282–283; King of Torts, 211, 250; trial lawyers and, 211–212, 215, 240; apartments of, 212, 213; Belli Building and, 212; celebration of favorable verdicts by, 212; courtroom theatrics of, 212, 235–237; Jack Ruby and, 212; personal injury law and, 212, 235–237, 238–239; offices of, 212; Policeman's Ball and, 212; push for increased damages and liability by, 212, 237–240, 242–243, 244–246, 261, 263–264; ATLA and, 214, 242, 246, 263, 268, 274, 275; fight against encroachment of administration on the common law by, 214–217, 242; NACCA and, 214, 242–243, 244, 245–246, 247, 249, 253; upbringing of, 234–235; early law career of, 235; education of, 235, 237; marriages of, 235, 278; *Escola v. Coca-Cola Bottling Company* and, 237–238, 245, 246; products liability law and, 237–239; *res ipsa loquitor* and, 237; contingent fee and, 238–239, 240; effect of other cases on, 240; suing tobacco companies, 240, 250; Belli Seminars, 243, 250; "The Adequate Award," 244, 270; Harvard Law School and, 247; *Modern Trials,* 250; New Orleans keys to the city given to, 251;

success of effort to uphold the common law, 264–266, 277–278; yacht, 264, 273; private administration, 270–271, 274–275; *Modern Damages,* 271, 274–275. *See also* Association of Trial Lawyers of America; Belli-Pound-NACCA relationship; National Association of Claimants' Counsel of America; Trial lawyers
Belli Building, 212
Belli-Pound-NACCA relationship, 9, 211, 212–217, 234, 246–254, 255–257, 259–263, 264, 266, 268, 277, 278, 280, 282–283; fight against encroachment of administration on the common law, 9, 214–217, 242, 246, 252–254, 254–262, 264–266, 277–278, 281–283; friendship of Belli and Pound, 211, 212–213, 248, 250; ATLA and, 214, 215–216, 234, 266, 277; NACCA benefits from Pound's prestige, 214, 249–252; Pound benefits from NACCA, 214, 247–249, 252, 253; Harvard Law School and, 249, 250, 251; Samuel Horovitz and, 249, 250, 251, 260; *Modern Trials* and, 250; suing tobacco companies and, 250; Pound birthday celebrations, 251–252, 260; Roscoe Pound–NACCA Foundation and, 251, 252; trial lawyers' associations and, 251; *Escola v. Coca-Cola Bottling Company,* 255; Pound shifts positions to accommodate NACCA, 255, 257; nationalist critique of administration by, 256–260, 277–278, 281–282; travel around the world in support of the common law by, 260; appropriating New Deal lan-

Belli-Pound-NACCA relationship
(*continued*)
guage, 261–262, 264; NACCA
successful in preserving the common law, 264–265, 373n94; economic regulation through the
courts, 265–266; private administration and, 266, 267–269, 275,
277; Roscoe Pound Papers, 277,
379n114
Belli Seminars, 243, 250
Bell Laboratories, 1
Benedict, Wallace, 170–171, 172,
184, 203
Bentham, Jeremy, 3
Berkeley. *See* University of California
at Berkeley
Berkeley, Bishop, 62
Berman, Nathaniel, 173–174
Bessey, Charles E., 218, 220, 221,
229, 234
Biddle, Charles John, 111
Bigelow, Herbert, 200
Bill of Rights, 4, 7, 109, 121, 122,
140, 144, 157, 159, 207, 218,
257, 262; Second Amendment,
121; Fourth Amendment, 121;
Fifth Amendment, 218. *See also*
First Amendment
Bingham, William, 30, 46, 76
Biology, 218, 221
Birth of a Nation, 87, 98, 142
Black, Charles, 144
Black, Hugo, 252
Black citizenship, 8, 86–87, 87–88,
99–100, 107, 109–110, 110–111,
111–114, 123, 126, 129, 134–
135, 141, 143
Black nationalism and nationhood,
101, 103, 105, 107–111, 114,
132–134, 139, 152–153; and
Book of Psalms, 105, 133, 139;

and Book of Romans, 133, 139,
153
Blackstone, William, 15, 28, 42, 45,
46, 49, 55–56, 57, 62, 74, 258;
Commentaries of, 49, 55
Blaine, James, 177
Blum, John, 193
Blyden, Edward Wilmot, 106, 108,
150
Bogusch, Ernst, 248
Bolshevik revolution. *See* Russian
Revolution
Boston Red Sox, 212
Botany, 218–219, 229, 230
Bourne, Randolph, 155
Bowditch, Nathaniel, 271
Boy Spies of America, 192
Bradley, Joseph P., 165
Bradwell, Myra, 165
Brandeis, Louis: Brandeis Brief, 228
Bratton, Rufus, 97, 115, 117, 118,
120, 128–129, 142, 144, 281,
314n20, 321n48
Brattonsville, 115
Brennan, William, 252
Brinkley, Alan, 215
Brooks, Preston, 97
Brown, Samuel G., 141
Brown v. Board of Education, 153
Brunswick, Georgia, 134
Bryan, William Jennings, 219
Bryant, Chester, 235–236, 361n40
Buckinghamshire, Second Earl of, 50
Burleson, Albert S., 191, 201
Butler, Pierce, 79

Cable Act, 345n47
Caldwell, Bob, 118
Calhoun, John, 96, 97, 144
California: Gold Rush country, 234;
Sonora, 234; products liability in,
237; Supreme Court of, 237, 245

California Law Review, 244
Cambridge, Massachusetts, 219, 248;
    Commander Hotel, 251
Campbell, Captain, 17–18
Canaan Company, 30–31
Canada, emigration to, 106, 128
Cape Mesurado, Liberia, 138,
    150
Capitalism, 208
Carnegie, Andrew, 176, 183; Carne-
    gie Endowment for International
    Peace, 176, 178, 188
Carroll, Milus S., 117–118
Carter, Jimmy, 278
Cary, Lott, 105
Catawba River, 85, 88
Cathcart, Andrew, 130–131, 138
Cather, Willa, 218, 229–231, 234,
    359n29
Catt, Carrie Chapman, 173
Central America, 106
Central American Court of Justice,
    178
Central American Peace Conference,
    178
Chafee, Zachariah, Jr., 204
Chamberlain, Daniel H., 121, 122,
    145
Chambers, Colonel, 17
Charfoos, Sam, 242
Charleston, South Carolina, 146;
    free blacks in, 93, 114, 146; attack
    on, 97
Charlotte, Columbia, and Augusta
    Rail Road, 86
Charlotte, North Carolina, 86, 88
Chase, Salmon P., 142
Cherokee (Indian tribe), 83
Chevrolet Corvair, 246
Chew, Benjamin, 42, 43
Chicago Juvenile Court, 227
Child Labor Act, 227–228

China lobby, 233
Chisholm v. Georgia, 73–75
Christianity, and black nationalism,
    105, 133, 139
Civil-law tradition of Continental
    Europe, 226–227. *See also* Admin-
    istration
Civil liberties, 157–158, 159, 160,
    193–194, 195–197, 199, 200,
    201–203, 204, 205, 206, 207,
    208, 259, 265, 266, 282, 283;
    American tradition of, 157–159,
    202; modern movement in Ameri-
    can law for, 157, 159, 160, 172,
    187, 206, 207, 208; moment of
    "creedal passion," 158–159; WWI
    and, 158–159, 193–203, 205–
    207. *See also* American Civil Lib-
    erties Union; American Union
    Against Militarism; Baldwin,
    Roger; Eastman, Crystal
Civil Liberties Bureau. *See* American
    Union Against Militarism
Civil Rights Act of 1866, 112
Civil Rights Act of 1964, 153
Civil War, 7, 8, 84, 86, 96, 102, 106,
    107, 110, 111, 134, 137, 143,
    150, 158, 161, 202, 221, 287n4
Clansman, The, 98, 142, 314n20
Clark, John Bates, 163–164
Clark, Tom, 252
Clay, Henry, 106
Clay Hill, 85, 88, 94, 113, 119, 127,
    128–131
Clay Hill congregation: and emigra-
    tion to Liberia, 85, 86–87, 88,
    104, 131–134, 135, 137–140,
    146–148, 149–150, 152, 153,
    155; relative prosperity of, 137–
    138; trip to Liberia, 138–139;
    mortality rate of, on passage to and
    in Liberia, 146–147; return of

Clay Hill congregation *(continued)*
members to U.S., 147. *See also*
Arthington
Clive, John, 23
Cobb, Frank, 190
Coca-Cola Company. See *Escola v.*
Coca-Cola Bottling Company
Coke, Sir Edward, 55, 56, 252, 258;
Institutes, 55
Cold War, 257, 350n70
Collectivism, 164, 214, 252
Columbia Law School, 165, 229
Columbia University, 163, 165
Columbus, Diego, 74
Commager, Henry Steele, 159
Committee on Public Information,
192
Common law. *See* American legal in-
stitutions; Belli-Pound-NACCA
relationship; Individualism
Commons, John, 225
Communism, 180, 206, 208, 233,
253, 257, 260. *See also* Council
Against Communist Aggression;
Marx, Karl; Socialism
Confederacy, the, 86, 89, 96, 97,
102, 117, 119, 121, 137, 145,
287n4, 314n20
Conference on international arbitra-
tion at Lake Mohonk, New York,
176
Congress, U.S., 182, 183, 185, 187,
190, 253, 254, 265
Conscription, 188, 190, 193, 202
Constitutional Convention, 8, 13,
16, 45, 47, 58–59, 60, 66, 67, 68,
69, 71, 76, 307n88
Constitutionalists, 16
Continental Congress, 5, 51, 65,
300n46
Convention of the Colored People of
the Southern States, 104

Corbin, Daniel T., 121, 122, 123,
144
Corcoran, Thomas, 228
Cornell University, 249
Corporation of the City of New
York, 1, 3
Cosmopolitanism, 155, 159, 160,
181, 187, 199, 207, 208, 209,
210, 218, 260, 279, 280, 283
Council Against Communist Aggres-
sion, 233
Councils of Safety, 116
Coxe, Tench, 62, 76
Creel, George, 192
Criminal law, 222
Cruikshank, U.S. v., 144
Crummell, Alexander, 106
Cuba, 178
Cuffe, Paul, 104–105
Currence, J. D., 135

Darnley, Fourth Earl of, 50
Darwin, 218, 220, 221
Davie, William, 75
Davies, Nelson, 135
Davis, Garrett, 110–111
Davis, Jefferson, 97, 115
Death penalty, 279
Debs, Eugene, 201
Decatur, Alabama, 134
Declaration of Independence of the
United States of America, 5, 15–
16, 39, 43, 45, 123, 283
Declaration of Sentiments, 161
Defense bar, 240–241, 245. *See also*
Insurance
Delany, Martin, 101, 106, 107, 108,
108–109, 114, 129, 133, 146
Democracy, 196, 202, 208, 209, 232,
278, 279
Democratic Party, 111, 114, 121,
125, 145, 219, 278

Department of Justice, 200
Dewey, John, 158, 179–180
Dickinson, John, 15, 24, 29, 43, 44, 55; *Letters from a Farmer,* 43
Discrimination, racial, 265, 283
Dixon, Thomas. See *Clansman, The*
Douglas, William O., 252
Douglass, Frederick, 103–104, 107, 114, 153
Draft. *See* Conscription
Dred Scott v. Sandford, 99–101, 106, 107, 110, 112, 116, 120, 123, 126, 316n23; response to, 100–101
Dyer, Benjamin, 26, 60

Eastman, Annis Ford, 161, 162, 163, 167, 170, 184
Eastman, Anstice, 161
Eastman, Crystal, 9, 160–170, 172, 189, 192, 203, 204, 208, 280, 281, 282; radical internationalism of, 155, 172–174, 180, 181–182, 183, 184, 185–186, 188, 193, 197, 207–208, 282, 345n49; American Union and, 160, 173, 192–193, 196–198, 200; Roger Baldwin and, 160, 196–199, 200; upbringing of, 160–162; woman's movement and, 161–162, 208; education of, 163–166; sociological law reform, 163–165, 166–170, 172, 208; Pittsburgh Survey and, 166–170, 198; workmen's compensation and, 167–170, 172, 198, 222; Wallace Benedict and, 170–171, 172, 184, 203; civil liberties and, 172, 195–196, 202, 206–208; rights skepticism of, 172, 195; Woman's Peace Party and, 173, 181, 183, 185–186;

Walter Fuller and, 184–185, 198, 203, 204; Woodrow Wilson and, 189, 193; health of, 197; Jeffrey Fuller and, 197–198; communism and, 208; women's suffrage movement and, 172, 199; feminism and, 208
Eastman, Max, 160–161, 162, 166, 169, 170–171, 172, 180, 189, 191, 197, 200
Eastman, Morgan, 197
Eastman, Samuel, 161, 162
Economic freedom. *See* New Deal
Economics, 163–164, 225, 227
Edinburgh, 23
Edith Rose, The, 86, 87, 138–139, 150
Edward II, laws of, 212
Edwards, Jonathan, 54, 65
Egypt: popularity of, in eighteenth century, 50, 51; courts of, 61; as source of African nationalism, 103. *See also* Psalms, Book of; Pyramids; Romans, Book of
Eisenhower, Dwight D., 233
Eleventh Amendment to U.S. Constitution, 75
Ellicott, Andrew, 67
Ellsworth, Olliver, 64
Elmira. *See* New York
Ely, Richard, 225, 227
Emancipation, 131, 135, 136
Emergency Peace Federation, 173
Employers' liability. *See* Tort law; Workmen's compensation
Enforcement Act, 141
Enlightenment, the, 53, 55, 62, 65, 71. *See also* Scottish Enlightenment
Equality of results, 225
Escola, Gladys, 237, 238

Escola v. Coca-Cola Bottling Company, 237–238, 245–246, 255

Espionage Act, 190–191, 201

Fairfield County, South Carolina, 314n20

Federal Code of Civil Procedure of 1938, 228

Federalist Papers, The, 20, 37, 66, 67, 68, 69, 70

Federal Trade Commission Act, 222

Fellowship of Reconciliation, 173

Feminism, 208. *See also* Woman's movement

Fernando Po, native labor trade in, 149

Field, Stephen, 144

Fifteenth Amendment to U.S. Constitution. *See* Reconstruction Amendments

Firestone Rubber Company, 149

First Amendment, 207; limitations on freedom of speech, 157, 158, 159, 190; freedom of assembly, 159, 190, 194, 195; freedom of petition, 159; freedom of the press, 159, 195, 196; freedom of speech, 190, 193–194, 195, 196. *See also* Bill of Rights

Foner, Eric, 127

Ford, Henry, 268

Fort Sumter, 86, 96

Fort Wilson, attack on, 17–18, 19, 20, 21, 38, 39, 44–45

Fosdick, Raymond, 158

Four Lights, 185–186

Four Minute Men, 192

Fourteenth Amendment to U.S. Constitution. *See* Reconstruction Amendments

France, 4, 50, 168, 202, 289n10; alliance with U.S., 50; jurists of, 226,

256–257. *See also* French Revolution

France, Joseph I., 196

Frankfurter, Felix, 102, 204, 228, 235, 252

Freed blacks: population of, in South Carolina, 89–90, 93–94, 282, 312n7, 313n13; South Carolina laws discriminating against, 90–91, 94–96, 113, 132–133

Freedman's Emigrant Aid Society, 134

Freedom Ride, 86

Freeman, M. H., 108

French Revolution, 19

Fugitive Slave Act, 101, 106

Fuller, Jeffrey, 197, 198

Fuller, Walter, 184–185, 194, 198, 203, 204

Fundamental Constitutions of Carolina, 25

Galloway, Joseph, 42

"Game, The," 248

Garnet, Henry Highland, 106

Garrison, William Lloyd, 83, 102

Garvey, Marcus, 151

George III, King, 39

Georgia Land Company, The, 30–31, 73

German school of historical economics, 163

Germany, 4, 163, 187, 201, 203. *See also* Nazi Germany

Gerry, Elbridge, 39, 47

Gibbon, Edward: *History of the Decline and Fall of the Roman Empire,* 31

Gibson, Mel: *The Patriot,* 115

Giddings, Franklin Henry, 163, 164–165, 167, 168, 169, 174, 204

Gilmore, Grant, 60

Ginn, Edward, 176
Glenora, New York. *See* New York
Goebel, Julius, 28
Goodell, William, 102
Grand Cape Mount, 138
Grand Rapids Press, 200
Grant, Ulysses S., 119–120, 141–142, 145, 329n93
Gratner, Abraham, 267
Gratz, Simon, 78
Gray, Hannah. *See* Wilson, Hannah
Gray, John Chipman, 219
Graydon, Alexander, 43
Great Chicago Fire, 136
Great Depression, 150, 151
Great Dismal Swamp Company, 30–31, 77
Great Migration, 150–153
Greaves, John, 52–54, 62, 81; *Pyramidographia,* 53, 62
Greece: ancient, 51, 52, 74; independence movement of, 108
Greener, Richard T., 152
Greenleaf, Simon, 319n38
Gregory, Thomas, 191, 201
Griffith, D. W. See *Birth of a Nation*
Griswold, Erwin, 249

Habeas corpus, 260, 281
Hague Conferences (of 1899 and 1907), 174–175, 177, 178, 182
Hague Protocol, 259
Hahn, Steven, 87, 152
Haiti, 106–107, 110–111; emigration to, 87, 105, 107, 108, 114; as symbol of black nationalism, 103, 107–108, 111
Hamilton, Alexander, 8, 21, 37, 64, 65–66, 68–69
Hamilton, Andrew, 29
Hammer v. Dagenhart, 227–228

Hammond, James Henry, 96, 97, 98, 102, 132
Hampton, Wade, III, 121, 145
Hand, Learned, 191, 228, 235
Hard, William, 227
Hartz, Louis, 5–6, 282; *The Liberal Tradition in America,* 5–6
Harvard College, 198
Harvard Law School, 204, 211, 212, 219, 227, 228, 229, 231, 241, 247, 249, 250, 251, 379n114; Langdell Hall, 249
Harvard University, 230, 249; Harvard-Yale football game, 248
Hayes, Rutherford B., 145
Hayne, Robert Y., 96
Haytien Emigration Society of Philadelphia, 105
Hemingway, Ernest, 158
Henkin, Louis, 186
Henry VIII, 212
Hensley Resolution, 182
Herodotus, 81
Hervey, James, 50
Hill, Andrew, 90
Hill, Daniel Harvey, 89, 91, 92–93
Hill, Dorcas. *See* Hill, Elias
Hill, Easter, 124, 324n65
Hill, Elias, 8, 155, 280, 281; as preacher, 85, 86, 113; status as freed slave, 85, 89, 90–91, 95, 100; disability of, 85–86, 91; as teacher, 86, 113, 320n43; birth of, 89; mother of, 89–91, 93, 95; family background of, 90, 132, 133; father of, 90, 91, 132, 133, 139; voice of, 113, 125; Union League and, 113, 124, 128; congressional testimony of, 124–126; attack on, by Ku Klux Klan, 124–126; and decision to emigrate to Liberia, 129–131, 131–132, 134;

Hill, Elias (*continued*)
    death of, 146–147; on conditions
    in Liberia, 147–148. *See also* Hill,
    Easter; Hill, Madison; Hill, Solo-
    mon (nephew); Johnson, Francis;
    Moore, June; Simpson, Thomas
Hill, Madison, 124, 147
Hill, Solomon (Elias's nephew), 129,
    130, 140, 149–150, 151, 154
Hill, Solomon (slaveholder), 89
Hill, William D., 89, 90
Hill & Moore, 149
Hillhouse, William, 50–51
Hillquit, Morris, 166
Hirschman, Albert O., 88, 102,
    153
Hitler, Adolf, 231, 256
Hobbes, Thomas, 34
Hofstadter, Richard, 233
Hohfeld, Wesley, 195
Hollingsworth v. Virginia, 73
Holmes, John Haynes, 193, 207
Holmes, Oliver Wendell, 157, 258
Honig, Bonnie, 209
Hopkinson, Francis, 43, 51
Hopper, Isaac, 78
Horovitz, Samuel, 241–242, 247,
    248–249, 249–250, 251, 260
Howe, General, 42
Howe, Mark DeWolfe, 249
Hughes, Charles Evans, 169
Hull, N. E. H., 230
Hull House, 227
Human rights, 188–189, 199,
    208
Hume, David, 23, 31, 32, 49, 62,
    68–69, 70, 304n67, 306n80
Huntington, Samuel, 158
Hutcheson, Francis, 23, 24, 31, 32–
    35, 36, 37, 47, 49, 56, 57, 67,
    68, 74
Hutchinson, Thomas, 27–28

Illinois, 165
Illinois-Wabash Land Company,
    30, 76
Immigration, in national tradition,
    83
Indiana (state), 87
Indiana Company, 30–31, 73
Indians, 40, 76; treatment of, as
    compared to treatment of blacks,
    94, 107
Individualism, of the common law,
    214, 217, 224, 255. *See also* Nine-
    teenth-century liberalism
Industrial accidents, 166–168, 169–
    170. *See also* Pittsburgh Survey;
    Workmen's compensation
Industrial Workers of the World,
    159, 201, 206
Ingersoll, Charles Jared, 44
Ingersoll, Jared, 42
Insurance, 168–169, 170, 172, 213,
    215, 221, 231, 238, 240–241,
    254–255, 262, 265, 267, 270,
    271, 274
Insurance Counsel Journal, 245
Interest groups, 209, 234, 242, 266,
    278
International Congress of Chambers
    of Commerce, 183
International Court of Justice, 280
International Criminal Court, 280
Internationalism, 155, 159–160,
    172–189, 192–194, 195–197,
    199, 200–208, 256, 260, 279,
    280, 282, 345n49; radical interna-
    tionalism, 155, 172–174, 179–
    188, 193, 197, 203, 204, 205,
    206, 207–208, 282, 345n49; in-
    ternational law and, 159, 174–
    176, 178, 181, 188; cosmopoli-
    tanism and, 160; Eastman's con-
    nection to the modern civil liber-

ties movement and, 160; movement for women's suffrage and, 172, 199; movement against the war and, 173–174, 186, 193, 194, 196, 206, 281; globalization, 174; technology and, 174; treaties and organizations, 174–175, 182; Hague Conferences of 1899 and 1907 and, 174–175, 177, 178, 182; American form of, 175–177, 182, 193, 203; Association for the Reform and Codification of the Law of Nations, 175; European form of, 175–176, 182, 199, 203; Institut de Droit International, 175; *l'esprit d'internationalité* and, 175, 177, 183; Permanent Court of Arbitration and International Prize Court and, 175, 177, 182; *Revue de droit international et de législation comparée* and, 175; American Society for International Law and, 176, 178, 179; associations and conferences on, 176; Carnegie Endowment for International Peace and, 176, 178, 188; orthodox type of, 178–179, 183; Christian-pacifist type of, 180; cosmopolitan democracy and, 181; WWI and, 187, 192–196, 197, 200–206, 207, 208; civil liberties and, 193–194, 195–196; decline of, 200–203, 204–205; socialism and, 201; women's branch of internationalist movement and, 203; Anglo-American Tradition of Liberty Conference, 203–205; human rights norms and, 208. *See also* Baldwin, Roger; Eastman, Crystal; National Civil Liberties Bureau; Root, Elihu; Wilson, Woodrow; Woman's Peace Party

International Prize Court, 175
International Telegraphic Union, 183
Interstate Commerce Act, 221
Interstate Commerce Commission, 221
Iredell, James, 41, 80
Israel. *See* Romans, Book of

Jackson, Robert, 281
Jackson Square, 212
James, Fleming, 252
Japanese internment camps, 83
Jay, John, 72, 76
Jefferson, Thomas, 42, 43–44, 50, 62, 80, 154, 158
Jews, 241
Jim Crow, 152
John Birch Society, 233
Johnson, Andrew, 112, 121
Johnson, Francis, 147
Johnson, Lyndon B., 265, 278
Johnson, Reverdy, 120–121, 121–122, 123, 126
Johnson, Samuel: *Rasselas, Prince of Abbisinia,* 50, 80–81
Joint Select Committee for investigating the Ku Klux Klan, 120, 128, 129, 135; testimony of black witnesses before subcommittee of, 123–126
Julien, Al, 243–244
Juvenile justice, 198, 222, 227

Kames, Lord, 33, 56, 67
Kansas (state), 87, 151
Kellogg, Paul, 166–167, 173, 183, 187, 199–200, 227
Kempe, John Tabor, 29, 43
King, James, 50
Knights of Liberty, 192

Ku Klux Klan, 127, 134, 144, 145, 281, 314n20, 321n48; in York County, 115–119, 123, 124–126, 128–131, 314n20; raids by, 116–119, 124–126, 134; attack on Jim Williams, 117–119, 128, 129, 142; attack on Elias Hill, 124–126; flight by members, 128; "pukes," 128; clemency for members, 141–142, 145, 329n93. *See also* Ku Klux Klan trials
Ku Klux Klan Act, 120, 121, 122, 128
Ku Klux Klan trials, 87, 90, 120–124, 126–127, 140, 141, 144, 145, 313n13, 329n93; testimony from black witnesses in, 126, 127; convictions resulting from, 126–127; legal grounds for prosecutions, 140–141; courts overwhelmed by volume of, 141; clemency given by Grant, 141–142, 145, 329n93
Kunstler, William, 229–231
Kyoto Protocols, 280

Labor movement, 265
Labor unions, 158, 176, 206, 207, 232–233
Laissez-faire, 158
Lambert, Thomas, 248
Lancaster County, South Carolina, 133
Landis, James, 228
Langdon-Davies, B. N., 204
Larsen, Arthur, 249
Law-and-society, 10–11
Lawyers (in eighteenth-century U.S.): status of, in American colonies and early U.S., 18–19, 24–25; Anglicizing tendencies of, 19, 27–28, 29; response to Revolution of, 19,

42; role of, in American constitutional mechanics, 21–22, 60, 61, 70, 82; wealth of, in colonies, 29; popular distrust of, 40–41; allegiances of, 41–42; success of, following Revolution, 45; political representation of, 45; League of Nations and, 149, 158, 160, 203, 205
Lee, Henry, 77
Lee, Robert E., 89, 97, 137
Legal Realists, 195, 228, 229, 230
Leslie, Robert, 62
L'esprit d'internationalité, 175, 177, 183
Lewis, John L., 86
Lewis, William, 43
Liberia: emigration to, 84, 85, 86–87, 88, 104–106, 106–108, 131–139, 140, 146–147, 151, 152, 153, 328n88; constitution of, 108–110, 154, 319n38; as independent nation-state, 108–109, 110, 111, 132, 134, 139, 153; Declaration of Independence of, 109, 153–154; American diplomacy with, 110–111, 150; social, political, and economic conditions in, 131–132, 147–150, 153–154, 332n104, 333n108; economic obstacles to emigration to, 136; opposition to emigration to, 136–137; rate of emigration to, 137; misinformation regarding, 146, 147, 332n104; exploitation of natives in, 148–150. *See also* Black nationalism and nationhood
Liberian Exodus Joint Steam Ship Company, 146
Liberty Boys, 41
Liberty League, 192
Life, 211

Limited liability. *See* Administration
Lincoln, Abraham, 96, 100, 110,
    142, 158, 161, 262, 281
Llewellyn, Karl, 229
Locke, John, 5, 25, 32, 179
Logan, James, 39–40
Louisiana, 143, 321n45
Louisiana State University, 249
Loyalists, 16, 42–43, 45, 299n41
Lusk Committee Raids, 201
Lycurgus, 45
Lynching, 158, 192. *See also* Ku Klux
    Klan

Machiavelli, 31
Machine, metaphor of, 21, 61–67,
    69, 70, 82, 305n78
Madison, James, 16, 20, 21, 22, 48,
    62, 65–70, 73, 74, 82, 106, 159,
    180, 209, 214, 222, 281, 305n78,
    306n80
Maires, Samuel Evans, 267
Malone, Wex, 249
Malthus, Thomas Robert, 163
Mandeville, Bernard de, 34
Manhattan Project, 1
Mansfield, Lord, 42, 43, 45, 258
Manumission of slaves, South
    Carolina laws impeding, 91, 94,
    95–96, 132–133
Marbury v. Madison, 74
Market Street Railway Company,
    235–236
Marshall, John (Chief Justice of U.S.
    Supreme Court), 74, 106, 154,
    258
Marshall, John (Liberian politician),
    154
Marshall, Thurgood, 265
Marx, Karl, 232, 256, 262
Marx, Leo, 63
Mason, George, 47–48

Mason, Scott, 133–134
Massachusetts Federation of Labor,
    241
Masses, The, 191, 200
Mays, Willie, 237
McAdoo, William, 192
McAfee, Leroy, 314n20
McCloskey, Robert, 72, 265
Mecklenburg County, North
    Carolina, 320n43
Merrill, Lewis, 119–120, 124,
    329n93
Militarism, 174, 181, 182, 185, 189,
    193, 194, 206, 345n49
Miller, Samuel, 142–144
Milwaukee, 171, 172
Milwaukee Leader, 191
Mississippi (state), 321n45
Missouri Compromise, 99
Mobile, Alabama, 134
Modern Damages, 271, 274–275
Modern Trials, 250, 262, 263
Monrovia, Liberia, 139, 147, 148,
    150, 151
Moore, June, 85, 124, 128, 129, 130,
    131, 135, 137, 140, 147, 149,
    150, 154, 333n107
Moore, Wallace, 149
Morris, Gouverneur, 16, 39
Morris, Richard, 19, 45
Morris, Robert, 16, 30, 43, 77
Moses, Wilson Jeremiah, 105
Mullins Depot, South Carolina,
    135
Murrin, John, 19, 27, 45

NACCA. *See* National Association of
    Claimants' Counsel of America
NACCA Law Journal, 244, 247, 248,
    249, 270
Nader, Ralph, 246
Napoleonic wars, 174

Nation, 191
National Association for the Advancement of Colored People, 199; Legal Defense and Education Fund, 265
National Association of Claimants' Compensation Attorneys. *See* National Association of Claimants' Counsel of America
National Association of Claimants' Counsel of America, 214, 240–244, 245–247, 248, 249–252, 253–254, 255–256, 257, 259–260, 261–262, 263, 264–265, 266–267, 268, 270, 271, 278, 379n114; Houston convention, 243, 247, 255; *NACCA Law Journal,* 244, 247, 248, 249, 270. *See also* Association of Trial Lawyers of America; Belli, Melvin Mouron; Belli-Pound-NACCA relationship; Private administration; Trial lawyers
National Civil Liberties Bureau, 201–202, 203–204, 205, 206
National Council for Civil Liberties, 194, 203–204, 205
National defense, 280
Nationalism, 2–12, 155, 160, 180, 181, 185, 189, 193, 201, 202, 203, 204, 205, 207, 257, 279, 281, 283; in WWI, 187–188, 190, 191–194, 199–200; legislation, 190–191; American, 209, 215, 256–259, 277–278; pan-African, 209. *See also* Belli-Pound-NACCA relationship, nationalist critique of administration by; Black nationalism and nationhood
National Labor Relations Act, 275–276
National Labor Relations Board v.

Jones & Laughlin Steel Corporation, 275–276, 277
National Liberty League, 192
National Peace Congress, 176
National Probation Officers' Association, 198
National Security League, 192
Nationhood, 2–12, 279–284; definition of, 7
Natural rights, 158, 164
Natural truths, 226
Naval Appropriation Act of 1916, 182
Nazi Germany, 231. *See also* Hitler, Adolf
Nebraska, 217; courts, 217; Lincoln, 217, 218, 219, 227, 234; Lincoln Bar Association, 217; state constitutional convention, 217–218; University of, 218–219, 219–220, 223, 229, 230, 234, 359n29
Nebraska Botanical Survey, 219
Newberry County, South Carolina, 119
New Deal, 213, 214, 215–216, 228, 231–233, 256, 257, 260–262, 264, 265, 266, 276, 277, 278, 281–282; Four Freedoms, 261–262. *See also* Administration
New Orleans, 251
Newton, Isaac, 53, 62, 63, 64, 65, 66, 305n78
New York: work accidents in, 169–170, 171; National Peace Congress in, 176; state employers' liability commission, 197; Crystal Eastman in, 199
New York Herald, 173
New York Peace Society, 176; associations similar to, 176
New York Times, 173
New York Tribune, 200

New York University School of Law, 165

New York World, 190, 191

Nicholas II, Czar, 175

Nineteenth Amendment, 345n47

Nineteenth-century liberalism, 162, 163, 164–165, 167, 168, 170, 195, 202, 206, 207, 262; institutions of nineteenth-century law and, 172, 198

Nineteenth-century woman's movement, 161–162, 184. *See also* Eastman, Crystal

Nobel Peace Prize for 1912, 178

No-fault compensation systems. *See* Administration

North Carolina Regulators, 41

Northwestern University Law School, 224, 227

Oberlin College, 161

O'Neall, John Belton, 99

Oklahoma (state), 87

Osgood, Samuel, 65

Oswald, Lee Harvey, 212

Paine, Thomas, 16

Palmer Raids, 201

Parisian Order of Barristers, 19

Paris Peace Conference, 203, 205

Park Church, Elmira, New York, 161

Parker, Enoch, 134–135

Parker, Reginald, 249

Partlow, J. B., 126

Patriots. *See* Nationalism

Paxton Boys, 40

Peace movement, 173. *See also* Internationalism

Peale, Charles Wilson, 17

Peal's of London, 236

Penn, William, 26

Pennsylvania. *See* Pittsburgh Survey

Pennsylvania Executive Council, 17, 20

Pennsylvania militia, anger toward rich Philadelphians, 15, 16. *See also* Fort Wilson

Pennsylvania ratifying convention, 48, 58, 59, 60, 71

Pennsylvania Society for Promoting the Abolition of Slavery, 65

Pennsylvania state constitution: Constitution of 1776, 16, 43, 65, 68; 1790 convention for a new state constitution, 48, 58, 71

People's Council, 173

Permanent Court of Arbitration, 175, 177, 182. *See also* Hague Conferences

Personal injury law. *See* Belli, Melvin Mouron; Belli-Pound-NACCA relationship; National Association of Claimants' Counsel of America; Tort law; Trial Lawyers; Workmen's compensation

Pettit, Charles, 63

Philadelphia: bar association of, 17, 24, 44, 45, 62; demographic change in, prior to Revolution, 40

Philadelphia, College of, 15, 24, 28

Philippines, 178

Piedmont (South Carolina region), 85, 86, 113, 145; free blacks in, 93–96, 282, 313n13; commitment to slavery in, 96–97; Ku Klux Klan in, 115–119, 124–126; flight of whites from, 127–128; voter intimidation in, 145; number of Confederate soldiers from, 314n20. *See also* Upcountry; York County

Pierce, William, 48

Piranesi, Giovanni Battista, 50; *Piramide di C. Cestio,* 52

Pittsburgh Survey, of industrial accidents, 166–167, 169–170, 198
Plaintiffs' bar. *See* Trial lawyers
Pliny, 81
Pocock, J. G. A., 21, 32, 58, 82
Policeman's Ball, 212
Polybius, 31
Ponsonby, Arthur, 204
Pound, Grace, 229, 247
Pound, Laura Biddlecome, 218, 226
Pound, Louise, 218, 247, 248
Pound, Lucy, 247, 248
Pound, Roscoe, 9, 29, 42, 204, 211, 212, 235, 238, 239, 280, 282–283; Dean of Harvard Law School, 211, 229, 231, 247, 248; Harvard Law School faculty and, 211, 227, 247, 249, 250; sociological jurisprudence and, 211, 220–221, 222–227, 255, 257, 261, 262, 273; American Bar Association and, 212; education of, 212, 218–219, 226; Policeman's Ball, 212; upbringing, 217–218; botany and, 218–219, 229, 230; practice of law by, 219; *Social Control through Law,* 220; sociology and, 220–221, 222; rise of administrative law and, 221; 1906 American Bar Association (ABA) address by, 223–224, 225, 227, 228, 230, 232, 239, 254; conservative turn of, 228–231, 232–234, 255, 256, 257, 261, 262; legal realists and, 228, 229, 230; family life of, 229, 247, 248, 249; psychological insight into, 230–231, 233, 359n29; Hitler and, 231, 256; New Deal and, 231–233; home of, 248, 251; Samuel Horovitz and, 248–249, 249–250, 251. *See also* Belli-Pound-NACCA relationship

Pound, Olivia, 218, 247, 249
Pound, Stephen B., 217–218, 219, 221, 230, 267
Pragmatism, 157, 159, 160, 180, 187, 195, 229
Price, Richard, 65
Princeton University, 188
Principles of Sociology, The, 220
Privacy, 279
Private administration, 215, 217, 266–275, 277, 278, 377n104
Products liability. *See* Tort law
Progressivism, 164, 172, 225, 227, 228, 230, 233, 265, 220
Prohibition, 234
Psalms, Book of, 105, 133, 139
Puerto Rico, 178
Pulaski County, Georgia, 134
Pure Food and Drug Act, 222
Push for increased damages and liability, 212, 237–240, 242–243, 244–246, 261, 263–264
Pyramids: metaphor of, 21, 47–51, 54–55, 57–60, 61, 63, 67–68, 69, 80–81, 82, 280–281; as means of synchronizing history, 51; as means of synchronizing measurements, 51–52; relation to Egyptian philosophy of, 54; relation to the common law of, 55, 57; as symbols of corruption, 81, 310n103; as symbols of African pride, 103, 105

Radical internationalism, 155, 172–174, 179–188, 193, 197, 203, 204, 205, 206, 207–208, 282, 345n49. *See also* Internationalism
Railroads, 219, 221, 253, 267
Randolph, Edmund, 71–72
Rawle, Francis, 72
Rawle, William, 43

Reaves, S., 135
Reconstruction, 7, 84, 86, 88, 89, 112–114, 116, 117, 138, 282; white response to, in South Carolina, 114–116, 119; end of, 144–146. *See also* Ku Klux Klan; Ku Klux Klan trials; Reconstruction Amendments
Reconstruction Amendments, 87, 112–113, 114, 119, 121–123, 140–141, 142–145; white response to, in South Carolina, 114, 116
Redpath, James, 114
Red Shirts, 145
Reed, Joseph, 17, 20, 42, 44
Reese, U.S. v., 144
Reform, 215, 228, 229, 256, 260, 265; reform-minded New York lawyers, 166; Chicago, 227
Reid, Thomas, 23, 34, 49, 74, 301n51
Republican National Committee, 232
Republican Party, 16, 111, 112, 114, 116, 117, 118, 119, 121, 125, 129, 131, 136, 142, 232, 233, 278
Republican Society, 16
Revolutionary War, 73, 89
Revue de droit international et de législation comparée, 175
Ricardo, David, 163
Riesenfeld, Stefan A., 249
Rights, 157–8, 159, 160, 163, 164, 167, 168, 169, 172, 186, 187, 189–190, 195, 196, 198, 206, 207, 225; of contract and liberty, employers' property rights, 170; negative and positive, 227; social, 232, 233. *See also* Bill of Rights; Sociological jurisprudence

Rights skeptics, 157, 172, 195
Rittenhouse, David, 62, 63
Roberts, Joseph Jenkins, 139, 147–148, 150
Rockefeller Center, 243
Rock Hill, South Carolina, 85, 86, 88, 119, 138, 145–146, 321n48
Rodgers, Daniel, 213
Roman law, 23
Romans, Book of, 133, 139, 153
Rome, ancient, 48–49, 51, 52
Roosevelt, Franklin Delano, 215, 228, 231–233, 233–234, 261, 262, 264, 265, 278, 281–282
Roosevelt, Theodore, 178, 192, 200–201
Root, Elihu, 178–179, 187–188, 189, 201
Roscoe Pound–NACCA Foundation, 251, 252
Roscoe Pound Papers, 277, 379n114
Rose Hotel, 115, 117, 120, 124
Ross, Edward Alsworth, 220–221, 223, 225, 227, 229, 234, 265; *The Principles of Sociology,* 220
Ross, H. Laurence, 269
Ross, John, 42
Roundtree, Tom, 116–117
Royal Academy, 50
Roye, James, 147–148, 150
Ruby, Jack, 212
Rule of law, 233, 252, 257–258. *See also* Belli-Pound-NACCA relationship: nationalist critique of administration by
Rule of thirds, 270
Rush, Benjamin, 16, 62, 76, 80
Rush, Jacob, 80
Russia, 173, 201, 208; Moscow, 257
Russian Revolution, 19, 201
Rutledge, John, 72

St. Andrews, University of, 15, 22, 23, 26
St. Clair, Andrew, 44
St. Paul's River, 139, 149, 150
San Francisco, 212, 256; Giants, 237
Sardis Baptist Church. *See* Clay Hill congregation
Saulsbury, Willard, 111
Scalia, Antonin, 279, 283
Scotland, legal system of, 23
Scott, Robert, 117, 128
Scottish emigration, "great flood" of, 24
Scottish Enlightenment, 20, 23, 31, 32–33, 57, 66, 209
Seamen, 253
Second Reconstruction, 152
Selma, Alabama, 134
Seneca Falls Convention, 161, 162
Shalev, Zur, 51
Shamrock Hotel, 243
Shays's Rebellion, 44
Shelley, Mary: *Frankenstein*, 65
Sherman, William Tecumseh, 97, 117, 119
Sierra Leone, 104–105
Silver Bullet Tour, 241
Simpson, Thomas, 90, 113, 147
Sindell, Joseph, 272
Sindell & Sindell, 270, 272
Sindell Formula, 270, 272
Skipwith, Robert, 80
Skowronek, Stephen, 276
Slaughterhouse Cases, 142–144
Slavery, 183; as part of constitutional scheme, 98–99
Slave trade: continuing in South Carolina after prohibition on, 90, 132, 326n79; as link between South Carolina and West Africa, 132
Smith, Adam, 23, 31, 32, 33, 35–36,

37, 62, 63; *Theory of Moral Sentiments,* 32, 33; *The Wealth of Nations,* 35
Smith, William, 24, 39
Social Control through Law, 220
Socialism, 163, 164, 166, 180, 201, 205, 206, 207–208, 231, 232, 252, 256, 257
Social sciences, 164, 220; statistics in, 164–165, 167, 169. *See also* Sociology
Social Security, 215, 261; Act of 1935, 231
Social welfare, 210, 213–214; through private entities, 213–215. *See also* Administration; Private administration
Sociological jurisprudence, 211, 220–221, 222–228, 255, 261, 262, 273. *See also* Pound, Roscoe
Sociological law reform, 164–165, 167–170, 171, 172, 198, 208, 263
Sociology, 163, 164–165, 167, 198, 220–221, 222, 224–225, 227, 261; social-utilitarian theory of justice, 225. *See also* Sociological jurisprudence; Sociological law reform
Socrates, 248
Solon, 45
South America, 106
South Carolina: colonial legal education in, 28–29; social, political, and economic conditions in, 96, 113, 321n45; black political representation in, 113–114; flight of whites from, 127–128
South Carolina General Assembly, 94–95
Spanish-American War, 178
Spartanburg County, South Carolina, 119

Speiser, Stuart, 259–260, 275
Stalin, 258–259
Stamp Act, 39, 40, 41, 42
Stanbery, Henry, 120, 121, 122
Stanford University, 220
State Department, 233
Steele, Max, 141–142
Stevens, John, 63–64, 65–66, 66, 67
Stowe, Harriet Beecher, 161, 162
Stuart monarchs, 252
Stuckey, Sterling, 132
Sumner, Charles, 97, 111

Takings Clause. *See* Bill of Rights:
    Fifth Amendment
Taney, Roger B., 100, 101, 107, 123,
    126, 316n23
Taylor, Frederick Winslow, 268
Telegraph Hill, 212
Temple, William, 49
Texas (state), 87, 267, 268–269
Thayer, Ezra, 227
Thayer, James Bradley, 219
Thirteenth Amendment to U.S.
    Constitution. *See* Reconstruction
    Amendments
Thomas, Joseph, 79–80
Thomas, Norman, 180, 187, 195,
    201, 205
Thompson, John, 99
"Three times three" rule, 270
Thurmond, Strom, 97
Tidewater Belt (region of South
    Carolina), 86, 93
Tilghman, Edward, 43
Tilghman, William, 26, 42–43
Tillman, "Pitchfork" Ben, 97
Titian, 50
Tocqueville, Alexis de, 222, 224
Tories, 16, 41–42, 43, 75
Tort law, 214, 215, 222, 237, 242,
    253, 254, 255, 258, 264, 266,
267, 269; employers' liability and,
    167–170, 267; lawyers shaping
    personal injury law, 212, 237,
    238–240, 242–243, 245; negli-
    gence in, 237–238; products liabil-
    ity in, 237–239, 245; *res ipsa
    loquitor,* 237; best cost avoider in,
    238; loss spreading in, 238; strict
    liability in, 238; tobacco compa-
    nies and, 240, 250; increased dam-
    ages awards and liberalized tort lia-
    bility, 245–246, 263; landowners
    in, 245, 246; medical malpractice
    in, 245, 246; auto manufacturers
    in, 246; consumer rights' advocates
    in, 246; emotional injury in, 246;
    automobile accidents in, 254, 269,
    271–272, 273; settlement and,
    268–275, 277, 377n104; adminis-
    trative costs in, 273–274. *See also*
    Association of Trial Lawyers of
    America; Belli, Melvin Mouron;
    Belli-Pound-NACCA relationship;
    National Association of Claimants'
    Counsel of America; Private ad-
    ministration; Trial lawyers; Work-
    men's compensation
Torture, 3, 280, 283
Totalitarianism, 252, 253
Trading with the Enemy Act, 191
Traynor, Roger, 237–238, 255
Treaty of Versailles, 203
Trelease, Allen, 115, 116
Trescot, Henry William, 98–99
Trial lawyers, 209–210, 211–212,
    215, 234, 235–237, 239, 241–
    242, 250, 252–253, 255, 256,
    259, 260, 261, 262, 263–264,
    265–266, 267, 271, 277–278;
    push for increased damages and li-
    ability, 212, 237–240, 242–243,
    244–245, 261, 263–264; contin-

Trial lawyers *(continued)*
gency fee, 238–239, 240, 264, 273–274; organizations of, 251, 262; success of, 264–266, 277–278; ambulance chasing and, 267. *See also* Association of Trial Lawyers of America; Belli, Melvin Mouron; Belli-Pound-NACCA relationship; National Association of Claimants' Counsel of America; Private administration; Tort law
Triangle Shirt-Waist fire, 171, 172
Turner, Henry McNeal, 114
Twain, Mark, 161, 162

Ulrika, Louisa, 50
Uncle Tom's Cabin, 161
Union army, 89, 97, 114, 117, 119
Union County, South Carolina, 119, 128–129, 135
Union for Democratic Control, 173, 204
Union League, 113, 114, 124, 128
United Nations, 199, 280
United States Court of Appeals, 235
United States Supreme Court, 5, 8, 16, 22, 41, 46, 73–75, 78, 99–101, 101–102, 120, 123, 128, 142–145, 157, 159, 165, 185, 204, 211, 228, 251–252, 265, 275–276, 277, 279, 280, 283
Universal History, 53
Universal Negro Improvement Association, 151
Universal Postal Union, 174, 183
University of Arkansas, 249
University of California at Berkeley, 235; School of Jurisprudence, 235, 237
University of Chicago, 227

University of Minnesota, 249
University of Minnesota Law School, 188
University of Pennsylvania, 48
Unsafe at Any Speed, 246
Upcountry (South Carolina region), 85, 87, 89, 97, 112, 115, 117, 132, 282; free blacks in, 93–96, 313n13; social, political, and economic conditions in, 96, 98–99, 125, 145; emigration from, 97, 133, 135; Ku Klux Klan in, 115–119, 121, 124–126; during the Revolution, 115; flight of whites from, 127–128; voter intimidation in, 145. *See also* Ku Klux Klan trials; Piedmont; York County

Vance, William R., 188
Van Trump, Philadelph, 125–126
Vassar College, 163, 169
Vietnam War, 278
Voltaire, 81
Voting Rights Act, 153

Wagner Act, 232–233, 276
Wainwright Commission, 169–170
Wald, Lillian D., 173, 174, 182, 183, 184, 198, 199–200, 201
Wallace, Alexander, 125, 131
Wallace, John, 135
Wall Street Journal, 212
Ward, Lester, 225
War Department, 200
Warren, Charles, 27, 28
Warsaw Convention, 259–260, 265, 373n94
Washington, Bushrod, 105, 143
Washington, George, 16, 46, 51, 71, 76, 77, 105
Washington Monument, 258
Washington Post, 236

Washington University, St. Louis, 198
Webster, Daniel, 96, 258
Wedgwood, Josiah, 50
Wells, H. G., 67
Westbeth Building, 1
White House, 204
Wigmore, John Henry, 224, 227, 229
Williams, George H., 141
Williams, Jim, 117–119, 124–125, 128, 129, 142
Wills, Gary, 63
Wilson, Bird, 79
Wilson, Hannah, 72, 79, 80
Wilson, James (U.S. congressman), 112
Wilson, James (U.S. Supreme Court Justice), 105, 209, 222, 226, 279, 280–281, 282; Constitutional Convention and, 8, 16, 47, 58–59, 60, 68, 71, 76, 307n88; as target of Pennsylvania militia, 15, 16; upbringing and education, 15, 22–23, 55–56; Declaration of Independence and, 15–16; shadowy business dealings of, 16, 308n95; attitude toward Revolution, 16, 44–45, 45–46; and Republican Society, 16; Philadelphia Tories and, 16; career on Supreme Court, 16, 46, 72–75, 76, 78–79; attacked at Fort Wilson, 17–18, 19, 20, 21, 38, 39, 44–45; Scottish Enlightenment and, 20, 23, 31, 32, 34–36, 57, 67, 209; pyramid metaphor and, 21, 47–51, 54–55, 57–60, 61, 63, 67–68, 69, 80–81, 82; financial difficulties of, 22, 75–80; early career of, 24, 29–30; land investments of, 29–31, 35, 36–38, 73, 76, 77, 78–79; and 1790

Pennsylvania state constitutional convention, 43, 48, 58, 71; and Pennsylvania Constitution of 1776, 43, 68; treatise-writing ambitions of, 46, 71–72; law lectures by, 46, 48–49, 58, 59, 71, 72; and Pennsylvania ratifying convention, 48, 58, 59, 60, 71; on custom, 55, 57–58, 59; on democracy, 56–57, 60; burned in effigy, 60; speech at the Pennsylvania State House yard, 71; death of, 80
Wilson, Woodrow, 160, 182, 183–184, 188–190, 191, 193, 201, 203, 204, 205; administration of, 159, 184, 198; "Fourteen Points" speech of, 188–189; internationalism and, 188–190; nationalism and, 189–190; "Peace without Victory" speech of, 189
Winstanley, William, 49
Winter, Jay, 206
Woman's movement, 161–162, 184, 208; discrimination against women, 185, 345n47
Woman's Peace Parade, 172–173, 203
Woman's Peace Party, 173, 183, 187, 189, 345n49; New York City branch, 181, 183, 185–186, 196
Woman's suffrage movement, 172, 199
Wood, Gordon, 19, 20
Workmen's compensation, 168–170, 171, 172, 198, 222, 227, 240–241, 242, 246, 253, 254. See also Tort law
World Peace Foundation, 176
World's Columbian Exposition, 104
World Trade Center, September 11 attacks on, 1–3

World War I, 7, 150, 155, 157, 158, 159, 160, 173, 180, 187, 197, 206, 208, 281. *See also* Civil liberties; Internationalism; Nationalism

Wright, Frank Lloyd, 243

Yale Law School, 195, 252

Yazoo land grant, 30–31, 73

York County, South Carolina, 85, 120, 328n87; Confederate troops from, 86, 97; support for Confederate values in, 97, 98, 119, 120. *See also* Ku Klux Klan; Piedmont; Upcountry

Yorkville, 89, 97–98, 115, 117, 120, 124, 127, 128, 135

Yorkville Enquirer, 127–128, 129, 137, 140, 147, 326n79

Zenger, John Peter, 26